The Sixties Experience

Hard Lessons about Modern America

D0815912

THE 60s EXPERIENCE

Hard Lessons about Modern America

EDWARD P. MORGAN

Temple University Press T Philadelphia

Temple University Press, Philadelphia 19122
Copyright © 1991 by Edward P. Morgan. All rights reserved
Published 1991
Printed in the United States of America

The paper used in this publication meets the minimum requirements of
American National Standard for Information Sciences—Permanence of Paper
for Printed Library Materials, ANSI Z39.48-1984

Library of Congress Cataloging-in-Publication Data
Morgan, Edward P., 1945–
The sixties experience : hard lessons about modern America / Edward P.
Morgan.
p.   cm.
Includes index.
ISBN 0-87722-805-1 (alk. paper)
1. United States—History—1961–1969.   2. United States—Social
conditions—1960–1980.   3. Social movements—United States—History—
20th century.   I. Title.
E841.M64   1991
973.92—dc20   90-43517

"We Shall Overcome," p. 3, by Zilphia Horton, Frank Hamilton, Guy
Carawan, and Pete Seeger. © Copyright 1960 (renewed) and 1963 Ludlow
Music, Inc., New York, NY. Used by permission.
"The Times They Are A-Changin'," pp. 5, 86, by Bob Dylan. © 1963 Warner
Bros. Inc. (renewed). All rights reserved. Used by permission.
"Chicago," pp. 21–22, lyrics and music by Graham Nash. © 1971 Nash Notes.
Used by permission. All rights reserved.
"Blowin' in the Wind," p. 35, by Bob Dylan. Copyright © transferred 1990 to
Special Rider Music. All rights reserved. International copyright secured.
Reprinted by permission.
"San Francisco (Be Sure to Wear Some Flowers in Your Hair)," p. 178. Words
and Music by John Phillips. © Copyright 1967 by MCA Music Publishing, A
Division of MCA Inc., New York, N.Y. 10019. Used by Permission. All Rights
Reserved.
"Lyndon Johnson Told the Nation," p. 127, by Tom Paxton. Copyright © 1965,
1968 United Artist Music Co., Inc. Rights assigned to EMI Catalogue
Partnership. All rights Controlled and Administered by EMI U Catalog, Inc. All
Rights Reserved. International Copyright Secured. Used by Permission.
"Masters of War," p. 133, by Bob Dylan. © 1963 Warner Bros. Inc. All rights
reserved. Used by permission.
"Ballad of a Thin Man," p. 187, by Bob Dylan. © 1965 Warner Bros. Inc. All
rights reserved. Used by permission.

For my mother and the memory of my father,

whose lives taught me from the beginning

that democracy is both personal and political—

and for Becky, Alex, Tim, and Lily,

in the hope that your world will be

far more democratic.

It was the best of times, it was the worst of times, it was

the age of wisdom, it was the age of foolishness, it was

the epoch of belief, it was the epoch of incredulity, it

was the season of Light, it was the season of Darkness, it

was the spring of hope, it was the winter of despair.

—Charles Dickens, *A Tale of Two Cities*

Contents

Part Three   **Since the Sixties: Lessons and Legacies**

Foreword

Howard Zinn

There are those who would like us to forget the Sixties, because they have not forgotten it, and the memory frightens them. It was a time of rebellion, defiance of authority, acting out of hopes and dreams. It was a time of reconsidering the way we lived, the way we behaved toward people in this country and abroad. And in every era, there are those who want to reconsider nothing, because they are doing well, and don't want their well-being disturbed.

For such people, it would be better if all histories of this country stopped at the end of the Second World War. Or, if such complete silence seems to them embarrassing, the Sixties could be passed over quickly, with brief references to the black movement, the antiwar movement, and the counterculture. What would be omitted would be the exhilaration, the excitement, the achievements of that time. Young people would be allowed to review the remains of that era, the desiccated skeleton of history, without its beating heart, thinking brain, flowing blood, aroused senses.

Some writers have been too angered by the Sixties to forget them. And so they present those years to us with smiling condescension, as a wall scrawled with obscenities, behind which are nothing but drug-befuddled youngsters and violent Weather people.

Fortunately, there are others who want us neither to forget, nor to remember with bile and fear. And so we have a growing literature of the Sixties, of personal reminiscence and thoughtful analysis, that captures the spirit of that era, and appreciates its contribution to American society.

Ted Morgan's book is a refreshing addition to that literature, an extraordinary achievement in its blending of vivid description and perceptive insight. He has the advantage of the participant–observer, one who was himself involved in a number of the movements of the Sixties. Yet he brings to his experience the perspective of the social scientist—not the detachment of the distant scholar, but the largeness of vision combined with passionate commitment to social justice that marked writers like C. Wright Mills.

He clearly shares the best of the values of the New Left, which arose in the

Sixties as a reaction to the racism and jingoism of the old order, while rejecting the dogmatism of the Old Left. He joins its effort to expose the gap between the democratic vision of this nation's most admirable citizens, and the reality of governmental policy and corporate greed.

However, he is totally sober in assessing the obstacles to radical change, and the inadequacies of the Movement as it desperately attempted to push those obstacles aside.

Many of the accounts of the Sixties are limited to the special vantage point of the writer, whether it is the academic fearfully watching student demonstrations from the window of his seminar room, or the participant centering the story of that time around his own group, his own experiences.

It is the special contribution of Ted Morgan to place the remarkable events of that time in a historical context that illuminates their importance. And he ranges widely across the movements of the Sixties: the black rebellion, the student upsurge, the cultural revolution, the women's movement, and the rising concern with the environment.

His descriptions are rich and full. His analysis is provocative and judicious. He understands the contradictions within each movement, but refuses to let the polarities batter themselves into meaninglessness. He does us all a great service by making the bold leap from that time to our own, extricating from that complex history a core of meaning for the future of our country.

Preface

In recent years, the 1960s have been placed under the magnifying glass of media retrospectives, anniversary commemorations, college and university courses, personal memoirs, and reassessments of specific events and personalities. This second wave of reflection makes it abundantly clear that the turmoil and emotions of that era maintain a powerful hold on the imaginations of many Americans, as well as those in other parts of the world.

Yet questions remain. "What did it all mean?" "Why did the Sixties happen?" And, "What do the 1960s mean for the contemporary world?" Today's young people bring a fresh perspective to these inquiries. They ask, "What *were* the Sixties?" "Why were students so idealistic, so active, and so angry?"

This book offers one kind of response to these questions—an interpretation grounded in the experiences and political education of 1960s movements in the United States. It represents my belief that Sixties experiences tell us a great deal about America and the modern world, that they speak to the struggles and crises of today and tomorrow. The Sixties were not the mythical time the mass media tend to recreate. Nor were they a time to be washed away and forgotten. The times are quieter today, but the problems are no less compelling.

Sixties movements were grounded in a democratic vision that is as compelling today as it was then: a belief that all people should be full members of society, that individuals become empowered through meaningful social participation, and that politics ought to be grounded on respect and compassion for the individual person. Sixties politics were infused with a quest for community—the sense of place, belonging, and purpose gained from engagement with others.

Through their agitation for change, Sixties movements exposed fundamental tensions between their democratic vision and the institutions of everyday life in the United States. Movement experiences demonstrated that the struggle for a truly democratic society is undermined by many forces: by a common fear of taking risks, by the cooptive preoccupation with self-advancement, and by the resistance of entrenched interests.

They also demonstrated how fleeting and vulnerable real community is.

Many Sixties activists envisioned a community built on sharing and learning from each others' experiences. With notable exceptions, however, the Movement fell far short of this goal in dealing with non-Movement people. Young activists contributed to their own isolation and ineffectiveness when they failed to recognize the shaping effect of differing experiences.

Another crucial lesson of the 1960s was that *how people make sense* of their experiences is heavily influenced by pervasive forces of everyday life: family interaction, social class, early schooling, corporate marketing, restricted access to information, and government propaganda. Many of these same forces have helped to obscure Sixties movements and their message. More generally, they are inimical to community and to the democratic vision that drew so many to activism in the Sixties; they keep people apart, in the dark, powerless.

The struggles and issues that came to a head during that decade haven't gone away; nor, thankfully, has the commitment to democracy that compelled so many to be active. For the most part, we still need to learn the lessons the Sixties can teach us.

As an interpretation of the 1960s, this book draws from the richly detailed accounts of others, synthesizing the many voices who have spoken and written about their experiences. This is not a comprehensive history of all social and political movements of the 1960s. Instead, my aim is to focus on major movements that contributed distinctly to the theoretical democratic vision of the Sixties. Thus, for example, I do not examine such important movements and groups as the Chicano movement, the Gay Liberation movement, the Puerto Rican Young Lords, the American Indian Movement, the National Welfare Rights Organization, or the Gray Panthers. Each echoed civil rights movement values and experiences in its distinctive cultural context.

The book also, invariably, reflects my own political education. I owe a debt of gratitude to the many students at Oberlin College who enriched my education during the crucial years of 1964 to 1968. This book reflects the sense of community I still feel with them. It also reflects my journey from youthful fascination with the awakening civil rights movement and the New Frontier, through modest involvement in civil rights activism, intense participation in campus politics, active engagement in the antiwar movement on many levels, a sustained embrace of ecological activism, and a personal dialogue with the feminist movement.

I am very grateful to George Katsiaficas, Carey McWilliams, Rick

Matthews, and Gary Olson, each of whom, at different times, read through the entire manuscript and made innumerable helpful suggestions. I thank Howard Zinn for his support and willingness to write a foreword to this volume. I also appreciate the helpful suggestions of many others who read sections of the manuscript: Bob Cohen, Morris Dickstein, Mary Hobgood, Kathleen Kelly, William Leuchtenburg, Bruce Moon, Christopher Morgan, Joan Morrison, Laura Katz Olson, Harlan Wilson, and Al Wurth. While their comments were very helpful, I absolve them of any responsibility for any flaws that remain in the book.

A number of people have contributed to this book's publication. Suzanne Irvine helped trim a voluminous early manuscript into a readable, coherent whole. Oberlin classmates Bill Kramer and Aaron Levin provided helpful advice in the search for publishers and photographs. Michael Ames of Temple University Press has edited with an instinctive feel for a book that is now much better than my original manuscript. Others at the Press—Jenny French, Henna Remstein, and Terri Kettering—were very helpful and supportive in expediting publication. I thank them all. I would also like to acknowledge John Hunt and Howard Whitcomb for supporting an early request for time off from teaching, Olive Stengel and her associates for providing me with a quiet space for writing, and the Lehigh Office of Research for assisting in manuscript preparation.

Finally, and most important, I am deeply grateful to my family. This book tells a story I want to share with my children, so I greatly appreciate their putting up with the innumerable times their father seemed distracted by distant thoughts or imminent deadlines. I am forever grateful to my wife, Mary Lou, who has lived with this project from the beginning. She knows best how engrossing and frequently stressful it has been. My heartfelt thanks to her for her love, support, and forbearance throughout the time we have shared it.

Chronology, 1960–1970

1960   John F. Kennedy announces his candidacy for the presidency. Student sit-ins spread from Greensboro, North Carolina, to Nashville, Tennessee, and much of the South. The Student Non-violent Coordinating Committee (SNCC) is organized to coordinate student civil rights protests. A San Francisco march protests Caryl Chessman's death sentence. University of California students are hosed and gassed as they protest the House Un-American Activities Committee (HUAC) hearings in San Francisco. U-2 spy pilot Francis Gary Powers is shot down over the Soviet Union. Elvis Presley is inducted into the Armed Forces. The Food and Drug Administration (FDA) approves the first birth control pill as safe for use. John Kennedy and Richard Nixon hold the first televised presidential campaign debates. The Kennedy–Johnson ticket narrowly defeats the Nixon–Lodge ticket. A congressional hearing exposes a disk jockey payola scandal.

1961   The United States breaks off diplomatic relations with Cuba. John F. Kennedy is inaugurated, and creates the Peace Corps by executive order. A ban against folk singing in Washington Square, New York City, is lifted after a successful protest. Soviet cosmonaut Yuri Gagarin becomes the first human being to orbit the earth. The American-sponsored invasion of Cuba founders at the Bay of Pigs. The Freedom Riders leave Washington, D.C., by bus to confront segregation throughout the South; buses are temporarily halted by violent white mobs in Anniston and Birmingham, Alabama. The black voter registration worker Herbert Lee is murdered in Mississippi. The Berlin Wall is built. Joseph Heller's *Catch-22* is published. Kennedy increases the number of American military advisers in South Vietnam. Student vigils protest the resumption of nuclear testing.

1962   American astronaut John Glenn orbits the earth. The Students for a Democratic Society (SDS) hold their first national convention in Port Huron, Michigan, and call for a "participatory democracy." Rachel Carson's *Silent Spring* is published, warning of the dangers of DDT.

Mass arrests of civil rights demonstrators take place in Albany, Georgia. The Supreme Court finds prayer and bible reading in schools unconstitutional. James Meredith becomes the first black to enroll at the University of Mississippi, forcing the Kennedy administration to send U.S. marshals and troops to protect him against segregationists' violence. The Twist becomes the latest dancing rage. Bob Dylan's first published song appears. The United States and the Soviet Union go "eyeball to eyeball" during the Cuban missile crisis. The number of U.S. military and technical personnel in Vietnam reaches 11,000.

1963   Michael Harrington's *The Other America* is published. A major voter registration drive begins in Mississippi, organized by the Council of Federated Organizations (COFO). The Reverend Martin Luther King, Jr., leads a peaceful march against segregation in Birmingham, Alabama; Sheriff Bull Connor unleashes hoses and police dogs against the demonstrators. President Kennedy introduces the most extensive civil rights bill since Reconstruction. The first exhibit of Pop Art opens at the Guggenheim in New York. Betty Friedan's *The Feminine Mystique* is published. The first of several Buddhist monks immolates himself in South Vietnam to protest religious persecution. Civil rights leader Medgar Evers is murdered in Jackson, Mississippi. The United States, Soviet Union, and Great Britain sign a test ban treaty halting all above-ground nuclear testing. An estimated 250,000 attend the civil rights March on Washington, which culminates in King's "I Have a Dream" speech. Harvard terminates the contracts of Timothy Leary and Richard Alpert (later known as Baba Ram Dass) for experiments with LSD. Four black girls are killed when a bomb explodes during a church service in Birmingham. Peter, Paul, and Mary's recording of Bob Dylan's "Blowin' in the Wind" makes the top-40 charts. The Commission on the Status of Women reports that there is discrimination against women in the United States. Over 80,000 black Mississippians vote in the "Freedom Ballot." South Vietnamese President Ngo Dinh Diem is murdered in a U.S.-supported coup. President John F. Kennedy is assassinated in Dallas. Lyndon B. Johnson assumes office as a stunned nation watches the events on television. Kennedy's accused assassin, Lee Harvey Oswald, is murdered by Jack Ruby. SDS begins the Economic Research and Action Project (ERAP), organizing poor communities in twelve northern U.S. cities.

1964   President Johnson declares an "unconditional war on poverty in America" in his State of the Union address. *Dr. Strangelove* is released. The Beatles' "I Want to Hold Your Hand" becomes the number one song, and the group makes its U.S. television debut on the Ed Sullivan show. *The Autobiography of Malcolm X* is published. The May 2nd Movement organizes against the War in Vietnam and begins gathering signatures pledging nonparticipation. LBJ signs the Civil Rights Act of 1964 into law. Arizona Senator Barry Goldwater wins the Republican nomination for president. The Mississippi Freedom Democratic Party clashes with Democratic party regulars at the national convention. A major riot occurs in the Harlem section of New York City. SNCC launches the Mississippi Freedom Summer Project; thousands of students from northern campuses flock to Mississippi for the summer voter registration drive. Three civil rights volunteers—James Chaney, Andrew Goodman, and Michael Schwerner—are murdered in Philadelphia, Mississippi. Congress passes the Gulf of Tonkin Resolution, authorizing "all necessary measures" to "prevent further aggression" by North Vietnam. Only two senators vote against the resolution. Congress passes the Equal Opportunity Act, the centerpiece of President Johnson's War on Poverty program. The University of California at Berkeley bans political activity on campus. The Berkeley Free Speech Movement erupts with sit-ins and a call for a campus strike. Martin Luther King, Jr., wins the Nobel Peace Prize. Lyndon Johnson wins a landslide election.

1965   Malcolm X is assassinated in Harlem. LBJ orders bombing raids on North Vietnam culminating in the massive Rolling Thunder campaign of "sustained reprisal." A young black man, Jimmy Lee Jackson, is killed during a mob attack on black marchers in Selma, Alabama. On "Bloody Sunday," Alabama state police storm civil rights marchers at the Edmund Pettus Bridge in Selma; Boston minister James Reeb is mortally beaten by white toughs. A mass civil rights march from Selma to Montgomery follows under National Guard protection. Civil rights volunteer Viola Liuzzo is murdered in Lowndes County, Alabama. LBJ sends the first U.S. infantry troops, the Ninth Marine Expeditionary Brigade, to Vietnam. The first campus teach-in on the Vietnam War is held at the University of Michigan. U.S. marines are sent to the Dominican Republic to help the military regime repel the return of reformist Juan Bosch to power. Three thousand join a SANE antiwar rally at the United Nations. Over 20,000 attend the SDS-sponsored Washington rally against the Vietnam war. Poet Robert Lowell and others boycott the White House Festival of the Arts in protest against the Vietnam War. Johnson signs the Voting Rights Act of 1965 into law. A major black riot erupts in the Watts section of Los Angeles. Twenty thousand attend a teach-in on the Berkeley campus, organized by the Vietnam Day Committee. The Los Angeles *Free Press* emerges as the first major underground newspaper of the 1960s, followed shortly by the Berkeley *Barb*, New York's *East Village Other*, Detroit's *Fifth Estate*, and East Lansing's *Paper*. The all-black Lowndes County Freedom Organization is founded in Alabama. Nguyen Cao Ky is appointed premier of South Vietnam. The Rolling Stones' song "Satisfaction" reaches number one on the charts. Bob Dylan "goes electric" at the Newport Folk Festival. SNCC's Julian Bond is elected to the Georgia state legislature, only to have his election invalidated because of his opposition to the War in Vietnam. Ken Kesey and the Merry Pranksters hold the first public "acid test." Barry McGuire's "Eve of Destruction" becomes the number one song. The largest draft call since the Korean War is issued. The first draft card is burned at a New York protest organized by the War Resisters League. Congress responds by passing a law making draft-card burning a crime. Quaker pacifist Norman Morrison burns himself to death in front of the Pentagon as an act of solidarity with the Vietnamese people. The Vietnam Day Committee organizes the First International Days of Protest against the war; more than 100,000 protest in over forty cities. Berkeley activists try to stop a train carrying troops en route to Vietnam. The U.S. death toll in Vietnam exceeds 1,000. A halt in the bombing of North Vietnam is ordered for Christmas.

1966   The bombing of North Vietnam resumes as "peace efforts" fail. Senate Foreign Relations Committee chairman J. William Fulbright opens hearings on the Vietnam War. SNCC denounces the war and supports draft resistance. A crowd of 50,000 attend the Second International Days of Protest march in New York City; nationwide participation doubles the previous year's totals. Four thousand protest outside as LBJ is given the National Freedom Award at a Freedom House dinner in New York. Johnson decries "nervous nellies" in a speech to a Chicago Democratic club. Students at the universities of Chicago and Wisconsin, and other campuses, stage sit-ins protesting the use of class rankings by the Selective Service. Three G.I.'s from Fort Hood, Texas refuse to go to Vietnam. Stokely Carmichael is elected chairman of SNCC and urges "black power." James Meredith is wounded by a sniper on his solitary march through Mississippi. Black leaders continue Meredith's March against Fear. "Black Power" slogan erupts during a Mississippi march following the attack on Meredith. Black riots erupt in Cleveland, Brooklyn, and Chicago. Twenty-thousand march down New York City's Fifth Avenue in antiwar protest. The Supreme Court hands down the *Miranda* ruling specifying the rights of the accused. The National Organization of Women (NOW) is established. Lenny Bruce dies of a heroin overdose in New York City. The San Francisco *Oracle* emerges as the voice of the burgeoning Haight-Ashbury community. A Buddhist uprising is crushed in South Vietnam. The SDS convention at Clear Lake, Iowa, signals return to campus organizing. General Motors apologizes for their ungrounded attack on safe car crusader Ralph Nader. Martin Luther King, Jr., leads an antidiscrimination march in Chicago and is stoned by the hostile crowd. The Black Panther Party for Self-Defense is organized in Oakland, California. Striking California farm workers march 250 miles to Sacramento. A sit-in takes place at the Dow Chemical Company, manufacturer of napalm and Agent Orange. *Ramparts* editor Robert Scheer runs for Congress on an antiwar platform and gains 45 percent of the vote. Ronald Reagan is elected governor of California. *Time* names the "under-25" generation Man of the Year (*sic*). The SDS national council condemns the Vietnam War and the antidemocratic draft. The U.S. troop level in Vietnam reaches 320,000.

1967   The first San Francisco "Human Be-in" is held. The first campus sit-in against Dow Chemical Company recruiters is held at the University of Wisconsin. The Resistance is organized in California and Massachusetts. *Ramparts* exposes Central Intelligence Agency (CIA) funding of the National Student Association. Over 100,000 attend an antiwar demonstration in New York City organized by the Spring Mobilization Committee to End the War in Vietnam; Martin Luther King, Jr., Dr. Benjamin Spock, Stokely Carmichael, and others condemn the war, while over seventy students burn their draft cards in Central Park. Sixty-five thousand march in a similar demonstration in San Francisco. Muhammad Ali is stripped of his heavyweight boxing crown for resisting the draft. The International War Crimes Tribunal, sponsored by the Bertrand Russell Peace Foundation, begins an investigation of the U.S. role in Vietnam. The "Summer of Love" attracts hordes of young people to San Francisco, and Scott McKenzie's song "San Francisco (Be Sure to Wear Flowers in Your Hair)" becomes a hit. John Lennon and George Harrison announce they have tried LSD. The Rolling Stones' Mick Jagger and Keith Richard are found guilty of minor drug charges. The *London Times* protests their jail sentences, which are later retracted. The Monterey

Pop Festival initiates the trend of large, outdoor rock festivals. The "long, hot summer" begins with a black riot in Boston's Roxbury section. Massive riots in Newark and Detroit leave sixty-nine dead, and millions of dollars in damage. Among the Detroit dead are three black youths murdered during a police raid on the Algiers Motel. From Havana, a Stokely Carmichael broadcast urges blacks to arm themselves for "total revolution." The first national Black Power conference is held in Newark. The Beatles' "Sgt. Pepper" album heads the pop charts. The National Conference for a New Politics meets in Chicago. Although it is the largest gathering to date of black and white liberals and radicals, the meeting is plagued by division and confusion. Arlo Guthrie performs "Alice's Restaurant" at the Newport Folk Festival. Reverend Philip Berrigan and three others raid a Baltimore draft office and pour blood on the draft files. The movie *Bonnie and Clyde* is released. Woody Guthrie dies. Che Guevara is killed in Bolivia. American troop levels in Vietnam reach 460,000. U.S. deaths in Vietnam total 13,000. Over 1,000 college students turn in draft cards during church services in New Haven, Cambridge, and sixteen other cities. The cards are then turned over to the Department of Justice by William Sloane Coffin, Dr. Benjamin Spock, Marcus Raskin, Mitchell Goodman, and Arthur Waskow. Over 100,000 attend the March on the Pentagon in Washington, D.C., organized by the National Mobilization Committee; its themes are "Confront the Warmakers" and "From Dissent to Resistance." A Ford Foundation study recommends a "community control" experiment in black sections of the New York City school system. The CIA, Federal Bureau of Investigation (FBI), and Army Intelligence begin surveillance of the antiwar movement. The Peace and Freedom party is organized in California. Allard Lowenstein organizes a "Dump Johnson" movement; Senator Eugene McCarthy is chosen as its candidate for President. The movie *The Graduate* is released.

1968   The U.S. intelligence ship *Pueblo* is captured off North Korea. Clergy and Laymen Concerned about Vietnam (CLCV) publish the report *In the Name of America*, condemning the United States' "consistent violation of almost every international agreement relating to the rules of warfare." LBJ calls up 14,787 Air Force and Navy reservists. The massive Vietcong Tet Offensive begins, stunning American decision-makers and the general public. Three black students are shot dead during a student protest at South Carolina State College; the "Orangeburg Massacre" is virtually ignored by the national media. Eldridge Cleaver's *Soul on Ice* is published. The Kerner Commission report on urban riots decries white racism and a rapidly polarizing society. Eugene McCarthy startles the press and the Johnson re-election campaign by finishing a close second in the New Hampshire primary. Robert Kennedy announces his candidacy for the presidency. LBJ stuns the American public by announcing he will not run for a second term. Students at Howard University seize a university building in protest against the institution's lack of "commitment to the black community." Martin Luther King, Jr., is assassinated in Memphis; violence erupts in cities across the country. Black Panther party member Bobby Sutton is killed in a police shoot-out in Oakland, California. Coffin, Spock, et al. are indicted for conspiracy for counseling draft resistance. Columbia University students strike and take over school buildings. One million college and high school students stay away from classes in a one-day boycott against the war. Student revolts erupt in Germany, Italy, and France; French students join with workers to bring the French government to the brink of collapse. One hundred thousand march in New York City. *Hair!* opens on Broadway. Hubert Humphrey announces his candidacy for president, calling for the "politics of joy." Norman Mailer's *Armies of the Night* is published. The Poor People's Campaign establishes Resurrection City in Washington, D.C. The Reverends Philip and Daniel Berrigan and seven others raid the Catonsville, Maryland draft board and destroy draft files with homemade napalm. The Vietnam War peace talks open in Paris. Robert Kennedy is assassinated at the end of a successful California primary campaign. The Vietnam War becomes the longest war in U.S. history. Protesting students and workers bring Paris to a virtual standstill. Richard Nixon and Spiro Agnew gain the Republican nomination. Black Panther party leader Eldridge Cleaver is chosen as the presidential candidate of the Peace and Freedom party–Black Panther party coalition. Soviet troops and tanks crush the liberalization movement in Czechoslovakia. The Democratic presidential convention in Chicago nominates Hubert Humphrey amidst massive demonstrations organized by antiwar groups and the Youth International party (Yippies); street disorders and police brutality ensue while demonstrators chant "the whole world is watching." A state of civil disaster is declared in Berkeley following recurring police–student confrontations. Olympic track stars Tommie Smith and John Carlos are suspended for giving the black power salute as the U.S. national anthem is played. Black Panther party leader Huey Newton is sentenced to fifteen years in prison for killing a policeman. Women's liberation activists picket the Miss America pageant. New York City teachers strike over the actions of the black Ocean Hill–Brownsville community board. G.I.'s and vets hold a peace march in San Francisco. The first women's liberation conference is held in Chicago. Richard Nixon is elected president by a very close margin.

1969   After weeks of publicized debate, negotiators at the Paris peace talks agree on the shape of the bargaining table. American troop levels in Vietnam reach a peak of 542,000. Ten thousand march against the tide on Pennsylvania Avenue during a "Counterinaugural" protest. The radical Catholic group the DC 9 break into the Dow Chemical Company, wreck equipment, pour blood on files, and post pictures of maimed Vietnamese victims on the walls. As police storm People's Park, created from vacant land in Berkeley, demonstrators are gassed and wounded and one student is killed; California governor Ronald Reagan applauds the police attack. The movie *Easy Rider* is released. President Nixon authorizes the development of an anti-ballistic missile (ABM) system against the prevailing advice of scientists. A Gallup poll shows 58 percent of Americans oppose the Vietnam War. Vice-president Spiro Agnew denounces the media's critical bias against the Nixon administration. American casualties in Vietnam exceed those of the Korean War. Black students exit an occupied building at Cornell University carrying guns. The Russell War Crimes Tribunal issues its report *Against the Crime of Silence*, condemning U.S. war crimes in Vietnam. A conference of the Underground Press Syndicate adopts a series of resolutions condemning male supremacy in the ranks of underground papers. Hundreds of black leaders from diverse groups gather for the Black Political Convention in Gary, Indiana. Neil Armstrong and Buzz Aldrin become the first human beings to walk on the moon. Four hundred thousand attend the massive Woodstock rock concert. The Chicago Eight (later the Chicago Seven) trial begins in the courtroom of Judge Julius Hoffman. An SDS splinter group, the Weathermen, organize the "Days of Rage" in Chicago, resulting in violent rampaging in the streets. The American Civil Liberties Union (ACLU) charges Chicago police with murdering Black Panther party leader Fred Hampton during a raid. The Vietnam Moratorium Day is observed by millions of Americans in thousands of cities, towns, and campuses across the country; one hundred thousand gather on the Boston Common. The New Mobilization Committee to End the War in Vietnam organizes the March Against Death in Washington; about 500,000 protesters attend weekend-long demonstrations. The American Indian Movement (AIM) occupies the abandoned Alcatraz prison. The American massacre of My Lai villagers in Vietnam is publicized by journalist Seymour Hersh. The first draft lottery of the decade is held. A black youth is stabbed to death by Hell's Angels during a Rolling Stones concert at Altamont. The Charles Manson gang goes on a murderous spree in Los Angeles.

1970   The militant Puerto Rican group the Young Lords issues a thirteen-point platform of liberation demands. Seven of the Chicago Eight are acquitted of conspiracy charges; convictions on lesser charges are later overturned. A University of Wisconsin Reserve Officers Training Corps (ROTC) building is fire-bombed, beginning a wave of some 500 bombings or arsons on college campuses. The Bank of America branch in Santa Barbara, California, is burned down by students. Nixon aide Daniel Patrick Moynihan urges "benign neglect" of racial issues in a memo to the President. Three are killed when a Greenwich Village townhouse is destroyed by a bomb being constructed by the Weathermen. The first Earth Day is held with environmental celebrations nationwide. Seventy-five thousand rally against the war on the Boston Common; subsequently, a splinter group rampages through Harvard Yard in nearby Cambridge. Amidst growing campus violence, Governor Reagan threatens: "If it takes a bloodbath, let it begin now." The Shea–Wells Bill passes the Massachusetts legislature, enabling Massachusetts men to refuse combat duty in the absence of a declaration of war. Thousands converge on New Haven to protest the murder trial of Black Panthers Bobby Seale and Erica Huggins. Yale President Kingman Brewster clashes with Vice-president Agnew over whether black revolutionaries can receive a fair trial in the United States. President Nixon announces the "incursion" of U.S. combat troops into Cambodia. Princeton University students organize an immediate protest; Oberlin College students occupy the administration building demanding a faculty meeting to discuss the invasion. An average of twenty campuses initiate strikes each day after Nixon's announcement. Four students are killed by the National Guard at a Kent State University protest. Two black students are killed and nine wounded by police gunfire at Jackson State College in Mississippi. Thirty ROTC buildings are burned or bombed during the first week in May. Over 450 colleges and universities close down. Hard-hat construction workers attack peace demonstrators in New York City. In Washington, D.C., 100,000 protest the invasion of Cambodia. Striking students converge on the Capitol to lobby for passage of the Cooper–Church and Hatfield–McGovern amendments to cut off funding for the Cambodian invasion and all Southeast Asian operations. U.S. troops withdraw from Cambodia. Black militants escape from the courthouse in San Rafael, California; a judge and three of his kidnappers are killed in the ensuing shootout. A warrant is issued for the arrest of Angela Davis. Twenty-five thousand attend the National Chicano Moratorium antiwar demonstration in Los Angeles. The Army Mathematics Research Center, an object of antiwar protests at the University of Wisconsin, is blown up during the night, killing graduate student Robert Fassnacht. Jimi Hendrix dies of a drug overdose in London. Janis Joplin dies of a drug overdose in Hollywood. The President's Commission on Campus Unrest issues its report calling the gap between youth culture and mainstream society a threat to American stability. FBI director J. Edgar Hoover accuses the East Coast Conspiracy to Save Lives of terrorist tactics and a plan to kidnap Henry Kissinger; the group is led by Catholic priests Philip and Daniel Berrigan.

PART ONE
Introduction

1 The Sixties Experience

We shall overcome, we shall overcome
We shall overcome some day.
Oh, deep in my heart, I do believe
We shall overcome some day.
—"We Shall Overcome" by Zilphia Horton, Frank Hamilton,
Guy Carawan, and Pete Seeger. ©

On February 3, 1960, one month after the junior senator from Massachusetts, John Fitzgerald Kennedy, announced his candidacy for President, the *New York Times* reported in a brief, back-page article from Greensboro, North Carolina, "A group of well-dressed Negro college students staged a sitdown strike in a downtown Woolworth store today and vowed to continue it in relays until Negroes were served at the lunch counter."

Ten years later, the *Times* devoted four front-page columns to a lead article headed, "4 Kent State Students Killed by Troops." Most startling of all was the photograph that appeared nationwide of a young woman screaming for help while kneeling over the body of a slain student.

These two events framed the decade of the 1960s. The Greensboro sit-in evolved out of the civil rights activities of the 1950s and was the spark that ignited a wave of student sit-ins across seventy cities of the South. The Kent State killings occurred during one of several hundred campus protests against the American invasion of Cambodia. After the shock of Kent State, and the subsequent deaths of two black students at Jackson State in Mississippi, over 450 college and university campuses shut down—fifty-one of them for the remainder of the academic year—in what proved to be the largest strike action in United States history. An estimated four million students were involved in the protests of May 1970.

Each event represented an important historical and psychological milestone in this era of protest. The Greensboro sit-ins marked the entry of students into full-scale participation in the civil rights movement. As sociologist Aldon Morris notes,

> Nineteen sixty was the year when thousands of Southern black students at black colleges joined forces with "old movement warriors" and tremendously increased the power of the developing civil rights movement. . . . From the privileged position of hindsight, it is clear that the student sit-ins of 1960 were the introduction to a decade of political turbulence.[1]

Similarly, although antiwar activity continued until the last American troops were brought home from Vietnam in 1973, the Kent State and Jackson State killings marked a psychological turning point in the student revolt. Many students realized for the first time that they could die because of their activism, that their government was capable of gunning them down in cold blood. The contrast between Greensboro and Kent State suggests the scale of change over the course of the decade—Greensboro symbolizing the hope and energy of the early Sixties, Kent State the nightmare of repression and social disintegration.

In between these events, the Sixties were stained by assassinations of public figures like John F. Kennedy, Medgar Evers, Malcolm X, Martin Luther King, Jr., and Robert Kennedy. They were years of mass protest, for civil rights and black power, for liberated education, for poor people, women's liberation, gay rights, Chicanos, American Indians, and against the Vietnam war. A host of activist groups of all persuasions materialized, from the Student Nonviolent Coordinating Committee (SNCC), Students for a Democratic Society (SDS), and the Women Strike for Peace, to the New Mobilization Committee to End the War in Vietnam (New Mobe), the Weather Underground, the Black Panther party, and the Radicalesbians.

The Sixties' claim for historical distinction rests on the combination of enormous cultural ferment and political upheaval within a single decade. In effect, the Sixties combined qualities of the 1920s and 1930s. Movements of the Sixties converged while grappling with the most pressing and intractable dilemmas of the post-war world—racism and poverty, pervasive dehumanization in the developed world, and Third World liberation. At their revolutionary peak in 1968, these movements sought to launch, in Daniel Cohn-Bendit's words, "an experiment that completely breaks with that society, an experiment . . . which allows a glimpse of a possibility."[2]

The Sixties were also years of enormous musical energy, from the folk revival in Greenwich Village in 1960 to the British invasion in 1963–1964 and the emergence of rock music in 1965 to the rock festival Age of Aquarius. Marijuana and hallucinogens like LSD were widely used by the young, and sexual experimentation was openly embraced by the youthful counterculture. Scores of underground newspapers appeared across the country, providing a community forum and network for various elements of the Movement. Rules, laws, and social norms changed with staggering speed. Traditional boundaries of acceptable expression were shattered in an enormous burst of innovation and experimentation in literature, theater, and the visual arts. As Michael Arlen described it, the Sixties represented the chaos of a world "coming more and more out from under wraps."[3]

From Martin Luther King's "Now is the time!" to the antiwar cry "Peace Now!" to the counterculture's query "Why wait?", movements of the 1960s were attuned to the present, the immediate. As the forces of change gathered momentum, the sheer barrage of events swept aside time for reflection. The world seemed upside down. Change became the only constant, and deviance became the rule. Sixties troubadour Bob Dylan put the fleeting feeling into his famous song, "The Times They Are A-Changin'."

> The line it is drawn
> The curse it is cast
> The slow one now will
> Later be fast.
> As the present now
> Will later be past
> The order is rapidly fadin'
> And the first one now
> Will later be last
> For the times they are a-changin'.

Although this book focuses on the United States, virtually all aspects of the decade's movements in the United States were echoed throughout the western world. The Sixties were, in brief, the West's "pro-democracy movement"—or at least its first phase. The civil rights movement inspired South African liberationists and the European disarmament movement. The United States and its war in Vietnam became prominent targets for international protest. University campuses in both capitalist and communist systems were the scene of growing student agitation, culminating in the upheavals of 1968. The counterculture spread throughout much of Europe. The women's movement began to emerge in much of the world at about the same time that it flourished in the United States. Ecology activism set the stage for the West German Green movement that arose in the latter 1970s.

■ Explaining the Sixties: A Movement Perspective

These tumultuous years have inspired reactions ranging from nostalgic recollection to fierce denunciation. In the heat of the times, many commentators attempted to explain the youthful behavior so strikingly characteristic of the age. Some argued that the values, attitudes, and behavior of young people in the Sixties were the product of immaturity and permissive upbringing. The youth revolt was a passing phenomenon; young people would soon grow up and embrace the society they rebelled against.[4] Others emphasized the distinctive generational socialization of those coming of age during the 1960s—the post-World War II environment and parental influences that encouraged personal honesty and moral antipathy toward discrimination and violence.[5] Each of these explanations contained a kernel of truth. Each observer could point to youthful behavior that corroborated his or her theory. However, each explanation was inevitably colored by the observer's ideological leanings.

Ideology that was sometimes subtle and unobtrusive in early scholarly works on the Sixties became overt and strident as the reformist legacy of that decade became part of the political battlefield of the 1980s. The resurgent American Right focused public discontent on excesses of the past, encompassing both liberal Democratic administrations and Sixties movements in their sights. Sixties-bashing was popularized by figures as diverse as President Ronald Reagan and philosopher Allan Bloom. At the same time, a host of twentieth anniversaries of Sixties events provided a focus for activists' reflection as well as mass media oversimplification.

We may distinguish three basic perspectives on the 1960s that reflect distinct social and political outlooks. Two of these—viewpoints we may call "liberal" and "conservative"—lie within the American political mainstream.[6] Citing factors like early socialization, changes in the institutional environment of American life, or simply the pendulum of history, American liberals tend to see the decade as a time when millions of Americans refused to tolerate the gap between institutional practice and the fundamental American ideals of equal rights, free speech, and a foreign policy grounded on universal human rights. Inspired by early civil rights activism and Kennedy rhetoric, young people demanded that their country live up to the values they had been taught.

To a considerable degree, the nation responded with liberal institutional reforms. Unprecedented civil rights legislation permanently changed the face of the Old South; the federal government launched a massive assault on poverty and inadequate education, housing, and health care; universities modified their curricular requirements and social regulations; the draft was replaced by a volunteer army; and the War in Vietnam—a tragic mistake in the view of many liberals—finally ground to a halt. In effect, despite mistakes and short-circuited social programs, the system worked.[7] The Sixties were essentially a noble era of reform.

With remarkable success in the mainstream media,[8] contemporary conservative critics have engaged in a sustained assault on the Sixties, determined to roll back its surge of liberal social and foreign policy: aggressive civil rights enforcement, federal involvement in social services for the poor, affirmative action policies, profit-reducing federal regulations, abortion rights, and most notably, public reluctance to support military intervention overseas, the so-called Vietnam syndrome.[9]

Conservatives argue that the liberal policies of the Sixties and the youth revolt were connected, and that both were carried to excess. The youth revolt was essentially apolitical and self-indulgent, spawned by post–World War II affluence and permissive childrearing. Liberal reformers in government and academia legitimized and thereby helped to unleash the self-indulgent impulses of the young. Liberal political values like free speech, equal rights, and individualism were distorted to justify excessive antisocial behavior.[10] During the early to mid-1980s, a handful of former radicals denounced their earlier political stance while embracing the rising tide of Reaganism.[11]

Both interpretations have merit. Liberals can point to significant accomplishments in civil rights and social welfare legislation. There is also ample evidence that many protesters espoused liberal values, denouncing the hypocrisy of government officials. Conservatives can point to flaws in Great Society programs and instances of excessively self-indulgent or violent behavior on the part of the counterculture and New Left.

However, to limit one's concern to the *relative* effectiveness of the era's liberal reforms, or to concentrate on the manifest behavior of young activists while overlooking the crucial events of that time, is to miss entirely the

point of the 1960s revolt. Since both are fully grounded in mainstream institutions, neither perspective can adequately explain movements that launched
a fundamental critique of those very institutions.

A third view, and one with many variants, has arisen from within the 1960s
movements themselves, and has emerged in a host of books that assess distinct movements or recount personal voyages through the Sixties. This view
is grounded in the *experience* of the decade's movements and the hard lessons
learned about modern America. For many, especially those who were young
during that time, the experiences of the Sixties were a formative political education that taught not only painful lessons about American institutions but
lessons about themselves.

What can be learned from a systematic review of the Sixties experience?
First, young people need to understand, rather than ignore or imitate, the
movements of the 1960s—where they came from, how they evolved, and why
they evolved as they did. Second, by examining the connections among the
movements of that time, we gain a more comprehensive understanding of the
meaning of the 1960s in history. And third, the experiences of Sixties movements can provide future movements of human liberation with important
lessons about the American political system and its potential for change.

What became known simply as the Movement began with two pro-
active struggles for change—the civil rights movement and the student New
Left. Both were rooted in the postwar world of the 1950s. Each contained
an expressive or prefigurative strain—an effort to build and enjoy new democratic social relationships—within an instrumental or political strain aimed at
transforming American society.[12] The electric combination of expressive and
instrumental strains is one main reason for the enormous energy unleashed
during the decade.

The two groups most synonymous with youthful Sixties activism, SNCC and
SDS, were acutely affected by the tensions between these two strains. Both
expressed an instinctive mistrust of authoritarian rule and hierarchy, a need
for loving connection with others, and an emphasis on individual creativity
and integrity. These values not only foreshadowed what a "post-revolutionary"
America should look like, but they prescribed how the movement to change
America should go about this instrumental task. Therein lay the fundamental
dilemmas that confronted all movements of the 1960s: how to effect change
on a national scale through movements founded on personal relationships and

grassroots organizing, a utopian vision, and personal spontaneity; what to do when confronted by a repressive state; how to extend a qualitative, post-scarcity critique of society to those still wanting to be included in that society.

As events unfolded in the 1960s, the relationship between expressive and instrumental politics changed. Initially, activists believed the two were compatible, that they could succeed in transforming society. The result was a contagious, hopeful energy and committed idealism. Over time, buffeted by evasion and resistance, the horror of the Vietnam War, and crushing repression, the hope for fundamental political transformation was shattered; the gap between prefigurative and instrumental politics widened. One outcome was disillusionment, rage, and either disassociation from or aggressive militance toward society. Another was a radicalized critique of modern America, a shift from liberal to radical democracy. The Sixties experience taught activists that their expressive democratic vision was fundamentally incompatible with the root assumptions of American institutions.[13] Let us examine these points in greater detail.

THE SIXTIES DEMOCRATIC VISION

The two seminal movements of the 1960s, civil rights and the student New Left, expressed a vision of democracy rooted in but distinct from prevailing political values in modern America. At their core, both movements were grounded on four primary values:[14]

(1) *equality*, or the full inclusion of society's dispossessed;

(2) *personal empowerment*, or the liberation of each person from psychological constraints as well as social oppression—a shift from the masculinist "power over" to the feminist "power to";

(3) a *moral politics* grounded on belief in individual growth, compassion for one's fellow human beings—indeed for all life—and intolerance of injustice; and

(4) the central importance of *community* as a locus for meaningful engagement in life and politics.

In sum, the Movement encompassed both a distributive and a qualitative critique of the United States. It railed against the exclusion of black Americans and other groups at the same time that it criticized deep-seated flaws in the very society that excluded these groups.

In its drive to bring American blacks into the mainstream, the civil rights movement insisted that the United States live up to its liberal democratic values of equal rights and universal citizenship. However, it sought equality in a manner that embodied the distinctive Sixties vision of democracy—through direct action that liberated black (and white) Americans from patterns of self-denial and accommodation, through an inspiring moral vision that insisted on justice instead of delay and evasion, and through participatory engagement in one's community.

From Rosa Parks' refusal to give up her seat on a Montgomery bus, to the young students who sat in at lunch counters in the face of white violence, to black sharecroppers' defiant determination to register to vote, direct action broke the bonds of accommodation to oppression and forged a commitment to work for justice. It also represented an inspiring "vision of citizenship and selfhood that assumes the free individual has the capacity to manage social affairs in a direct, ethical, and rational manner"[15]—an implicit statement of belief in direct or participatory democracy.

The civil rights movement derived much of its persuasive power from a moral vision of politics based on love rather than an instrumental politics of self-interest, a vision articulated most forcefully by Martin Luther King, Jr. Often overlooked in the post-1960s mass media adulation of King was his, and the civil rights movement's, stubborn insistence on "freedom now" rather than business as usual.

Finally, the civil rights movement sought to transform the experiences of everyday life through engagement in the institutions of community, whether these were the church-based communities of Montgomery's bus boycott, the churches and schools of Birmingham, or the "beloved community" sought by the field workers of SNCC. Community building was an inherent part of working for democracy. As one Freedom Summer volunteer recalled, "You've got to build community above all else. If you give people a taste of it, there's nothing you can't do. It's that rich and, I should add, that rare an experience in our society. I never had it until I went South and I . . . *haven't been able to live without it since.*[16]

The civil rights movement was the formative catalyst for sustained activism throughout the rest of the decade. For many white student activists, the call to heal one of America's deepest wounds was the primary inspiration for their own political activism. In the early to mid-1960s both black and white students flocked to the civil rights cause. The other influential student organization of the decade, SDS, was closely tied to SNCC in its formative years and was responsible for the community organizing effort Economic Research and Action Project (ERAP) in a variety of inner city communities. Indeed, the early years of SDS were patterned after SNCC's emphasis on participation and organizing for empowerment. Like SNCC, SDS was pulled in different directions by its expressive and instrumental objectives.

In addition to racial and social differences, three qualities distinguished SDS and the New Left from SNCC and the civil rights struggle: the articulation of a New Left manifesto in the *Port Huron Statement*, concentration on the political implications of college and university life, and its transformation to a mass movement in the wake of the Vietnam War. While unremarkable in its policy recommendations, the *Port Huron Statement* nonetheless captured the distinctive flavor of youthful dissent: generational disaffection with an impersonal and acquisitive society, an emphasis on values and human relationships, and the unifying vision of participatory democracy. Reflecting the initial rumblings of campus discontent, SDS decried student apathy, in loco parentis university regulations, and an academic experience that prepared students to adapt to the corporate economy. The latter two themes would be played out on college campuses throughout the rest of the decade. It remained for the war in Vietnam to sharpen the student critique at the same time that it drew thousands of new recruits into the New Left, exacerbating its internal tensions.

Colored by experiences within the civil rights movement and New Left, and battered by the war in Vietnam, all major 1960s movements—from civil rights and New Left to the black power and antiwar movements to the counterculture and the women's and environmental movements—converged in embracing variants of these values.

The antiwar movement rejected a foreign policy that elevated instrumental rationality above moral compassion, and corporate and strategic interests above the right of national self-determination. The counterculture embraced the intuitive wisdom of the people over the technocratic rule of experts, the liberation of the physical and spiritual person from psychological repression, and the quest for loving union with a community of others. The women's movement championed the liberation of women from masculine domination and patriarchy in all cultures. It came to advocate the transformation of society according to a feminist ethic of caring and a community-based feminist praxis.

The ecology movement broadened the definition of domination to include human exploitation of nature, and it extended the notion of community to the entire ecosphere.

From a perspective outside the mainstream, Sixties movements expressed the voices of those whom society had systematically treated as "other"—black Americans, Latinos, the poor, Native Americans, women, gays, Vietnamese peasants, the intuitive and spiritual primitive, and nonhuman nature. In opposing domination, the rape metaphor applied not only to women, but to nonwhites, Vietnamese, and nature.[17] In place of domination, the Movement sought community and celebrated eros, or the union of equals.

In addition to the decade's turbulence, this convergent vision is what distinguishes the 1960s and lays the groundwork for its democratic legacy. The energy from all these movements revitalized the critical left at the same time that prevailing powers were shifting rightward.

PRECONDITIONS FOR THE SIXTIES: POST-WAR MODERNITY

The great sinfulness of the modern way is that it renders concrete things abstract.
—Daniel Berrigan, Jesuit peace activist

This is the age of machinery, mechanical nightmare,
The wonderful work of technology,
Napalm, hydrogen bomb, biological warfare.
This is the Twentieth Century, too much aggravation,
This is the age of insanity,
I'm a Twentieth Century man, but I don't want to be here.
—The Kinks, "Twentieth Century Man," © Davray Music, Ltd.

Both the specific issues and movements of the 1960s and the distinctive combination of expressive and instrumental politics can be traced to conditions in postwar America. World War II was a watershed in modern history, a turning point that unleashed many of the contradictory impulses of the modern world. The experience of the Holocaust and the destruction of Hiroshima and Nagasaki left an indelible mark on the human psyche. The introduction of biological, chemical, and atomic weaponry erased forever the notion of combat essentially limited to military personnel. The triumph over Nazism, exclusive possession of the bomb, and the resurgence of capitalist affluence left the United States in a position of economic and military preeminence in the world. The result was a heady belief in the "American Century" and a prevailing liberal consensus in American politics.[18]

The experiences of the Second World War triggered a variety of phenomena that emerged (or re-emerged) over the following twenty years: resurgent anticommunism, Keynesian management of economic growth fueled largely by defense expenditures, rising prosperity, the spread of American economic and strategic interests throughout the noncommunist world, the growth of mass marketing and the medium of television, the entry of millions of Americans into the home-owning middle class, a major investment in scientific and technical research, and the baby boom. Neocapitalism, or the postwar corporate system, was firmly in place.[19]

Yet all was not rosy. As Langdon Winner has observed, life in the 1950s "tended to inspire a fast belief in the religion of progress. Modern was always thought to be superior to 'old fashioned.' The pattern, however, was certainly not one of tailoring technology to suit human needs. Instead, the practice was that of renovating human needs to match what modern science and engineering happened to make available."[20] And, as Richard Flacks has argued, the contradiction between the "technological capacities and social organization of society" under advanced corporate capitalism feeds aspirations it cannot satisfy. Specifically, the liberating promise of modernity held out by technological capitalism is grounded on imperatives—profit, consumption, and uninhibited economic growth—that undermine the very promise of human liberation. The resulting "irrationalities and barbarities," in turn, feed a heightened desire for liberation. Nowhere were these contradictions more apparent than in the university, where students simultaneously became aware of an alternative future while being channeled into existing and narrowing career opportunities.[21]

The Second World War unleashed forces that would kindle fundamental challenges to the mainstream consensus. The war set in motion the unraveling of the colonial empires of Western Europe, a surge in Third World independence that would ultimately clash with American corporate and strategic interests. The war also wove science, industry, and government together in the management of American foreign policy. These developments would bear bitter fruit in Vietnam.[22]

The boom of suburban living spawned a young middle-class generation comfortably affluent but troubled by a gnawing sense that something was missing from the lives that lay before them. As Greg Calvert and Carol Nieman have contended, this postscarcity outlook ultimately posed a fundamental challenge to postwar capitalism

> When Establishment sources express the fear that a new generation of young Americans is rejecting consumption as a goal and definition of their lives, it expresses a very real concern on the part of the corporate establishment about its economic future and its historical *raison d'être*. In place of isolation, powerlessness, meaningless work, and lives defined as the production, ownership, and consumption of commodities, they are demanding community, love, creativity, and power over their own lives.[23]

In the postwar era, the social and physical landscape of traditional communities was being uprooted at the same time that television mesmerized children with shows like "Lassie" and "Leave It to Beaver." The post-Sputnik education boom spawned a new emphasis on efficiency that accentuated the bureaucratization of schooling. Fathers were caught up in the rat race, while middle-class mothers were encouraged to abandon their wartime employment for the new full-time job of housewife and primary parent. Working-class mothers, of course, could not afford such a luxury, and instead were bumped down to unskilled jobs by returning male workers.

These changes bore fruit. Dr. Benjamin Spock and the new domestic realm of middle-class motherhood encouraged child care approaches that focused attention on the individuation of each child, yet the constraints of mothers' sex roles would later generate a rebellion by their daughters. A booming mass-market economy accelerated the environmental crisis that erupted in the early 1970s.[24] Perhaps most important for the political struggles to come, the war made many aware of the price of racism, stimulating resurgent racial consciousness and assertiveness among black Americans. Both culminated in the modern civil rights movement.

Although the 1950s seemed like a Great Sleep in which millions of Americans went about the business of providing for themselves, and social scientists proclaimed the "end of ideology," both strains of the Sixties revolt—its push for democratization of American society and its expressive emphasis on personal relationships, community, and moral politics—were evident. The civil rights movement, most especially the Montgomery bus boycott and the *Brown v. Board of Education* decision, anticipated and stimulated much of the democratic impulse that was to come. The antimaterialism of the Beats, the emergence of rock and roll music, the rebellious personas of Elvis Presley, Marlon Brando, and James Dean, and the appearance of *Mad* magazine all tapped into the discontent of the young that snowballed into the expressive, countermodern culture of the 1960s.

Although the Old Left had been decimated by the Truman–McCarthy anticommunism purges and deeply fractured by both the Soviet invasion of Hungary and Nikita Khrushchev's denunciation of Joseph Stalin's brutality, journals like *Dissent* and organizations like the Young People's Socialists' League (YPSL) nurtured a critical perspective that influenced young New Leftists. A variety of left and pacifist figures—C. Wright Mills, Herbert Marcuse, Michael Harrington, A. J. Muste, I. F. Stone, Norman O. Brown, Paul Goodman, Staughton Lynd, Howard Zinn, and others—articulated critical insights that continued to inform activists throughout much of the Sixties.[25]

The seeds of a radical rebellion were present. The contradictions of modern technocratic institutions spawned movements that would struggle to contain their own internal tensions.

JOHN F. KENNEDY AND THE PROMISE OF THE EARLY 1960S

There was a definite flowering-out of positive feelings when John Kennedy became President. The Civil Rights movement was giving off positive vibrations. There was a great feeling of reform, that things could be changed. . . . Things looked incredibly promising.
—Phil Ochs, folksinger

It is precisely when things are beginning to go better that the contradictions and demands of the situations will explode at once.
—Andre Gorz, *Capitalism in Crisis*

Several forces came to a head with the election of John Kennedy as president in 1960. The resurgent civil rights movement gained new steam, feeling it had found a sympathetic ear in the White House. Young Americans were inspired by the personable young president's call to serve their country's best interests. A new wave of managerial technocrats were drawn to the analytical pragmatism of the new administration, while died-in-the-wool liberals found government niches from which they could advance the cause of human justice. In effect, Kennedy's pragmatic liberalism (followed by the early years of Lyndon Johnson's Great Society) activated the heady promises of liberal government and scientific progress: social problem solving and a compassionate welfare state, assertion of U.S. preeminence in defense of the "free world," and a belief in economic growth as the key to opportunity for society's dispossessed.

Much of Kennedy's impact derived from his distinctive personality—his mastery of rhetoric and his ability to inspire the public with his vision; the constant image of an administration in motion, tackling crises (some of his own creation) and solving problems that obstructed social progress; his quick intelligence and ability to appear in command of an enormous flow of information; his personal charm and ready wit, especially effective in encounters with the press; and the important fact that he seemed to be responsive to a world in flux.

Kennedy had a particularly poignant effect on the disaffected young who, in Paul Goodman's terms, had been deprived of the romance of patriotism during the 1950s. As Goodman remarked in the mid-1960s, "John Kennedy hit on the Posture of Sacrifice, which was what young people wanted to hear, something to give meaning to the affluent society."[26] Novelist Norman Mailer also sensed the significance of a Kennedy election for the America that was emerging from the 1950s. As he wrote in 1960,

> Since the First World War Americans have been leading a double life, and our history has moved on two rivers, one visible, the other underground; there has been the history of politics which is concrete, factual, practical, and unbelievably dull if not for the consequences of the actions of some of these men; and there is a subterranean river of untapped, ferocious, lonely and romantic desires, that concentration of ecstasy and violence which is the dream life of the nation. . . . I knew if he became President, it would be an existential event; he would touch depths in American life which were uncharted . . . and we as a nation would finally be loose again in the historic seas of a national psyche which was willy-nilly and at last, again, adventurous.[27]

Significantly, Kennedy's rhetoric awakened hope for an expansion of liberal democracy; more Americans would be able to enjoy the benefits of full participation in public life and more people around the world would be able to live and breathe free from poverty and oppression. Despite Kennedy's conventional politics and his cautious pragmatism, his administration gave "unwilling charge," in Mailer's term, to energies previously underground.[28]

Initially, the confidence that things *could* change came from leaders like

John Kennedy and Martin Luther King, Jr. In different ways, these two men were gifted with an remarkable ability to convey confidence to their audience; their leadership was a catalyst for many to discard habitual accommodations to the deprivations or petty preoccupations of everyday life. Thus the fight for justice seemed more plausible and rewarding than the more typical flight from injustice. Young people drawn to activism could for a time believe (or want to believe) that their expressive politics would ultimately prevail, that democracy grounded on community and moral purpose was possible. Expressive and instrumental politics were joined.

The result was the high-energy, optimistic early Sixties, the time Carl Oglesby called the Heroic Period of the Movement, its Bronze Age.[29] It seemed, in short, as if America were reclaiming its idealistic heritage, its moral purpose, its promise. Martin Luther King's memorable "I Have a Dream" speech captured the infectious feeling of the time. The vitality and optimism that came to pervade American society is precisely what seems so remote and so improbable when viewed from afar. For many, these qualities define the Sixties they recall fondly. Tom Hayden recalls, "I still don't know where this messianic sense, this belief in being right, this confidence that we could speak for a generation came from. But the time was ripe, vibrating with potential."[30] As Morris Dickstein has observed of the primary form of cultural expression during these years,

> Folk music was the perfect expression of the green years of the early six-
> ties, the years of integration, interracial solidarity, "I have a dream," and
> "We shall overcome": the years of the Port Huron statement and the early
> New Left; the years of the lunch-counter sit-ins and ban-the-Bomb dem-
> onstrations. Folk music was living bridge between the protest culture of
> the New Left and the genuinely populist elements of the Old Left of the
> 1930s and after.[31]

Few in the shining moment of 1960 could anticipate the degree to which the awakening of the Sixties would come to pervade all areas of American society in the decade to come. A significant source of energy came from the expressive side of emerging activism. As Wini Breines observes, young people were caught up in the creative spirit of defining new forms of social relationship: "The release of suppressed expression was liberating. Most had never experienced anything like it. It went against all the formal and controlled notions of liberal politics, releasing genuinely political, democratic instincts while underscoring the manipulated and anti-political nature of the American political system. . . . Participatory visions and experiments were the fuel that fired the movement's grass roots. . . .[32] Over time, the Movement produced endless alternative or counterinstitutions: co-ops and communes, grassroots and community organizing efforts like ERAP, the Mississippi Freedom Democratic party, free universities and experimental colleges, community control experiments, store-front schools, underground newspapers, feminist consciousness-raising groups and collectives, and ecology action alliances.

Again and again, activists testified to the powerful emotions unlocked by their engagement in community. Jack Weinberg recalled of the Berkeley Free Speech movement, "The FSM . . . has been the most complete experience of my life, the most all-encompassing. . . . It gave me a sense of comradeship we had not known existed."[33] Freedom Summer volunteer Neil McCarthy described his time in Mississippi as "the most frightening and rewarding thing I've done in my life . . . the richest part [of the experience] was the bond you felt with everyone in the project. We were really a family."[34]

In their initial forays into activism, the young began a journey that, as Kenneth Keniston observed, would later evolve into a quest for new pathways of personal development, new values for living, new ways of knowing, new kinds of learning, new formulations of the world, new types of social organization, new tactics of political action, new patterns of international relations, and new controls on violence.[35]

This journey brought them increasingly into conflict with the social and political mainstream, for the Kennedy–Johnson legacy also lay the foundation for the democratic revolt of the disillusioned. As Allen J. Matusow argues, "By his heroic poses, his urgent rhetoric, his appeal to idealism and the nation's great traditions, Kennedy inadvertently helped arouse among millions a dormant desire to perfect America. . . . Only later, during Lyndon Johnson's term as president, would the limits of liberal good will become apparent and the flaws of liberal reform be exposed."[36] Kennedy's was a legacy of rising expectations and shattered illusions, of magnificent promises yet modest results. For many dispossessed people, it was an experience much like opening a long-locked door only to have a chain-lock snap the door back in their face. Sixties movements began *within* the system they were trying to change and ended up struggling *against* that system.

THE PROCESS OF RADICALIZATION

Through our involvement in specific struggles, then, we came to
understand that what we were opposed to was a system.
—Dick Cluster, *They Should Have Served that Cup of Coffee*

The process of radicalization began with three crucial ingredients—
belief in a community-based, egalitarian democracy; a sharp personal awareness of social ills; and a feeling of confidence that something could be done.
As new activists joined the civil rights movement in the South (or the Peace
Corps overseas), they came face to face with the compelling need to uproot
and eliminate appalling conditions of oppression and powerlessness. Others
were moved by the suffering they witnessed at greater distance. For both, what
had once been vague and abstract, even invisible, became more immediate
and concrete as oppressive conditions came to the surface. In parallel ways,
those in other movements were moved by the contrast between their own concrete awareness of suffering, and the inadequacy, even callousness, of society's
normal operations. The result was a powerful, personal sense that things had
to change.

The combination of moral values, awareness of injustice, and confidence
in change produced action, what George Katsiaficas has referred to as the "*eros
effect*, the massive awakening of the instinctual human need for justice and
for freedom."[37] In the 1960s, this meant joining activist organizations or more
established service agencies like the Peace Corps, or, most profoundly, engaging in direct action or "putting your body on the line." Black sharecroppers
risked death to register to vote, young men refused draft induction, women
dared to leave abusive mates.

In a variety of forms, personal action set in motion the remaining stages of
the radicalization process, although obviously not everyone traveled the same
path or the same distance in that process. Initially, direct action produced a
heady sense of empowerment, described by participants as a combination of
fear and ecstasy resulting from taking risks to change one's environment. It also
reinforced the personal commitment to work for justice. Out of this profound
personal engagement came the distinctive personal politics of the Sixties.[38] In
contrast to the more compartmentalized, abstract mainstream process, political action was bound up with personal authenticity.

The moral catalyst for change therefore came from outside the institutions
of government. During the early years of the civil rights movement, the inter-

play between activists and liberal officials in the federal government was the primary dramatic setting for the contradictions of liberal democracy, a process later played out in the antiwar movement. For those who had been optimistic, disillusionment began to set in. Endangered SNCC field workers came to see the federal government as a disinterested observer rather than a participant in remedying the injustices of Southern racism. College students came to see the traditional curriculum reflecting the vested interests of future employers. Antiwar activists rejected the authority of an administration that continually promised "light at the end of the tunnel." Hippies fled from the nightmarish violence of society while also rejecting the increasingly violent tactics of the New Left. Women activists were appalled to discover that their New Left boy-friends mirrored oppressive strains of the larger society. Ecologists despaired at society's perpetual "progress" toward ecological disaster.

For activists, the encounter with official evasion and resistance often became a catalytic event, triggered by an existential act that forever changed the way the actor viewed the system. One such act was getting arrested. As writer Hans Koning recalls, "Getting arrested is a salutary experience. When it has happened to you, you have lost your political virginity and gained new perspective. . . . A political arrest here means a falling-out between an individual and the state on a moral issue, and with the individual rather than the state and its police force on the side of morality."[39] Similarly, demonstrators found themselves assaulted by police at nonviolent sit-ins or by National Guard troops marching into their ranks.[40] These were moments of remarkable moral clarity about one's self in relation to the larger society. They produced a deepening commitment and a sharpened awareness of society's determination to resist change. They fostered a growing sense of being outlaws in America.

TRANSITION TO THE "HIGH SIXTIES"

> This generation was unique in the conviction that it could do something about war, racism, and economic justice. We never asked, "Jesus, what are we talking about?" The assumption was, "Of course." We were never in doubt.
> —Rennie Davis, SDS leader

While the process of radicalization took place at different times within each movement, it also colored the tone of the decade as a whole. In 1964–1965, events coming on the heels of the president's assassination signaled a basic shift in the national dynamics of change. In 1964, Congress passed the Civil Rights Act, followed by the Voting Rights Act and an avalanche of social legislation including the War on Poverty. Yet civil rights activists involved in the Mississippi Freedom Summer campaign were sharply alienated by the failure of the Democratic party to seat the Mississippi Freedom Democratic party at the 1964 convention. The first major urban riots of the decade exploded in Harlem and Watts, and in 1965, the first cries of "black power" were heard. Freedom Summer veterans also returned to college campuses in the North and began to mobilize the student movement, beginning with the Berkeley Free Speech movement.

Most crucially, the United States unofficially declared war on Vietnam through the Gulf of Tonkin Resolution, and began massive bombing and deployment of the first wave of ground troops. Nothing alienated, and in many cases radicalized, a broader segment of the young more than the war in Vietnam. The government's promise of winning the hearts and minds of the Vietnamese was shattered by the hideous experience of the war and of the young men who were shipped home in coffins or with broken bodies or damaged spirits.

These events helped usher in the "high Sixties," a time of mass movement characterized by two ultimately incompatible traits: a growing radical awareness of society's deeply rooted resistance to change, coupled with activists' still confident commitment to bring about change. As faith in leaders and the political process faded, the sense of efficacy came from participation in a momentous collective enterprise. As Ann Oakley recalls,

> The extraordinary intimacy experienced by people who have fallen in love is akin to that felt by participation in great political movements: one's sensory world expands, becomes more intense, the boundaries between people become diffused, ordinary human selfishness is replaced by an unusual altruism, and everyday routines and language become inappropriate to the description and working out of a relationship that cancels time by becoming "an eternalization of the present."[41]

The euphoria was powerful. Yet the seeds of an apocalyptic vision and an exaggerated belief in one's own power lurked beneath the surface. The tensions of a darkening decade were captured in Graham Nash's lyrics to "Chicago":

> We can change the world,
> Rearrange the world,

It's dying

To get better.

As the promise of the early Sixties disintegrated, activists experienced what Todd Gitlin has called "radical disappointment." They came to see their liberal allies as morally hypocritical, and the system as deeply entrenched and in need of more fundamental or radical change. They discovered that liberal rhetoric obscured a determination to maintain prevailing institutional arrangements. The liberal establishment spoke the language of democracy, but meant a democracy in which the powerful continued to hold most of the power. When push came to shove, those who held power rebuffed the claims of those who sought change. In short, activists came to be radicalized when they realized that liberalism inspired a form of personal activism and democracy that it ultimately could not tolerate, much less satisfy.

The tension between expressive and instrumental politics became too strong. As SDS national secretary Clark Kissinger asked, "How can one live his values in the movement and yet change an industrial society of 180,000,000 people?"[42] Activists increasingly felt the urge to disassociate from a society that seemingly expected them to "sell out" as a price for their participation. Many exercised a "great refusal," rejecting participation in society on society's terms. At different times, radical disassociation emerged in the black separatist movement, the creation of counterinstitutions like experimental colleges and free schools, the noncooperation or expatriation of draft resisters, the amazing and sometimes bizarre array of lifestyles in the counterculture, the creation of radical and lesbian feminist communities, and the total rejection of commercial technologies exhibited in elements of the counterculture and ecology movements. The only recourse, many felt, was to remove the stain of cooperation with a society that demanded amoral complicity in immoral acts.

Radical disappointment also fed activists' anger, not only at the system's injustice but at sympathetic liberals' willingness to compromise with the perpetrators of injustice. The result was renewed activism with a harder edge, a growing militance that in turn sharpened the conflict with society. Camus' words, "There are times . . . when the only feeling I have is one of mad revolt," describe a growing feeling in the decade's later years. As Todd Gitlin recalled, "The war was driving us nuts."[43] Something had to give.

TRANSITION TO THE LATE SIXTIES—1968

On August 28, 1963, the President welcomed civil rights leaders and
250,000 people to Washington for a sort of joyous celebration. On
August 28, 1968 we were gassed in front of the Conrad Hilton and both
Kennedys were dead. The difference between those two things, although
they're only five years apart, is too staggering to sort out and fully
understand right now.
—Tom Hayden, interview in *The Movement*, October 1968

In 1968, it all came apart. The bloody Tet Offensive exploded administration myths about the "light at the end of the tunnel" in Vietnam. Senators Eugene McCarthy and Robert Kennedy challenged the President for the
Democratic nomination, and Lyndon Johnson withdrew from the presidential race. Martin Luther King, Jr., and Robert Kennedy, the two mainstream
political figures who held out the greatest hope for change, were shockingly, yet
almost predictably, assassinated. Students took over five buildings at Columbia University and defiantly held them until a brutal police assault ended
the occupation. Americans became aware of the global extent of revolt as a
student–worker strike immobilized Paris, and Soviet tanks rolled into Prague
to crush the Czech uprising. Finally, the Democratic National Convention
in Chicago itself grimly recalled Prague as National Guardsmen patrolled the
barbwired city and Chicago police assaulted protesters and reporters outside
the convention hall. As Hans Koning recalled, "The essence of 1968 was a
clarity of perception. It was as if a curtain had been raised, a veil lifted. The
clichés, platitudes, and myths of our public life . . . were suddenly seen as
such." [44] The late Sixties were ushered in by the election of Richard Nixon and
Spiro Agnew. The Movement began to spin out of control.

While the mid-Sixties had taught activists that the system was capable of
enormous evil, it had also seemed responsive to mass movements that clearly
demanded change, especially as the numbers of those demanding change
swelled. The late Sixties taught activists that the system was only symbolically
responsive. Also, as Richard Flacks argued in 1966, the Vietnam War revealed
a fundamental dilemma for the New Left:

It has helped to build the Left. But people on the Left can't responsibly
worry about much else as long as it goes on. And the more they accept the
responsibility for trying to end the war, the more militant they become—
and the more they sense their own impotence, isolation, and alienation

from the larger society. . . . The war helps to build the radical movement, but the necessary obsession to work to end it is, in many ways, incompatible with *achieving* such a movement.[45]

By this time, the system was fighting back, seemingly determined to crush the Movement. Government repression was pervasive. Under Director J. Edgar Hoover, the FBI not only kept Movement activists under surveillance, they used provocateurs to instigate violence at innumerable demonstrations, and infiltrators who fanned the flames of factionalism within the black power movement and underground press. They pressured corporations like Columbia Records not to advertise in the underground papers, and planted damaging disinformation about Movement activists in the mainstream press. Local police, most notoriously in Chicago and Oakland, harassed and arrested black and white radicals, shut down underground newspapers, and even killed several Black Panthers in dubious shoot-outs. The conspiracy trial of the Chicago Seven provided an insane kind of comic relief within the Movement, yet sent the clear message that there *was* a conspiracy by the Nixon administration to eradicate the Movement.[46] Movement paranoia increased apace. It all became terribly real at Kent State in 1970.

As society's resistance stiffened, the tendency to disassociate led to a splintering of Movement alliances. Black militants clashed with feminists, as did one SDS faction with another, hippies with politicos, men with women, straights with gays—each with its own agenda. Ultimately the disassociation could not be sustained. Abe Peck recalls,

> Movement politics had taken on an edge of violence and frustration. Talented underground staffers chafed under collectivity. Music, sweet rock music, was slipping away from political ties that had been amorphous even at their peak. Underground-press staffers felt besieged. Various alliances—acidheads and Panthers, gays and socialists—were forming, then blowing apart. The Panthers—the very vanguard party—had finally suffered a split caused by ideology, ego, the isolation of their militant position, and ceaseless government repression.[47]

More generally, the Movement's twin strains, the prefigurative creation of a new democratic community and the instrumental drive to transform institutions, fractured. As hope died late in the decade, the personal politics of the 1960s tended to become *either* personal *or* political, either expressive or instrumental. The movements of the Sixties evolved toward two opposite extremes. One extreme expressed a militant perseverance to change society even if it meant abandoning the personal morality that originally inspired Sixties movements. The organized New Left, the heirs of SNCC and SDS, emphasized an instrumental revolutionary politics in which the ends justified the often violent means. The politics of experience was replaced by borrowed dogma from the Marxist–Leninist tradition. Amidst squabbles over "Revolutionary Korrectness," in Abe Peck's phrase, the New Left embraced "tyrannies in the name of democracy." It thereby left itself open to the accusation that it mirrored the moral degradation of the system it opposed so violently. And the New Left provided an obvious scapegoat for the effort to turn the United States to the right.[48]

The opposite extreme, represented by counterculture dropouts, championed an abandonment of political concerns and a preoccupation with inner or private reality. Recoiling from the heavy turbulence of political struggle, many young people (especially the younger phalanx of the Sixties generation) abandoned the Movement's declining political hopefulness and demonstrated little awareness of the economic roots of the social mores they rejected. This was the key to the counterculture's vulnerability, the reason it deteriorated into excessive disassociation only to be largely absorbed by the mainstream culture. However short-sighted, excessive, or naive the counterculture may have been, it represented a deeply felt need to escape the alienating mainstream culture, to turn inward and explore personal qualities repressed in conventional society, and to live in more intimate connectedness with others, all of which were elements at the core of Sixties prefigurative politics.

Most of the young did not move to either extreme. Seasoned activists clung to whatever sense of community they could find, even if that community was largely defined by what it was not. Many continued to turn out for massive antiwar protests while grappling with issues closer to home. The period of radical disassociation also provided the psychological space that enabled many to see society more clearly, thereby revitalizing a Left critique. It nourished a vast multitude of experiments and meetings of the mind, all exploring visions of democracy, community, and personal empowerment. Together with feminism and ecology, which were the two new pro-active movements of the late 1960s and early 1970s, these participatory experiments are part of the unfinished democratic legacy of the Sixties.

Meanwhile, as America went back to business, the Movement licked its wounds and began to take a look at what it had and had not accomplished, where it had gone wrong, ways in which the system perpetuated itself, and the reasons for this perpetuation. As Hans Koning put it,

> It is tiring to look reality in the eye, nearly as hard as looking at the sun, looking at death. No one can keep that up. Challenging it may be, but no one wants seven days a week of challenge.
>
> The powers-that-be, whose empire had been shaken and threatened by our sixties insight, took advantage of our weariness and invited this nation to relax and feel good.[49]

Since the Sixties, society has gone in two directions, one effectively rejecting the democratic and communitarian vision of the Sixties, the other continuing to embrace that vision in various forms.

■ Hard Lessons

For many activists—those who come together to reflect on Sixties movements and events, those who continue to embrace the prefigurative democratic vision of the Sixties in their lifestyles and their work, and those who are actively committed to any of the myriad movements that reflect those values—the Sixties experience is part of a continuing path of political commitment and personal growth. In large part, this movement for democracy is grounded on lessons learned through the experiences of the 1960s.

Many activists' experiences forged their consciousness of the underside of American life that has not been and cannot be obscured by politicians' rhetoric about standing tall, government propaganda about overseas ventures, or mass media hype about winning the Cold War. If the Sixties experience demonstrated anything, it was the dramatic difference between the "advertisement" and the "product." The intensity and emotion of Sixties experiences have, over time, led to radical assessment of American culture and institutions.[50]

At the core of Sixties' lessons was the awareness that, whatever virtues they might possess, American institutions are fundamentally incompatible with the democratic vision that inspired and drew so many to activism. Instead of eradicating racial oppression, a system under fire cautiously removed its most blatant forms of expression, ultimately rendering invisible those who bore the double burden of racism and class inequality. Instead of eliminating poverty, this system, amidst great flourish and for a limited period of time, produced program after program that softened the cruelest edge of suffering for those fortunate enough to benefit. Instead of empowering people, the system relied increasingly on experts who in the best of times provided the needy with incremental material and psychological gains. Instead of a politics grounded on moral compassion, activists encountered resistance to their moral claims justified by the "higher good" of system maintenance. Instead of a culture that valued the full flowering of individuality, they found a society that purports to leave people alone yet barrages them daily with inducements to fit into the mass culture. Instead of the flourishing of community, they encountered faceless bureaucracy, distant arenas of political decision-making, and a marketplace that accelerated the extinction of traditional communities and the natural landscape. And, of course, instead of an America making the world safe for democracy, they discovered a bipartisan, elite-driven foreign policy virtually crushing the life blood out of a small Asian nation, all to prove its commitment to sustaining the American empire. These lessons were pounded home by the traumatic shocks of the decade: assassinations, sell-outs by party politicians, arrests, violent assaults by police or National Guard, and the searing reality of Vietnam.

These experiences converged to teach two deeper lessons. First, the oppression and dehumanization targeted by Sixties movements were not so much the result of bad men as they were sustained by the incentives and rewards that characterize America's most hallowed institutions—free elections, two-party competition, representative democracy, a free press, universal education, a capitalist economy, and the American tradition of political liberalism. Second, these institutions are inherently incapable of eradicating the ills that so galled activists—poverty, racial and sexual inequality, narrowly technocratic education, an aggressive foreign policy, and the destruction of community and the environment.

In part, these institutional limitations are rooted in a liberal political system sustained in the aggregate by the individual pursuit of self-interest. From John Kennedy's inauguration to Lyndon Johnson's call for a Great Society, Sixties activists encountered a political process that brimmed with hopeful rhetoric yet repeatedly responded to the imperative of system maintenance. All of the most hopeful and seemingly idealistic programs, from Kennedy's Peace Corps and Alliance for Progress to Lyndon Johnson's War on Poverty, reflected not only an effort to do good but also an insider's response to threats to the system. Overseas crises rested on the "hoariest of Cold War myths: the idea of a monolithic communist drive, headed by the Soviet Union, to achieve world domination."[51] The antipoverty bill was, in the words of the *New York Times*, an "anti-riot bill."

The objective of defending the system repeatedly overrode more progressive intentions whenever the two came into conflict, which they invariably did. Thus when Peace Corps volunteers began to protest publicly against the war in Vietnam, the Johnson administration tried to silence them. When military dictatorships were seen as the only alternative to social revolutions in Latin America, they were found to be compatible with U.S. intentions despite their brutality and systematic oppression of peasants. When community action agencies articulated the demands of poor people against big-city Democratic mayors, the Johnson administration placed them under the authority of mayors, and the Nixon administration later targeted the Office of Economic Opportunity (OEO) for elimination.

In the case of Vietnam, successive administrations deceived their antiwar critics and manipulated public support with increasing intensity and vindictiveness. Again and again, the purpose of executive action and rhetoric was to limit awareness of U.S. policy and its effects. Examples of executive deceit, suppression of information, and manipulation of the public during the Vietnam War were legion.[52] The result was that traditional liberal–democratic checks like congressional oversight and a free press were rendered virtually impotent until late in the 1960s when antiwar sentiments had spread to a majority of the public and elite groups were themselves sharply divided over the wisdom of continuing the war.

A second reason for the primacy of system maintenance is procedural; innovative and redistributive policies have traditionally been designed and implemented through a pluralist process dominated by powerful interest groups. Thus the Alliance for Progress, advertised as lifting Latin America out of poverty and desolation, was sold to skeptical American corporate interests with guarantees that loan recipients would maintain a good investment climate, which meant, for example, no deficit spending for agrarian reform or unemployment compensation.[53] For their part, the participation of Latin American officials was secured with generous economic and military aid. Thus, progressive reform in Latin America was stifled while military aid increased by 50 percent. Domestically, both Kennedy and Johnson instinctively resisted civil rights demands because they feared alienating the white South.[54] The one truly participatory segment of the poverty program, the Community Action Program, was rapidly scuttled when big-city mayors complained that the program empowered poor communities independently of city hall. The potentially destabilizing demands of the poor were co-opted by those with a stake in the very institutions within which the poor were voiceless.

Finally, the liberal politics of the 1960s were permeated by the now dominant ethos of managerial technocracy. Problem areas like poverty, juvenile delinquency, illiteracy, Third World underdevelopment, and American strategic interests were isolated and studied through an allegedly objective social science. The poor were viewed abstractly as merely lacking in sufficient skills and motivation—which could be provided through programs engineered by trained professionals—rather than empathically as caught in systemic oppression. Third World nations were seen as simply lacking in the knowledge and investment capital for development based on the American model; these, too, could be provided by American experts. Programs were designed from the top down by an elite realm of decision-makers cut off from the world of their subjects, by insiders righteously unaware that their own subjectivity distorted the object of their analysis and policy. The Alliance for Progress, the vast Great Society programs, and, most blatantly, the war in Vietnam were suffused with a technocratic mindset caught up in its own logic and captive to its distorted world of statistics.[55]

The combination of euphoric liberal rhetoric, programs designed and implemented by technocrats, and the resistance of powerful elite interests sharpened radical perceptions in the Sixties. When public officials pursued their technocratic visions in the face of mounting contradictory evidence, government policy seemed completely irrational. Again, the Vietnam War was the most blatant example of seemingly contradictory, illogical, and counterproductive policies. Perhaps the ultimate metaphor for the war was the oft-quoted commander's report, "We had to destroy the village in order to save it."[56] Similar examples of irrationality could be seen in the effort to end poverty through an educational process designed to separate "winners" from "losers," or the short-sighted effort to quell urban riots with band-aid public services but no meaningful job opportunities, or the never-ending quest for technical fixes to solve environmental problems or meet energy needs.

The perception of government policy as permeated by irrationality suggested that either American policy makers *were* irrational or that there *was* a rationale for U.S. actions different from what most Americans were told.

Both explanations contain some truth. In the case of Vietnam, for example, the war's irrationality reflected the degree to which individuals deceived themselves in order to retain their belief in the rightness of their actions (and to avoid intensely uncomfortable self-scrutiny). Its rationality, on the other hand, reflected the superordinate goal of maintaining American hegemony, a willingness to use force to crush a war of national liberation and leave a nation so effectively disabled that it posed no danger of inspiring other Third World nations to follow a similar path.

Insights into the logic of seemingly irrational patterns of government behavior brought critics face to face with functional imperatives of a capitalist economy—a fourth and, some would say, ultimate reason for system maintenance. In the wake of Sixties experiences, a revitalized Left has scrutinized ways in which virtually all targets of Sixties concern are tied to imperatives of global capitalism.

This radical critique brings home some of the most enduring hard lessons of the 1960s, especially as these were confirmed by the rightist agenda of corporate retrenchment and Third World intervention during the 1980s. If anything like the hopeful democratic vision of the 1960s is ever to be realized, I would suggest that these are among the most important lessons to learn from that decade's experience.

At the same time, movements for human liberation, community, and ecological sanity can learn from the shortcomings of Sixties movements themselves. The day may come again when it seems feasible to "speak truth to power" with effective results. Yet the Sixties experience taught again and again that this is an unrealistic expectation that fueled painful disillusionment and self-defeating outbursts of rage and violence. The naiveté of early-Sixties hopefulness was one side of the emotional experience of the Sixties; apocalyptic rage late in the decade was another. Other things being equal, there is a crucial difference between controlled anger that produces determined activism and rage that strikes out at any and all targets.

Similarly, base-building is probably more fundamentally important than gaining short-term concessions or reforms from powerful elites, except as these demonstrate the efficacy of political mobilization. Put somewhat differently, progressive action should focus its attention and energy laterally as well as vertically—addressing the need to build connections with others in the process of demanding change from "above." At least, all forms of political action should bear in mind a lesson from their most successful Sixties predecessors:

for action to be persuasive, the psychological distance between activists and audience must be smaller than the distance between audience and target.

Finally, the rapidly changing world offers expanding opportunities for mobilization in small communities and across national borders. In the absence of a powerful communist "menace," a truly global capitalist economy is likely to highlight the contradictions of capitalism—providing glimpses of human liberation while undermining its achievability, requiring the exploitation of many for the benefit of relatively few, and, driven by market and growth imperatives, progressively destroying the ecosphere. Unless persuasive new demons are promulgated to divert attention from these contradictions, an aroused public will be more likely to demand human and social control of market forces, both at the global level and in the local community.

All this is, of course, conjectural. It is, however, a good deal more realistic than the myopic optimism of those who, like their "end of ideology" predecessors in the 1950s, assert that we are at the "end of history." They would have us ignore history—including the history of the 1960s.

PART TWO
Movements of
the Sixties

2 The Struggle for Racial Justice
The Sixties Catalyst

How many years can some people exist,
Before they're allowed to be free?
How many times can a man turn his head
Pretending he just doesn't see?
The answer, my friend, is blowin' in the wind.
The answer is blowin' in the wind.
—Bob Dylan, "Blowin' in the Wind"

The Civil Rights Movement exposed the basic structure of the
country which, as it's set up, cannot sustain itself without
oppressing someone.
—Bernice Reagon, SNCC activist

The movement for civil rights and racial equality was the
single most important catalyst for the awakening liberal activism in the Sixties
and the subsequent democratic revolt against modern, liberal America. Beginning in the 1950s, the modern civil rights movement reflected a new assertiveness among black Americans and awakened a fresh moral consciousness
among the white majority. For many, especially the young, it spawned a growing awareness of the vast gap between liberal rhetoric and social reality. The
movement both inspired other movements of the Sixties and foreshadowed
their experience and evolution.

The struggle for racial justice consisted of two often inseparable movements.
One was an instrumental, liberal movement that focused primarily on the
extension of social, legal, and political rights in the South. This movement
was grounded on faith in liberal institutions, extending constitutional rights
to blacks through class-action litigation, mobilizing public pressure on elected
representatives to enact civil rights legislation, and improving blacks' marketplace opportunities through government action. In classic liberal–democratic

fashion, extending these rights was seen as the path to realizing full racial equality.

The other movement was more democratic and ultimately more radical. It spawned the expressive politics of the 1960s. Initially, the emphasis on personal liberation and empowerment, moral politics, and community engagement was implicit in the tactics of the liberal movement to extend rights; eventually, these became explicit goals, carrying over into other movements of the decade. The vision of racial equality also transcended traditional liberal reformism to target the class-based inequality inherent in a capitalist economy. Full inclusion of the dispossessed meant addressing the economic forces that made widespread inequality inevitable.

In essence, the liberal civil rights movement was an effort to bring the South into the liberal American mainstream, while the democratic movement, which incorporated black power, attempted to reorder that mainstream. The liberal movement for civil rights succeeded to a remarkable degree, making it one of the great movements for emancipation in American history. Passage of the Civil Rights Act of 1964 and the Voting Rights Act of 1965 were instrumental in transforming southern society from a feudal caste system to one resembling that of the North.[1] De jure school segregation was abolished, replaced by the de facto segregation pattern that prevails in Northern urban areas.[2] Black registration and voting increased dramatically as federal enforcement made its mark.[3] These changes have produced far greater black representation in the American political system.[4] The election of black mayors in Birmingham and Atlanta, and Jesse Jackson's presidential campaigns of 1984 and 1988, were scarcely imaginable at the beginning of the struggle for civil rights. Or, as David Garrow argued in 1978, "In 1965 very few could have imagined that little more than a decade later a white former governor of Georgia from Sumter County would accept the presidential nomination of the Democratic Party on a platform containing the Reverend Martin Luther King, Sr., and Coretta Scott King, and to the strains of the civil rights movement's favorite anthem, 'We Shall Overcome.'"[5] Middle-class blacks have been the civil rights movement's primary beneficiaries, taking advantage of their hard-won access to mainstream institutions.

The democratic movement for racial justice had quite different effects. First, its prefigurative strain had a powerful impact on its participants, the black Americans who cast off years of accommodation to oppression and those white Americans who joined in their struggle. As Jerry Watts observed, "The act of

becoming politicized, of claiming a space and identity, where there had previously been only silence, was, given the historical and social circumstances
of southern blacks, as radical an act as occurred in the 60s."[6] Direct action,
putting one's body on the line, meant that people had to overcome or sus-
pend palpable fears of isolation, violence, and death. As Ralph Abernathy
recalled of mass meetings in Montgomery's bus boycott, "The fear left that had
shackled us across the years—all left suddenly when we were in that church
together."[7] Abraham Wood recalled of the Birmingham protests of 1963,

> When you get caught up in the Movement, you just lose some of your
> fear. It's an amazing kind of thing. I can look back now at some of the
> situations we got involved in and I didn't think about it to be afraid. At the
> time. But when you look back at some of the situations we were in, you
> kind of shudder afterwards. But when you are caught up in the emotion
> of the Movement and you commit yourself, you really don't worry about
> what's going to happen to you.[8]

For the first time in American history, masses of black Americans shook
off the burden of years of internalized oppression and justifiable fear of white
police power to act for their own emancipation. In the northern ghettoes,
young blacks rebelliously asserted that they would no longer submit quietly to
the hopeless oppression of slum life. The contagious intensity of empowerment became the explicit goal of the black power movement.

White students who traveled south to join in the Mississippi Freedom Summer campaign often found themselves cut off from their pasts, even their
families. They found inspiration in the Student Non-violent Coordinating
Committee (SNCC) activists who, in one volunteer's recollection, "have a free-
ness of spirit that I've rarely seen. . . . I feel like I've finally come home."[9]
They embarked on a journey of personal liberation as well as political action,
inspired by the "high moral purpose, adventure, and rich community"[10] they
encountered in the project. Those who took action in conjunction with hundreds of others felt empowered by making history.

Besides requiring the existential decision to act, the prefigurative civil rights
movement was grounded on a powerful moral force articulated most emphati-
cally by Martin Luther King, Jr. As Vincent Harding has observed,

> Love was the answer. Not sentimentality, but the tough and resolute love
> that refused bitterness and hatred but stood firmly against every shred of

injustice. Few brands of black radicalism had ever required so much. Men were not only urged to stand and face the menace, they were called upon to be true to themselves and to reject the very weapons that had destroyed them for so long. They were called upon to transform American life by substituting moral and spiritual courage for its traditional dependence upon violence and coercion.[11]

The moral tenor of civil rights activism had a powerful impact not only on participants, but on innumerable white observers. In the early weeks of the Montgomery bus boycott, Juliette Morgan, a white librarian, wrote to the local newspaper, "It is hard to imagine a soul so dead, a heart so hard, a vision so blinded and provincial as not to be awed with admiration at the quiet dignity, discipline and dedication with which the Negroes have conducted the boycott."[12]

For participants, the sense of doing what was clearly right reinforced the determination to act and intensified the exhilaration of joining in a momentous collective experience. As Doug McAdam described the 1964 Freedom Summer, "The combination of fear, history-making media attention, exposure to new lifestyles, and sense of political mission that suffused the project had produced for many the type of transcendent, larger-than-life experiences that would bind them to the movement for years to come."[13] The sense of community was everywhere present, from the mass church meetings in Montgomery to the "freedom" communes and voter registration efforts of SNCC. Where community wasn't present—as, for example, in the beleaguered Northern ghettoes—it was sought through community organizing and the community control movement.

The democratic struggle for racial justice influenced and anticipated the rest of the 1960s in two ways. First, its infectious spirit stimulated a revived liberalism in the political mainstream and a rich diversity of ethically rooted liberation movements among other outcast minorities in the United States. Civil rights agitation marked the beginning of white America's awakening, a process that was to continue painfully through the Sixties. As James Baldwin wrote in 1963:

The American Negro has the great advantage of having never believed that collection of myths to which white Americans cling: that their ancestors were all freedom-loving heroes, that they were born in the greatest country the world has ever seen, or that Americans are invincible in battle and wise in peace, that Americans have always dealt honorably with Mexicans and Indians and all other neighbors or inferiors, that American men are the world's most direct and virile, that American women are pure.[14]

The movement was also a powerful, experiential catalyst for other struggles of the 1960s—the moral activism against the war in Vietnam, student unrest on college campuses, agitation to liberate public education and eliminate poverty, the experimental counterculture, and the women's liberation movement.[15]

Northern white students who joined SNCC's Mississippi Freedom Summer project in 1964 returned to northern campuses with a burning sense of urgency about the social struggles of the day. As Mario Savio, who returned to Berkeley and became one of the leaders of the 1964 Free Speech Movement, asserted, "Last summer I went to Mississippi to join the struggle there for civil rights. This fall I am engaged in another phase of the same struggle, this time in Berkeley."[16] Before long many of these same students were concentrating their moral indignation and direct action tactics on the war in Vietnam. The Freedom Schools of the Freedom Summer project helped awaken an educational liberation movement that spanned the rest of the decade. The intense communal living, work shirts and dungarees, and breakdown of sexual inhibitions and taboos of the Freedom Summer set in motion a process that was to flower in the counterculture. Finally, the civil rights experience inspired the awakening women's movement of the later Sixties through leadership roles played by black women and the contradictory second-class citizenship often experienced by female SNCC field workers.

More than anything else, the civil rights movement galvanized the phenomenon known as "the Sixties." The heightened sense of moral awareness, the loneliness of breaking from one's social roots, the exhilaration of being part of history, the bonds of kinship reinforced by music and communal work, and the courage gained from collective effort, all became characteristics of the activist "Sixties generation" as it broadened its assault on American society.

The civil rights struggle also taught many young activists their first hard lessons about America. Despite the constant threat of violence and terror in the largely hostile South, civil rights workers believed they could "speak truth to power" and national political leaders and institutions would respond. Yet their experiences taught them otherwise. Assaulted by white violence, buffeted by two-party politics and legislative delay, often denied federal enforcement and protection, civil rights activists tasted the bitter fruit of radical disillusionment.[17] The year 1964 was the watershed.

The struggle for racial justice revealed the basic incompatibility between the Movement and the system. Direct action contained a vision of participatory democracy inherently at odds with pluralistic, interest group liberalism. The moral creed of nonviolence and the moralistic stance against compromising with injustice were ultimately incompatible with the modern notion of value free public space, the amoral relativism of interest group exchange, and the instrumental incentives fed by the market economy. Furthermore, the civil rights movement was grounded on cultural and political institutions of community that were threatened by the impersonal, atomistic culture of modernity.

The embryo of radical disassocation was present from the beginning of the liberal movement for equal rights. It became more overt when racial equality emerged as the overriding goal. Black activists from Martin Luther King to the Black Panthers recognized the central importance of economic inequality and its roots in American capitalism.[18] More and more radicalized blacks felt driven to disassociate from a decadent system. The black power movement encompassed the culturally grounded drive for black separatism, the democratic emphasis on community power, and a critique of corporate capitalism. The assault on inequality moved toward militant confrontation with local and national institutions. It also encountered more effective resistance and repression by mainstream America.

Thus, over time, the civil rights struggle evolved from a mainstream, liberal vision to a more democratic, and ultimately radical, perspective; an evolution captured in the shifting ground among leaders and groups that were preeminent in the movement. Through it all, the movement confronted white violence, first from the terrorism of southern sheriffs, police dogs, and notorious vigilantes like the Ku Klux Klan and White Citizens Council and later, from police brutality in Northern cities and systematic harassment and repression by the FBI.

■ The Beginnings, 1953–1960

A bill is coming in that I fear America is not prepared to pay.
—James Baldwin, *The Fire Next Time*

After the conclusion of the Second World War, two preconditions for the modern civil rights struggle were in place. One was the system of oppression that permeated the South, most viciously in the deep southern states of Alabama, Mississippi, and Louisiana. While racial prejudice and discrimination existed in the North, racial oppression in the South was more total, less legitimized by liberal values and institutions. Or as a black saying put it, "In the North the white man says, 'Negro, go as high as you can but don't come close,' and in the South the white man says, 'Negro, come as close as you can but don't go up.'" A tripartite system of economic, political, and personal control prevailed. Blacks who were fortunate enough to find employment filled jobs at the bottom of the work hierarchy, subject to white supervisors and managers. Prohibitive legal sanctions systematically excluded them from the political process. Social segregation denied them personal freedoms enjoyed by whites. And they were subjected to humiliating self-denial by the norms of interracial relations.

Throughout the South (and much of the North), white violence and terror against blacks always lurked in the background, ready to erupt if any blacks became "uppity," which meant displeasing the arbitrary whims of whites. A black male who failed to lower his eyes in the presence of a white female ran the risk of a brutal beating or death. It "just wasn't done." Anyone daring to be assertive faced physical harm at the hands of white vigilantes, from house bombings and arson to assault on the roadways to death by lynching. No place was safe, even those limited rural areas where black farmers carried weapons for their self-defense.

The second precondition for the modern civil rights movement reflected changing social and attitudinal patterns spawned by the Second World War. The accelerated migration from rural to urban areas meant that blacks lived in more concentrated segregated areas, so it became easier to perceive their collective predicament as well as their collective strength. The anticolonial revolt of African nations also provided an inspiring example for African-Americans, as well as a fitting metaphor for their experience.

Furthermore, the Second World War itself heightened black assertiveness and white consciousness. The struggle against the Nazis made many white Americans more sensitive to racism and discrimination in the United States. James Baldwin maintained that Nazism forever erased any claim of white superiority and demonstrated that the "ultimate, genocidal expression of racism" was possible in a nation that claimed to be "civilized and Christian."[19] Meanwhile, black servicemen who "fought for democracy" alongside white servicemen returned to the jarring reality of southern oppression. The war gave existing civil rights groups new impetus for action.

THE NAACP AND *BROWN V. THE BOARD OF EDUCATION*

The modern civil rights movement began with the seminal role played by the National Association for the Advancement of Colored People (NAACP), the oldest modern civil rights group. An integrated and bureaucratic national organization headquartered in New York City, the NAACP used litigation to win for southern blacks the same constitutional rights enjoyed by other Americans. Of all the civil rights groups, this was the most purely liberal, relying as it did on legal petition to hold in check oppressive white majorities in the South.

The NAACP strategy dated back to 1915, when it succeeded in overturning the grandfather clause of southern Jim Crow laws, a technical ploy used to deny southern blacks the right to vote. Over the years, NAACP chapters spread throughout the South while the national organization continued its constitutional assault on segregation in education and public transportation and its effort to eradicate white terrorism.

In 1950, a national conference of NAACP lawyers decided to wage an all-out assault on segregated education in the South. The five lawsuits filed in federal courts between 1950 and 1952 culminated in the landmark *Brown v. Board of Education* decisions in 1954 and 1955 overturning de jure segregation and the notion of separate but equal education in the South.

The *Brown* decision had mixed results. Most black leaders and newspapers were "pleased but cautious" in their remarks,[20] hopeful for a break in southern oppression but wary of the good intentions of white America. The reaction in the white South was more forceful, with cries of outrage and defiance issuing from Governors Herman Talmadge of Georgia and James Byrnes of South Carolina and Senators Harry Byrd of Virginia and James Eastland of Mississippi. Southern legislatures took advantage of the Supreme Court's "all deliberate speed" mandate to evade desegregation. Between 1954 and 1959, southern NAACP chapters were assaulted by terroristic attacks, FBI surveillance, and state bans on NAACP membership.

Ultimately, however, the *Brown* decision provided southern blacks with an institutional ally in the federal government, with the resulting legitimacy grounded in national values. It generated new hope that the American political system might respond to their petition for an end to segregation and centuries of oppression. In conjunction with the rising postwar assertiveness of black Americans, it provided an impetus for the direct action strategies of black activists in southern communities.

DIRECT ACTION I: THE MONTGOMERY BUS BOYCOTT

The spark that ignited the second wave of civil rights activism was the nationally visible Montgomery bus boycott. The immediate catalyst for the boycott occurred on December 1, 1955, when Rosa Parks refused to give up her seat in the white section at the front of a city bus. Parks had been the first secretary of the Alabama state NAACP, had recently attended racial consciousness seminars at the Highlander Folk School in Tennessee, and had previously been ejected from buses for refusing to comply with segregation regulations.

Initial leadership for the boycott was provided by E. D. Nixon, head of the local unit of A. Philip Randolph's Brotherhood of Sleeping Car Porters. Local groups coalesced under an umbrella organization called the Montgomery Improvement Association (MIA) and met in Reverend Ralph Abernathy's First Baptist Church. They selected the relative newcomer, the Reverend Martin Luther King, Jr., as their president. In addition to his charismatic personality and impressive speaking and organizational skills, King brought with him links to the southern black church network, to northern civil rights sympathizers, and to the nonviolent activism of Glenn Smiley and Bayard Rustin of the Fellowship of Reconciliation.

The MIA responded to Parks' arrest by organizing a full boycott of Montgomery buses and demanding an end to Montgomery's bus segregation. The local NAACP attorney, Fred Gray, appealed Parks' arrest and filed a complaint against the city in the federal district court. The boycott began when the well-prepared Women's Political Council distributed to the black citizenry 35,000 copies of an appeal to "stay off the buses." With the active cooperation of black ministers and their churches, bi-weekly mass meetings, a sophisticated car-pool system that transported 17,000 people to work each day, and considerable financial support from the black congregations and outside sympathizers, the boycott succeeded; remarkably, over 95 percent of Montgomery's black popu-lation cooperated with the boycott for over a year. On November 13, 1956, the Supreme Court upheld a lower court ruling that the municipal bus segregation ordinance was unconstitutional. On December 21, King, E. D. Nixon, and other leaders tested the court order and were treated courteously by the city's bus drivers.

Although litigation formed an important backdrop to the bus boycotts, direct action was a new and distinctly democratic strategy in the civil rights struggle, a shift from the bureaucratic organization and liberal litigation strategy of the NAACP to local organizing coordinated by black clergy. The participation of clergy not only generated a charismatic style of leadership that appealed to the populace, but strengthened grassroots involvement through the black minis-ters' contact with the personal concerns of their parishioners, most of whom were relatively poor.[21] The black churches also brought together blacks of all classes and forged a sense of racial solidarity.

Furthermore, the black church embodied the affective, moral, and spiritual ties of community. Powerful spiritual exhortation, direct personal testimony, uplifting music, and strong interpersonal relationships fused together a deter-mined community. In Lerone Bennett's words, "Under the impact of the Old Negro Spirituals, of hand-clapping, shouting, 'testifying,' and 'amend-ing,' personality shells dissolved and reintegrated themselves around a larger, more inclusive racial self."[22] All of these qualities combined with the church's fund-raising and institutional strengths to give the movement a strong organi-zational base.

The central place of music anticipated subsequent movements of the Six-ties. As E. D. Nixon explained, "If you are going to continue to lead a group of people you are going to have to put something into the program that those people like. A whole lot of people came to the MIA meetings for no other reason than just to hear the music, some came to hear the folks who spoke."[23] All, however, joined the community boycott.

The leadership of black ministers like King and Abernathy in Montgomery, T. J. Jamison in Baton Rouge, and Fred Shuttlesworth in Birmingham, di-rected the aroused "frenzy" of the black church to new political ends. By merging Mohandas Gandhi's philosophy of nonviolence with Christian theology, King linked the Christian ethic of love to an assertive assault on evil and injustice. Religion became the basis for action rather than "turn the other cheek" submission. Thus King articulated the crucial distinction between nonviolent direct action and passive nonresistance.

In contrast to the laborious process of litigation, direct action emphasized the immediate. James Lawson, of the Southern Christian Leadership Conference (SCLC), observed of the differences between the new direct action organization and the NAACP,

> When people are suffering they don't want rhetoric and processes which seem to go slowly. . . . Many people, when they are suffering and they see their people suffering, they want direct participation. They want to be able to say, what I'm doing here gives me power and is going to help us change this business. . . . That's one of the great successes when you do something like a school boycott . . . or an economic boycott. Because here I am, mad already, with a racism I see, and now you tell me, okay . . . here's a chance for us to do something. So you stay out of that store until they do XYZ. . . . Just stay out of that store. So you put into the hands of all kinds of ordinary people a positive alternative to powerlessness and frustration. That's one of the great things about direct action.[24]

Direct action also involved the simple yet courageous decision to take physical steps to accomplish political goals, to use one's body as a political weapon. Politics became something as real and immediate as one's own body. The decision to act therefore involved a concrete commitment to one's political goals.

The community boycott also effectively employed collective economic power.[25] It motivated the white elite to sit down and negotiate with black leaders. As Aldon Morris observes,

> The collective power of the masses was generated from the instant that the entire black community boycotted Montgomery buses. Indeed, once the mass boycott was under way, the Mayor, the city commissioners, and officials of the bus company were forced to meet continuously with protest leaders to discuss grievances and demands. These meetings contrasted sharply with earlier sessions between black leaders and white authorities. The boycott made it clear that black demands could not be easily ignored, because the entire black community was mobilized.[26]

The boycott's effectiveness gave the black community a sense of its own power. It also spurred an increase in white violence and harassment. Riders in Montgomery's car pools were regularly subjected to abuse, boycott leaders received threatening letters and phone calls, and a bomb was thrown into King's house. After the federal court decision, the White Citizens Council and Ku Klux Klan initiated a terrorist campaign against the black activists; Ralph Abernathy's house and the First Baptist Church were both bombed.

At the same time, the boycott reached a larger and more sympathetic white audience through news coverage and direct appeals of leaders like King. In stressing the nonviolent involvement of local blacks in direct action against localized segregation, the MIA hoped to spark a national response to southern oppression, and ultimately to effect federal enforcement of integration.

In sum, the *goals* of the bus boycotts were entirely compatible with American liberal democracy. They sought an end to arbitrary racial segregation that excluded blacks from full and equal participation in common public activities. However, the *tactic* of direct action went beyond the normal liberal–democratic approach of petitioning the government for legal redress of grievances. The direct action campaign energized a community-based notion of politics. From the perspective of boycott participants, the politics of desegregation were not something abstract, programmatic, and grounded in rational self-interest. They were concrete, deeply felt, and moral, even religious. They were as personally meaningful as anything could be. As MIA member Jo Ann Robinson said of the boycott victory, "We felt that we were somebody." [27]

After the success of the Montgomery boycott, black ministers gathered in Atlanta in 1957 and organized the Southern Christian Leadership Conference (SCLC) as a regional umbrella organization that would facilitate the spread of similar actions. In effect, this meeting expanded the informal network that already existed among Alabama clergy. The Montgomery experience became a model for subsequent organizing, generated important support from black churches in the North, and facilitated links to other organizations like the Fellowship of Reconciliation, the Highlander Folk School, and the Southern Conference Educational Fund (SCEF).

From 1957 to 1960, the civil rights struggle revolved around two developments. First, the SCLC formulated a plan for confronting desegregation throughout the South through direct action. At its initial meeting, the SCLC discussed a series of working papers written by Bayard Rustin that stressed the disruptive potential of nonviolent boycotts, marches, and filling the jails throughout the South. It also expanded the scope of future activities to include voter education and registration. The first organized attempt to mobilize black voters was the SCLC's Crusade for Citizenship program, begun in 1958. While this program stimulated the crucial growth of local movement organizations, it also encountered a campaign of white evasion and repression. As a result, little tangible progress was made in black voter registration.

Second, the national NAACP continued its strategy of litigation, focusing on school segregation and noncompliance with *Brown*, a strategy that came to a head in Little Rock, Arkansas, in 1957. While the NAACP moved ahead, the white power structure retaliated. In a pattern that would become familiar throughout the Sixties, cries of "communists," "outsiders," and "subversives" were raised in an effort to eliminate the new threat to regional white supremacy. These charges were also raised against groups loosely affiliated with the efforts of the SCLC, especially the Highlander Folk School and the SCEF, both of which were racially integrated efforts to confront racism and oppression in the region. While the Eisenhower administration stood by, the escalation of white hostility virtually closed the door to additional desegregation during the remaining years of the decade.

■ Gaining Momentum, 1960–1961

Little tangible change had occurred in the system of southern segregation, yet, the momentum for change was building by the end of the 1950s. The landmark *Brown* decision and the subsequent success of local direct action had activated collective black consciousness.

The struggle for racial justice was marked by two main developments between 1960 and 1965. One was the continuing activism of the SCLC and other civil rights groups, notably the Congress of Racial Equality (CORE). This older generation of civil rights activists evolved toward increasingly aggressive, nonviolent direct action aimed at obtaining federal civil rights legislation to eliminate southern segregation.

The second development was the entrance of a new generation of black youth into the civil rights struggle through the student sit-in movement and the Student Non-violent Coordinating Committee. Of all the civil rights groups, SNCC was most synonymous with the prefigurative democratic vision of Sixties movements. From 1960 to 1965, SNCC grew from a loosely organized community of black and white field activists committed to mobilizing poor blacks (what Vincent Harding called the "shock troops of the non-violent movement") through a series of personal and organizational tremors, to the floundering, divided group that first asserted black power in 1966.

In effect, while the SCLC introduced the here-and-now, community-based tactic of direct action into the civil rights struggle, SNCC extended that tactic further. Direct confrontation of the most vicious white racism, community organizing among poor rural blacks, growing impatience with an evasive and uncooperative federal government, a sense of moral righteousness, and a life-style that reflected its commitments—all were trademarks of SNCC at its peak. Because of its members' age and approach, SNCC was more likely to clash with the deliberative process of federal legislation and bureaucracy, thereby evolving toward greater militancy. Emphasizing the community basis of black empowerment, SNCC units were also the first to disassociate from whites.

The combined efforts of older and younger civil rights groups produced a climate of turmoil and change in the first half of the Sixties. The growing determination and militance of civil rights activists of both generations ensured that civil rights and racial justice would be at the forefront of the nation's domestic political agenda.

DIRECT ACTION II: THE STUDENT SIT-INS

The new generation of college-aged black youth came into contact with the new racial consciousness of the late Fifties through such avenues as church youth groups, campus YM–YWCA's, and the local NAACP Youth Councils.[28] And they did so at a crucial age for the formation of their social identity.

Although isolated sit-ins had occurred in the late 1950s, it wasn't until Greensboro, North Carolina, that student sit-ins catapulted into public awareness. On February 1, 1960, four students from North Carolina Agricultural and Technical College—Ezell Blair, Jr., Franklin McCain, Joe McNeil, and David Richmond—sat down at the Woolworth's lunch counter in Greensboro, a direct challenge to southern laws that prohibited whites and blacks from eating together. With the aid of national news coverage and the network of SCLC movement centers, the effect of the sit-in was immediate and electric.[29] The original four protesters in Greensboro were joined the next day by hundreds of students from nearby colleges. One week later, the sit-ins had spread to neighboring Durham and Winston-Salem. Through the organizing efforts of the NAACP Youth Division head Floyd McKissick, along with Reverend Douglas Moore and CORE's Gordon Carey, movement activists were contacted throughout North Carolina, South Carolina, and Virginia. By the end of February, sit-ins had spread throughout these states. By the end of March, they had spread to about seventy southern cities, including the deep-South cities of Birmingham, Montgomery, Baton Rouge, New Orleans, Tallahassee, and Savannah.

The sit-ins gave the civil rights movement a new surge of youthful energy. They were the first evidence that the SCLC organizing efforts were bearing fruit. The local SCLC movement centers not only helped spread the sit-ins, but also provided critical local support to students beleaguered and assaulted by violent whites.[30] In some communities, where local support for the sit-ins was present and where sit-ins were combined with a boycott, the pressure on local businesses caused the practice of lunch counter segregation to give way. For white elites who found that their world had not fallen apart, the effect was eye opening. For young blacks, it was exhilarating.

The student sit-ins resembled the direct action tactics of the bus boycotts, but with two distinctions. They were more aggressive and more spontaneous. Although the spread and effectiveness of the sit-ins required considerable organization, individual students were readily caught up in the enthusiasm of collective action. They often joined impulsively, casting aside personal fears and years of repressive socialization. The result was a newfound feeling of empowerment and optimism. For many young blacks it was a heady experience that forged their commitment to the struggle.

> Once seized by the "freedom spirit," young blacks experienced an intense need to become deeply engaged. Ruby Doris Smith, only seventeen years old and a sophomore at Spelman College in Atlanta, convinced her older sister that she should take her place in the sit-in at Rock Hill, South Carolina. She explained to her uncomprehending mother that she just "had to go." Once there, she spent thirty days in jail as part of the first group to act on the "jail-no-bail" tactic.[31]

Like the boycotts, however, the sit-ins concentrated on the liberal goal of integration. As Clayborne Carson notes, at this early stage the students "protested against the pace rather than the direction of change."[32]

THE FORMATION OF SNCC

Taking advantage of the energy and enthusiasm generated by the sit-ins, the executive director of the SCLC, Ella Baker, organized a conference of young sit-in leaders from April 16 to 18, 1960, in Raleigh, North Carolina. In addition to the SCLC, conference participants included CORE, the Fellowship of Reconciliation, the National Student Association, the nascent Students for a Democratic Society, and the National Student Christian Federation. Reflecting her dissatisfaction with the leader-oriented authority structure of the SCLC, Baker emphasized the low-key information-sharing function of the conference in her letters to student activists. The largest student contingent, and one that was to dominate the early SNCC, came from Nashville.

After hearing Martin Luther King, Jr., and James Lawson urge them to mobilize a nonviolent campaign to spread the freedom struggle into all parts of the South, the students voted to establish a temporary Student Non-violent Coordinating Committee and elected Marion Barry its first chairman. The primary function of the new organization was to link local groups so that common concerns and information could be shared. The organization was explicitly independent of any of the older civil rights groups. From the start, SNCC reflected Baker's group-centered notion of leadership and a resistance to planning by elites.[33]

A subsequent October conference established a permanent organization that reflected the students' predilection for expressive politics and resistance to bureaucratic structure. As Howard Zinn wrote, "The twig was bent, and the tree grew that way. For SNCC . . . managed to maintain an autonomy in the field, an unpredictability of action, a lack of overall planning which brought exasperation to some of its most ardent supporters, bewilderment to outside observers, and bemusement to the students themselves."[34] Events would help determine what course SNCC would follow. Within months of the fall meeting, fifteen SNCC members voted to support a sit-in in Rock Hill, South Carolina, to demonstrate movement unity. The four who traveled to Rock Hill were arrested and joined the local students in jail. The jail-no-bail tactic reflected a refusal to cooperate with an evil system (a strategy echoed later by the antiwar Resistance movement), and an effort to revitalize the student protest movement. The jail experience also heightened group solidarity and individual commitment. Jailed SNCC activist Charles Sherrod recalled, "You get ideas in jail. You talk with other young people you've never seen. Right away we recognize each other. People like yourself, getting out of the past. We're up all night, sharing creativity, planning action. You learn the truth in prison, you learn wholeness. You find out the difference between being dead and alive."[35] It wasn't until after the Freedom Rides that SNCC gained the energy and momentum it had been seeking.

DIRECT ACTION III: THE FREEDOM RIDES

Exactly one year after the Greensboro sit-in, James Farmer was named the new national director of CORE. As CORE's first black director, Farmer's appointment symbolized a shift within the northern-based organization. Previously, CORE had been an organization dominated by whites and devoted to the philosophy of nonviolent direct action outside the deep South. The most noteworthy example was the Journey of Reconciliation, organized by Bayard Rustin to test compliance with a Supreme Court ruling against segregation on interstate trains and buses. A small, integrated group of activists had traveled through the border states of the upper South without any significant incidents.

Reflecting CORE's past, Farmer hatched the idea for the Freedom Rides, an effort to confront segregation in interstate bus facilities throughout the South from Washington, D.C., to New Orleans. The Freedom Rides were designed to provoke a reaction from white segregationists in the South, thereby drawing northern (and government) attention to the harsh realities of southern segregation.

On May 4, 1961, a biracial group of thirteen embarked from Washington, D.C., and traveled through Virginia, the Carolinas, and Georgia, encountering relatively mild reactions along the way. One rider was arrested for demanding a shoe shine in Charlotte, North Carolina; two others were attacked by whites in Rock Hill; and two were arrested in Winnsboro, South Carolina. However, when the buses left Georgia, they encountered mob violence in Anniston, Alabama.

> The Greyhound bus carrying the first contingent, scheduled for a half-hour rest stop there, was attacked as it pulled into the depot by thirty or forty whites carrying chains, sticks, and iron bars. They broke windows in the bus, dented the body and slashed the tires. While policemen stood by watching, they pulled Freedom Riders from the bus and badly beat them. Policemen finally waved off the attackers and escorted the bus from the

depot to the street. As it drove away toward Birmingham, the assailants jumped into their cars and gave chase.

One of the cars kept ahead of the bus to keep it from gathering speed. Then, about six miles out of Anniston, the bus was forced to stop when a damaged tire gave way. The mob attacked again, shattered several windows, and threw a fire bomb, which exploded inside. At first the attackers kept the door closed, trapping the passengers amid the smoke and flames. After the doors were opened, they administered more beatings as the passengers fled.[36]

Meanwhile, the second bus was subsequently stopped and riders were forced to the rear; those who refused were beaten. One rider, Walter Bergman, a sixty-one-year old professor, was knocked to the floor and clubbed. He suffered permanent brain injuries. Despite warnings of trouble ahead in Birmingham, no police were visible when the bus reached the city.[37] Riders were attacked with clubs as they disembarked; one rider, James Peck, was hospitalized and required fifty-three stitches to close a head wound.

By this time, the Freedom Rides had captured national attention because of the brutality encountered by the small group of courageous riders. Fearing additional violence, Greyhound bus drivers in Birmingham refused to take the riders on to Montgomery. Heeding Attorney General Robert Kennedy's request for a cooling off period, the original CORE riders decided to terminate the remaining bus travel and flew to New Orleans where they declared the Freedom Ride a success.

SNCC activists felt it was critical that the rides be continued in the face of white violence. Nashville SNCC coordinator Diane Nash organized a group including ten students who traveled to Birmingham to complete the Freedom Rides. At the Birmingham city limits, the bus was commandeered by whites who put newspaper over all the windows before driving to the bus station. The terrorized riders waited inside, unable to see out, until Birmingham Police Commissioner Bull Connor arrived and ordered them into protective custody in the city jail. The next night, Connor and the police drove the riders 150 miles to the Alabama–Tennessee border where they were left in a deserted rural area to find their way back to Nashville. Instead, Diane Nash sent a car that returned the riders to Birmingham where they awaited a bus to Montgomery.

Meanwhile, the Kennedy administration finally responded to appeals for protection of the Freedom Riders. Robert Kennedy dispatched a special assistant, John Seigenthaler, to plead with Governor John Patterson. With bus drivers reassured and Seigenthaler aboard, the riders embarked at Birmingham for Montgomery. Despite a police escort en route, a white mob appeared in Montgomery and attacked the riders and any blacks or sympathetic-looking whites in the area. John Seigenthaler was among those knocked unconscious and left lying on the sidewalk. Shortly thereafter Robert Kennedy, acting on the President's orders, sent federal marshalls to Montgomery and sought an injunction against the Ku Klux Klan and other groups. The riders and their supporters gathered the next night in the First Baptist Church where Martin Luther King, Jr., again called for nonviolence in the face of white terrorism. Surrounded by an angry mob of whites outside the church, the meeting reflected the courageous determination aroused by the Freedom Rides. As in earlier meetings, the assembled group gained strength from singing freedom songs and hymns.

King and the Freedom Riders rejected Robert Kennedy's call for a cooling off period, and the rides proceeded to Jackson, Mississippi, under heavy National Guard escort. In Jackson, police arrested the riders as they tried to use the white rest rooms. The Jackson confrontation drew additional national attention, and white liberals from the North joined the protests. Behind the scene, Attorney General Kennedy requested the Interstate Commerce Commission (ICC) to issue antisegregation regulations for bus and train terminals. Four months later, the ICC handed down such an order.

The Freedom Rides were a dramatic and aggressive form of nonviolent direct action that confronted racial segregation throughout the South. Clearly instrumental in nature, they aimed at provoking national awareness of oppressive racial segregation and the ugliness of white violence against a nonviolent, integrated group bent on using facilities that were integrated in the North. With the help of media coverage, they raised white consciousness of the brutality that lay behind racial segregation in the South. Because of the protesters' persistence in the face of violence, and because a sympathetic though wary administration could implement change through administrative action, the Freedom Rides were largely successful in their immediate objective of integration.

As Clayborne Carson notes, the rides also "contributed to the development of a self-consciously radical southern student movement prepared to direct its militancy toward other concerns. . . . [The participants] suddenly became aware of their collective ability to provoke a crisis that would attract international attention and compel federal intervention." [38] Federal intervention also brought to light tensions between a sympathetic administration attuned to the give and take of party politics and the young protesters whose moralistic perceptions and personal commitment made them impatient with political expediency. It was a conflict that reappeared throughout the decade. Perhaps more than any other factor, the tension between young protesters who sought full administration support and the Kennedy and Johnson administrations who were wary of losing the white Democratic vote in the South fed the growing radical perspective of SNCC.

Shortly after the end of the Freedom Rides, Robert Kennedy suggested that SNCC and the other civil rights groups shift their focus from direct action to voter registration. He even promised financial support. From Kennedy's perspective, this strategy seemed less likely to draw the federal government into clashes with white southerners. It was also likely to increase voting support for the administration. In time, however, the SNCC voter registration drives took on a more radical, democratic meaning, focusing on empowering poor blacks to take control of local institutions. The path to voter registration proved to be at least as dangerous and violent as the direct action campaigns.

■ The Growing Schism: Rights versus Power

> The *act* of registering to vote does several things. It marks the beginning of political modernization by broadening the base of participation. It also does something the existentialists talk about: it gives one a sense of being. . . .
> The black person begins to live. He begins to create his *own* existence when he says "No" to someone who contains him.
> —Stokely Carmichael and Charles V. Hamilton, *Black Power*

After the Freedom Rides, the struggle for civil rights moved to the center of the nation's political agenda. The Kennedy adminstration had responded to the concerns of black Americans, and four civil rights groups were actively challenging racial oppression. The NAACP, SCLC, CORE, and SNCC differed in their strategies and constituencies and often acted autonomously. However, prior to 1962, they were essentially supportive of each others' efforts.

As civil rights gained prominence in the nation's political consciousness, conflicts gradually intensified between the priorities and personalities of the different groups. [39] The NAACP continued to emphasize litigation to extend the constitutional rights of blacks, as it had prior to the Freedom Rides. CORE, which was momentarily invigorated by the Freedom Rides, continued to mobilize southern blacks through local CORE offices. Before long, it slipped into the background only to re-emerge during the black power era. After the Freedom Rides, the SCLC concentrated on a black Citizenship Education Program and searched for a community in which to launch a new direct action assault on local segregation.

The shifting focus of civil rights activism was felt especially keenly by SNCC. Some SNCC members, notably Charles Jones and field staffers Charles Sherrod and Robert Moses, advocated switching to voter registration. Others like Diane Nash and Marion Barry advocated continuing the direct action campaign against segregation. At an August meeting, SNCC members adopted Ella Baker's suggestion that the organization pursue both strategies by establishing two wings. At about the same time, SNCC regained its cohesion and forcefulness when it hired James Forman as executive secretary. Eventually, the locally based voter registration effort prevailed as SNCC's distinctive approach.

Although the SCLC and SNCC were not pure models of liberal–instrumental and democratic–prefigurative politics, the two groups came closest to representing two distinct perspectives on the struggle for racial justice. The SCLC was by no means oblivious to the need for a psychological breakthrough by previously submissive blacks. In fact, it addressed this concern through the Citizenship Education Program. Nor was it unaware of the crucial significance of economic inequality for blacks. However, the SCLC's *emphasis* was instrumental and liberal, an approach that depended on its alliance with the federal government, focusing on legislation to ensure availability of liberal–democratic rights for all black Americans.

After 1965, Martin Luther King, Jr., showed an inclination to move in a more radical direction while maintaining his personal devotion to nonviolence. In 1966, he encountered the violence of white racism in the North as well as congressional resistance to open housing legislation. In 1967, he split with the administration by speaking out against the Vietnam War. In his final years he expressed his disillusionment with capitalism, which he viewed as the root of enduring racial inequality.[40]

Meanwhile, SNCC became more directly involved in empowering poor blacks to control their local political and economic institutions. The difficulty of overcoming entrenched feelings of inferiority among poor rural blacks eventually led SNCC to exclude white volunteers. At the same time, encounters with the virulent white violence in rural Mississippi reinforced SNCC's collective identity, and several angry activists came to see armed self-defense as necessary. Most SNCC workers lost faith in an administration they saw as disinterested when blacks were killed but aroused by the death of whites. White liberals' "sell-out" of the Mississippi Freedom Democratic party only furthered SNCC's alienation, causing it to shift in an increasingly militant and radical direction. The result was the black power movement.

THE FIRST SPLIT: FAILURE IN ALBANY, GEORGIA

Immediately after its August 1961 meeting, SNCC launched its initial voter registration drive in McComb, Mississippi, a campaign that instantly provoked the specter of extralegal Mississippi justice and culminated in the 1964 Mississippi Freedom Summer project. Shortly thereafter, two SNCC workers, Charles Sherrod and Cordell Reagon, arrived in Albany, Georgia to open a SNCC office. The two were youthful veterans of the Freedom Rides with an awakened sense of racial pride. They devoted their efforts to organizing the people to confront segregation and register to vote. They succeeded in persuading students from Albany State College to sit in at the white bus terminal, thereby galvanizing the support of the entire black community. An umbrella organization called the Albany movement was formed with Dr. William Anderson as its president. Its goal was to end all forms of racial discrimination in Albany.

When three members of the NAACP Youth Council were arrested by Police Chief Laurie Pritchett, a mass meeting was called at the Mount Zion Baptist Church. The meeting once again generated a sense of collective strength through song, prayer, and inspirational speech. Subsequently, SNCC staffers including James Forman arrived to strengthen the activist forces. As SNCC actions continued, additional arrests fanned the flames of determined protest.

Mass arrests and jailings followed. Though personally spiteful toward "niggers," Chief Pritchett carefully avoided the provocative violence later exhibited by his counterparts Bull Connor of Birmingham and Jim Clark of Selma. "Pritchett's method was to arrest quickly and to refrain from using overt violence against the protesters. The South had not seen a total community mobilized on such a wide scale since the Montgomery bus boycott. The usual activities of the city were severely disrupted by continuous demonstrations. The jails were full, and merchants were filled with anxiety."[41]

Ultimately, however, the Albany movement failed to achieve an end to segregation and discrimination. After negotiations between movement leaders and city elites collapsed, William Anderson invited Martin Luther King, Jr., to Albany, a move that was vehemently opposed by SNCC leaders who viewed King's presence as a shift away from their "people's movement." SNCC leaders were particularly resentful of SCLC Executive Director Wyatt Walker, who assumed command of protest organization. As they had predicted, King's arrival brought increased media attention (and outside funding) to Albany. King, Abernathy, and Anderson were arrested two days later along with two hundred protesters.

Subsequently, King was maneuvered out of the city by an agreement arranged (but not honored) by city leaders. While the boycott and lunch counter demonstrations continued, President Kennedy finally responded to activists' pleas for support by urging local leaders to negotiate a settlement.[42] However, the settlement never came; a federal court injunction against unlawful demonstrations caused King to cease his involvement at a critical juncture, since he was unwilling to flout the order of a crucial civil rights ally. The city held out until the energy and enthusiasm of the movement waned. As SNCC worker Bill Hansen observed, "We ran out of people before [Chief Pritchett] ran out of jails."[43]

SNCC workers came away from the 1961–1962 protests with growing mistrust toward older civil rights leaders in the SCLC, and aware that protesters' suffering would not bring federal intervention. King came away aware of the need to persist in the face of court injunctions and the importance of white violence as a provocation for federal intervention. The Albany experience also demonstrated that an entire community could be mobilized to participate in civil disobedience. However, such an effort would require more effective and unified organization. Less than a year after the end of the Albany movement, these lessons were applied in the SCLC's demonstrations in Birmingham.

DIRECT ACTION IV: BIRMINGHAM

In selecting Birmingham as the next target, King chose a city in which the SCLC had a strong organizational presence and an inspirational local leader, Reverend Fred Shuttlesworth. It was also the city reputed to be the most racist in the South, and one in which law enforcement was in the hands of an unsophisticated "redneck," Bull Connor.[44] All of these characteristics worked to SCLC's advantage, although the price paid in punishing brutality was high.

Birmingham was arguably the high point of SCLC effectiveness. Fortified by substantial funding and a core of experienced, determined leaders including King, Abernathy, Shuttlesworth, and James Lawson, and coordinating their efforts with SNCC activists James Bevel and Diane Nash, the direct action campaign was well prepared and highly organized. The movement was seeking full integration of downtown lunch counters, public facilities, parks and playgrounds; establishment of fair hiring procedures in retail stores; and creation of a biracial commission and timetable for integrating city schools.

The SCLC instituted a cumulative, three-tier strategy designed to split the white economic elite from political officials and white mobs and to elicit federal support. Phase 1 involved a full boycott of downtown stores, accompanied by small sit-ins and picketing. Phase 2 involved mass marches on City Hall. Phase 3 called for elementary, secondary, and college students to go to jail in massive numbers. In addition, King and the SCLC had decided in advance to violate a court injunction if one were handed down.

The SCLC held nightly mass meetings for sixty-five consecutive nights, rotating the meetings among the city's black churches. As in previous cases, these meetings provided the solidarity and determination needed in the face of expected violence. King recalled the important role of music.

> In a sense the freedom songs are the soul of the movement. They are more than just incantations of clever phrases designed to invigorate a campaign; they are as old as the history of the Negro in America. . . . I have stood in a meeting with hundreds of youngsters and joined in while they sang "Ain't Gonna Let Nobody Turn Me 'Round." It's not just a song; it is a resolve. A few minutes later, I have seen those same youngsters refuse to turn around from the onrush of a police dog, refuse to turn around before a pugnacious Bull Connor in command of men armed with power hoses. These songs bind us together, give us courage together, help us to march together.[45]

Phase 1 of the protests began slowly, but arrests were a catalyst for mobilizing the black community. Sensing that the white businesses would not respond unless pressured, Phase 2 was instituted. Increasing numbers were arrested, the jails began to fill, and the boycott gained momentum. Bull Connor sought and acquired an injunction against the protests, but King announced the protesters' determination to continue with the ringing proclamation "we've got an injunction from heaven." King and Abernathy led a march in violation of the injunction on Good Friday, and subsequently King penned his famous "Letter from Birmingham Jail." Addressed to eight white clergymen who had called King's activities "unwise and untimely," King's response was an articulate defense of nonviolent civil disobedience in the face of evil:

> We know through painful experience that freedom is never voluntarily given by the oppressor; it must be demanded by the oppressed. Frankly, I have yet to engage in a direct-action campaign that was "well timed" in the view of those who have not suffered unduly from the disease of segregation. For years now I have heard the word "Wait!" It rings in the ear of every Negro with piercing familiarity. This "Wait" has almost always meant "Never." [46]

He went on to decry his critics' "blame the victim" mentality: "We who engage in nonviolent direct action are not the creators of tension. We merely bring to the surface the hidden tension that is already alive. We bring it out in the open where it can be seen and dealt with." [47]

With financial pressure on white businesses growing,[48] Phase 3 was initiated on May 3, 1963. Thousands of students gathered in the Sixteenth Street Baptist Church, prepared to protest. As they left the building, the teenagers were attacked by Bull Connor's police and firemen armed with fire hoses, billy clubs, and dogs. The news media transmitted dramatic photographs of the attack around the world, attracting instant attention to the shocking violence. President Kennedy was reported to have told the Americans for Democratic Action that a photograph of a leashed dog lunging at a young demonstrator made him "sick." The immediacy of the brutality seems to have galvanized the President to act.

Kennedy mobilized the National Guard in Birmingham after a bomb exploded at King's headquarters at the Gaston Motel and incited an angry black mob to rage through the streets. In addition, powerful and well-connected northerners in the Kennedy administration contacted their business colleagues to bring pressure on Birmingham's economic elite. Later Kennedy warned Governor George Wallace that he would use "all necessary force" to override

Wallace's obstruction of black students bent on attending the University of Alabama. And on June 11, the president went before a nationwide television audience to propose his major civil rights initiative. "We are confronted primarily with a moral issue. It is as old as the Scriptures and is as clear as the American Constitution. The heart of the question is whether all Americans are going to be afforded equal rights and equal opportunities; whether we are going to treat our fellow Americans as we want to be treated."[49]

Despite the violent backlash, the Birmingham movement was a high point for civil rights direct action. Superb organization and the inspired determination of the black population sustained the confrontation with local elites, producing an agreement with the businessmen and new mayor that promised to fulfill the SCLC's demands. The publicity given the demonstrations raised national consciousness of intransigent racism in the deep South and stimulated a wave of local movements throughout the region. These added to the mounting pressure for national civil rights legislation. Finally, the Birmingham movement reinvigorated the white student movement on northern campuses, as student groups mobilized to support the protesters in Birmingham.

Nonetheless, white violence continued in Birmingham, as did efforts by Bull Connor and George Wallace to destroy the agreement. More civil rights workers were killed, including the widely respected Mississippi NAACP field secretary Medgar Evers. A few months later, in one of the most jarring outrages of the civil rights struggles, four young black girls died when a bomb was thrown into their church.

THE MARCH ON WASHINGTON

The massive March on Washington held on August 28, 1963, was one of the most memorable moments of the civil rights movement. The march is best known for Martin Luther King's impassioned "I Have a Dream" speech and the powerful sense of community felt by the 250,000 blacks and whites in attendance. Perhaps its most significant effect was to bring the civil rights movement physically and psychologically close to the Kennedy administration and the halls of Congress, where the civil rights bill was being debated.

Beneath the surface, however, civil rights unity was disintegrating. Inspired by A. Philip Randolph and organized by Bayard Rustin, the march was a tactic not totally welcomed by all groups. The more conservative civil rights leaders like Roy Wilkins of the NAACP and Whitney Young of the Urban League were initially concerned that a march might get out of hand. The more aggressive leaders like John Lewis of SNCC and James Farmer of CORE felt the idea of a march was too tame. All, however, joined in the united effort once Martin Luther King, Jr., was recruited to speak.

President Kennedy initially tried to discourage Randolph and the other leaders from holding the march, suggesting that it might harm rather than help passage of the civil rights bill. When convinced that the march would be peaceful, the President came around to publicly welcome the "peaceful assembly for the redress of grievances." With somewhat tenuous support from the administration, march leaders were eager to avoid rhetoric or actions that might embarrass the administration or alienate members of Congress. By the time of the march, SNCC had become increasingly skeptical of administration sympathies, even engaging in sit-ins at the Department of Justice to push for federal protection of their voter registration efforts.

John Lewis, the new SNCC chairman and one of the scheduled speakers, had prepared a militant speech that reflected SNCC's shifting orientation. In a text leaked later to the press, Lewis asserted, "We will march through the South, through the Heart of Dixie, the way Sherman did. We will pursue our own 'scorched earth' policy and burn Jim Crow to the ground—nonviolently. . . . We will take matters into our own hands and create a source of power, outside any national structure, that could and would assure us a victory." [50] Lewis also withheld SNCC backing for the administration's civil rights bill, noting that it provided insufficient protection for voter registration. When notified that the Catholic Archbishop of Washington would not give the opening invocation if Lewis gave his speech, the march leaders prevailed on the SNCC chairman to tone down his remarks; the final version was softened but still bore the SNCC trademark of concern for the poor blacks of the deep South, disassociation from the politics of expediency, and a call for blacks throughout the nation to join "the great social revolution sweeping our nation."

Although some disillusioned SNCC workers stayed away from the march, others were caught up in the event's infectious glow. One remarked that, despite its shortcomings, the march was a tremendous inspiration to the poor blacks who were brought from the deep South by SNCC workers: "It helped them believe they were not alone." [51] While there were discordant notes within the movement, the appearance of unity and solidarity at the march made a powerful impression on those who joined in or watched on television. The march also inspired similar efforts by the antiwar movement later in the decade.

SNCC IN MISSISSIPPI: FROM THE BELOVED
COMMUNITY TO BLACK POWER

The SNCC story is the most distinctly Sixties phenomenon of the civil rights movement.[52] As Howard Zinn wrote, "For the first time in our history a major social movement, shaking the nation to its bones, is being led by youngsters. . . . But in one important way these young people are very much like the abolitionists of old: they have a healthy disrespect for respectability."[53]

Emily Stoper has described SNCC as a redemptive organization, using a term more commonly applied to religious sects. In SNCC's early years, the redemptive ethos prevailed in a set of attitudes toward the world, exemplified by the moral courage and personal integrity of leaders like Robert Moses in Mississippi, and a strong sense of intimacy, solidarity, and loyalty. SNCC workers' attitudes were more than an ideology in that they embraced personal lifestyles as well as ideas, and less in that they were imprecise and not authoritatively established. The conflict between SNCC's sect-like qualities—the expressive politics of the "Freedom High" contingent—and its instrumental political goals may have contributed to its downfall.

One redemptive trait of SNCC was its decision to carry out a major voter registration drive in Mississippi and rural counties elsewhere in the deep South. As Stoper suggests, this decision had "some of the appeal of the conversion of the worst sinner," for Mississippi was reputed to be the most racist state in the nation.[54] Other civil rights groups concentrated their efforts elsewhere, partly because of the history of white terrorism in Mississippi. By organizing poor blacks in the rural deep South, SNCC chose a path strewn with roadblocks, from constant white harassment and arrest to violence and death. The hostile environment helped forge solidarity among SNCC field workers. It also generated repeated conflicts with the Johnson administration over federal protection, and growing tensions between black staffers and northern white volunteers.

Robert Moses, who led the initial Mississippi project in McComb, epitomized the qualities of SNCC workers. Moses left his teaching job in New York and joined SNCC after seeing a photograph of the determined Greensboro students in the first 1960 sit-in. He quickly became one of the most inspirational of the SNCC leaders, partly because of his quiet courage in the face of danger and partly because he studiously avoided the limelight of visible leadership. In the fall of 1960, Moses met with Amzie Moore, a local NAACP chairman in Mississippi. Reflecting Moore's preference for voter registration over desegregation efforts, Moses planned the rural campaign that began in August 1961. He selected Pike County in the Mississippi Delta, a region where only 200 of 80,000 blacks were registered.

The campaign began with a citizenship school aimed at teaching poor blacks the necessary skills to pass Mississippi's literacy test. Moses and two other SNCC workers walked door to door trying to overcome the natural suspicions of impoverished blacks. Shortly after Moses and a small core of SNCC staffers began the project, a black who tried to register was shot. On August 15, Moses was arrested for interfering with police officers while escorting three blacks to the courthouse to register. A phone call to the Justice Department failed to elicit a pledge of support or protection. On August 29, Moses was beaten by angry whites while assisting two more blacks. The black community was aroused. About 200 attended a rally while black high school students held a sit-in at a bus station lunch counter. Five teenagers were arrested and jailed for over a month.

Blacks continued their efforts to register; white resistance mounted. Less than a month after the sit-in, an NAACP field worker, Herbert Lee, was killed by a white state representative in front of several eyewitnesses. The white official was absolved by the coroner's jury. A black witness told Moses that he had lied at the inquest because he feared retaliation, but would tell the truth if he were promised protection. Moses' appeal to the federal government was rebuffed.[55] Later, SNCC workers Moses, Charles McDew, and Robert Zellner were sentenced to four months in jail for their voter registration efforts.

After the SNCC workers were released, planning for a more extensive voter registration campaign began. The initial efforts had attracted several students who dropped out of college to become full-time SNCC staffers. The impetus for SNCC activism had shifted from the original coordinating committee to its grassroots field staff, and with this shift came a sense of collective identity—what the more religious saw as a "beloved community" of blacks and whites, men and women, confronting and altering the evil ways of racial oppression. The redemptive organization was growing. "Day-to-day interactions with each other and with politically awakened blacks in communities with SNCC projects made staff members more willing to look at their own experiences in the struggle as a source of alternative values."[56]

The emerging SNCC became increasingly unwilling to compromise. While the term "revolutionary" was uttered more frequently and self-consciously in discussions among staffers, SNCC still retained the reformer's faith that their efforts of speaking truth to power would cause racial oppression to disappear. As Julian Bond remarked, they were still "operating on the theory that here was a problem, you expose it to the world, the world says 'How horrible!' and moves to correct it."[57] Yet the seeds of SNCC's transformation were growing. As Stoper observes,

> The SNCC outlook stands most sharply in contrast to that of the liberal—the person who makes a point of seeing every issue from all perspectives and of being always prepared to trade off his or her values. . . . The liberal is a specialist living with a minimum of conflict in a complex, atomized, shifting world. Without the liberal, the American system could hardly exist. . . .
>
> It was to this society that the early SNCC offered an alternative.[58]

During the winter, a group of SNCC staffers rented a house in Jackson, Mississippi that soon became the hub of renewed activity throughout the Delta. The following spring and summer voter registration efforts spread throughout the region. SNCC staffers were organizing in communities like Greenwood, Cleveland, Holly Springs, Laurel, Hattiesburg, Vicksburg, and Ruleville. An umbrella group, the Council of Federated Organizations (COFO), was organized to coordinate funding for the voter registration activities of SNCC, CORE, SCLC, and NAACP. Robert Moses was named director of the COFO voter registration drive.

As before, field workers encountered white violence. Many were beaten severely by white mobs or by police. Stories of courageous confrontations with white violence spread, infecting the poor blacks with a growing spirit of determination. Amzie Moore recalls when he "stood at a courthouse . . . and watched tiny figures [of the SNCC workers] standing against a huge column . . . triggermen and drivers and lookout men riding in automobiles with automatic guns . . . *how they stood* . . . how gladly they got in front of that line, those leaders, and went to jail! It didn't seem to bother them. It was an awakening for me."[59]

In one incident, Moses, Jimmy Travis, and Randolph Blackwell were assaulted while driving from Greenwood to Greenville. Howard Zinn writes,

> A 1962 Buick with no license tags had been sitting outside the SNCC
> office all day, with three white men in it—nothing unusual for SNCC. As
> they pulled away, the Buick followed. They stopped at a filling station
> for gasoline, and the Buick followed and circled the block. Then they
> headed out on the main highway toward Greenville, all three sitting in
> front: Jimmy Travis at the wheel, Bob Moses next to him, Blackwell on
> the outside. It was about 10:30 p.m., and there was a good deal of traffic
> on the road. As the traffic began to thin, the Buick pulled up alongside
> and then came the deafening sound of gunfire. Thirteen 45-calibre bul-
> lets ripped through the car shattering the front left window, missing Bob
> Moses and Randolph Blackwell by inches, smashing through the window
> on the other side. Two bullets hit Jimmy Travis. The Buick sped off, and
> Moses grabbed the controls to pull the car to a stop as Travis crouched in
> his seat, bleeding.[60]

Travis narrowly missed death.

The SNCC efforts stirred local residents to break from their oppressed past at
great personal risk. One older black farmer, Hartman Turnbow, joined a registration effort at the Holmes County courthouse. After the usual delay tactics,
evasion, and harassment on the part of county officials, Turnbow completed
the registration procedure. A few days later, his house was shot up and fire-
bombed with considerable damage. Turnbow fought off two assailants with his
rifle. The next day, while waiting for an FBI investigator, he was arrested by
the local sheriff for arson.

Fannie Lou Hamer was a forty-seven-year old sharecropper in Ruleville.
After hearing SNCC workers James Bevel and James Forman speak at a local
meeting, she went to register. "Well, after I'd gotten back home, this man that
I had worked for as a timekeeper and sharecropper for eighteen years, he said
that I would just have to leave. . . . So I told him I wasn't trying to register
for him, I was trying to register for myself. . . . I didn't have no other choice
because for one time I wanted things to be different."[61] Ten days later, while
staying with a friend, a car drove by the house and fired sixteen bullets into
the bedroom in which she was sleeping. Hamer survived by hiding and later
escaped.

During 1962–1963, the voter registration drive continued in the face of persistent white violence and with almost no federal presence. Increasing numbers of SNCC staffers were recruited from local black residents, reflecting Moses' view that white staffers increased the danger to black residents and also failed to counteract the poor blacks' sense of inferiority.

After the murder of Medgar Evers in 1963, white activists were recruited to participate in demonstrations in Jackson, Mississippi. One of them, Allard Lowenstein, suggested the idea of a "freedom vote" to Robert Moses: Blacks would vote at a convenient polling place for an independent slate of candidates for statewide office. Through his contacts at Yale and Stanford Universities, Lowenstein recruited about one hundred students to help in the voting drive. In November over 80,000 blacks participated in this symbolic protest vote. As the first statewide effort, the freedom vote lay the groundwork for the creation of the Mississippi Freedom Democratic party and the Freedom Summer project in 1964.[62]

Soon after the freedom vote, Lowenstein and Moses began planning the daring effort to register masses of black voters the following summer. From the start there was ambivalence about white participation. Some SNCC workers like James Forman had reservations about the anticipated wave of northern student volunteers. On the other hand, SNCC activists like Marion Barry and John Lewis believed that an influx of hundreds of white students blanketing the state would create a crisis that would finally bring in the federal government. Most of SNCC's older black staffers appreciated the determination of white workers like Bob Zellner who proved themselves in the line of fire from white racists and still saw SNCC as the idealized integrated community.[63]

As increasing numbers of white activists joined the SNCC effort, the sense of kinship and communal solidarity declined. Pressures for increased organizational efficiency became more pronounced, leading to conflicts between the freedom high idealists and the effectiveness advocates. More pervasively, tensions between black and white staffers came to the fore, reflecting the radical contrast between each group's experience. While blacks understood that the involvement of whites meant that the nation's attention would be captured by the Mississippi movement, they resented the lack of national attention and federal protection when whites were not involved.[64] Some of the blacks recruited from poorer backgrounds felt intimidated by the more aggressive and articulate whites from affluent backgrounds. They also realized that, unlike themselves, white students were free to return to their comfortable environment whenever they wished. And they were quick to disparage the naiveté of northern students who were unconscious of the dangers SNCC workers had lived with for months or years—dangers that were highlighted by the brutal June murder of three volunteers, James Chaney, Andrew Goodman, and Michael Schwerner. Sexuality between whites and blacks, especially black men and white women, also aggravated tensions while reflecting efforts of both races and sexes to break through ingrained taboos and inhibitions.

For their part, northern white students were attracted by the sense of commitment to idealistic moral action posed by the civil rights struggle. Many southern white women who joined SNCC in the early years were motivated by their religious backgrounds. One volunteer, citing John Kennedy's inaugural call to action, noted, "I want to do my part. There is a moral wave building among today's youth and I intend to catch it!"[65]

The effect of Freedom Summer was electric. As Doug McAdam observes, few of the volunteers had ever experienced conditions like those they encountered in Mississippi:

> But it wasn't the discrimination alone—the "colored only" drinking fountains and KKK billboards—that made such an impact. . . . It was the depths of the problem and the broader implications of what they saw. It was the poverty of black Mississippi and what that said about the inherent goodness of America. It was the endemic quality of official lawlessness and the blatant contradiction it posed to their "law and order" upbringings. But perhaps what shocked the volunteers most was the depths of federal complicity in maintaining Mississippi's system of segregation.[66]

Gradually many volunteers came to the sobering realization that they were at war with their own culture. One student wrote, "A relatively short time ago, I began to awake after at least an eighteen-year sleep. . . . I have said *no* to almost all of my past. . . ."[67] Another remarked, "The summer moved me light years beyond where I had been politically."[68]

The federal government's detached "sympathy" for field workers and black residents was the biggest thorn in the side of SNCC activists. The rhetorical claims of federal officials became more remote, less credible. "Living day by day in situations that amounted to mortal combat with an unprincipled enemy, the assurance that federal authorities would take action *later* represented the equivalent of the U.S. government siding *now* with the brutality being meted out by white racists."[69] Even the Kennedy legacy lost some of its shine. As Paul Cowan recalls of the week after the murder of the three civil rights workers:

Bob [Moses] became, for me, the embodiment of the America for which I had been searching. . . . I compared my admiration for Bob with my attitude toward John Kennedy. Kennedy might have inspired a generation by talking about courage; Bob was trying to transform a state by living courageously. Kennedy had won great power for himself through the skillful use of wealth and influence; Bob's example, his endurance, had helped Mississippi Negroes gain a little power for themselves. John Kennedy talked about the value of democracy. Bob Moses tried to be a democrat. . . . While Theodore Sorensen and Burke Marshall conferred in Washington about the "Negro problem," Bob stayed in Mississippi through four cold, lonely winters organizing black people to demand things for themselves.[70]

SNCC's insistence on direct, empowering democratic control—an insistence expressed in the activists' lifestyle—stood in stark contrast to the more abstract rhetoric of administration officials. The latter may have been sincerely committed to effecting systematic progress for blacks, but their commitment emanated from the detached and necessarily abstract realm of national politics. It was tempered by a commitment to pluralistic party and legislative politics. Liberals in the federal government came to be viewed as too easily co-opted, too ready to sell out the struggle in political compromise. Nowhere was the growing chasm between the radicalized field activists and federal government liberals more pronounced than in the Mississippi Freedom Democratic party.

THE MISSISSIPPI FREEDOM DEMOCRATIC PARTY (MFDP)

At a 1963 meeting, SNCC staffers decided to organize an insurgent Democratic slate to challenge the party regulars for seating at the 1964 Democratic national convention. The MFDP became the mobilizing symbol for the Freedom Summer voter registration effort. It also received strong lobbying support within the Democratic party from United Automobile Workers' counsel Joseph Rauh, a long-time liberal activist and vice president of the Americans for Democratic Action. While blacks in Mississippi convened precinct meetings (in the absence of any public meetings by party regulars) and attempted unsuccessfully to join county nominating conventions, Rauh prepared a legal brief to present to the party's credentials committee. Rauh's activities drew the increasingly anxious attention of President Johnson's campaign workers who worried about potential backlash support for Barry Goldwater in the South.

The resulting political showdown occurred in an arena dominated by Lyndon Johnson. On one side were the determined MFDP activists who believed their grassroots delegation represented the expressed values of the Democratic party far better than did the party regulars who had abandoned John Kennedy in 1960 and would likely desert the party again.[71] On the other side were Johnson loyalists, including Rauh's old ally and current vice presidential hopeful Hubert Humphrey. Determined not to lose the white South, Johnson feared a dramatic split at the televised convention.

The MFDP took its case directly to the credentials committee hearings. One of the most memorable moments occurred when network television cameras honed in on Fannie Lou Hamer's vivid account of her efforts to register and the violence she encountered in jail. The moment was short-lived, however, for President Johnson called a sudden press conference that drew away the network cameras. Yet, Hamer's impact was electric. Party delegates were deluged with telegrams urging their support for the MFDP.

With control slipping away, the Johnson forces urged a compromise that would allow the MFDP to participate but not vote on the convention floor. Pressure mounted on credentials committee members. Congresswoman Edith Green suggested a compromise in which all members of both delegations who signed an oath of loyalty to the national ticket would be seated, with votes divided among them. The MFDP quietly agreed to this compromise and had convinced a majority of the committee to recommend it to the convention floor when the Johnson forces suggested another, weaker compromise. According to the latter, two at-large seats would be given to Aaron Henry and Ed King of the MFDP while all members of the regular delegation would be seated if they agreed to support the party candidates. Zinn describes the tense meeting that followed:

> Joseph Rauh and Edith Green now met with the Freedom Democratic Party delegation to urge them to accept the Administration offer. Green and Rauh were clearly shaken and uneasy. They were being pressured by Humphrey, Walter Reuther of the United Auto Workers, and the hierarchy of the Democratic Party. On the other side, they faced not only the anger of the SNCC youngsters who had helped organize the FDP, but that of the FDP delegates, for whom this token offer of recognition was too

much like the usual bone thrown to Negroes who showed signs of revolt. And perhaps a third pressure was simply their own traditional view that politics is "the art of the possible."

But SNCC and the FDP were born in struggles for "the impossible."[72]

The MFDP delegates unanimously rejected the compromise. After a sit-in on the convention floor and concerted pressure by civil rights leaders like King, Farmer, and Rustin, the FDP voted not to reconsider the compromise proposal. SNCC Executive Director James Forman recalls the gap between the MFDP rank-and-file and the national liberal leaders:

[The NAACP's Roy] Wilkins had told Mrs. Hamer, after her testimony, that she and the other people from Mississippi had made their point— they should go back home now and leave politicking to those who knew how to do it. . . . But the people in Mississippi . . . knew that none of those distinguished ladies and gentlemen had lain on the floor with them during the nights when the Klan rode by their houses firing guns. They knew that none of those fast-talking politicians had picked cotton with them to earn a meal, or lived on corn bread and grease and Kool Aid, or faced a sheriff like Jim Clark with murder in his eyes. They knew what party had sold them out before—the Democratic Party. And they knew the same party was trying to sell short their struggle again.[73]

Many MFDP members left the convention embittered. As Forman observed,

[The convention] was a powerful lesson, not only for black people from Mississippi but for all of SNCC and many other people as well. No longer was there any hope, among those who still had it, that the federal government would change the situation in the Deep South. . . . Five years of struggle had radically changed the thought processes of many people, changed them from idealistic reformers to full-time revolutionaries. And the change had come through direct experience.[74]

The convention clash reflected SNCC's growing distance from traditional party politics and the federal government. While the Johnson compromise was intended as a safe gesture of support for the MFDP, it was viewed as empty symbolism by SNCC workers and delegates who had risked their lives to organize the MFDP and come to the convention. For them, it epitomized the administration's unwillingness to take seriously racist violence in the South. SNCC activists were particularly galled that the administration compromise treated them worse than the Mississippi regulars whom they viewed as totally immoral. In effect, the administration had rejected the principle that racism had no place in the Democratic party. As Forman recalled of the confrontation with national leaders, "Bob Moses said we had to bring morality into politics. That's what was wrong with the country now. There is no morality in politics, otherwise we would not be here."[75]

The conflict over the MFDP revealed the contrast between a redemptive organization living its political values and confronting injustice on a daily basis, and sympathetic liberals detached from the daily dangers of the voter registration drive and accustomed to the snail-like pace of change within a bureaucratic national party. From the SNCC perspective, token or symbolic change was equivalent to no change. Their decision was itself symbolically significant. As Charles Sherrod maintained, in language that foreshadowed the future struggle, "We want much more than token positions. We want power for our people. [Acceptance of the compromise] would have said to blacks across the nation and the world that we share the power, and that is a lie! The 'liberals' would have felt great relief for a job well done."[76] From the liberals' perspective, the compromise represented all the change that could realistically be expected at the time. Although party leaders skirted an effort to block the seating of Mississippi congressmen in January 1965, by the time of the 1968 convention, party regulars from Mississippi and Georgia were denied their convention seats because of discriminatory selection procedures.

SNCC IN TRANSITION

After the summer of 1964, SNCC passed through a period of soul-searching and organizational renewal. Painfully disillusioned by the MFDP experience and the apparent betrayal by whites, Robert Moses recommended that the MFDP organization establish an independent state government in Mississippi—a secessionist idea later echoed in parts of the urban North.[77] Moses subsequently drifted away from SNCC, eventually ending up in Africa. A contingent of SNCC leaders traveled to Africa during the fall of 1964 and were greatly inspired by the example of black self-rule.[78] Many were influenced by the pan-African socialism of leaders like Sekou Toure of Ghana, and were dismayed at U.S. government propaganda that portrayed black progress at home in a deceptively positive light. They also encountered Malcolm X, who had recently broken with Elijah Muhammad's Nation of Islam. SNCC's contact led to Malcolm's subsequent support for SNCC efforts in Selma.

At home, SNCC activists debated the future of their organization. On one side stood those who, inspired by the example of Moses, embraced the freedom high belief that individuals should break free from hierarchical authority and centralized structure. On the other stood those like James Forman who advocated more effective organization to enhance the political power of black people. (The same prefigurative–instrumental debate was being waged within SDS at about the same time.) As this debate continued, it was clear that SNCC was moving in a more radical direction; broadening its critique of U.S. society. The redemptive organization had reached a turning point. The SNCC that emerged was more centralized and almost exclusively black. Before long, it would shift its attention to the urban North, largely abandoning community organization among the disenfranchised poor in the rural South.

Simultaneously, SNCC came under fire from many of its earlier allies in the civil rights movement. Liberals were alarmed at news columns that denounced SNCC activists as subversives and even communist sympathizers. Despite a total lack of supportive evidence for these claims, SNCC was singled out for denunciation because it followed a nonexclusionary policy in its field activities (as did SDS in the antiwar movement). SNCC's prefigurative democracy was, however, totally incompatible with the doctrinaire ideology and hierarchy of the Communist party.

DIRECT ACTION V: SELMA, 1965

Meanwhile, other civil rights groups were inspired by congressional passage of the Kennedy–Johnson Civil Rights Act, the most aggressive federal civil rights legislation since Reconstruction. The new law provided federal support for an assault on segregation in public facilities. However, it did relatively little to advance black voter registration and, as the Freedom Summer campaign demonstrated, effective voter registration required federal support. The Southern Christian Leadership Conference (SCLC) was developing plans with its liberal allies in Congress for a new campaign to wrest strong voting rights legislation from the federal government. At the time, President Johnson's civil rights advisers favored a breathing period to demonstrate the effect of the Civil Rights Act. The SCLC, however, anticipated a faster timetable.

The Birmingham experience had reinforced Martin Luther King's belief that southern violence helped the civil rights movement gain support from northern liberals and the federal government. Selma, Alabama, was a natural site for the next campaign. Sheriff James Clark of Selma was noted for his violent temper in dealing with blacks. In addition, SNCC field workers had been organizing in Selma since early 1963. They had succeeded in drawing Clark's ire to such an extent that the federal government had interceded in court to constrain the sheriff. SNCC had also mobilized the local black population.

After organizing a direct action protest in St. Augustine, Florida, in 1964, King turned his sights on Selma and announced the new campaign. The demonstrations that followed in early 1965 were a crucial and well-orchestrated catalyst for passage of the Voting Rights Act of 1965. They were also the last large-scale civil rights action involving the combined efforts of the SCLC and SNCC. The use of white violence to expedite effective legislation proved to King that his strategy was right. However, it also confirmed SNCC workers' belief that appeals to the national conscience required unacceptable levels of suffering.

The crucial confrontation occurred after the death of Jimmy Lee Jackson, a young black man who was killed by a state policeman while coming to the aid of his mother, who had been beaten by police.[79] King announced what was to become the first of three attempts to march from Selma to Montgomery. With King away preaching a sermon in Atlanta, the marchers were led by the SCLC's Hosea Williams and SNCC's John Lewis and Robert Mants. At the Pettus Bridge at the edge of town, they were confronted by Sheriff Clark, the deputies, and the state police, who ordered them to disperse. When the marchers refused, they were attacked in one of the bloodiest assaults of the civil rights era, which later came to be known as "Bloody Sunday." The police charged into the marchers swinging billy clubs and throwing tear gas. Scores were injured, and several required hospitalization.

The attack at Pettus Bridge attracted reinforcements from SNCC workers in Mississippi. As Cleveland Sellers remarked, "We were angry, and we wanted to show Governor Wallace, the Alabama State Highway Patrol, Sheriff Clark, Selma's whites, the federal government and poor southern blacks in other Selmas that we didn't intend to take any more shit. We would ram the march down the throat of anyone who tried to stop us."[80] The violence also had a larger audience. News photos and graphic accounts of the assault flashed across the country, triggering an outpouring of condemnation among congressional liberals. Two days later, King led a second march that again confronted a police barricade outside of town. After Ralph Abernathy led the marchers in prayer, King told them to return to Selma, leaving many SNCC workers angry and frustrated.[81] After the march, an angry white mob attacked and beat three white ministers who had been in the march; one was James Reeb, who died several days later.

A national outcry resulted. Congressional leaders demanded action on voting rights. Memorial services and rallies attracted thousands in Washington and Boston where Reeb had served. That night, President Johnson went before a joint session of Congress with his "We Shall Overcome" address calling for adoption of his new voting rights bill.

The Selma demonstrations continued. On Wednesday, a federal injunction restrained Governor Wallace and the state troopers from interfering with the march. Preparations for the third effort to march to Montgomery were underway. Meanwhile, the House of Representatives began hearings on the voting rights bill. On Sunday, under the protection of federalized national guardsmen, the marchers crossed the Pettus Bridge and began the fifty-four-mile trek down U.S. 80 to Montgomery. On the following Thursday, King led the triumphal entry into Montgomery. At the afternoon rally in front of the state capitol on Thursday, he roused the crowd with an inspirational address using the familiar cadence of repeated phrases, "We are on the move now. . . . How long? Not long. . . ."

The Selma march achieved precisely what King had hoped—swift passage of the Voting Rights Act. Media coverage played an important role as TV stations interrupted the network film "Judgment at Nuremburg" to show dignified, nonviolent blacks brutally attacked while marching to petition for their right to vote, and white racists willing to commit murder in their effort to prevent this basic right from being enjoyed by blacks. Northern sympathies were fully aroused in support of the protesters.[82]

Reflecting their redemptive vision of alternative politics, SNCC workers were ambivalent toward the Voting Rights Act. On the one hand, it provided undeniable assistance in the voter registration drive. On the other hand, it seemingly co-opted the very people SNCC had hoped would build a new politics by luring them into reliance on the federal two-party system.[83]

SNCC workers had been registering voters and organizing poor blacks in rural Lowndes County, between Selma and Montgomery. The day after white volunteer Viola Liuzzo became the third activist killed in the Selma action,

SNCC worker Stokely Carmichael arrived in Lowndes County to help mobilize the voter drive. Carmichael joined militant local blacks, many of whom were prepared to use weapons in self-defense. In August 1965, aided by the arrival of a federal registrar under the newly passed Voting Rights Act, blacks began registering in large numbers. Carmichael helped form an independent political party, the Lowndes County Freedom Organization. The emblem for the LCFO was a black panther. The stage was set for the black power movement.

◼ Black Power

> Once you gain control of the economy of your own community, then you don't have to picket and boycott and beg some cracker downtown for a job in his business.
> . . . In areas where the government has proven itself either unwilling or unable to defend the lives and the property of Negroes, it's time for Negroes to defend themselves.
> —Malcolm X, "The Ballot or the Bullet"

After Selma, the civil rights movement had achieved its primary objectives: passage of civil rights and voting rights legislation aimed at ending Jim Crow and bringing the South into the liberal mainstream. Through these successes, the movement began to eradicate the two forms of oppression most contrary to the principles of liberal democracy: racial segregation in public environments like schools, bus terminals, lunch counters, and rest rooms (though not in housing); and denial of the right to vote. By isolating the extreme and regionally contained form of racial oppression in the South, King's appeal to the white conscience of mainstream America had succeeded.

However, severe racial inequality and poverty remained untouched by the civil rights legislation. As the Johnson administration turned its attention to the war on poverty, the civil rights agenda shifted to the North and the nation as a whole. Johnson proposed the civil rights bill of 1966, an attack on housing discrimination. King traveled to the outskirts of Chicago with a march aimed at the same goal. Meanwhile, the SNCC leadership began to change hands, bringing in activists who were increasingly responsive to an urban constituency; militant rhetoric replaced local community organizing and black frustrations began to explode in violence.

This second wave or black power phase of the movement for racial justice failed to eradicate, or even substantially reduce, racial inequality. The civil rights bill of 1966 was defeated. By his own account, King encountered the most virulent white hatred of his career in Chicago. The War on Poverty was trimmed back when it posed a threat to local politicians, and was later scrapped by a Nixon administration that recognized its potential for empowering the poor.

The black power phase confronted, rather than cooperated with, the institutions, power, and ideology of the liberal mainstream. It was rooted in SNCC's emphasis on enabling poor people to achieve real power through participation in their local communities, rather than abstract power provided by legislated guarantees. It was echoed in the SDS Economic Research Action Project (ERAP) efforts in urban ghettoes and the community organizing tactics of Saul Alinsky and others. Power was gained through the collective action of ordinary people, resulting in both external and internal transformation.

From this more radical perspective, party politics and legislative log-rolling in a distant capitol only diluted the drive for justice until it was rendered largely cosmetic. Educational institutions, those alleged halls of opportunity for the downtrodden, were viewed as credentialing agencies that legitimized existing inequalities while denying the subjective cultures of minority groups. City halls were responsive to powerful business interests and, when conflicts erupted, to white ethnic groups hostile to racial minorities. When push came to shove, labor unions were responsive to their membership, most of whom were economically or historically so close to society's edge that they viewed the entry of a new group as threatening. Finally, the changing occupational structure of corporate capitalism and the service economy closed off the paths of advancement to any who had not pursued proper credentialing. In sum, white society gave blacks the message that they had to be white to succeed, and that success was reserved for only a few. But to be white, if you were black, was to deny your culture.

The radical consciousness was fueled by growing anger at a white mainstream that mouthed empty rhetoric when it preached democracy and equality for all Americans. Malcolm X had been expressing militant sentiments to growing audiences for several years before his assassination in 1965. The previous year, he had asserted, "What we need in this country is the same type of Mau Mau here that they had over there in Kenya. . . . If they were over here, they'd get this problem straightened up just like that."[84]

Anger underlay the direct action campaign in the South even while it was channeled into nonviolent expression. However, the continued violence encountered by blacks in the South provoked a turn toward aggression in the black struggle. The rhetoric of SNCC leaders like Stokely Carmichael and H. Rap Brown became increasingly hot. At a Newark Conference on Black Power, Brown proclaimed, "Straighten up America, or we'll burn you down." Aggressive denunciations of such sacred institutions as the presidency, the Congress, or the police were commonplace, as were scathing dismissals of Uncle Toms and white liberals, and taunting calls for armed self-defense.[85]

One key development in the latter part of the racial struggle was the explosion of the black ghettoes in northern cities, beginning with Harlem, North Philadelphia, and Rochester, New York in 1964. It dramatically escalated in the Watts section of Los Angeles in 1965; spread through Chicago, Omaha, Cleveland, and numerous other cities in 1966; and culminated in the devastating destruction in Newark and Detroit in 1967, only to reemerge on a national scale after the assassination of Martin Luther King, Jr., in 1968.[86]

The growing mood of black rage was fueled by shattered hopes—hopes once inspired by political rhetoric and legislation that spawned the so-called revolution of rising expectations, and dashed by backlash against the more radical Community Action Program. Growing ideological support for violence came from the aggressive rhetoric of black leaders and the anticolonial struggles of black Africa. The initial spark for urban insurrection was usually an isolated incident between young blacks and the police. In general, the changing mood was voiced by a militant constituency that could not be ignored by black leaders.

The angry mood also matched the increasing black separatism of SNCC. In early 1966, Stokely Carmichael succeeded John Lewis as chairman of SNCC, and Floyd McKissick replaced James Farmer (who subsequently joined the Nixon administration) as national director of CORE. Both groups were moving toward excluding whites. While some militants may have wished whites dead, others, like Julius Lester, believed "the white man is simply to be ignored, because the time has come for the black man to control things which affect his life."[87]

The black power slogan first emerged into public view in June 1966, during the March against Fear to mobilize black determination after James Meredith had been shot while marching alone across Mississippi. Along the way, Carmichael and SNCC worker Willie Ricks aroused the crowd with the cry "black power." The slogan was picked up by the media and immediately evoked a national response. Mainstream whites felt threatened and even some civil rights leaders felt that black power sounded like anti–white power.

In any event, the slogan captured the changing mood of blacks, and that mood determined the direction black power would travel. Carmichael noted that

> we couldn't control what was happening in America. I had seen spontaneous rebellions, been involved in spontaneous rebellions, since the early sixties. Cambridge, Maryland, was where I first saw it, where black people not only threw bricks and bottles, but shot at the National Guard. I saw it in Birmingham, in Jackson, in Greenwood. I saw the feeling. I saw the energy, and I was myself nervous about it. But it was building and there was no way to stop it.[88]

As it turned out, there was a way to stop it. About three years later, the Nixon administration instituted its counterintelligence program of repression of black militants and the antiwar movement called "COINTELPRO." At the same time it promoted the co-optive notion of black capitalism. In the meantime, a white backlash had begun to emerge. The urban revolt proved to be highly disruptive but essentially short lived.

The notion of black separatism drew on blacks' contempt for a white society that was viewed as amoral, fearful, and repressed. As James Baldwin wrote,

> The only thing white people have that black people need, or should want, is power—and no one holds power forever. White people cannot, in the generality, be taken as models of how to live. Rather, the white man is himself in sore need of new standards, which will release him from his confusion and place him once again in fruitful communion with the depths of his own being. And I repeat: the price of the liberation of the white people is the liberation of the blacks—the total liberation, in the cities, in the towns, before the law, and in the mind.[89]

Malcolm X put it more bluntly. "You don't integrate with a sinking ship."

The idea of black power encompassed several meanings: black entry into the American tradition of ethnic and interest-group pluralism, a local emphasis on separatist community power and black self-determination, black cultural pride or cultural nationalism, identification with other peoples oppressed by capitalism and American imperialism, and a leftist vanguardism that sought to effect revolutionary change. One common strain in the black power movement was the psychological dimension of empowerment, the self-esteem gained through direct participation in shaping one's destiny. In this respect, the prefigurative politics of the civil rights movement persisted.

During the year that Stokely Carmichael and Charles Hamilton collaborated in writing *Black Power*, the New York City school system embarked on its community control experiment. After years of struggle for integration of New York schools, black parents shifted strategies in 1966. When the city failed to live up to its promise that a new school would be opened with an integrated student body, parents threatened to boycott the schools.

Fearing adverse publicity, the school administration (assisted by the Ford Foundation), opted to open three experimental community controlled school districts within the city. Each community elected a lay board that would have discretionary power over personnel, curriculum, and budget. When the Ocean Hill–Brownsville district board transferred nineteen teachers out of the district, the American Federation of Teachers (AFT) protested against the violation of contractual due process rights; eventually, the AFT went out on strike. The schools remained in turmoil for the balance of the school year, and the situation grew ugly. Racial epithets were slung back and forth between the black and Jewish communities in the Ocean Hill–Brownsville area, and tensions mounted between the teachers union and young college graduates who continued to teach in the maverick districts. The following year, the schools reopened under a new state decentralization law that divided the city schools into large sub-districts with watered-down parent advisory councils.[90]

In their emphasis on cultural nationalism black Americans reached back into the past to embrace their African roots. Through various forms of expression—music, hairstyle, dress, the selection of African names, and the use of black English—they asserted the notion that black is beautiful. This cultural awakening echoed Marcus Garvey's separatist movement of the early twentieth century and was a direct attack on self-demeaning forms of personal expression that had emerged from centuries of oppression. Cultural nationalism emerged in many forms, from the political black separatism expressed in some SNCC organizing projects and Elijah Muhammad's Nation of Islam, to the rhetoric of Carmichael and his supporters, to the rise of the black student movement and the push for Afro-American studies on college and university campuses. According to a publication of SNCC's organizing effort in Atlanta, *Nitty Gritty*,

We can see no meaningful, long range social changes coming about for [the masses of black Americans], until we can change each individual's belief in himself. We can see no long standing structures created by Blacks who are emotionally, socially, politically and economically dependent upon those individuals who are non-black. [The staff hoped to awaken in blacks] . . . a sense of pride in their beauty, strength and resourcefulness; and also a meaningful sense of self-respect that they can only gain when they see Black people working together accomplishing worthwhile programs—without the guidance and/or direction and control of non-Blacks.[91]

Cultural nationalism gravitated toward black Africa as the hub of a new pan-African revolution. Like the largely white counterculture, it embodied the expressive side of New Left politics, emphasizing personal liberation and authenticity. Similarly, it embraced separatist impulses, a rejection of and disassociation from the mainstream culture.

The other face of black power moved closer to the instrumental movements of the traditional Left and was less separatist. With roots in the effort of local southern blacks to achieve political and economic power, the ultimate expression of this movement came with the Black Panther Party for Self-Defense, formed in Oakland, California in late 1966. Panther co-founders Bobby Seale and Huey Newton had grown dissatisfied with the cultural nationalism and middle-class orientation of the Afro-American Association they had joined at Merritt Junior College. They left and went to work in the urban black community, "knocking on doors and asking the residents of Oakland's ghetto what they needed and wanted."[92]

THE BLACK PANTHER PARTY

To most white Americans, the Black Panther party no doubt conveyed the image of an "anarchistic band of gun-toting, white-hating thugs," in Philip Foner's parody of average Americans' views,[93] partly because of their inflammatory rhetoric and street style, but also because the media and the Nixon administration were quick to scapegoat threatening Panther behavior. In actual practice, the Panthers' version of black power was a blend of left-influenced ideology, community-based activism, and incendiary rhetoric and behavior.

At its origin, the Black Panther party promulgated a ten-point program entitled "What We Want—What We Believe." The program was a laundry list of demands by the dispossessed, concluding with a lengthy quote from the Declaration of Independence. The first and most basic demand was for democratic freedom, the "power to determine the destiny of our Black community." Some demands were economic—a call for full employment of black Americans, business reparations, and an end to "robbery" of the black community. Other demands reflected the view of the black ghetto as a colony of white America. These included an end to police brutality and murder, a call for armed self-defense against the outside occupying power, the release of all blacks held in jail because they had not received a fair and impartial trial, and a U.N. plebescite for the black colony in the United States.

The Black Panther party's new leaders were influenced by the writings of Malcolm X and Franz Fanon, both of whom stressed the need for blacks to overcome the paralysis of accommodation to white society by fighting back, violently, if necessary. In subsequent years, their awareness of solidarity with oppressed peoples around the world was informed by reading Marx, Engels, Lenin, Mao, Ho Chi Minh, and Che Guevara. They became particularly outspoken in their attack on the U.S. war in Vietnam and the recruitment of blacks to fight the war. They knew of Malcolm's conversion away from black separatism when he traveled to Africa and the Middle East; they realized that not only could whites be allies in the struggle against oppression, but blacks could be obstacles to that struggle. As Eldridge Cleaver wrote to black nationalist Stokely Carmichael after Carmichael's brief tenure as prime minister of the Black Panther party,

> You should know that suffering is color-blind, that the victims of Imperialism, Racism, Colonialism, and Neo-Colonialism come in all colors, and that they need a unity based on revolutionary principles rather than skin color. . . . In short, your habit of looking at the world through black-colored glasses would lead you, on the domestic level, to close ranks with such enemies of black people as James Farmer, Whitney Young, Roy Wilkins, and Ron Karenga; and on the international level you would end up in the same bag with Papa Doc Duvalier, Joseph Mobutu, and Haile Selassie.[94]

Much of the Panthers' early activity emphasized armed self-defense. The original Oakland branch established a system of legal patrol cars that followed police through the ghetto area, armed with both guns and lawbooks to ensure that the constitutional rights of black residents were not violated. The patrol cars enraged the Oakland police, but greatly impressed the ghetto youth, especially when incidents of police harassment tapered off. Word of the Panthers spread among ghetto residents.

In 1967, the Panthers dropped the Self-Defense portion of their title, a change that reflected not only their broadening political ideology but also a variety of community programs instituted earlier that year. They had protested rent evictions, set up educational programs informing welfare recipients of their rights, established schools that taught black history, lobbied successfully for new school traffic lights, and begun a free breakfast for children program. These local programs echoed the community control movement that reached its peak in New York City schools in 1967–1968; both emphasized policy-making power in the hands of indigenous inner city populations.

At the same time, the Panthers were increasingly engaged in provocative, militant behavior. When the California legislature considered a 1967 bill aimed at curbing the Panthers' heretofore legal possession of weapons, thirty legally-armed Party members marched up the steps of the Capitol building and into the visitors' gallery. While television cameras whirred, all were arrested for disturbing the peace. The specter of armed blacks invading the legislature was transmitted across national news media, triggering near hysteria in some quarters, and a subsequent massive campaign of repression. As Bobby Seale noted, however, the action represented the Panthers' constituency of young ghetto blacks:

> Now the papers are going to call us thugs and hoodlums. . . . But the brothers on the block, who the man's been calling thugs and hoodlums for 100 years, they're going to say, "Them's some out of sight thugs and hoodlums up there." . . . Who is these thugs and hoodlums? Huey was smart enough to know that the black people were going to say, "Well, they've been calling us niggers, thugs and hoodlums for 400 years, that ain't gon' hurt me, I'm going to check out what these brothers is doing!"[95]

SNCC leaders Carmichael and Brown demonstrated a similar appreciation of their shifting constituency. In effect, if black activists were to truly represent the urban black underclass, militant rhetoric and actions were a necessary part of their communication.

In fact, the Panthers broke new ground in personifying the pent-up rage of the most oppressed urban blacks. Whereas the largely spontaneous riots often lashed out at the most convenient targets in the black community, the Panthers focused on white oppression. Armed with an increasingly revolutionary ideological awareness, they came to be viewed as a dangerous threat by the white power structure, despite the fact that Panther leaders (unlike some black militants) had long emphasized armed self-defense rather than a suicidal armed revolution.

The system fought back. The response to Panther bravado was a systematic and ultimately successful effort to eliminate the Black Panther party. This effort included rhetorical assaults by officials like FBI Director J. Edgar Hoover, Vice-president Spiro Agnew, Attorney General John Mitchell, and presidential advisor (later senator) Daniel P. Moynihan. It encompassed surveillance, infiltration, and provocation under the Nixon administration's COINTELPRO program. It involved continuous police harassment and arrest of Panther leaders like Huey Newton and Bobby Seale. And it erupted in violent police attacks on the homes and offices of Panther members. An ACLU report found a prima facie case of a systematic nationwide law enforcement drive against the organization. As Ronald Fraser recalls,

> The single most shocking facet of the Nixon era's political repression was the nationwide campaign to crush the Black Panther Party. From coast to coast, wherever a Panther group appeared, the police moved quickly to force it out of existence. Hundreds of Panthers were jailed on charges ranging from illegal use of sound equipment to resisting arrest to attempted murder. Police raided Panther headquarters, shot up the walls, smashed typewriters and furniture and destroyed the food destined for the Panther's food for children [program]. Gun battles between police and Panthers erupted in many cities. At least ten Panthers were killed, and another ten wounded by police, between 1967 and 1969.[96]

After the murder of Fred Hampton and Mark Clark by the Chicago police, even the staid *New York Times* declared,

> The story unfolded by the Chicago grand jury makes it appear that the law-enforcement agencies, more than the Panthers, were acting out of a conspiracy. The police, following Federal tips, sprayed the Panthers' lodging with massive gunfire, even though no more than one shot was found to have been fired from the inside. Chicago officials subsequently

engaged in a deliberate publicity campaign to depict the Panthers as the aggressors. Police laboratories, lacking either in competence or integrity, provided erroneous findings to serve the same purpose.

Against a background of doctored evidence and coached police wit-nesses, it is not surprising that the State's Attorney, who initially had played a leading role in building the public case against the Panthers, finally dropped all charges against them.[97]

Given society's assault against them, the enormous resources required for their community mobilizing efforts, and their own escalating rhetoric of "revolution," it is hardly surprising that the Black Panther party eventually faded from view. In the polarized, violent times of the late Sixties and early Seventies, revolutionary rhetoric became overemphasized at the expense of political foundation-building. (The same could, of course, be said for the white New Left). As SDS leader Carl Oglesby observed in 1969:

> The Panthers did not *organize* the ghetto, they only apostrophized it. So far as I know, the breakfast-for-children program represents the only serious attempt to relate concretely, practically, broadly, and *institution-ally* to the black urban community as a whole. . . . There ought to be dozens of programs like the breakfasts. Nothing else, in fact, gives stature, credibility, and social meaning to the gun; for the ghetto, as such, neither can be nor should be defended. Only when that ghetto is being transformed, de-ghettoized, by the self-organized activity of the people does its militant, self-defense become a real *political* possibility.[98]

For the most part, the inner city ghettoes faded from public visibility, as the urban black underclass, increasingly decimated by drugs and gang wars, returned to the hopeless and desperate condition of what Ralph Ellison called the "invisible man."

■ Legacies of the Civil Rights Struggle

The racial struggles of the 1950s and 1960s produced three outcomes of great consequence. They liberated millions of black Americans from the psychological devastation of racial oppression; they changed forever the social and political face of the South; and they had a profound effect on white consciousness, most directly on that of student activists. They did not, however, produce significant and lasting changes in race-related economic inequality.

By the end of the 1960s, substantial progress had been made in bringing race relations in the South closer to those of the rest of the nation. At least most of the autocratic personal control of white racists had been eradicated by the courageous and persistent efforts of civil rights activists who risked violence, ostracism, and death. Both the Voting Rights Act and the segregated residential patterns in urban areas have contributed to the growing numbers of blacks who hold public office.

However, the problems of racial inequality persist to this day.[99] As the black middle class becomes more visible in mainstream institutions, racial inequality is increasingly *class* inequality compounded by racism. Many people in the racial struggles of the Sixties came to realize that addressing this inequality required far more than extending civil rights to blacks or funding equal opportunity programs. It also meant confronting the roots of class inequality in a capitalist economy. As SNCC realized perhaps best of all, for poor blacks to gain the same power as that of poor whites was insufficient. Gaining a sense of control over one's destiny meant far more than being able to use previously white lunch counters or being admitted to white schools. It meant being able to share in decisions governing living and working environments; it meant finding one's place in (not at the fringes of) one's community; it meant gaining power over one's destiny. The vision that emerged from the struggle for racial justice was far more expressive, democratic, and radical than the vision that informed support for the Kennedy and Johnson administrations. As Emily Stoper maintains,

> SNCC's ethos served a kind of prepolitical role by presenting a model of an alternative politics to the New Left and a critique of America's values that is of potential interest to many more people—though very few outside the New Left heard the message. . . . SNCC is of interest because it attempted to do both things: to be political and to offer its members the satisfactions of a redemptive ethos. The story of how it failed provides an illustration of the reason the American political system is not likely to provide its citizens with a sense of community or meaning for their lives.[100]

3 Political Education
The New Student Left and the Campus Revolt

The employers will love this generation. They aren't going to press many grievances. . . . There aren't going to be any riots.
—Clark Kerr, 1959

Come mothers and fathers,
Throughout the land
And don't criticize
What you can't understand.
Your sons and your daughters
Are beyond your command
Your old road is
Rapidly agin'
Please get out of the new one
If you can't lend your hand
For the times they are a-changin'.
—Bob Dylan, "The Times They Are A-Changin'

Probably the most distinctive feature of the decade from 1960 to 1970 was the unprecedented scale of student protest. The student revolt swept across much of the globe with major student upheavals occurring in France, West Germany, Great Britain, Czechoslovakia, Poland, Italy, Japan, Mexico, Brazil, Venezuela, Senegal, and other nations.[1] This distinctively New Left rose up against the bureaucratic and imperial institutions of both advanced capitalism and state socialism, expressing what Greg Calvert and Carol Nieman have called the "critique of the programmed society."[2]

After initial rumblings on selected campuses in the late 1950s, the American student revolt erupted in 1960 with four signal events: the initial student sit-in at Greensboro, North Carolina; student protests against the House Un-American Activities Committee hearings in San Francisco; the formation of the Student Non-violent Coordinating Committee (SNCC); and the creation of the Students for a Democratic Society (SDS) from the moribund Student League for Industrial Democracy. In their distinctive blend of expressive and instrumental politics and their emphasis on politics grounded on the "authority of experience," SNCC and SDS symbolized what was new about the New Left more than any other activist organizations.

The student revolt came to an end in 1970. In March, an explosion shattered a Greenwich Village townhouse, killing three members of the Weathermen and effectively driving the remnants of this SDS faction underground for the next decade. Two months later, students were killed by the National Guard at Kent State University and by police at Jackson State College. What remained of campus activism dissipated as the academic year came to a chaotic end. The following fall, a University of Wisconsin graduate student was killed when young militants blew up the Army Mathematics Research Center, which had been implicated in war-related research. These events were the final, deadly spasm of confrontational campus politics.

In the interim, unprecedented numbers of students participated in on- and off-campus protests against racism, university rules and regulations, academic bureaucracy, and university complicity in the war in Vietnam. Because of the vehemence of some protests, and because unprecedented numbers of young Americans attended college during the Sixties, the campus revolt drew substantial media and public attention—so much so that in 1966 *Time* magazine pronounced the entire under-25 generation "Man [sic] of the Year." SDS membership alone grew from approximately 250 in late 1960 to an estimated peak of 80,000 to 100,000 on 350 to 400 campuses in 1968.[3]

■ The New Student Left

We had begun by trying to find an answer to our own loneliness and despair through action and the building of political community. We were unwilling to adopt the stance of cynicism. We continued to insist that the revolution which we wanted to make, which we were engaged in making, was about our lives and for life. We refused to defer existence and the search for new freedom and new life until some mythical future. To succumb to such mystification would have been to fall totally victim to capitalist ideology in its purest form; for capitalism *is* the ideology of deferred existence, of the ethics of accumulation for future power rather than production for present enjoyment. Nothing contradicts the capitalist ethic more thoroughly than

the spirit of the New Left, a spirit embodied in the slogan, "Now The Revolution!" The Community of Free Persons will not be built tomorrow if we do not begin to embody its values today.
—Greg Calvert and Carol Nieman, A *Disrupted History*

College students in the 1960s came of age at a time when the contra-dictory impulses of American society were in full sway. The activist student generation was shaped by the successes of postwar American capitalism—access to material affluence and comfort—but also by the wastefulness of mass consumption, the emptiness of suburbia, and the alienating prospect of climb-ing the corporate ladder. Material comfort enabled many students to look beyond the quest for security, and they did so instinctively, envisioning a post-scarcity society responsive to human values. They eagerly sought meaningful engagement in the larger society. Their expressive politics were a quest for what was missing—moral purpose, the bonds of community, and a sense of individual selfhood. Initially, their instrumental politics were generated on one hand by the civil rights struggle, and on the other by residues of McCarthyism and fifties repression on university campuses.

THE POLITICAL ROLE OF EDUCATION

Universities brought unprecedented numbers of young people into an environment segregated by age, suspended in time and place, and focused on an intellectual encounter with critical minds. The dynamics of university life encouraged students to imagine a society freed from the inequities and im-peratives of production and consumption. Yet universities themselves reflected society's contradictions. "On the one hand, the university offers considerable time, freedom, opportunity, and resources for self-expression, personal devel-opment, and the free play of imagination, intellect, and feeling. But on the other hand, its formal educational program, its structured competitive disci-pline, its impersonality, its authoritarianism, serve to continuously corrode the liberating possibilities one glimpses within it."[4] Being young, skeptical, and, in many cases, receptive to the moral power of the civil rights movement, many were predisposed to respond to activist initiatives. Yet the technologically based, postwar economy had begun to transform higher education from its classical liberal arts focus to one of training the scientific, technical, and pro-fessional employees of advanced capitalism. In this context, students became a potential oppositional force within the technocratic society; they became restive within the constraints of mass education. For a decade, they sought to make learning meaningful and relevant to a world in ferment.

The campus revolt was the more volatile part of a broader critique of education at all levels. Stimulated by pioneering models like the Highlander Folk School, the Mississippi Freedom Schools, and A. S. Neill's Summerhill School in England, Sixties critics embraced a democratic rather than paternalistic vision of education, which viewed learning as growth-enhancing experience rather than conformity to top-down imperatives. A host of critics denounced schooling as antieducational, dehumanizing, oppressive, discriminatory, and intensely destructive of students who performed poorly.[5] Many provided powerful images of what was wrong with American schools. A few conveyed a sense of what learning should look like in a democratic context. John Dewey's theory of democratic education, which involved the interaction between learner and a socially useful purpose, was rediscovered; Paolo Freire articulated a vision of liberating education grounded on the concrete conditions of oppression. Innumerable experimental or "free" schools cropped up throughout the nation, developing and testing democratic or libertarian educational theories.

Through it all, education was recognized as a process with significant political implications, a fact borne out by students' experiences on college and university campuses. Inclined by economic security and parental support toward the liberating tendencies of universities, students looked on their university learning environment with critical eyes. Inspired by the civil rights struggle, students began to act. Participating in mass meetings, they grappled with the purpose of their campus experiences. Their efforts to open things up, in turn challenged the authority of university officials who responded with institution-protecting instincts and sometimes with authoritarian discipline. The civil rights movement's tension between idealistic activism and institutional defense was replicated on the nation's campuses.

THE EDUCATIONAL ROLE OF POLITICS

Students' experiences taught them not only that education is inherently political, but that political action is intensely educational. As Wini Breines put it,

Participants in the student revolt were quickly struck by the fact that in the university, as in the society at large, talk leading to political action was discouraged or trivialized. . . . As soon as they had *acted on* their own loss of democracy or liberty, the university stepped in. Words in the classroom, meaningless with respect to their desire for relevancy and freedom, were unsatisfactory. When the connection was made between words and actions, students understood by the university's response that they were becoming relevant.[6]

The educational process of mobilization, action, reaction, and deliberation proceeded on campuses nationwide during the decade. Through it, students became aware of the functional connection between their college education and the larger society.

In the early years, civil rights was the primary external stimulus for student activism. The Mississippi Freedom Summer, in particular, provided a radicalizing training ground for the activists who started Berkeley's Free Speech Movement in 1964. More generally, sympathetic civil rights support groups formed on many northern campuses, and SNCC served as a model for the early SDS. Students began to confront racism and inequality on their campuses and surrounding communities. As Berkeley's Free Speech Movement learned, some university administrations were loathe to disturb local or state political waters.

Then, in Breines' words, "Everything changed in 1965. The escalation of the war in Vietnam and the development of the anti-war movement, created a mass movement in the space of several months."[7] The war also sharpened student awareness of the university's role in the larger society. The draft resistance movement discovered "manpower channeling": Working-class youth were channeled into combat while middle-class students who were given deferments were expected to embrace the competitive ethic of capitalism and fit into functional roles in the corporate and technical hierarchy. SDS Vice-president Carl Davidson wrote the 1967 pamphlet *The Multiversity: Crucible of the New Working Class*, exploring a theory of students-as-vanguard in the transformation of technological capitalism. About the same time, students uncovered war related research on campuses like Stanford, Wisconsin, and Columbia, a discovery that brought home the university's complicity in American foreign policy.

Feeling growing anguish over the war and increasingly powerless to stop it, students demanded that their institutions cease all activities linked to the war effort, if not take a stand against the war. For their part, university administrators were caught in their instinctive concern for institutional maintenance, and some decried students' demands as a violation of their institution's "neutrality." In its early stages, student activism was framed in liberal terms like "free speech"; in the later, more confrontational stages, the cry of free speech was also heard on the other side among those opposed to the activists' moralistic stance.[8]

RADICALIZATION IN THE NEW LEFT

Activism on the part of the young, and resistance on the part of their elders, sharpened activists' critical consciousness, emboldened them, and pushed their strategies in an increasingly confrontational and militant direction, from witness to protest to confrontation to resistance to self-proclaimed revolution. Ultimately, the contradiction between the liberating and constraining impulses of university life came more and more to feel like an either-or choice, either to change society or to join it. This was a *radical* choice in the sense that students came to view "the system" as the primary obstacle to human liberation and justice, and because it broke their psychological bond to that system. By the end of the decade, the heirs of SDS were self-consciously revolutionary in their ideology and violent in their strategies. A Gallup poll of college students in 1970 indicated that 44 percent felt violence was justified to bring about social change in the United States, while 37 percent described themselves politically as "far left" or "left."[9]

The radicalization of student activists and the growth of a mass movement exposed tensions within the New Left. Chief among these was the fundamental tension between their instrumental drive to transform society and their expressive, morally grounded activism. As Barbara Myerhoff observed in her study of a 1970 campus protest, "The accomplishment of their political goals necessitates self-sacrifice, determination, delayed gratification, and rational, calculating, efficient organization. Yet these very qualities and actions are antithetical to the way life is to be lived in their view—spontaneously, openly, for the present, for its own sake, in unanalyzed, uncategorized, urgent subjectivity."[10] Historically, proponents of radical visions have chosen one of two routes: a revolutionary path in which the *end* of changing the existing social order justified *means* that violate the very values that motivated the radicalism in the first place; or a utopian path of withdrawal from the corrupt and intransigent social order. The more resistance students encountered, the more their belief in personal compassion and open, direct personal relationships seemed at odds with their hopes for realizing a just and humane social order.

In effect, the contradictions of postindustrial society spawned an oppositional movement that itself contained contradictions. These tensions were reflected in pervasive divisions within the Movement. Additional organizational tensions plagued the New Left. SDS struggled repeatedly with the paradox of base-building through campus organization versus direct off-campus confrontation of social ills. As the Movement swelled, the prefigurative–instrumental strain was played out between the spontaneity of grassroots campus activity and the demand for national organization.

However, the distinctiveness of the New Left stemmed from its refusal to embrace a purely instrumental politics. Except for a few deviations like the Progressive Labor party it never subscribed to a Leninist version of vanguardism.[11] As Theodore Roszak observed, the intense personalism of the New Left meant it was unwilling "to reify doctrine to the extent of granting it more importance than flesh and blood."[12]

As numerous critics have pointed out, the expressive side of the New Left was not without its flaws: a mistrust of authority that led to excessive collective soul-searching and self-indulgence, a resistance to organization that hampered efforts to mobilize a national movement, and an intense subjectivity that blinded activists to their impact on others. On the other hand, the abandonment of the New Left's prefigurative politics led in an even more ominous direction. The apocalyptic adventurism of the late 1960s, while mirroring the violence of the war and police repression, became a useful symbol in the hands of those who wished to discredit the New Left in toto.

THE RISE AND FALL OF SDS

No group was more central to or symbolic of the turbulence of the 1960s than the Students for a Democratic Society. The rise and fall of SDS embodied the evolution of the New Left. In the early stages, the left critique tended to be hopeful and reformist, activism focused on direct mobilization of the dispossessed, and the lifestyle of student activists reflected a kind of intense, communal esprit. In the middle years, the critique shifted to a more radical separatism, activism was more emotion-laden and confrontational, while life-styles began to embrace countercultural influences like drugs and rock music. In the later years, the Movement unraveled. The critique became more explicitly radical, and activism ranged from withdrawal to electoral participation, from mass protest to violent outburst, while lifestyles continued to reflect the communal tug of the counterculture. In the late Sixties, SDS was devoured by bitter internal strife, systematic political repression, and its isolation from others in the Movement.

The groundwork for SDS was prepared on several campuses during the late 1950s. A student party called SLATE was founded at Berkeley in 1957, anticipating the formation of other student activist groups like VOICE at Michigan, POLIT at Chicago, TOCSIN at Harvard, the Progressive Student League at Oberlin, and the Political Action Club at Swarthmore. From these campuses and others, like Columbia, Wisconsin, and Yale, came the early generation of SDS leaders: Al Haber, Tom Hayden, Todd Gitlin, Rennie Davis, Bob Ross, Sharon Jeffrey, Paul Booth, Dick and Mickey Flacks, and Paul Potter, among others. The Student Peace Union was founded in 1959, while the first issue of *Studies on the Left* was published that same year. The reactivated Student League for Industrial Democracy, the junior member of the muckraking League for Industrial Democracy (LID), became the organizational predecessor of SDS. These were years when "something was struggling to be born." [13]

As numerous early leaders have testified, the inspirational spark for SDS came from the 1960 black student sit-ins and the subsequent activities of SNCC. Rennie Davis recalled of the first sit-ins, "Here were four students from Greensboro who were suddenly all over *Life* magazine. There was a feeling that they were us and we were them, and a recognition that they were expressing something we were feeling as well, and they'd won the attention of the country." [14] At its seminal conference in Ann Arbor in 1960, SDS was addressed by civil rights leaders Bayard Rustin, James Farmer, Marvin Rich, and James McCain. Tom Hayden and Paul Potter joined the SNCC voter registration drive in McComb, Mississippi, in 1961, and returned north not only with bruises from beatings at the hands of whites but with ideas for the SDS community organizing campaign known as the Economic Research and Action Program (ERAP). As Hayden told his compatriots, black students were "miles ahead of us." [15] In a 1965 speech, Carl Oglesby observed,

> At our best, I think we (SDS) are SNCC translated to the North and trained on a somewhat different and broader set of issues. Our best concern comes

from SNCC. Some may find that concern a bit shocking, but I'll name it anyway. It is to make love more possible. We work to remove from society what threatens and prevents it—the inequity that coordinates with injustice to create plain suffering and to make custom of distrust. Poverty. Racism. The assembly line universities of this Pepsi Generation. The ulcerating drive for affluence. And the ideology of anti-communism, too, because it smothers my curiosity and bribes my compassion.[16]

Port Huron: The visionary trumpet call for the rest of the decade was sounded at the first national SDS convention at Port Huron, Michigan, in 1962. Fifty-nine participants represented eleven SDS chapters from ten campuses and a New York city at large delegation. Bob Ross's recollection of the Port Huron conference echoes the intense feeling of community recalled by SNCC and Freedom Summer activists "It was a little like starting a journey. We all felt very close to each other. I remember singing freedom songs all night, and Casey [Hayden of SNCC] singing 'Hold On' so that I'll never forget it."[17]

The *Port Huron Statement*, ratified at the 1962 convention, became the manifesto of the emerging New Student Left. The initial draft was written by Tom Hayden after poring through the writing of C. Wright Mills, Harold Taylor, Albert Camus, Erich Fromm, and other liberal, leftist, and existentialist critics of modern society. The document reflected the social environment of middle-class youth—"We are the people of this generation, bred in at least modest comfort, housed now in universities, looking uncomfortably to the world we inherit,"[18] and proceeded to catalog the social ills that filled the students' vision, primarily those of racial injustice, the cold war, growing social alienation and helplessness, and the inadequacy of mainstream party politics. Little in this account was new, although one of the more controversial strains of the SDS critique was its suggestion that the United States' responsibility for the cold war at least matched that of the Soviet Union. Despite the relatively modest language, the mainstream press coverage of SDS distorted the organization's principal thrust. In Jack Newfield's recollections, "They cartooned it, they made it look like a melange of beatniks, potheads, and agents of international Communism; they did everything but explain the failures in the society that called it into being."[19]

The *Port Huron Statement* reflected the distinctive imprint of the New Left in two ways. First, it was a ringing declaration of moral politics, reflecting an ethical rather than historical perspective. The root of the students' moral outlook was an optimistic faith in the potential of human beings—a rejection of liberalism's inclination to set faction against faction as a check against humanity's darker instincts.

> We regard men [*sic*] as infinitely precious and possessed of unfulfilled capacities for reason, freedom, and love. In affirming these principles we are aware of countering perhaps the dominant conceptions of man in the twentieth century: that he is a thing to be manipulated, and that he is inherently incapable of directing his own affairs. We oppose the depersonalization that reduces human beings to the status of things—if anything, the brutalities of the twentieth century teach that means and ends are intimately related, that vague appeals to "posterity" cannot justify the mutilations of the present. . . .
>
> Men have unrealized potential for self-evaluation, self-direction, self-understanding, and creativity. It is this potential that we regard as crucial and to which we appeal, not to the human potentiality for violence, unreason, and submission to authority.[20]

Like SNCC, SDS embraced the philosophy of nonviolence and a moralistic rather than instrumental stance toward politics—much to the consternation of liberals. As Newfield observed, "When SDSers are posed with a possible strategy they ask themselves not, 'Is it workable?' or 'How much support can we get on this from the liberals?' They ask themselves, 'Is it right to do this?'"[21]

Through its emphasis on the potential development and fulfillment of each human being, the New Left's moralism led to the *Port Huron Statement*'s most notable and implicitly radical exhortation—its call for participatory democracy:

> In a participatory democracy, the political life would be based on several root principles:
>
> that decision-making of basic social consequence be carried on by public groupings;
>
> that politics be seen positively, as the art of collectively creating an acceptable pattern of social relations;
>
> that politics have the function of bringing people out of isolation and into community, thus being a necessary, though not sufficient, means of finding meaning in personal life; . . .

The economic sphere would have as its basis the principles:

> that the economic experience is so personally decisive that the individual must share in its full determination;
>
> that the economy itself is of such social importance that its major resources and means of production should be open to democratic participation and subject to democratic social regulation.[22]

Left intentionally vague in Tom Hayden's effort to "speak American," participatory democracy meant a quality of life that went well beyond the formalistic procedures of liberal democracy as well as the top-down social control of private enterprise. For some, it implied a participatory vision of democratic socialism.[23]

Participatory democracy became, in James Miller's term, the lodestar of the New Left, the guiding principle and inspiration for both political vision and action. It was rooted in the notion of personal empowerment. Breines observes,

> Participatory democracy was a means of transforming powerlessness into shared competence and responsibility and rested on operationalizing the participation of everyone in the group. New left participatory democrats assumed that everyone was equal in their potential understanding and contribution, and sought to create both a community within the movement and structural transformation in the larger society. Large-scale change, whether it was called economic democracy, independence for ordinary people, or socialism, was unsatisfactory if achieved from the top down. Participation was crucial.[24]

Two additional themes of the *Port Huron Statement* are noteworthy. While their notion of participatory democracy was implicitly at odds with Soviet-model state socialism, New Leftists refused to subscribe to the anticommunism of most older American liberals and social democrats. This stance of nonexclusion toward participation in SDS-sponsored activities was a source of friction throughout SDS's history, from early clashes with the parent LID to Progressive Labor's later bid to take over SDS through its communist-style party discipline. For the most part, the early SDS saw the Communist party as a potential ally on individual issues but otherwise as largely irrelevant, or obsolete in Daniel and Gabriel Cohn-Bendit's phrase.

The other aspect of the *Port Huron Statement* that anticipated the activities of the New Student Left was the focus on education and the role of the student and university. In words that anticipated the Berkeley Free Speech Movement and the campus revolt, as well as the movement to liberate elementary and secondary education, SDS decried student apathy and narrow academicism.

> The real campus, the familiar campus, is a place of private people, engaged in their notorious "inner emigration." It is a place of commitment to business-as-usual, getting ahead, playing it cool. It is a place of mass affirmation of the Twist, but mass reluctance toward the controversial public stance. Rules are accepted as "inevitable," bureaucracy as "just circumstances," irrelevance as "scholarship," selflessness as "martyrdom," politics as "just another way to make people." [25]

Within this social milieu, education was seen as paternalistic and divorced from the reality of experience:

> The academic life contains reinforcing counterparts to the way in which extracurricular life is organized. The academic world is founded on a teacher-student relation analogous to the parent-child relation which characterizes *in loco parentis*. Further, academia includes a radical separation of the student from the material of study. That which is studied, the social reality, is "objectified" to sterility, dividing the student from life— just as he is restrained in active involvement by the deans controlling student government. [26]

The SDS critique would be expanded on the nation's campuses throughout the decade.

The early SDS anticipated an emerging New Left led by an awakened student population, enriched by interaction with faculty (especially liberals and socialists) and emanating outward from an idealized university viewed as a "community of controversy." [27] It was a vision that reflected C. Wright Mills' conception of the revolutionary role of students and anticipated the new working class formulation of Carl Davidson, Richard Flacks, and others.

Expressing the extraparliamentary stance of Sixties activism, SDS soon outpaced the student-government–oriented National Student Association and became the primary national organization for student activists. Campus chapters focused on education and the political role of the university. Among their objectives were the elimination of campus restrictions on communist or "subversive" speakers, the abolition of social restrictions and the principle of *in loco parentis*, increased curricular flexibility and the development of relevant new courses, and disclosure of ways in which the university served the status quo, especially, in later years, the war in Vietnam. The early idealistic notion of a community of controversy began to be supplanted by critical awareness of the university's role in the larger society. At a 1963 conference on university reform, Paul Potter commented,

> We recognize that the Universities are currently concerned with the development of none of these [humane] approaches and are in fact, because of their historic commitment to the nourishment of the existing system, a commitment intensified ultimately by the Cold War, in some sense in opposition to their development. And we recognize that the only course for us is to stand outside the existing traditions and on our own intellectual, economic, political, and human resources develop alternatives to the system so compelling as to obtain basic concessions from it.[28]

Simultaneously, the radical vision of many SDS leaders led them to confront societal ills off campus. In 1963, Tom Hayden argued that President Kennedy's New Frontier was not "coping with problems in ways that will guarantee acceptable levels of democracy and peace," and asked, "Can the methods of SNCC be applied to the North?"[29] The SDS answer came when a contingent that included Hayden, Sharon Jeffrey, and Rennie Davis organized the Economic Research and Action Program (ERAP), an effort to realize the empowerment goal of democracy through community organizing in the urban ghettoes. An early ERAP brochure declared, "We are young people in search of effective forms of action and new possibilities for change. We have chosen to work with people who most desperately need alternatives to poverty and economic voicelessness, and to devote ourselves to the development of a community organization capable of achieving a better deal for the poor in a democratic fashion."[30] As James Miller recounted, "In the summer of 1964, some 125 members of SDS fanned out into the slums of nine American cities in an effort to organize the poor, pressure established liberals and stimulate 'the new insurgency.'"[31] Others within SDS, like Al Haber, criticized the newfound "cult of the ghetto."[32] As Maurice Isserman has observed, "Seldom in history has a group of political visionaries been so swiftly rewarded by the appearance of a movement [on college campuses] that so neatly fit their original vision; perhaps never before has anyone so blessed then proceeded to abandon that movement just as it began to realize its potential in favor of other pursuits."[33]

ERAP embraced a philosophy of organizing both black and white poor around economic issues and felt grievances. Field activities were largely concentrated in black ghettoes, and tackling inner-city powerlessness proved to be a staggering and decidedly long-term task. ERAP organizers encountered variations of the prefigurative–instrumental dilemma: tensions between indigenous grassroots democracy and outside leadership, and between long-term social change and concrete, short-term gains. In typical New Left fashion, the organizers worked without a road map, learning as they went.

Though the ERAP projects lasted at most a few years, they were a vital part of the movement for participatory democracy, and inspired later community organizing efforts. Perhaps most of all, the experience of living and working with the poor demystified the liberal poverty programs of the Kennedy–Johnson administration. As Hayden recalled of his time working with the Newark Community Union Project, "The difference between NCUP and the area [antipoverty] boards was the difference between a supportive community and a bureaucracy, between participatory democracy and administrative management, between power for poor people and services for poor clients."[34] Many came away from their experiences convinced that the political system, including its labor and liberal allies, was totally unresponsive to the demands of the poor.

At its base, however, SDS was a student organization, which meant that leadership tended to turn over annually. As a result, the tenor of the national organization as well as its campus chapters shifted as younger cohorts moved into positions of prominence. Each new wave of leadership came of age at a later date, influenced not only by unraveling social norms and institutions but also by the actions of previous leaders. Thus, for example, the events of 1963 and 1964—the Birmingham bombing, the assassination of President Kennedy, the Mississippi Freedom Summer and the deaths of Chaney, Goodman, and Schwerner—caused a significant leftward swing in SDS rhetoric and in the establishment of two new leftist organizations, the May 2nd Movement and Progressive Labor. When Clark Kissinger was elected SDS's new national secretary, he reactivated the organization's campus focus, leaving ERAP at the margins of the organization. The Berkeley revolt subsequently provided the crucial catalyst for the student movement during the rest of the decade.

SDS as a Mass Student Movement: As U.S. involvement in Vietnam escalated, SDS helped to organize the early national demonstrations against the war. Within the antiwar movement, the dilemma recurred: long-term social change or tangible results (an end to the war)? SDS consistently militated for the broader focus of social transformation. Yet, the war sharpened SDS's critical perception of the political role of the university; it also affected the makeup of SDS, turning it into a loosely-structured mass organization.

In December 1965, the SDS "old guard" called a "rethinking conference" at the Champaign-Urbana campus of the University of Illinois. Through a series of leaflets and debates, the conference addressed the need for improved organization, the dilemmas of participatory democracy, and SDS's role in the antiwar movement. Also, new currents were emerging; a workshop on women anticipated the women's movement that spread rapidly in subsequent years. The effects of the burgeoning mass movement were even more visible at the SDS convention at Clear Lake, Iowa, in the summer of 1966. A new wave of students attended the conference in unprecedented numbers, and prefigurative politics were again in full swing. The new students were different. SDS chronicler Kirkpatrick Sale describes them:

> The new breed brought to SDS a new style and a new heritage. For the first time at an SDS meeting people smoked marijuana; . . . blue workshirts, denim jackets, and boots were worn by both men and women. These were people generally raised outside of the East, many from the Midwest and Southwest, and their ruralistic dress reflected a different tradition, one more aligned to the frontier. . . . They were non-Jewish, nonintellectual, nonurban, from a nonprofessional class, and often without any family tradition of political involvement, much less radicalism. . . . they emphasized "morals" and "values," action and bodies-on-the-line, honesty and courage, not ideology and theory and what they called "Old Leftism". . . . Their notions of politics had been formed *ab ovo* in the civil-rights struggle or with the impact of the Vietnam escalation, so most of them had yet to make radical connections, to develop much beyond a moral view of race and war.[35]

As the war heated up and draft calls mounted, SDS became increasingly militant. By 1967, the Resistance was formed, representing a new stage of disassociation from institutions connected to the war; many came to see their outlaw status as the only alternative to cooperating with a corrupt system. Students began using tactics like sit-ins and building seizures to prevent military and corporate recruiters from perpetuating the war effort by recruiting new

The early to mid-sixties were alive with hope, idealistic action, and a growing sense of urgency.

1. Rosa Parks refused to give up her seat to a white man in 1955. Her arrest sparked the Montgomery bus boycott. The Bettmann Archive. UPI/Bettmann Newsphotos

2. The young, charismatic John F. Kennedy on the campaign trail. © Jacques Lowe, from Woodfin Camp & Associates

3. Martin Luther King, Jr., delivering his "I Have a Dream" speech at the 1963 March on Washington. Copyright Bob Adelman, from Magnum Photos Inc.

4. The Students for a Democratic Society (SDS) gather at a 1963 National Council meeting. Photo by and © C. Clark Kissinger

5. Protesting students at Sather Gate during the 1964 Free Speech Movement at the University of California at Berkeley. Photo courtesy of *California Monthly* magazine

6. Police attack peaceful civil rights marchers in Birmingham. © 1963 Charles Moore, from Black Star

7. With the help of Student Non-violent Coordinating Committee (SNCC) field workers, thousands of black Mississippians registered to vote in the face of white violence. © Charles Moore, from Black Star

8. Vietnamese Buddhist monks protesting the oppressive Diem regime by burning themselves to death. AP/Wide World Photos

9. Malcolm X addresses a 1963 Harlem rally in support of civil rights efforts in Birmingham. The Bettmann Archive. UPI/ Bettmann Newsphotos

10. After James Meredith was shot during his "March against Fear" across Mississippi, Stokely Carmichael rallied black marchers with the call for "black power." © Bob Fitch, from Black Star

11. An occupying army of U.S. troops enforced the curfew in devastated inner-city Detroit, one of a series of cities torn by black rage during the "long hot summers" of 1964–1967. The Bettmann Archive. UPI/Bettmann Newsphotos

12. A few of the two dozen casualties of napalm accidentally dropped on a U.S. infantry position by American planes. AP/Wide World Photos

soldiers or employees. The war drew more and more of the attention of the young, especially as the black power movement went its own way. The perennial tensions between on- and off-campus activism and between decentralized spontaneity and organizational effectiveness intensified.

Campus politics and radical national change were momentarily fused at the Columbia uprising of 1968. However,

> It became clear to many SDSers in a very direct way that it was not the *reform* of the university that they really wanted, not the limiting of complicity [in the Vietnam war], not the *restructuring* of the evil complex, but something much vaster, more significant, more, well, revolutionary. "To student rebels," wrote Dick Greeman . . . , the lessons of Columbia were that "allies must be sought in the black ghettos and in the ranks of labor, not on campus. . . .
>
> The seeds of Weatherman are planted here.[36]

The violence of 1968—the Tet Offensive, the protester–police confrontations at Columbia and Chicago, the assassinations of King and Kennedy—severed the remaining emotional ties that connected SDS leaders to the system they denounced.[37] Simultaneously, the Nixon administration led an all-out assault against the New Left through surveillance, infiltration and provocation, police harassment and brutality, and arrest.[38]

While campuses remained embroiled in grassroots antiwar activities, the national office of SDS moved leftward and devoted increasing attention to a direct assault on the system viewed as responsible for the Vietnam War. Ronald Fraser recalls,

> Student radicals raced to read Lenin, Trotsky, Mao. David Gilbert, one of a small group of SDSers who had studied Marxism seriously over a number of years, observed that SDS "went from being students with a moral vision to realizing that we were up against the heaviest power structure in the world. We were seeing blacks that we associated with killed by the government. It was life and death serious. There was a sense that either we get some sort of power base or we have to retreat. So people looked around for almost magical solutions, and within the left, in SDS in 1968–69, the magical answer became a regurgitation of the Marxist formulation of the working class."[39]

As self-described revolutionaries, these leaders were far less sanguine about the fruitfulness of campus revolt. Advocating a "revolutionary youth movement," Mike Klonsky wrote, "The main task now is to begin moving beyond the limitations of struggle placed upon a student movement. We must realize our potential to reach out to new constituencies both on and off campus and build SDS into a youth movement that is revolutionary."[40]

Two factions that had been most active in the national organization struggled for control of SDS. At the 1969 convention in Chicago, the Revolutionary Youth Movement (RYM) and Progressive Labor party (PL) fought to convince neutral or unaffiliated members that *they* represented the truest traditions of the Left. As former SDS leader Carl Oglesby observed of this struggle, "The general adoption of some kind of Marxism–Leninism by all vocal factions in SDS means, certainly, that a long moment of intellectual suspense has been resolved—but much less in response to experience than to the pressure of the *tradition*."[41] The prefigurative–instrumental tension within SDS was resolved—in favor of the latter.

RYM produced a Weatherman manifesto,[42] advocating dramatic actions against U.S. imperialism at home, actions likened to the struggle of Third World guerrilla movements. For its part, PL rejected hints of prefigurative politics still present in RYM, along with the adventurist tactics of guerrilla warfare and the separatism of the Black Panthers. For several years, PL had advocated a more classical Leninist notion of a disciplined party vanguard, and had focused its energy on mobilizing the working class rather than organizing students. In the convention fury following a Black Panther call to expel PL from SDS, the Weathermen (or Weatherbureau as they soon began calling themselves) walked out. After long deliberation, climaxing in a rousing speech by the charismatic Bernardine Dohrn, the Weatherbureau decided to claim the SDS mantle for themselves, expelling PL from the organization. The newly separate PL naturally countered with its own claim as the true SDS.

In the months that followed, communal Weatherbureau groups experimented with sexuality, drug use, and violent bravado, most notably the Chicago "Days of Rage" in October. Cathy Wilkerson recalls that the Weatherbureau's confrontational style "was trying to reach white youth on the basis of their most reactionary macho instinct"[43]—a strategy that not only failed but alienated SDS women. As Ronald Fraser observes,

> Having failed in its effort to build a revolutionary movement among white working-class youth and alienated from the existing radical student movement—the entire Wisconsin SDS chapter physically turned their backs on Weatherman speakers who came to address their chapter—Weather-

man's response was to go into clandestine armed struggle. Two months after the Days of Rage, its leaders and about three hundred followers went underground.[44]

For its part, the PL strategy of a student-worker alliance also failed; in its abrasive, sectarian approach, PL became increasingly irrelevant to the vast majority of students. Except for sporadic bombings claimed by the Weather-bureau and the self-destructive explosion in Greenwich Village, the remnants of SDS became all but invisible.

■ The Campus Revolt

> People are getting up there and talking, and people are listening. And people are voting on this and people are voting on that. . . . It's almost enough to make you believe that if it were given a chance, the democratic process might work. It just might work. People quoted books as if books were relevant. They talked about the Greeks, and they talked about theories of politics, as if it all *meant* something. And listening to them, I almost believed for the first time in years that it did mean something.
> —Michael Rossman, "The Birth of the Free Speech Movement"

Although external forces like civil rights and the Vietnam War stimulated students' critical awareness, colleges and universities were the most direct, convenient, and vulnerable targets of this awareness. Initially, students used the campus as a base of discussion and organization from which to launch their challenges to society. As the decade passed, colleges and universities themselves came under increasing attack, first because they resisted student efforts to awaken others to social ills, then because students came to see universities as instruments of the larger culture. Becoming increasingly critical of the technocratic society, students sharpened their attack on the institution whose task it was to mold them for technical, professional, and corporate occupations. As the Vietnam War heated up in the later Sixties, students concentrated much of their ire on the universities' complicity in perpetuating the war, while simultaneously pursuing university curricular reform and relaxation of social regulations.

A portent of future unrest occurred in May 1960, when several hundred Berkeley students, calling themselves Students for Civil Liberties, protested against hearings being held by the infamous House Un-American Activities

Committee in San Francisco. After failing to gain admission to the hearings, most students sat in the corridors and sang. Police appeared with fire hoses and clubs and attacked the students, sending bodies sprawling and sliding down the slick concrete steps. The incident became known as "Black Friday,"[45] and anticipated student–police confrontations of later years.

Influenced by civil rights activity in the South, students on several campuses began to mobilize support for the movement.[46] Many traveled south to help, especially during the Freedom Summer of 1964. Others organized local picketing of chain stores like Woolworth's that were targeted by the student sit-ins in the South. Students invited provocative and controversial speakers to campus, and organized protests against nuclear testing, the death penalty, and the presence of ROTC on campus. In a number of cases, especially at public universities, student initiatives encountered resistance by university officials. At Berkeley, for example, the administration rejected the students' bid to invite Malcolm X to speak on the grounds that to do so would violate university and state regulations protecting the separation of church and state!

Student activism percolated on campuses throughout the early years of the decade. Then, in the fall of 1964, the Free Speech Movement erupted on the Berkeley campus, signaling the emergence of a new stage of student activism and awareness.

THE BERKELEY FREE SPEECH MOVEMENT

Like most movements of the Sixties, the University of California at Berkeley revolt began with an essentially liberal agenda: confrontation and elimination of university restrictions on student political activity.[47] Since the time of the southern sit-ins, Berkeley students had engaged in a number of civil rights protests against San Francisco Bay area businesses. Off-campus activity picked up during the 1963–1964 school year and took a more aggressive turn in the fall of 1964 after several students returned from the Mississippi Freedom Summer project.

Though the Mississippi project had resulted in a leftward shift among student activists, the California political environment had moved to the right after Barry Goldwater's primary victory. The balance had shifted from the moderate Earl Warren wing of the Republican party to a group identified with Ronald Reagan and hostile to the university. Reflecting growing pressure from the right, particularly from former Senator William Knowland, whose family owned the powerful, conservative *Oakland Tribune*, university president Clark Kerr invoked campus regulations to prohibit student leafleting on the twenty-six-foot long Bancroft Strip at the entrance to the campus. For several years, students had set up tables on the Bancroft Strip to solicit members and support for various political groups and activities. The area had become like a colorful Hyde Park of political oratory and leafleting, and was responsible for much of Berkeley's reputation as a magnet for uninhibited activity of all sorts.

Reflecting the new activist predisposition, student political groups ranging from the Young Socialists to Youth for Goldwater formed a united front to protest the ban. After several days of rallies, picketing, and vigils outside of Sproul Hall, students set up advocate tables on the strip in a direct challenge to the administration's directives. A total of eight students, including Mario Savio, were cited by campus police for violating the university's rules. After several hundred students held a sit-in inside Sproul Hall, the administration suspended the eight students, and the fledgling Free Speech Movement (FSM) took off. When former graduate student Jack Weinberg was arrested for continuing to violate the Bancroft Strip ban, students surrounded the police car containing Weinberg, holding it captive for thirty-two hours. Their numbers swelled. Michael Rossman recalled:

> The news of 600 police, late in the second afternoon, massed on the other side of Sproul Hall, about to reposses their car; and no word at all from our negotiators, let alone from the faculty. . . . "Take off your pierced earrings, remove your ties," advised the microphone, "if we link arms, it is likely they will club us apart." Someone standing by the car in those closing minutes, with a big box of green pippin apples, tossing them out to faces without appetite but lit by sudden beams, as we sang "We are not afraid" in voices shaking with fear, and waited, free.[48]

Under Savio's leadership, and with a bungling administration as a catalyst, the Free Speech Movement broadened its focus to confront the "multiversity machine." As Berkeley professors Seymour Martin Lipset and Sheldon Wolin observed, the Free Speech Movement convulsed the campus:

> Before the dispute had run its course, the faculty was drawn in, and the effects of the controversy were registered throughout the entire state. The governor became involved; members of the state legislature began to take sides; thousands of letters and telegrams were sent by alumni,

prominent citizens, and interested individuals and groups. Meanwhile the campus was the scene of many unacademic events. There were the endless protest meetings, rallies, and silent vigils, with crowds sometimes reaching as many as 7000; there were repeated violations of university rules and civil laws; on two occasions hundreds of police were massed on campus, and the threat of violence seemed immediate and inevitable; three sit-ins occurred, the last culminating in the occupation of the central administration building by 800 students and their forcible removal by an almost equal number of police; and a sympathy strike, launched by teaching assistants, severely interrupted classroom routines. One of the world's largest and most famous centers of learning was brought to the edge of collapse.[49]

In a manner that anticipated government officials' responses to antiwar activists, some mainstream liberals denounced the activists' tactics. Lipset told the students surrounding the police car that their civil disobedience tactics were "like the Ku Klux Klan," while Clark Kerr engaged in red-baiting, announcing to a press conference that "up to 40 percent of the hard-core participants" in the FSM came from off campus and were "very experienced and professional people . . . tied in with organizations having Communist influences."[50]

It became clear that there was more at stake than the free speech issue, or as one student slogan put it, "The issue is not the issue." Many, including the students themselves, were amazed at the scale of the Berkeley upheaval. Observers sensed that the movement tapped a deeper disenchantment felt by many students regardless of political persuasion. One campus minister wrote of the "modern isolation and alienation of the spirit" and the students' effort to restore a lost sense of community.[51] Students caustically likened themselves to IBM cards and decried the narrowness and specialization of required university courses. Education bureaucratized was education corrupted.

As Breines suggests, free speech had two meanings:

> "Free" in the civil liberties sense, so that citizens and students were able to express their political ideas and platforms without fear of punishment; and "free" in the sense of liberated, unrestricted communication that may foster political visions and political forms that transcend the existing framework, enabling utopian ideas to inspire individuals toward becoming political actors on the basis of their unmet collective and individual needs.[52]

The former could, in theory, be embraced by the liberal mainstream; the latter reflected the prefigurative and more radical democratic vision of the New Left. It also posed a fundamental challenge to the University of California and president Clark Kerr's vision of the future of higher education. Kerr had proclaimed that, with the coming of the "multiversity," higher education was undergoing its "second great transformation"

> to educate previously unimagined numbers of students; to respond to the expanding claims of national service; to merge its activities with industry as never before; to adapt to and rechannel new intellectual currents. . . . Basic to this transformation is the growth of the "knowledge industry," which is coming to permeate government and business and to draw into it more and more people raised to higher and higher levels of skill. . . .
>
> The university and segments of industry are becoming more and more alike. As the university becomes tied into the world of work, the professor—at least in the natural and some of the social sciences—takes on the characteristics of an entrepreneur.[53]

Student critics could not have described the integrative function of university education any better. They would later echo Kerr's claim that Department of Defense contracts were an increasingly important symbol of the university's function. The night before the Bancroft Strip protest, FSM activist Hal Draper delivered a speech on "Clark Kerr's View of the University as a Factory."

Kerr's vision expressed the hope for a technocratic future in which continued progress required highly specialized knowledge in corporate and governmental institutions. It was a vision that was as uncomfortable to liberal arts traditionalists as it was to the student critics. The former emphasized the purity and timelessness of intellectual inquiry through detachment from society and its utilitarian demands; the latter embraced the integration of the university in society as a critical agent responsible for awakening and sustaining society's humane vision.

True to his own view of the university presidents' role as mediator, Kerr took what he saw as a middle position between the ivory tower, elitist view and the change-oriented "socialist view" of student activists. As with technocratic visions generally, the managerial position is self-consciously neutral in the struggle among diverse power centers.[54] Kerr's own words echoed the end of ideology claims of social scientists: "the ends are already given. . . . The means must be ever improved in a competitive dynamic environment."[55]

Students saw things differently. Former graduate student Bradford Cleaveland published an open letter to the undergraduates, maintaining that "the university pushed the myth that you, as undergraduates, are 'training for leadership,' when in fact you are training for obedience," and citing Bertrand Russell's comment, "We are faced with the paradoxical fact that education has become one of the chief obstacles of intelligence and freedom of thought." [56] In another article, Cleaveland charged, "The salient characteristic of the multiversity is massive production of specialized excellence. The multiversity is actually not an educational center but a highly efficient industry engaged in producing skilled individuals to meet the immediate needs of business or government." [57] It was a critique that intuitively appealed to masses of students who found their narrow studies increasingly irrelevant to their awakening concern for questions of morality and justice. It also echoed the concern of many faculty and administrators at Berkeley and other institutions. [58]

A broadened confrontation was brewing. The multiversity represented the "triumph of the American dream, a public university acknowledged to be perhaps the finest in the country, the perfect postideological mixture of government, private industry, academia, computers, managerial skills, brains, and money—and the whole thing was being called into question. The young, upon whom the future of course would depend, were being given the American dream—*and they didn't want it*. More: they *attacked* it." [59] The students, in short, were beginning to criticize the *role* of the university in the larger society, an instrumental role supporting prevailing institutional arrangements and closely tied to society's power relations. Observers noted that one persistent characteristic of the New Left was that its leaders were often among the most intelligent and imaginative students of their generation and that campus protests occurred predominantly at what were acknowledged to be the best institutions. Thus rebellion occurred not because students were exploited and left out of society's reward structure, but because they were most privy to those rewards. They imagined what did not exist instead of concentrating on gaining what did. They were not in the same position as the children of working- and lower-class families, who naturally were eager to gain a share of what society offered. [60]

Activist student leaders initially came to this view because their political experience had exposed them to both the *possibility* of progressive social change and the *resistance* of those in power. Mario Savio compared the Berkeley movement to his experience in the Mississippi Freedom Summer:

The two battlefields may seem quite different to some observers, but this is not the case. The same rights are at stake in both places—the right to participate as citizens in a democratic society and to struggle against the same enemy. In Mississippi an autocratic and powerful minority rules, through organized violence, to suppress the vast, virtually powerless, majority. In California, the privileged minority manipulates the University bureaucracy to suppress the students' political expression. That "respectable" bureaucracy masks the financial plutocrats; that impersonal bureaucracy is the efficient enemy in a "Brave New World."[61]

The politicized campus increased students' awareness of the interconnection between university life and the larger society. In 1967, SDS vice president Carl Davidson stood Kerr's analysis on its head:

Irrelevancy, meaninglessness, boredom, and fragmentation are the kinds of attributes that are becoming more and more applicable to mass education in America. We are becoming a people required to know more and more about less and less. . . .

Primary, secondary, and university systems are fusing together, thoroughly rationalizing and dehumanizing their internal order, and placing themselves in the service of the state, industry, and the military. Kerr is quite clear about this when he speaks of the "multiversity". . . . From this perspective, we can begin to understand that the educational malaise we as students and teachers have felt so personally and intensely is no aberration, but firmly rooted in the American political economy.[62]

The Berkeley revolt became the watershed for subsequent campus activism. Students discovered that they had resources with which to fight back against the multiversity and its demands. They learned that the university was vulnerable to bold action and rhetoric that appealed to the moral sensibilities of the academic community. They found that their mass actions attracted wide attention and were deeply disturbing to powerful elements in society. SDS adopted the slogan "A Free University in a Free Society," and student membership soared after Berkeley. The campus upheaval of the ensuing years was all but inevitable; the war in Vietnam only ensured that it would be highly emotional and sometimes violent.

AFTER BERKELEY

In the aftermath of the Free Speech Movement and the Mississippi Freedom Summer, student activism grew on campuses across the country. The Berkeley example inspired similar organizing efforts on other campuses; activist students at Oberlin College, for example, ran for student government positions under a SLATE banner, borrowing the name of Berkeley's activist organization. Students and faculty at San Francisco State College organized the decade's first "Free University," a typical New Left counterinstitution that offered courses students believed were more relevant to their lives. On many campuses, students challenged the hidden curriculum. On the academic front, they railed against the gamesmanship encouraged by grading and time pressures as well as the intellectual conformity and docility that resulted. On the social front, they confronted what they perceived as archaic and petty regulations governing interactions between the sexes. In both areas they accused universities of a fundamental hypocrisy.[63]

In 1965–1966, the civil rights struggle was largely supplanted as the moral magnet for activism by the war in Vietnam. The escalation of American involvement in 1965 spawned the nationwide teach-in movement that spread from the University of Michigan to eastern campuses and culminated in a virulent denunciation of the war at a Berkeley teach-in. As noted earlier, SDS leaders were disinclined to stress the war as the focal point for protest. As a result, after 1965, SDS largely vacated the leadership of the antiwar movement.

As the U.S. combat role intensified in 1966, the Johnson administration sought to increase the pool of potential draftees. In February, General Lewis B. Hershey, director of the Selective Service System, announced that local draft boards would for the first time be able to induct college students of low class ranking. University officials were required to report the class ranking of all their male students and a national draft examination was scheduled. The reaction was instantaneous. SDS organized a counterdraft exam with questions about the U.S. role in Vietnam. The SDS chapter at the University of Chicago formed a Students Against the Rank group and held a sit-in as part of their effort to persuade university officials to defy the Hershey order.[64] Although they failed in the latter, ranking proved to be so controversial that it was scrapped within a year. The sit-in tactic caught on at other campuses.

From the draft ranking controversy it was a short step to the perception of university complicity in the war in Vietnam. Investigative research into investment portfolios and faculty research activities at a number of universities confirmed the perception that colleges and universities were not the independent, benevolent institutions they claimed to be. The exposure of private profiteering, support for CIA counterinsurgency activities in Vietnam, vast quantities of research supported by defense and corporate contracts, and exploitative investments in South Africa and Latin America all sharpened the critical consciousness of student activists.

Through 1966 and 1967, student activism grew and assaulted a widening array of targets on a variety of campuses. Some focused on local campus issues: a tuition increase at New York University, high prices and poor quality at the cafeteria at San Francisco State, a student bill of rights at the University of Nebraska. More focused on connections to the war. Students at Antioch, Oberlin, City University of New York, Cornell, Columbia, Howard, Stanford, Iowa State, and other campuses targeted the student rankings and the college's role in aiding the war machine. At the University of Pennsylvania, students uncovered extensive faculty research on biological and chemical warfare, while their peers at New York University revealed a link between the university and corporations involved in the war. In several cases, student anger intensified when it was revealed that some university officials had reported their protest activities to the FBI.

Among the primary targets for war-related protests were speakers representing the Johnson administration, and campus recruiters for the military services or for the Dow Chemical Company, manufacturers of the napalm used in Vietnam. At Berkeley, students from the campus SDS chapter sat in around the table of a Navy recruiter, while angry Harvard students cornered defense secretary Robert S. McNamara in a chilling confrontation.

Surveys of the nation's campuses confirmed the spread of the campus revolt.[65] Across the nation, students sought to exercise greater influence over their educational experiences and asserted the need for "student power." The free university or experimental college movement spread to a growing number of campuses. Meanwhile, the alternative education movement began to spread into the secondary and elementary schools.

In the aftermath of the Newark and Detroit riots, and with antiwar militance on the rise, the 1967–1968 academic year was marked by a sustained level of intense campus protest. During the week before the March on the Pentagon, students at the University of Wisconsin held a sit-in against Dow Chemical recruiters that led to one of the decade's most notable confrontations between police and students, with predictable results. Sale describes the clash:

> Giving a final warning to the students that they faced arrest, [campus police chief Ralph Hanson] moved outside, gathered around him a force of fifty policemen, and charged the front entrance to the building. Suddenly, chaos. Hanson and the first ranks of cops were pushed aside by the students inside, but in their wake the Madison riot squad rushed wildly, flailing and pelting, using sticks and fists, without supervision. . . . Students poured out of the building, their heads oozing blood, groaning and crying, limping and bruised. . . . In a matter of twelve minutes, by official estimate, the building was cleared.
>
> Not so the area outside. There the thousands of students gathered were shocked at the brutality before them. . . . More shoving, hitting, taunting, and then, tear gas—tear gas for the first time on a major college campus. . . .
>
> Within an hour a mass rally was begun on the library mall to fashion a student response to the invasion. An estimated five thousand students and perhaps two hundred faculty members showed up, and the mood was bitter, angry, militant: overwhelmingly they agreed not to attend any classes until recruiters from the Dow Chemical Company were forever banned from the university. The student newspaper, the *Daily Cardinal*, supported the strike, then the student government, finally even a right-wing campus party. The student front was solid.[66]

Two weeks later, students at Oberlin College surrounded a Navy recruiter's car only to be dispersed by town and state police using tear gas and fire hoses. As with the more violent Wisconsin response, the police reaction to the Oberlin demonstration galvanized the campus and led to a broader-based student sit-in, cancellation of classes, and a day-long campus-wide debate over the appropriate use of college placement facilities.

COLUMBIA UNIVERSITY

> There's this tremendous ferment. You get up in the morning and you look for the demonstration. You look for the protest. You look for something to be different before nightfall. It was natural.
> —Bill Sales, Columbia student

Probably the most widely publicized campus protest of the late 1960's was the student takeover at Columbia University in the spring of 1968. The two immediate issues raised by the students were the university expropriation of public land for construction of a new gymnasium in Harlem's Morningside Park, and the university's links to the Institute for Defense Analysis (IDA), a government-funded military research project. In addition, the students demanded amnesty for six SDS leaders charged with violating university regulations in a previous demonstration.

As was the case at Berkeley, however, it soon became clear that student disenchantment ran far deeper; at stake were basic questions about the university's role in the local community, the need for radical change in the larger society, and the power of students as a revolutionary vanguard for change. Echoing the words of the Berkeley slogan, from the student activists' perspective, "The issue was not the issue," or as Abe Peck has put it, the Columbia action was an effort to "organize energy" as well as accomplish political goals.[67] Campus protest had come to represent symbolically the students' urge to transform society. The Columbia protest was further complicated by dual actions, one led by SDS and the Strike Coordinating Committee, the other led by black militants representing the West Harlem community.

Students employed just about every tactic that had been used in earlier campus protests, staging teach-ins, rallies, picketing, a sit-in, a strike, and the takeover of five university buildings. SDS leaders stormed into the administration building and confronted president Grayson Kirk; they held a dean hostage, and ransacked university files, uncovering correspondence that belied university officials' claims that there were no institutional ties to the IDA. The New York underground paper, the *Rat*, published papers detailing the university's business and defense relationships "in the belief that information which concerns the public welfare should be made available to the public and should never be maintained as the privileged right of those who wield power over us all."[68]

For a time black militants acted in solidarity with the white radicals; after the seizure of campus buildings, they insisted that the white students leave Hamilton Hall so as to dramatize the racial character of their grievances.[69] The university administration tried to negotiate separately with the black group in order to isolate the white radicals; in the view of some observers, the black militants effectively controlled the protest because the administration's and the city's greatest fear was a riot in neighboring Harlem.[70]

As negotiations broke down, the administration decided to call in the police. Vice-president David Truman announced to an ad hoc faculty mediating group that the police had been invited to clear the campus.

> His announcement was greeted by shouts of "Shame! Shame!" and "Resign!" Evicted by the faculty from the hall, the Vice President fled back into Low Library pursued by a score of angry, shouting professors.
>
> One hour later plainclothes police forcibly entered Low Library, using their night sticks to break through the crowd of professors who had blockaded the entrance to the building. Many teachers were hurt. . . . SDS had won a clubbed and outraged faculty to its side.[71]

As it had at Berkeley, Wisconsin, and other campuses, the police action triggered a groundswell of sympathy for the protesters. Faced with threats of cancelled pledges and growing numbers of nonstudent notables inside the occupied buildings, the administration announced that construction of the gymnasium would be suspended pending official action by the Board of Trustees. The latter, however, gave little indication that they supported this protest objective. Negotiating efforts continued until an impasse developed on the issue of amnesty and judicial proceedings for the protesters.[72] Tensions grew as a self-proclaimed student majority coalition blockaded Low Library to keep food and supplies from the students inside.[73]

In the early morning hours of April 30, 2000 police moved onto the campus and methodically cleared the five occupied buildings. Black students occupying Hamilton Hall were, by previous arrangement, quietly ushered to waiting police wagons. The effort to clear the remaining buildings became violent. In one account,

> The president's office was cleared in less than 30 minutes. Police violence was unprovoked and unlimited. A pregnant girl was dragged by the hair down Avery's steps. Professors were beaten senseless. In Mathematics, the students were dragged down six flights of concrete steps, leaving blood so thick the cops were slipping in it. A male student, thrown to the ground, had his eye gouged by a plainclothesman. Horsemen on Broadway rode into terrified crowds, trampling spectators. For two and a half hours, faculty watching through the windows, and wounded students still unremoved from the buildings, witnessed the police destroying furniture, urinating on rugs, dumping files on the floor.[74]

Following the police bust that resulted in 692 arrests, a student strike, supported by a petition signed by 340 faculty members, disrupted normal university classes for nearly a month. In late May, students again took over Hamilton and Fayerweather Halls. While most of the disturbances occurred outside the buildings, fires were reported in each building and research papers of one professor were destroyed. The administration again called the police. In the words of the normally restrained Cox Commission:

> Hell broke loose. One hundred students locked arms behind the barricades at Amsterdam Avenue. Hundreds more were crowded close to the gate. The police swiftly dismantled the obstruction. The hundred broke and ran. But 2,000 students live in dormitories facing South Field. Many of them and hundreds of other persons were crowded on the campus. For most, the character of the police action was a profound shock; neither they nor others in the Columbia community appreciated the extent of the violence which is the probable concomitant of massive police action against hundreds, if not thousands, of angry students. As police advanced, most students fled. . . . Some police first warned the students; others chased and clubbed them indiscriminately. But not all students went to their dormitories and some who fled came back out to attack the police. Bottles and bricks were hurled by students. A number of police were injured. The action grew fiercer . . . then 50 plainclothesmen and non-uniformed police came onto the campus. They charged into Livingston and Hartley Halls, clubs swinging. In Furnald Hall they chased and clubbed students as high as the fourth floor landings. By 5:30 a.m. the campus was secured.[75]

The violence at Columbia left a bitter residue. For a time, it obscured ongoing efforts of many students and faculty to reform university regulations and governance. However, liberal reforms eventually carried the day. The more radical students saw that university reform and limited complicity in the war machine were not their primary objectives; they turned their sights to direct action off campus. For many students, hardened by the climate of violence in 1968, the incentive to work within a system viewed as totally unresponsive and brutally repressive was rapidly fading.

AFTER COLUMBIA—THE ROAD TO KENT STATE

After Columbia, student strikes and building takeovers multiplied as protests convulsed campuses nationwide. The threat of violence was always present. At San Francisco State, black and Hispanic students, together with white radicals and sympathetic faculty, boycotted classes for four and one-half months; 700 were arrested and countless numbers were injured. At Cornell, black students took over a campus building, armed themselves in self-defense, and later walked out carrying rifles in plain view of press cameras. At Harvard, PL occupied the administration building in protest against the campus ROTC program. Police were immediately called, and, after removing their badges, cleared the building with clubs swinging—an event that generated a bitter student strike. A custodian at Santa Barbara State College was killed by a bomb he picked up on the patio of the faculty club. And Berkeley police opened fire on white demonstrators connected to the People's Park protest, killing visitor, James Rector, blinding a student, and injuring at least one hundred demonstrators. As Kirkpatrick Sale recounts, "All told, there were major protest demonstrations at nearly three hundred colleges and universities, in every part of the country, at a rate of nearly two a day, involving a third of the nation's students, roughly 20 percent of them accompanied by bombs, fires, or destruction of property, a quarter by strikes or building takeovers, and a quarter more by disruption of classes and institutional functions."[76]

During this period, campus reform passed through a phase of uninhibited experimentation and innovation. Social rules had been greatly liberalized if not abolished; academic regulations were eased to enable greater individualization of study; and black and Afro-American studies courses were added to university curricula. Students and interested faculty created alternative learning opportunities. Many were legitimized as experimental colleges or free universities within the regular curriculum. Others were more spontaneous outgrowths of student protests. In a pattern running from Berkeley's Freedom School in the Sproul Hall sit-in of 1964, to Brandeis's Malcolm X University created by black students occupying Ford Hall, students created "liberated" education zones in buildings they seized.

What had not changed was that the United States continued to carry on its war in Vietnam despite electoral upheaval, bloodshed, and the highly publicized peace negotiations of 1968. Students' frustration with all institutional supports for the war grew apace. In addition, the Nixon administration escalated its surveillance and repression of student activists, and sought to isolate them by direct appeal to public resentment against, in Nixon's words, student "bums" "blowing up the universities."

The final and most extensive phase of the campus revolt was ushered in by Nixon's decision to invade Cambodia in late April of 1970. In the immediate aftermath, students at sixty institutions went on strike, and demonstrations, sometimes accompanied by violence, occurred on nearly forty of these campuses. A Gallup poll showed that campus unrest was the number one concern of the American public.

Shortly after noon on May 4, 1970, a National Guard contingent, called out to maintain order on the Kent State campus, knelt in formation and without warning opened fire on a crowd of about 200 unarmed students. The latter had been protesting the war and the presence of ROTC on campus; some had been taunting the Guardsmen. As recounted by one observer, "A girl was screaming, 'They're not using blanks. They're not using blanks.' Another student fell over, dead. A student collapsed to the ground, hit. Suddenly, after about 30 seconds, the shooting stopped. One girl was lying on the ground, holding her stomach. Her face was white. There were others, lying on the ground. Some moved. Some didn't. The whole area was one of panic."[77] Four students were killed instantly, two of whom were simply walking across the campus to lunch; nine others were injured, one of whom would be paralyzed for life.[78]

The national response was instantaneous shock and dismay. In the next four days, Sale recalls, "There were major campus demonstrations at the rate of more than a hundred a day, students at a total of at least 350 institutions went out on strike and 536 schools were shut down completely for some period of time, 51 of them for the [rest of the academic] year."[79]

Ten days after the Kent State deaths, and after 500 Jackson State College students had rallied against the Cambodian invasion, police moved to secure the campus ROTC building. Opening fire against a women's dormitory, they killed two students and wounded twelve others. Again, students and civil rights activists mobilized protests on major university campuses and the high schools of big cities like New York and Chicago. A coalition of civil rights and antipoverty groups organized for self-defense as the Mississippi United Front.

In September, the President's Commission on Campus Unrest declared,

The crisis on American campuses has no parallel in this history of the nation. This crisis has roots in divisions of American society as deep as any since the Civil War. The divisions are reflected in violent acts and harsh rhetoric, and in the enmity of those Americans who see themselves as occupying opposing camps. Campus unrest reflects and increases a more profound crisis in the nation as a whole. . . . We fear new violence and growing enmity. . . . If this trend continues, if this crisis of understanding endures, the very survival of the nation will be threatened.[80]

Yet, the trend did not continue. The campus revolt had come to a violent end. While self-styled revolutionaries may have predicted the inevitable use of weapons against students, most students were stunned by the escalation of government violence on campus, and by the realization that they could die if they continued confrontational politics. Another way of agitating for an end to the war seemed closed off. And as the President's Commission on Campus Unrest had recommended, campus reform and police professionalization were employed to reduce the "tinder of discontent on the campuses."

Never before and never since have American campuses seen so much turmoil as they did during the 1960s, and many breathed a sigh of relief as the turmoil came to an end. A great deal of student activism was motivated by the drive to make the university learning experience more meaningful for students coming of age in a world marked by major social and political transformation. Implicit in this activism, and often explicitly stated, was the notion that students should play a more active role in selecting and shaping their learning experiences, and more generally that students should have more power over their lives. This democratic localism was largely superceded by student reactions to the civil rights movement and Vietnam War. As a result the impulse for democratic education emerged more clearly in the movement to liberate elementary and secondary schools.

Nonetheless, both civil rights and Vietnam drew attention to the university's role in the larger society. In both instances, students were sensitized to moral challenges to prevailing institutions, and in both cases, college and university policies confirmed students' perception that these institutions were not independent and neutral as they claimed, but instead reinforced society's status quo. In asserting that education meant the opposite of indoctrination, students moved inexorably in a radical direction.

4

The Vietnam War
A Nation Divided,
A Movement Radicalized

Lyndon Johnson told the nation,
Have no fear of escalation,
I am trying everyone to please.
Though it isn't really war,
We're sending fifty thousand more
To help save Vietnam from the Vietnamese.
—Tom Paxton, "Lyndon Johnson Told the Nation"

To kill on military orders and be a criminal, or to refuse to kill
and be a criminal is the moral agony of America's Vietnam
war generation.
—Jan Barry, Vietnam Veterans Against the War

The war in Vietnam changed everything—the uplifting
struggle for civil rights, the hopeful New Left, the Great Society. Dreams of a
liberated America turned to ashes. Disassociation from American culture accelerated. The war shaped consciousness by what it revealed about America,
about its politicians and military brass, about G.I.'s facing impossible combat
conditions, about hundreds of thousands of young men refusing to serve. As
Loren Baritz has noted, the war served as a "magnifying glass that enlarged
aspects of some of the ways we, as Americans, think and act."[1] Millions of
lives were deeply affected by the war's destructive power.

The war also generated the largest antiwar movement in the nation's history. In the eyes of those who opposed it, the war stands to this day as the
United States' most savagely aggressive and self-destructive action of the twentieth century. Numbers—the official language of the war's policy makers—
conveyed only a superficial impression of the war's effects. Still, they were
sobering and, for grieving Americans, too real.

Of the 3.78 million armed servicemen and women who served in the war
zone in Vietnam, 303,652 were wounded (6,655 lost limbs) and nearly 58,000

died. The war's psychological costs were also heavy.[2] An estimated 27 million relatives of those who served in Vietnam were scarred by the war. Thirty-eight percent of married veterans were divorced within six months after their return from Vietnam. Of those who fought in the war, an estimated 500,000 to 700,000 suffer from post-traumatic stress symptoms. Nearly a quarter of the men who saw heavy combat have been arrested on criminal charges since returning. About the same proportion used drugs after their return; an estimated 30,000 to 40,000 Vietnam veterans in New York City alone are heroin addicts.[3] In all these figures, a disproportionate number are black; most are from lower socioeconomic levels.

Those who protested against the war had a different experience: 172,000 men were conscientious objectors, while over half a million committed draft violations, like burning draft cards or resisting induction, that could have sent them to prison for up to five years; 3,250 went to prison. Military deserters numbered 93,250, with more than a fifth deserting *after* completing a full term in Vietnam. At the war's peak, one American soldier was going AWOL every two minutes, and deserting every six.[4] Between 60,000 and 100,000 Americans emigrated to Canada, Sweden, and other countries.

The war created a deep and emotional polarization in American society. Parents were alienated from children, soldiers from students, young people from nearly all older authority figures, and veterans from much of American society. Although many in the antiwar movement were critical of the class-based exploitation built into the draft—indeed, their banners read "Support Our G.I.'s . . . Bring Them Home Now"—the inherent tension between military service and opposition to war triggered excessive personal attacks on both servicemen and activists.[5] Reconciliation between these "brothers and sisters" of the Vietnam generation has proceeded at a snail's pace in the years since the war.

For millions of Americans moved by the promises of the early Sixties, faith in the American dream was painfully shattered. The war revealed the power of political rhetoric and propaganda to mask an ugly reality. It exposed the degree to which the U.S. government would willingly and openly engage in repressive and inhumane actions, both overseas and at home, when the system itself was challenged. Public trust in authoritative institutions like Congress, the presidency, the military, business corporations, labor unions, even the medical profession, plunged. Distrust and cynicism soared after Watergate, itself an heir of Vietnam.

While the war's effects on the United States were tragic, what happened to the nation of Vietnam was criminal. At least 16 percent of Vietnam's 40 million people were killed or wounded. An estimated 400,000 *civilians* were killed, 900,000 wounded, and 6.5 million turned into refugees. The country itself was turned into a barren, poisoned landscape. In 1981, British journalist John Pilger wrote on his return to Vietnam that

> in Cu Chi, near Saigon, which I remember as a thick forest, there is today a shimmering horizon of wilderness which has been poisoned, perhaps for generations. Eleven million gallons of the herbicide Agent Orange were dumped on Vietnam; its chief ingredient, dioxin, is estimated to be a thousand times more destructive than thalidomide. . . . Blind and deformed babies are now common in those areas sprayed during Operation Hades, later re-named Operation Ranch Hand.[6]

As Ngo Vinh Long reported, "Much of the land in central Vietnam had been destroyed by chemical defoliants, bombs, and salt water which invaded the paddyfields after American forces destroyed the sea dikes."[7] Widespread starvation resulted, and today little of economic value remains in either the North or South. The United States has continued to punish Vietnam with economic and diplomatic isolation ever since the war ended.[8]

■ The Antiwar Movement

The reason for much of the Sixties turmoil was the growing realization that the United States was largely responsible for this carnage. Americans differed in how much they were willing to assign the responsibility to their own government, but people across the political spectrum came to see their nation engaged in activities for which they could find no adequate justification. As this realization grew, so did anger, antiwar activism, and social disintegration. The war in Vietnam was the watershed for the mass upheaval that occurred in the later Sixties. In a speech given to the first major antiwar demonstration in Washington, D.C., in 1965, Paul Potter of sds articulated this view:

> The incredible war in Vietnam has provided the razor, the terrifying sharp cutting edge that has finally severed the last vestige of illusion that morality and democracy are the guiding principles of American foreign policy. . . . The further we explore the reality of what this country is doing

and planning in Vietnam the more we are driven toward the conclusion of Senator Morse that the United States may well be the greatest threat to peace in the world today. That is a terrible and bitter insight for people who grew up as we did—and our revulsion at that insight, our refusal to accept it as inevitable or necessary is one of the reasons that so many people have come here today.[9]

The history of the antiwar movement is the history of the gradual yet inexorable progression of many Americans toward increasingly militant behavior and radical consciousness. This progression mirrored the growth of American involvement in the war. As horrifying images of war and suffering filtered home, the antiwar movement took root; as the United States escalated the war, dissent grew. Outside of traditional leftists and New Left radicals, early expressions of antiwar sentiment were largely moralistic in tone, addressed in the form of petitions to public officials. The latter responded with rhetorical pronouncements framed in official language. In time, as evidence of atrocities mounted, it became clear that officials were incapable of speaking the same moral language as the protesters; occasional "regrettable" actions were justified by the "higher morality" of American purpose.

As the war expanded and activists became more aware of contradictions between government claims and Vietnam realities, increasing numbers in the Movement came to see not only American behavior but American *purpose* in the war as immoral and undemocratic. They shifted to a more aggressive, radical, and democratic stance—radical in the sense that they perceived the war as *systemic* in its roots,[10] democratic in the sense that they embraced an American tradition of self-determination rooted in the Declaration of Independence (which, ironically, was also cited by Ho Chi Minh in his declaration of Vietnamese independence from colonial rule in 1945).[11] As the war ground on and on, despite protest after protest and seemingly futile forays into electoral politics, movement frustrations grew. Feeling no adequate outlet for their anger, encountering increasing government repression and police violence, and reeling in disbelief with each new escalation, protesters acted out their rage against public authorities. Alienated from an apparently fruitless political process, large numbers dropped out; others explored a more systematic critique of the institutional underpinning for the war.

Throughout the antiwar decade of 1963–1973, the Movement spanned an enormous breadth and diversity of people and perspectives: morally grounded church activists and long-time pacifists, committed New Left radicals, young men mobilized by an impending draft, housewives and grieving mothers, veterans who experienced first hand the numbing horror of the war, socialists of various stripes, alienated young people, labor unions, and businesspeople.[12]

Movement unity was perpetually threatened by strategic concerns like the exclusion or nonexclusion of communists; the call for immediate withdrawal versus negotiations, the use of illegal tactics like civil disobedience or seizure of university buildings; the emphasis or deemphasis on electoral politics and major-party antiwar candidates; the legitimacy and effectiveness of violence; and the single issue of ending the war versus the more profound task of transforming American society. Movement planning conferences sometimes collapsed over these conflicts; at other times, government escalation would trigger newfound unity and a new wave of demonstrations. Each new action brought new people into active mobilization against the war, thereby repeating the process of commitment and radicalization.

Although they traveled different ideological paths, more and more Americans came to view the war from an *outsider's* perspective. Men who fought the war realized the gratuitous distortions they had been taught by schoolteachers, the government, and military brass.[13] Veterans later realized their government was more interested in them as symbols than as people suffering from psychological or physical disorders resulting from service in Vietnam. Probing antiwar activists or an occasional journalist discovered atrocities that recalled the infamous war crimes of World War II. These realities—the first hard lessons of Vietnam—awakened the antiwar movement's moral outrage and spawned widespread alienation.

For many, the war in Vietnam came to symbolize the system they felt so alienated from. Potter noted in his 1965 speech that "the war goes on; the freedom to conduct that war depends on the dehumanization not only of Vietnamese people but of Americans as well; it depends on the construction of a system of premises and thinking that insulates the President and his advisors thoroughly and completely from the human consequences of the decisions they make."[14]

Furthermore, increasing numbers of activists came to see that the system that produced the war was the same system targeted by the black power critique, the campus upheavals, the counterculture, and the women's and environmental movements. The war revealed to black activists the pervasiveness of American racism, from the disproportionate burden of combat borne by black men, to the government's failure to provide adequate protection for civil rights workers in the South while "protecting freedom" in Vietnam, to white America's racial assumptions about the culture of Vietnamese "gooks" and "slopes." Student activists saw in the detached quantitative analysis and unquestioning loyalty of government decision makers the products of the same technocratic education they resisted. To countercultural seekers of inner peace, love, and community, Vietnam came to embody the repressive violence of a culture gone mad. From battlefield bravado and Presidential toughness to the self-proclaimed objective systems analysis of technocrats, feminists saw in Vietnam the ultimate expression of male machismo and the perils of a segmented, masculine personality detached from feelings, morality, and experience. Finally, ecologists saw in the war the same corporate priests of technological progress that threatened the ecosphere. With an arrogant belief in their own legitimacy and effectiveness, and seemingly ignorant of the human cost of their policies, these technocrats expressed an ultimate faith in the "technical fix." As Carl Oglesby summed up, "What sets Vietnam aflame is the same force that brutalizes the black population and poisons everybody's air."[15]

The years since the war in Vietnam have been marked by contortions of the national psyche reminiscent of post-war Germany's struggle with the loss of a costly war and the knowledge that their government knowingly committed atrocities. Needless to say, Americans differ now as they did then in how they view the Vietnam War. From *within* the decision-making process, almost any action could be, and was, justified when coated with the gloss of noble intentions. Official terminology and quantitative measures masked the realities of Vietnam and facilitated enormous self-delusion on the part of many decision makers. More pervasively, this rhetoric also resulted in the gross manipulation of the American public.

From *outside* the decision-making process, the experiences of the antiwar movement led some to a more radical awareness of systemic forces that made Vietnam, or a war like it, inevitable. Briefly, these include (1) an ideological mythology that views systems like the government, the marketplace, and the "free world" as neutral and therefore just; (2) the convergence of corporate, strategic, and political interests in a system of American hegemony or domination over the non-Communist world; (3) technocratic decision-making that emphasized disinterested analysis, a logic of escalation, and belief in its own universality; and (4) a veil of rhetoric, secrecy, and distortion—in a word, propaganda—designed to maximize efficient management and minimize public awareness and participation.[16] Awareness of these systemic forces, confirmed by post-Vietnam U.S. intervention in Central America, are among the ultimate hard lessons of the Vietnam War.

■ The Evolution of American Policy and Opposition to It

You that hide behind walls
You that hide behind desks
I just want you to know
I can see through your masks . . .

You fasten all the triggers
For the others to fire
Then you sit back and watch
While the death count gets higher
You hide in your mansion
As young people's blood
Flows out of their bodies
And is buried in the mud . . .

I think you will find
When your death takes its toll
All the money you made
Will never buy back your soul

—Bob Dylan, "Masters of War"

United States policy toward Vietnam can be divided into four distinct stages. The first stage pre-dates the 1960s, spanning the period from 1945 to 1961. It marks the crucial time in which the basic framework of American policy toward Vietnam was established—that of fighting a proxy war to stalemate the perceived threat of communism. The remaining three stages correspond to the three administrations of the 1960s: the Kennedy years of transition from a war of proxy to an American war, the Johnson escalation to a massive assault on Vietnam, and the Nixon years of "Vietnamization," with its attendant deceits, deteriorating morale, and intensification of violence.

In light of this book's focus on the experiences of the Sixties, the initial stage is relevant only as a backdrop that prepared the way for the war years of

1961–1973.[17] The American policy inherited by Presidents Kennedy, Johnson, and Nixon was most directly shaped by three developments of the post–World War II years: the strategy of global American interventionism, the rising crescendo of anticommunism in the Truman–McCarthy era, and the Vietnam-specific stalemate policy that evolved out of the Geneva Conference of 1954.

Reflecting the World War II experience and the imperatives of American corporate expansion overseas, postwar American policy was interventionist from the start. Nonetheless, the shape, extent, and location of that intervention would be determined by U.S. policy decisions in the postwar years. The groundwork for intervention was laid by the Truman Doctrine, which provided aid to anticommunist forces in Greece and Turkey, placing this policy in a global framework aimed at containing communism. The Truman Doctrine was a public declaration[18] reflecting the objectives outlined in the National Security Council document "NSC 68," which asserted that the United States needed to "foster a world environment in which the American system can survive and flourish"—in short, American hegemony.

The grand design of American interventionism did not by itself necessitate intervention in Vietnam. Perhaps the greatest missed opportunity to avoid the war in Vietnam came when the Truman administration rebuffed overtures from Ho Chi Minh, the leader of the intensely nationalistic Vietminh.[19] However, it didn't take long for American policy makers to take the counterrevolutionary position of supporting efforts by the French to hold onto their Indochina colony. The Truman administration recognized the regime of Emperor Bao Dai as the legitimate government of Vietnam,[20] and provided economic and military aid to the French, who were fighting the anticolonial Vietminh. The Eisenhower administration built on and reinforced these initial commitments by increasing American economic and military support for the French to 78 percent of the cost of the French effort, and adopting the infamous domino theory, which publicly linked all leftist or populist insurgencies to Moscow and Peking and all efforts to crush these insurgencies to the vital interests of the United States. In the wake of the catastrophic French defeat at Dien Bien Phu the Eisenhower administration committed U.S. support directly to the regime of President Ngo Dinh Diem of South Vietnam. That support, and Diem's reign of terror, resulted in the deaths of an estimated 80,000 South Vietnamese by the time the Kennedy administration took office in 1961.[21]

A second major development in this period was the virulent wave of anticommunism that tinged virtually all American politics during the 1950s. The McCarthy phenomenon had a direct impact on early Vietnam policy, causing the purge of the China and East Asia experts in the State Department (who were blamed for the "loss" of China), thereby reducing the likelihood that informed analysis of nationalist and anticolonial movements would influence policy deliberations.[22] More generally, it created a climate of fear and repression that scapegoated virtually all challenges to status quo arrangements, and made it politically suicidal for liberal politicians to appear soft on communism.

Finally, the signing of the 1954 Geneva Accords called for a temporary division of Vietnam at the 17th parallel, with internationally supervised elections to decide Vietnam's fate within two years. It also limited the number of foreign support personnel in both North and South. The United States publically refused to sign the Geneva agreement because the document legitimized North Vietnam as "new" communist territory. Instead, the administration supported President Diem's refusal to hold elections. With this refusal and support for the tyrannical Diem, the United States, in effect, created the nation of South Vietnam and committed itself to maintaining a stalemate against the communist forces in the North. Shortly after the United States took this action, an indigenous opposition movement with roots in the Vietminh, labeled the Vietcong by Diem, arose in the South. From 1954 to 1959, the official North Vietnamese Communist party policy regarding South Vietnam was to avoid the use of violence "except in limited circumstances." In 1959, after years of repression in the South, the party decided to support a campaign of organized guerrilla activity, and in 1960, the National Liberation Front (NLF) was formed by the Third Congress of the Vietnamese Communist party with the aim of reunifying Vietnam. The stage was set for the events of the 1960s.

THE KENNEDY TECHNOCRATS TAKE CHARGE

The Kennedy administration took office conveying to the public a sense of energy and mission and a combination of toughness and flexibility. While other arenas occupied most of President Kennedy's attention, Vietnam policies were formulated within the larger context of the Kennedy foreign policy. Most significant were the president's uncertain dealings with Soviet Premier Nikita Khrushchev, the Bay of Pigs fiasco, his fear of the right wing, and his infatuation with the strategy of counterinsurgency as a method of combatting Third World national liberation movements. John Kennedy's administration took significant steps that began the transition from a proxy war in Vietnam to the fully Americanized war that it became in 1965. Not surprisingly a nascent antiwar movement emerged during these years.

In addition, the members of the Kennedy team brought with them a new, technocratic toughness that distinguished them from the "fuzzy ideologues" of the Eisenhower administration.

> [They] were tough, unsentimental, and embarrassed by idealism, do-goodism, and other forms of what they called empty rhetoric. . . . They thought of themselves as muscular realists, disciplined, potent, demanding hard facts, never pieties, connected with the way the world actually works, decisive, never vacillating or timorous, vigorous, and never tedious. They thought of themselves as above narrow or petty interests of mere politics in their dedication to the larger national interest. They believed that they knew what was good for the country. They were cool and confident, and did not trust emotion. They preferred intellectual speed, agility, and precision. They were rationalists. And they embraced power as if it bestowed immortality.[23]

The new administration made two crucial decisions regarding Vietnam. The first of these, the deployment of Green Beret Special Forces and increasing numbers of "advisers," reflected the administration's preference for counterinsurgency as a weapon in the struggle to preserve U.S. hegemony in the Third World. Significantly, when President Kennedy sent 400 Green Berets and 100 additional advisers to Vietnam in 1961, he violated Geneva agreement limitations that previously had been tacitly observed by the United States. State Department official Paul Kattenburg asserted that "something intangible but immensely important went out of our Indochina policy," for "Geneva had presented a type of hidden but nonetheless real restraint."[24]

During 1961–1962, counterinsurgency activities and the widespread bombing of NLF-controlled countryside in South Vietnam grew as the Kennedy administration sent an additional 15,000 U.S. military men to Vietnam. The escalation of bombing, defoliation, and "advising" was designed to move large numbers of Vietnamese peasants into "strategic hamlets" where they would be confined by barbed wire and armed guards and "protected" from the guerrillas that approximately 50 percent of them supported anyway. A pattern that was to become only too familiar was emerging. Faced with competing pressures from the Defense Department (for more military personnel) and the State

Department (for more pressure on Diem to seek popular support), Kennedy initially chose the middle ground—a conditional pledge of more troops and an ultimatum to Diem. When Diem defied U.S. demands, the troops were sent anyway. The United States was allowing itself to be trapped by its fear of Diem's autonomy (he might negotiate on his own with the North, as General Nguyen Khanh threatened to do later on), by its belief that American hegemony in the "friendly world" depended on the willingness of the United States to stand by its commitments, and by the fear that withdrawal from Vietnam would trigger another McCarthyist Red Scare.

The Kennedy administration's second crucial step was its decision to support the generals' coup against Diem in 1963. As Diem's tyrannical regime tried to expand its hold on South Vietnam with U.S. support, protests by Buddhists grew, including hunger strikes and acts of self-immolation. The horrifying, searing image of Buddhist monks doused in gasoline and set on fire was conveyed to the American public by the mass media. Public discontent grew, not only in Vietnam but in the United States, and a vacillating president told Ambassador Henry Cabot Lodge to give tacit U.S. approval to the generals plotting against Diem.

U.S. support for the Diem overthrow reflected a state department objective of improving the political stability of the South Vietnamese government, an emphasis viewed unfavorably by both Secretary of Defense Robert McNamara and CIA Director John McCone. However, the coup also led to deeper and more violent involvement by the United States in South Vietnam. Among other things, it signaled to future South Vietnamese rulers how far the United States was willing to go to pursue its own objectives in Vietnam. It also destabilized the South Vietnamese government, leading to seven more coups over the next two years, and spawned a small trickle of public doubt in the United States.

The Diem assassination reportedly shook President Kennedy into awareness that Vietnam was a foreign policy failure that called for far greater attention than it had been given. Three weeks later, President Kennedy himself was assassinated, and the transition to the Johnson presidency began.

The years 1963–1964 are described by antiwar chroniclers Nancy Zaroulis and Gerald Sullivan as years of lonely dissent for the antiwar movement,

> The years when a few isolated voices began to cry out against American involvement in Vietnam. They came mostly from organizations on the fringes of American political life, largely unknown to the ordinary citizen.

This fragile, embryonic peace movement was comprised of pacifist, religious, civil rights, disarmament, and student groups, as well as elements of the "Old Left." Many of them had been working since the mid-1950's to achieve nuclear disarmament; others had been newly energized in the civil rights struggle.[25]

One reason for this trickle of dissent was the lack of public awareness about the U.S. presence in Vietnam, a lack reinforced by upbeat official pronouncements and optimistic news accounts that passed on administration reports without question.[26]

Early dissent toward American involvement first appeared at an Easter peace rally held by SANE at the United Nations in 1963. The rally focused on SANE's proposed nuclear test ban treaty. However, some marchers carried signs denouncing the American presence in Vietnam, and long-time peace activists David Dellinger and A. J. Muste spoke out on Vietnam.

The first organized demonstrations against U.S. involvement in Vietnam were held in Philadelphia and New York in August 1963, during the annual commemoration of the Hiroshima–Nagasaki bombings. Additional signs of dissent appeared in letters to the *New York Times* criticizing the McNamara–Taylor fact-finding report on Vietnam. At a Harvard Law School forum in October, about one hundred demonstrators booed Diem's sister-in-law, Madame Nhu, when she appeared to plead for support for the South Vietnamese leader.

There were few other omens that segments of the public were unhappy with U.S. policies in Vietnam, although the self-immolation of Buddhist monks made a deep impression on at least three Americans, each of whom later burned him or herself alive in anguish over America's role in the war. At the time, no one could have predicted how turbulent the next ten years would become.

AMERICA'S WAR, 1964–1968

We are not about to send American boys nine or ten thousand miles away from home to do what Asian boys ought to be doing for themselves.
—President Lyndon Johnson

After John Kennedy's death, Lyndon Johnson took on the mantle of executor of the slain president's will. In addition to his more obvious inheritance of Kennedy's civil rights initiative, Johnson was heir to the legacy of

American involvement in Vietnam, a path leading directly back to the end of the Second World War. He inherited the Kennedy team of technocrats, the "best and the brightest." He also inherited the mythical belief that South Vietnam was a nation rather than an American invention. As a consequence, the South Vietnamese government would have to "win the hearts and minds" of the Vietnamese people while simultaneously defeating the insurgent National Liberation Front.

Johnson's signal contribution to the Vietnam struggle was to make it a full-scale war between the armed forces of the United States and the forces of both the National Liberation Front and North Vietnam. He began active escalation of this war in 1965 by approving Operation Rolling Thunder, the bombing of North Vietnam, and by dispatching the first American ground troops to Vietnam.

Planning for Escalation, 1964: The groundwork for these two pivotal decisions was laid during the transition year of 1964. In fact, it was begun almost immediately after President Kennedy's death, as the new president ordered planning for secret operations against North Vietnam. The result was Operation Plan 34A, a secret proposal for "progressively escalating pressure" against the North. Escalation was motivated in part by growing administration concern that the South Vietnamese government was showing interest in premature negotiations with the National Liberation Front, or as Gabriel Kolko put it, "The war would soon end unless the Americans entered it with their own troops."[27] The plan was also part of a conscious design to characterize the struggle in Vietnam as an invasion sponsored by the North. The escalation of American involvement was built on a rationale that Vietnam was the first real test of the United States' ability to "defeat the communist wars of liberation." Operation Plan 34A called for espionage and sabotage in the North, a secret air war in Laos, and intelligence operations by U.S. destroyers in the Gulf of Tonkin.

In August, an apparent attack by North Vietnamese torpedo boats against patrolling U.S. destroyers in the Gulf of Tonkin provided the justification for U.S. reprisals against North Vietnam. The next day, U.S. planes bombed the torpedo boats' bases and an oil storage depot, and President Johnson prepared Congress for the Gulf of Tonkin Resolution, the blueprint for presidential escalation of the war in the years to come.[28]

As Johnson's momentum increased, the trickle of antiwar dissent began to swell. Although largely ignored by congressional colleagues and much of the mainstream press, the only two congressional opponents to the Gulf of Tonkin Resolution—Senators Wayne Morse and Ernest Gruening—helped bring doubts about U.S. involvement into the public limelight. In April, the Women's International League for Peace and Freedom condemned the use of napalm and defoliants in Vietnam and lobbied against U.S. involvement. Eighty-seven young men from the leftist Progressive Labor party signed an advertisement declaring their refusal to fight in Vietnam; many liberal publications reportedly refused to publish the ad. The May 2 Movement, a coalition of groups including the Young Socialist Alliance and Socialist Workers party, began a campaign to collect funds for medical supplies to be sent to North Vietnam; they also held two small rallies in New York City. On the very day that President Johnson signed the Civil Rights Act of 1964, veteran peace activists David Dellinger, A. J. Muste, and the Reverends Daniel and Philip Berrigan held a demonstration across from the White House to publicize a "Declaration of Conscience," a pacifist call for draft resistance and noncooperation with military research and production.

Additional rallies and vigils against the war occurred throughout the summer and fall. At a memorial service for the three slain civil rights workers in Mississippi, SNCC leader Robert Moses compared administration willingness to use force to "protect freedom" in Vietnam to its tolerance of violence against civil rights activists in the South. On December 29, 1964, the relatively young Students for a Democratic Society began planning for a march on Washington on April 17, the Saturday of Easter weekend. During the following months, as the government escalated the bombing and sent combat troops to Vietnam, more and more groups signed on for the April demonstration.

America Expands the War, 1965: On February 7, 1965, the U.S. air base at Pleiku was hit by a Vietcong mortar attack. Eight American men were killed and 126 were wounded. Within twelve hours, U.S. bombers attacked a suspected Vietcong camp just north of the demilitarized zone in North Vietnam. As he returned that day from an observation tour in Vietnam, national security adviser McGeorge Bundy drafted a memorandum for President Johnson calling for a policy of sustained reprisal. The campaign of massive bombing of North Vietnam, devised the year before and code-named Operation Rolling Thunder was put into operation; Pleiku was the pretext.[29]

The ultimate outcome of that decision was that the United States dropped four times the tonnage of bombs on the tiny nation of Vietnam that U.S. forces dropped everywhere during all of World War II.

After the bombing began, public criticism of U.S. policy spread on college campuses and in newspapers. The administration responded by issuing the State Department White Paper on February 27, documenting North Vietnamese aggression against South Vietnam and providing a public rationale for the bombing campaign. A week later, using State Department data from the unpublished appendix to the report, journalist I. F. Stone rebutted the report by showing that the Vietcong received very little equipment, arms, or ammunition from the North, 80 percent of their weapons being captured from U.S. or South Vietnamese forces.

Thus the battle lines were drawn between the administration and its critics in what was to become "the war at home." The first battlefields were the college campuses where the short-lived teach-in movement took place in the spring of 1965. Two hundred and sixteen faculty members at the University of Michigan placed an ad in the *Michigan Daily*: "We the faculty are deeply worried about the war in Vietnam. We think its moral, political and military consequences are very grave, and that we must examine them and find new alternatives before irreparable actions occur. We are devoting this night, March 24–25, to seminars, lectures, informal discussions and a protest rally to focus attention on the war, its consequences, and ways to stop it." [30] Three thousand students attended, including women students who needed special university permission to stay out all night. Students and faculty probed State Department arguments and materials through the night in an intensely educational experience that recalled the "real discussions" of the Berkeley Free Speech Movement.

The teach-in movement spread rapidly to colleges and universities of all sizes and types. In response to the growing criticism on campuses across the country, the administration dispatched a State Department "truth team" to the Midwest. Hostile confrontations with college students revealed the beginning of a moral and emotional chasm that would separate the administration from antiwar critics for years to come. [31] Thomas Powers recalls one such exchange that demonstrated the gulf: "Like [State Department official] Conlon, the students wearing black armbands at the University of Wisconsin had decided the basic issues of the war before the State Department team arrived.

The moral intensity that infused their questions about napalm, tear gas, and torture could never be quieted by reference to Eisenhower's letter to Diem or President Johnson's offer of unconditional negotiations."[32]

With the SDS-sponsored demonstration looming in Washington, President Johnson spoke at Johns Hopkins University in an effort to placate the growing number of critics, offering "unconditional negotiations" with North Vietnam while "helping South Vietnam defend its independence." The two claims were contradictory. The notion of an independent, that is, U.S.-dominated, South Vietnam was diametrically opposed to both North Vietnam and National Liberation Front objectives, which largely conformed to the Geneva Conference agreement. It effectively precluded negotiations and exposed the real meaning of Johnson's promise of unconditional talks—North Vietnamese acceptance of U.S. conditions.[33]

Three days later, Dr. Benjamin Spock, co-chair of SANE, responded to Johnson's speech at a march and rally at the United Nations. Spock called for an immediate cease-fire in Vietnam and warned that administration policy was "still based on mistaken views of the fundamental realities there."[34]

The next weekend marked the first nationwide demonstration against the war in Vietnam, with roughly twenty thousand people attending in Washington, D.C. Long-time pacifist A. J. Muste smoothed over a split among demonstration sponsors over SDS policy of not excluding communist-inspired groups like the May 2 Movement (M2M) and Progressive Labor. Speakers included Yale historian Staughton Lynd, Senator Gruening, I. F. Stone, SDS president Paul Potter, and SNCC leader Robert Moses. In his stirring speech, Potter articulated the growing awareness of an emerging New Left:

> What is exciting about the participants in this march is that so many of us view ourselves consciously as participants as well in a movement to build a more decent society. There are students here who have been involved in protests over the quality and kind of education they are receiving in growingly bureaucratized, depersonalized institutions called universities; there are Negroes from Mississippi and Alabama who are struggling against the tyranny and repression of those states; there are poor people here—Negro and white—from Northern urban areas who are attempting to build movements that abolish poverty and secure democracy; there are faculty who are beginning to question the relevance of their institutions to the critical problems facing the society. . . .
>
> What we must do is begin to build a democratic and humane society

in which Vietnams are unthinkable, in which human life and initiative are precious. . . . That means that we build a movement that understands Vietnam in all its horror as but a symptom of a deeper malaise . . . , a movement that will wrench the country into a confrontation with the issues of the war.[35]

Potter called on the demonstrators to name the system that spawned the war in Vietnam, but later acknowledged that he refused to label it capitalism "because capitalism was for me and my generation an inadequate description of the evils of America—a hollow, dead word tied to the thirties."[36] Fred Halstead of the Socialist Workers party recalled of the rally's end:

> The crowd stood and applauded [Potter's speech], then moved down the wide, grassy mall between the monument and the capitol. Those at the front of the march, looking over their shoulders, viewed a spectacular sight of the throng making their way, banners and placards aloft with the low afternoon sun streaming through them, down the long slope towards the steps of the capitol. There the march stopped as a petition to Congress was delivered.[37]

The petition called for immediate U.S. withdrawal from Vietnam and reconvening of the Geneva conference.

From all outward appearances, the administration ignored the nearby rally. At the end of April, President Johnson approved direct use of U.S. ground forces in the war, with plans for gradual escalation to 150,000 troops by the end of 1965—gradual, so as to avoid the appearance of a dramatic planned escalation. He also ordered a stepped-up draft call: 180,000 men were drafted in 1965, and 341 cases of draft resistance were recorded. By taking this momentous step, the President was refuting his own earlier public pronouncements and the oft-quoted advice of General Douglas MacArthur against fighting a land war in Asia.

On May 22, about 30,000 people attended the 36-hour-long Vietnam Day teach-in at Berkeley. The tone of teach-ins had changed since Michigan. Antiwar organizers established the terms of the teach-in by stating, "The purpose of Vietnam Day is to present to the Bay Area community alternatives to current U.S. policy. The information and ideas that will be related on these days cannot be found in the mass media, the State Department *White Paper*, or even in university classrooms. We are contributing to democratic dialogue by expressing views which, although widespread in Asia and Europe, are rarely presented to the American people." [38] Gone was the tone of academic debate. In its place was an instinctive disassociation from mainstream institutions and their "truths." As Norman Mailer warned in his remarks to the Vietnam Day gathering,

> Listen, Lyndon Johnson, you've gone too far this time. You are a bully with an Air Force, and since you will not call off your Air Force, there are young people who will persecute you back. It is a little thing, but it will hound you into nightmares and endless corridors of night without sleep. . . . They will go on marches and they will make demonstrations, and they will begin a war of public protest against you which will never cease. It will go on and on and it will get stronger and stronger. [39]

Mailer's prediction was accurate. Gradually, as administration claims were repeatedly refuted by events, more and more young people came to this instinctive disassociation. President Johnson's crucial 1965 escalation lay the groundwork for the next three tumultuous years, a time in which over 30,000 Americans would die in Vietnam, the United States would become convulsed in social upheaval, and the president would leave office with his administration and his foreign policy in shambles. In the end, Johnson's policy accomplished precisely what he dreaded most—humiliation.

In August, several groups—the Committee for Non-Violent Action, the War Resisters League, the *Catholic Worker*, and the Student Peace Union— held a march and sit-in near the Capitol in Washington. They called it an Assembly of Unrepresented People. Three hundred and fifty were arrested, the largest mass arrest ever to have taken place in that city. [40] In October, the Vietnam Day Committee (VDC) mobilized antiwar groups in the absence of SDS and organized the First International Days of Protest against the war. The largest demonstrations, with 20,000 to 30,000 protesters, were held in New York and Oakland; smaller demonstrations were held in some sixty cities across the United States and in over fifteen foreign countries. Other actions dramatized the growing antiwar sentiment: an official-looking truck warning "napalm bombs ahead" followed shipments to and from a napalm manufacturing plant in California, and the VDC organized well-publicized efforts to stop troop trains from reaching their destination in Oakland.

Counterdemonstration rhetoric heated up. The protests were denounced as extremist, treasonous, and communist by wide-ranging critics, including moderate columnists. Attorney General Nicholas Katzenbach gave notice that the Justice Department might have to investigate "some Communists" involved in the protests. *Time* magazine ran its story under the title "Vietniks—Self-Defeating Dissent," while J. Edgar Hoover was more blunt in dismissing the "halfway citizens who are neither morally, mentally nor emotionally mature."[41]

By the year's end, the National Coordinating Committee to End the War in Vietnam (NCC) was organized in an effort to bring order to the proliferating antiwar groups scattered across the country. The first NCC conference split over the question of whether to call for immediate withdrawal from Vietnam. About the same time, 35,000 attended a SANE "march of concern" in Washington, notable for SDS president Carl Oglesby's words:

> The original commitment in Vietnam was made by President Truman, a mainstream liberal. It was seconded by President Eisenhower, a moderate liberal. It was intensified by President Kennedy, a flaming liberal. Think of the men who now engineer that war. . . . They are all liberals. . . .
>
> Our dead revolutionaries [of 1776] would . . . wonder why their country was fighting against what appeared to be a revolution. The living liberals would hotly deny that it is one: there are troops coming in from outside, the rebels get arms from other countries, most of the people are not on their side, and they practice terror against their own. Therefore, *not* a revolution.
>
> What would our dead revolutionaries answer? They might say: "What fools and bandits, sirs, you make then of us. Outside help? Do you remember Lafayette? . . . . Did you never hear what we did to our own Loyalists? Or about the thousands of rich American tories who fled for their lives to Canada? And as for popular support, do you not know that we had less than one-third of our people with us? . . ."
>
> We have become a nation of young, bright-eyed, hard hearted, slim-waisted, bullet-headed make-out artists. A nation—may I say it—of beardless liberals. . . . others will make of it that I sound mighty anti-American. To these, I say: Don't blame *me* for *that*! Blame those who mouthed my liberal values and broke my American heart.[42]

Fragmentation and the Liberal Antiwar Movement, 1966: In 1966, the liberal wing of the antiwar movement pushed for

limited objectives through *limited* means. For the Movement, limited objectives meant a "peaceful solution" or a negotiated settlement; limited means proved to be vigils, newspaper ads, fasts, teach-ins, "read-ins" and an occasional orderly march of protest. Students at Bryn Mawr, Haverford, and Swarthmore colleges began symbolic fasts; others at CCNY, Wesleyan, Amherst, and elsewhere followed suit. In Washington four hundred Quakers conducted a two-hour vigil at the White House and Women Strike for Peace began a continuous lobbying of Congress for "a peaceful solution." In New York City members of Clergy and Laymen Concerned about Vietnam tolled the bell of St. Mark's-in-the-Bouwerie [*sic*] Church. A national campaign under the auspices of SANE for the election of congressional candidates who favored scaling down the war in Vietnam was announced.[43]

As diverse, small-scale actions were taken against the war machinery, it became more difficult to hold the movement together, especially in planning major demonstrations.

In addition to the immediate withdrawal controversy, the movement was plagued by the single–versus–multiple issue dilemma. The ever-present concern for racial justice raised the delicate question of relations with and within the civil rights movement. After Stokely Carmichael, the militant SNCC leader, appeared at a press conference announcing a New York City march, old-line pacifists began to pull back from the young movement, claiming that "being linked to the civil rights movement would hurt the infant anti-war movement: the American people might accept peace in Vietnam but they would never accept racial equality. Similarly, many black leaders shunned the anti-war movement. What one commentator called the "fateful merging of anti-war and racial dissension" never happened."[44]

Despite these divisions, the antiwar movement continued to grow. A March 26 Second International Days of Protest march in New York City drew an estimated 50,000 diverse citizens including Afro-Americans Against the War in Vietnam, the Women Strike for Peace, and the Teacher's Committee. American flags were conspicuous among the marchers. A variety of smaller demonstrations took place in over 100 American cities as well as dozens of locations around the world. The first of many draft board raids took place in Big Lake, Minnesota, when a father and his twelve sons poured two buckets of human feces on draft records. Senator J. William Fulbright broke with the administration, decrying the "arrogance of power." Three G.I.'s from Fort Hood went AWOL and issued a statement that challenged the constitutionality of the war and declared their refusal to go to Vietnam. Their courageous stand earned them two years in prison but triggered increasing G.I. unrest. Public opinion polls showed that Vietnam had become the voters' number one concern. In the working-class suburb of Dearborn, Michigan, slightly more than 40 percent of November voters approved a resolution calling for immediate withdrawal of American troops. Twenty thousand turned out for a New York City rally. Jerry Rubin turned hearings of the House Un-American Activities Committee (HUAC) into a theater of the absurd by appearing dressed as a Revolutionary War soldier.

For his part, President Johnson blasted the "nervous nellies" who criticized his policies. Johnson soon found protesters appearing wherever he traveled, even outside the White House gates while his daughter Luci was married on the lawn. He became more and more a prisoner in the White House. In his isolation, he escalated American involvement by bombing oil depots near Hanoi and Haiphong and sending another 200,000 troops to Vietnam. He also promised a willingness to negotiate troop withdrawals with Hanoi whenever they ceased *their* "aggression."

Later in the year, planning for a major mass mobilization in 1967 began at a National Leadership Conference called in Cleveland by A. J. Muste, Sidney Peck, and other activists. The plan called for a Spring Mobilization Committee to End the War in Vietnam to plan demonstrations in both New York and San Francisco in April. Older groups like the anti-nuclear SANE pulled back from active participation in demonstration planning, and in a telling move, SDS chose to downplay the war in order to stress the need for broad social transformation.

Meanwhile, at Harvard, Secretary of Defense McNamara was cornered in a grim confrontation with antiwar students. In December, *New York Times* correspondent Harrison Salisbury reported from Hanoi that U.S. bombing had killed civilians and destroyed hospitals, churches, homes, and factories. The credibility gap became a permanent fixture on the political landscape. By the end of 1966, there were 389,000 American troops in Vietnam, and 6,644 Americans had died there.

1967: The War at Home: The year 1967 saw continued escalation of both U.S. actions in Vietnam and the antiwar movement at home. The latter began to shift from protest to resistance, from a stance of moral witness against the war to a more active confrontation and nonviolent obstruction of the war effort. The University of Wisconsin student sit-in against Dow Chemical recruiters brought a violent response from Madison police dressed in riot gear; its fallout typified confrontations that were to come. Students and faculty were shocked by the police violence; many called for a campus strike. Thirteen students were subsequently suspended and three faculty members fired for joining the strike. Dow Chemical was temporarily banned from campus, but vowed to continue campus recruitment and the manufacture of napalm.[45] Subsequent demonstrations were fueled by increasing anger against the war policymakers, against corporations like Dow, and against the police.

Planning for the Spring Mobilization demonstrated the vulnerability of the antiwar movement to liberal political and economic support. David Dellinger recalls that his efforts to recruit civil rights activist James Bevel and Martin Luther King, Jr., hit the familiar snag of nonexclusion:

> [Bevel's] first demand was that the Communists be taken off the letterhead. Now, we had a policy of nonexclusion. . . . And King demanded that Arnold Johnson, who was the public relations director of the CP [Communist party], be taken off the letterhead. Fred Halstead and I led the debate to say we would not take Arnold Johnson off the letterhead. Even if we lost Martin Luther King. . . . All the traditional antiwar organizations thought that we ought to compromise.
>
> Then toward the end, King said he wouldn't speak unless we dropped Stokely Carmichael. Right up to the end we were afraid we were going to lose him. One time he came up to New York and said everything was OK and then there was a fund-raiser and a bunch of his financiers said that if he took part in the demonstration they were going to withdraw their money. That same night, Jim Bevel, Andy Young, Ivanhoe Donaldson, Bob Greenblatt and I just had a down-to-earth no-holds-barred discussion and I believe that I convinced Andy Young that we were going to have the biggest antiwar march that ever took place on April 15, 1967, with or without Martin Luther King and that Martin Luther King was going to be left behind in history if he didn't come.[46]

King attended the protest. His speech against the war marked a major break with the Johnson administration, which he had long and successfully courted for civil rights legislation; for his part, Johnson was stung by King's rebuke. A *Washington Post* editorial of April 6 mouthed the mainstream liberal response. "Dr. King has done a grave injury to those who are his natural allies in a great struggle to remove ancient abuses from our public life; and he has done an even graver injury to himself. Many who have listened to him with respect will never again accord him the same confidence. He has diminished his usefulness to his cause, to his country, and to his people." For his part King explained his decision. "I knew I could never again raise my voice against the violence of the repressed in the ghettos without having first spoken clearly to the greatest purveyor of violence in the world today—my own government." [47]

Well over 100,000 people came to New York, and comparable numbers demonstrated in San Francisco. After gathering in Central Park they marched to the United Nations, although there were so many people that some never arrived for the speeches. Signs and banners revealed the changing times and diverse perspectives involved: "Stop the Bombing—Bring the Troops Home," "Children are Not Born to Burn," and "No Vietnamese Ever Called Me Nigger." Chants of "Hell no, we won't go," and "Hey, hey, LBJ, how many kids did you kill today?" resounded through New York's streets. Mothers pushed baby carriages, while hippies painted themselves with poster paint, carried flowers, and chanted "flower power." In addition, seventy young men, many from Cornell University, gathered in Central Park and burned their draft cards, declaring their intention to resist the draft.

The two wars were escalating. American soldiers continued to die in the Vietnam jungle as troop numbers reached 463,000. Tales of horror filtered home with returning veterans. Some G.I.'s who experienced the horrors of battle became combat-numb,[48] detached from feeling, and therefore capable of normally unimaginable atrocities, a psychological repression many paid for in later years with post-traumatic shock syndrome.[49] Increasing numbers saw through the mask of official rhetoric. In Myra MacPherson's account, one soldier recalled,

"I don't believe in heroes. They felt so guilty about us being there, they gave medals out like candy. Everybody come home lookin' like Georgie Patton. I told one reporter the truth and he didn't believe me. They wanted to write what a big hero I was. A buddy was still on fire and I carried, I crawled with him twenty-five feet. It had nothin' to do with heroism. It was because I did not want to be alone. Everybody else was dead and I was sittin' there cryin'." Eddie spaces his words out for emphasis. "And . . . I . . . did . . . not . . . want . . . to . . . be . . . alone." [50]

Another veteran later remembered, "I just lost respect for everything after Vietnam. Now I feel politicians are as crooked as the day is long. Everything I learned as a kid turned out to be a damn lie." [51]

Compounding the repugnance of the war was a politically functional but inequitable draft. For most of the early years of U.S. involvement in combat, college students were deferred from the draft, leaving the burden of service on young men from working- and lower-middle-class families where values such as military patriotism were more likely to be emphasized. And with less promising futures ahead of them, these teenagers were susceptible to military marketing. [52] In the racially conscious mid-Sixties, black servicemen were keenly aware that they served and died in disproportionate numbers; in 1967, blacks made up 20 percent of combat forces, 25 percent of the elite troops, and up to 45 percent of the airborne rifle platoons. Dick Gregory commented, "If you died in the jungle, the VC would have buried you and the white boy in a common grave. But if your two bodies had been shipped back to the U.S., you couldn't be buried in the same cemetery in many cities." [53] Mindful of political ramifications, President Johnson resisted calling up the reserves because most were the college-educated sons of politically vocal upper-middle-class families.

Immediately after the Spring Mobilization, Johnson approved the bombing of industrial and power plants and air bases in the Hanoi area. Shortly thereafter, a secret memorandum from Secretary McNamara observed, "There continues to be no sign that the bombing has reduced Hanoi's will to resist or her ability to ship the necessary supplies south." [54] Senators J. William Fulbright, Frank Church, George McGovern, and Robert Kennedy attacked the escalation, while members of the Spring Mobilization denounced the "genocide and mass butchery" perpetrated by American bombers.

The Resistance was announced at the April San Francisco mobilization with release of the statement "We Refuse to Serve." Declaring their opposition to the war, the draft, and "all American military adventures," the signers stated:

> We all agree on one point: the war in Vietnam is criminal and we must act together, at great individual risk, to stop it. . . .
>
> Most of us now have deferments . . . but all these individual outs can have no effect on the draft, the war, or the consciousness of this

country. . . . We have chosen to openly defy the draft and confront the government and its war directly.

This is no small decision in a person's life. Each one realizes that refusing to cooperate with Selective Service may mean prison. . . .

The Resistance confronts the government with an unresolvable dilemma: to prosecute and imprison us, which will generate new waves of protest and dissent . . . ; or to set us free, which will provide greater impetus for the expansion of the movement.[55]

The Resistance combined prefigurative and instrumental politics in "a seizing of control of our own lives and a conscious effort to redirect the movement of American society." It embraced community: "Many Resistance members are deeply concerned with the formation of community, and in some instances our common commitment is leading to the development of strong communal bonds. If radicals are to remain faithful to their own values, then they must create mechanisms in which those values, can not only be expressed but also *experienced* in the present."[56]

Meanwhile, the American social fabric began to unravel in 1967. During the summer, massive riots erupted in Newark and Detroit, heightening awareness that something was grievously wrong with the system. As New Left journalist Andrew Kopkind wrote, "To be white and a radical in America this summer is to see horror and feel impotence. It is to watch the war grow and know no way to stop it, to understand the black rebellion and find no way to join it, to realize that the politics of a generation has failed and the institutions of reform are bankrupt, and yet to have neither ideology, programmes, nor the power to reconstruct them."[57]

As increasing numbers of antiwar activists distanced themselves from the political mainstream, others pursued liberal paths toward the 1968 elections. The community organizing faction of SDS veterans helped develop a Vietnam Summer modeled on the Mississippi experience. Large numbers of students engaged in door-to-door canvassing and electoral planning with the war as an organizing device. Allard Lowenstein began to explore the possibility of an electoral challenge to President Johnson in 1968, and eventually landed Eugene McCarthy as his candidate. In September, the National Conference for a New Politics met, marking the biggest and quite possibly the most hopelessly divided gathering of activist, radical–liberal, black power, and peace group leaders to date. In October, a group of clergy, professors, and others issued "A Call to Resist Illegitimate Authority."

The process of radicalization continued. Rennie Davis returned from a trip to Hanoi and reported,

> North Vietnam had an impact on me. I saw that these people were about something that I could not even comprehend. . . . In Hanoi we saw things that *no one* in this country was aware of. It was a combination of factors: the magnitude of the war and the incredible human struggle and the widespread [positive] Vietnamese attitude toward the American people.
> . . . The Vietnamese really did identify with and believe in the American Revolution. Because of our own origins, they seemed to genuinely believe that the American people understood the meaning of "freedom and independence."[58]

An Oakland Stop The Draft Week leading up to the March on the Pentagon included a draft card turn-in, supportive sit-ins, campus rallies, and violent confrontations at the Oakland induction center.

On October 21, the first massive assault on Washington, D.C.—the March on the Pentagon—occurred. Its theme, "Confront the Warmakers," was expressed in a rally at the Lincoln Memorial, a march to the Pentagon, and nonviolent civil disobedience at the Pentagon. By most accounts, government security was extraordinary, especially at the White House. March organizer David Dellinger noted that it marked the end of peaceful protest and the beginning of civil disobedience and confrontation in the effort to end the war. He also cautioned the demonstrators to "confront the troops without hostility" in order to "carry the antiwar message to them."

Over 100,000 gathered at the Lincoln Memorial and proceeded toward the Pentagon. At the head of the march across the Potomac a huge banner read "Support Our GIs, Bring Them Home Now!" The large numbers contributed to small-group actions. Mobilization leaders who were supposed to lead the civil disobedience were still at the rally when a small radical group called the Revolutionary Contingent charged the Pentagon. Some taunted troops who responded angrily. Many were beaten; all were quickly arrested. Those that remained behind in the agreed-upon parking lot confronted a new and frightening specter. Dellinger recalls that

> this was the first time they brought out federal troops, and that was the big debate, about how to respond to them. . . . All of a sudden the troops came marching out as if a door opened. The three of us [Dellinger, Spock, and Monsignor Charles Rice] addressed them on the agreed-upon

theme: "You are not our enemies, you are people like us. Join us. . . ." Then another door opened and I said [to our people] "Get on your knees," or "Sit down . . . ." And they were coming in military formation and the sergeant said something like "Bloody up the motherfuckers." I was down like this [he bends over and puts his arms over his head], like [civil right demonstrations] in the South waiting to be hit and they came up and a lot of them just went [gestures a tap] on me, they were like love taps even with batons. Now who knows? At the time the interpretation I made was that they had responded to our thing and they technically fulfilled what they had been asked to do but they were trying not to hurt us.[59]

The confrontation continued late into the night. Some protesters advocated an all-out confrontation. Others, like Green Beret veteran Gary Rader, explained his antiwar sentiments to the troops in a rare moment of direct, personal communication between the two sides. Finally,

Around midnight things quieted down. It was a crisp, clear fall night; the sky was filled with stars. People huddled under blankets in their little affinity groups. There was [Sidney Peck recalls] a "sense of quietness." Then someone began to sing. The song that she chose was not a rousing anti-war chant, or a mournful folk paean to brotherhood and peace, but the old Christmas hymn, "Silent Night." It was, says Peck, "a moment I will never forget. Before you knew it, it was picked up by everyone. It was truly a moment of religious awe. We had a tremendous feeling that what we were doing was a good thing, it was the right thing to do, and it was a profound expression of ending the killing and restoring the peace."[60]

Not surprisingly, the administration responded to the massive confrontation by blaming the antiwar demonstration for delaying successful peace negotiations with Hanoi. President Johnson, now a captive in the White House, asserted that peace would come sooner "if the American people were united rather than divided"—an increasingly effective tactic of isolating the antiwar movement from the mainstream of public opinion. Right-wing critics of the administration, like Congressman Gerald Ford, went further, claiming preposterously that Hanoi not only applauded the Pentagon march but had actually organized it. The administration also stepped up surveillance and subversion of the peace movement in a strategy later escalated by the Nixon administration.

Shortly before the end of 1967, an increasingly disenchanted and beleaguered Robert McNamara resigned as secretary of defense, urging the president to halt the ineffective bombing of North Vietnam and announce that no additional U.S. troops would be deployed. In the months before his departure, McNamara had ordered the systematic study of U.S. policies in Vietnam, setting in motion the document that became known as the Pentagon Papers.

The Pivotal Year, 1968: In William O'Neill's account of the Sixties, 1968 was "The Hard Year,"[61] the year of violent assassinations, campus take-overs, the Democratic convention in Chicago, and crushed hopes for electoral change. It was also a crucial turning point for American policy in Vietnam and the war at home. In Zaroulis and Sullivan's characterization, "Nineteen sixty-eight was the fulcrum year, the year the balance scales tipped against the American effort in Vietnam. It was a year in which events happened so quickly, hammer blow after hammer blow, that in retrospect it seems astonishing that the national psyche survived intact. Perhaps it did not."[62]

On January 21, North Vietnamese units placed the Marine combat base at Khe Sanh under a continuous and bloody siege that would ultimately last until April 14.[63] Ten days later, with American forces diverted to defend Khe Sanh, Vietcong guerrillas undertook a massive, simultaneous assault across South Vietnam, attacking five of the six major cities, thirty-six of forty-four provincial capitals, sixty-four district capitals, some fifty hamlets, and several airfields and munition dumps. They temporarily overran the U.S. embassy in Saigon and occupied the ancient capitol city of Hue with brutal force.

The Tet Offensive was a calculated gamble by the Vietcong and Hanoi that a massive ground assault, which they knew would be costly, would convince Americans that they could not be ground down. Despite U.S. claims of military victory,[64] the real casualty of Tet was the administration's credibility, which was effectively destroyed for the vast majority of Americans. As Zaroulis and Sullivan observe, "Americans had their most terrifying glimpse to date of how far from reality were the official reports on the progress of the war."[65]

One result of the television coverage of the bloodshed was an administration attack, maintained to this day, against the media for misrepresenting Tet as a defeat for the United States. This accusation misses the point, for most Americans didn't see Tet as a defeat of U.S. troops, but rather an unbelievable demonstration of Vietcong and North Vietnamese determination and staying power.[66] Through televised accounts, Americans witnessed the lie in the administration's constant claims about wearing down the enemy and proverbial promises of "light at the end of the tunnel." As critic Loren Baritz observed,

"America was never to recover from this victory."[67] From Tet onward, it became clear to most Americans that the goal of U.S. policy had to be extraction from Vietnam.

Much of the rest of 1968 revolved around the race for President: McCarthy's surprising near-victory in New Hampshire, Robert Kennedy's controversial announcement of his candidacy a week later, President Johnson's stunning announcement that he was withdrawing from the race, the entry of Hubert Humphrey and his forced "politics of joy," the Kennedy–McCarthy competition in Oregon and California, Robert Kennedy's assassination at the end of the victorious California campaign, and of course Chicago.

For the most part, the presidential race absorbed the energies and attention of the antiwar movement. The mass media paraded stories about peace negotiations, violence in the cities, and campus protests across the public's vision. Activists of all movements, but especially the black youth of America's cities, were devastated by the murder of Martin Luther King, Jr., on April 4, four days after President Johnson's withdrawal from the presidential race. Less than three weeks later, the local chapter of SDS seized and occupied the administration buildings and library of Columbia University, ushering in the most violent period in the history of American higher education. As Zaroulis and Sullivan recall, "The bitterness and violence at Columbia were in accord with the year itself. Everything had gone sour—the war, the campuses, the civil rights struggle, the war on poverty."[68] That same week the musical *Hair* opened, romanticizing the escapist Age of Aquarius.

Nonetheless, spring brought another round of mass actions against the war. On April 26, in the midst of the Columbia takeover, one million students, including some two hundred thousand in the city colleges and high schools of New York, engaged in the first national student strike since the 1930s. Thousands of students demonstrated in Japan, France, Germany, Denmark, Canada, Mexico, and Czechoslovakia, the last then in the midst of the Prague Spring. On the 27th, massive demonstrations took place across the United States. Two hundred thousand gathered in New York's Central Park to hear Martin Luther King's widow, Coretta Scott King, carry forward her slain husband's commitment to the antiwar movement.

The Democratic presidential convention scheduled for Chicago became the focal point for antiwar planning and debate. Activists like David Dellinger, Rennie Davis, Tom Hayden, Carl Oglesby, Sidney Peck, Robert Greenblatt, and Ron Young met to plan for Chicago amidst talk of massive confrontation and attack on the Democratic convention on the one hand, and fears that widespread violence would alienate mainstream antiwar sentiment on the other. Amidst the unprecedented build-up of police, National Guard, and other security forces, thousands of liberal activists and traditional peace groups stayed away from Chicago. Ideologically radical groups like the Socialist Workers party refused to participate in an illegal action, especially one that symbolically legitimized the Democratic party. The Yippies announced plans to nominate Pigasus, a pig, for President.

Violence, chaos, and countercultural inanity all occurred, and the Chicago police lost all restraint. Images of the convention remain stuck in the memories of all who witnessed them. As Todd Gitlin observes of television audiences, "Viewers drew wildly different conclusions from the Chicago coverage: antiwar and movement sympathizers were everlastingly horrified by police violence, while the Right accused the networks of bias and rallied to the side of the police."[69]

For many in the antiwar movement, Chicago was a radicalizing watershed. As Kirkpatrick Sale argues,

> Because it was televised, because it occasioned the unmuzzled brutality of the Chicago police, because it displayed the bankruptcy of American liberalism, and because it exposed once again the decrepitude of the American two-party system, the Democratic National Convention in August was one of the most propelling and influential events of the sixties, becoming very quickly the symbolic watershed for the end of the resistance period. . . .
>
> Chicago proved once and for all, for those still needing proof, that the country could not be educated or reformed out of its pernicious system, even by establishmentarian reformers like [Eugene] McCarthy. It showed that even resistance, open and defiant resistance, was not enough to wrest changes, for the institutions of American society, grounded in violence, would use violence in their own defense when the threat was regarded as serious enough.[70]

The antiwar movement was seemingly stuck. The electoral process was a dead end; the 1968 election provided a choice between incumbent Vice-president Humphrey, who symbolized more of the same, and the resilient Richard Nixon, whom most in the Movement had learned to mistrust if not hate in the Fifties and early Sixties. Third-party efforts appeared doomed.

Advocates of nonviolence had to withstand a police assault, much as the civil rights movement had to do when it tried to expand to the northern cities. Some fought back, but it was becoming clear that increasing violence in the movement would isolate it from a base of mass support among troubled Americans of all ideologies. It was tempting to throw up one's hands in despair.

It remained for Richard Nixon to assume the presidency of a deeply fractured America. Nixon's presidency was noteworthy for its conscious effort to manipulate the polarization of the American people.[71]

■ Nixon's War and the End of the Sixties

> It all seemed so senseless. We'd kill and they'd kill and it didn't mean anything.
> —Tom Hagel, Vietnam veteran, in MacPherson, *Long Time Passing*

The years from Richard Nixon's election through the final withdrawal of U.S. troops in 1973 and Nixon's resignation in 1974 marked the third and final phase of the Sixties era. It was characterized by three significant developments: the war in Vietnam took on the peculiar signature of the Richard Nixon–Henry Kissinger team; the antiwar movement expanded, became more divided, and eventually lost its momentum; and many Sixties activists began to focus on issues closer to home.

Each of these developments was paradoxical. First, Nixon "ended" the war in Vietnam. In the process however he greatly intensified the war, unleashing massive suffering among civilian populations in North Vietnam, Laos, and Cambodia. He engaged in a massive deception of the American people that encompassed not only the peace movement, but the "silent majority," Vietnam veterans, and even his Republican colleagues in the Congress. Finally, despite campaigning on the promise of a secret plan to achieve peace, Nixon extended the war for more than four years, resulting in more than 20,000 additional American deaths.

Second, although the electoral dead end of 1968 was an emotional blow to the antiwar movement, the Nixon years saw some of the most remarkable antiwar actions of the entire Vietnam period. A nascent G.I. antiwar movement took off in October 1968, following a march and rally in San Francisco. The Vietnam Moratorium Days of October and November 1969 were by far the largest nationwide antiwar actions ever. Millions of Americans confronted the war not only in a huge Washington demonstration, but in rallies, vigils, poetry readings, religious services, and funerals in local communities across the nation. Similarly, the aftermath of the Cambodian incursion and the Kent State killings in 1970 disrupted more college campuses than any earlier protest activities.

Finally, as the movements of the Sixties came to a frustrating and seemingly impotent end, and mainstream American politics swung to the right, the evolution of Sixties activism was greatly influenced by the personal politics implicit in its prefigurative side. The women's movement had emerged and environmental consciousness began to stir during the Sixties, yet both were largely obscured by the heat of civil rights and Vietnam. In the Seventies, both movements came to the fore, partly because they spoke to compelling concerns of millions of Americans, and partly because they offered new and more personally achievable avenues for change.

The Nixon Touch: As a Republican with secure red-baiting credentials, Nixon theoretically had an opportunity to end the war when he assumed office. In actuality, the election period revealed the distinctive Nixon–Kissinger touch. In the late stages of the 1968 election campaign, President Johnson telephoned both candidates to inform them that secret peace talks were taking place in Paris and that a settlement might result. Since peace was the one event that might deny Nixon the election, the final weeks of the campaign were marked by a sordid trail of deceit and maneuvering by the Nixon–Kissinger team to avoid a last-minute settlement that might hand Hubert Humphrey the presidency.[72]

Perhaps the primary distinction of Nixon–Kissinger policy in Vietnam was the shift from a war of attrition, in which the goal was to wear down the adversary by killing enough of them, to a war that might be ended sooner with more massive and dramatic killing. The Nixon–Kissinger team saw Vietnam as an albatross that obstructed their larger foreign policy objectives, especially those involving détente with the Soviet Union and China. Their goal, quite simply, was to end the war by whatever means it took (short of withdrawal) as long as these were not so visible and offensive that they destroyed any semblance of public support.[73] Hence, the plan that emerged involved four strategies: pressure on the Soviet Union to influence North Vietnam; use of "madman" behavior that suggested to Hanoi that Nixon was capable of doing anything to get his way; a "better" offer to North Vietnam than the Johnson administration had given them; and Vietnamization, the gradual replacement of U.S. troops with Vietnamese troops.[74]

The secret plan failed to achieve peace within the promised year. It also included the infamous secret bombing of Cambodia and Laos, the invasion of Cambodia in violation of congressional limits, the mining of Haiphong harbor, and several waves of massive bombing in North Vietnam, the most barbarous of which was the so-called "Christmas bombing" of Hanoi and Haiphong ordered by an enraged Nixon. The latter failed to change the ultimate peace agreement, yet resulted in enormous destruction and civilian casualties in Hanoi, an incensed and recalcitrant North Vietnamese adversary in Paris, additional U.S. casualties, a new wave of U.S. prisoners of war, damage to détente, and worldwide condemnation of the United States.

The domestic battlefield during the Nixon years was a bewildering vista of contradictory tensions. The war gradually wound down as troops were withdrawn and draft calls reduced. Yet examples of overt deceit and manipulation repeatedly surfaced, and government repression increased dramatically. Antiwar actions grew more desperate. In May 1969, the "Catonsville 9," a group of radical Catholics, burned draft files in Catonsville, Maryland with homemade napalm. In October, timed to dramatize government repression in the Chicago Eight trial, the Weathermen held the "Days of Rage" in Chicago—an outburst of street violence by the Weathermen, the "Crazies," "Youth Against Fascism," and "Mad Dogs."

In November 1969, in the midst of the Vietnam Moratorium Day demonstrations, and at a time when the majority of Americans were antiwar, Nixon gave his infamous "silent majority" speech in which he portrayed the antiwar movement as a minority trying to impose its will and threaten the nation's "future as a free society." "North Vietnam cannot defeat or humiliate the United States. Only Americans can do that. . . . [I appeal] to you, the great silent majority of my fellow Americans—I ask for your support."[75]

Nixon's divide-and-rule strategy was applied to the antiwar movement itself. In the early days of his administration he authorized what became a massive campaign of surveillance, harassment, and provocation of the antiwar movement. Subsequent investigations showed that many of the more violent outbursts in antiwar demonstrations were actually instigated by government provocateurs. The goal of these actions was clear—to further fragment the antiwar movement and to isolate it from mainstream public opinion. These techniques were not new; however, Nixon intensified the level of illegal sur-veillance and tried to bring all domestic intelligence into the centralized con-trol of the White House through the aborted Huston Plan, an initial step toward a police state.[76] The Movement haunted the minds of Nixon and Kissinger even as they ignored public opinion against the war.

The Broadening Movement: At times when it seemed as if the war could not be more devastating, news of atrocities or a new round of escalation dealt the antiwar movement a fresh emotional blow. Each time, thousands took to the street in protest, each an example of what George Katsiaficas calls the *"eros* effect."[77] In November 1969, Seymour Hersh's exposé of the My Lai massacre that had occurred twenty months earlier caught the attention of the mass media. The grim story of the search and destroy mission that seem-ingly went haywire shocked the public and reverberated for years afterward. As described by Neil Sheehan,

> Some of the troops refused to participate in the massacre; their refusal did not restrain some of their fellows. The American soldiers and junior offi-cers shot old men, women, boys, girls, and babies. One soldier missed a baby lying on the ground twice with a .45 pistol as his comrades laughed at his marksmanship. He stood over the child and fired a third time. The soldiers beat women with rifle butts and raped some and sodomized others before shooting them. They shot the water buffalos, the pigs, and the chickens. They threw the dead animals into the wells to poison the water. They tossed satchel charges into the bomb shelters under the houses. A lot of the inhabitants had fled into the shelters. Those who leaped out to escape the explosives were gunned down. All of the houses were put to the torch.[78]

My Lai was the most gruesome of the American atrocities to come to light during the war. It revealed the total dehumanization of American G.I.'s who "lost it" under the extreme stress of faceless combat. But it could also be seen as a metaphor for a war that systematically assaulted the people of Vietnam. Sheehan observed:

> Had [the American platoon] killed just as many over a larger area in a longer period of time and killed impersonally with bombs, shells, rockets, white phosphorus, and napalm, they would have been following the nor-

mal pattern of American military conduct. . . . Further brutalized by the cycle of meaningless violence that was Westmoreland's war of attrition, and full of hatred because his comrades were so often killed and wounded by mines and booby traps set by the local guerrillas and the peasants who helped them, [the soldier] naturally came to see all Vietnamese of the countryside as vermin to be exterminated. The massacre . . . was inevitable.[79]

The impact of a constant barrage of gruesome news about the war was inflamed by perceptions of an administration single-minded in its desire to save face, remorselessly manipulative of the American public, and eager to crush dissent. Increasing numbers of antiwar activists were radicalized, and the antiwar movement spread into sectors of the population that had been less vociferous in the past. During the summer of 1970, the National Chicano Moratorium held a march in Los Angeles attended by some 25,000 marchers and innumerable onlookers. The state legislatures of Massachusetts and Wisconsin passed bills challenging the federal government's right to send their citizens to fight in an undeclared war. Four labor councils representing hundreds of thousands of workers in northern California rebuffed the prowar position of AFL-CIO President George Meany and endorsed the massive 1971 demonstration in San Francisco. Even FBI and CIA personnel engaged in antiwar activity around the time of the 1971 protest. The voters in Madison, Wisconsin voted two-to-one for a resolution calling for immediate withdrawal, while a Harris poll showed that 60 percent of the public favored withdrawal from Vietnam "even if the government in South Vietnam collapsed." A series of demonstrations were held around the country on April 15, 1970; at the largest of these, nearly 100,000 gathered on the Boston Common. Subsequently a spin-off group of "plate glass revolutionaries" trashed the storefronts in Harvard Square.

Meanwhile, G.I.'s themselves had become more outspoken against the war. One effect of the Nixon plan of Vietnamization was the total demoralization of those troops unfortunate enough to serve in Vietnam from 1969 to 1973. As reporter Neil Sheehan described it,

[The U.S. Army of 1969] was an Army in which men escaped into marijuana and heroin and other men died because their comrades were "stoned" on these drugs that profited the Chinese traffickers and the Saigon generals. It was an Army whose units in the field were on the edge of mutiny, whose soldiers rebelled against the senselessness of their sacrifice by assassinating officers and noncoms in "accidental" shootings and "fraggings" with grenades.[80]

It was already demoralizing to battle against an unseen enemy for territory that was quickly seized and just as quickly abandoned. It became intolerable when a strategy of troop withdrawal deprived the troops of any plausible purpose for engaging in combat.[81] The newly organized Vietnam Veterans Against the War took their message to Congress and participated in national demonstrations. In the days preceding the massive April 1971 demonstration, the Vets engaged in mock search and destroy missions in Washington's streets, held a silent march past the White House, and turned in their medals at the Capitol steps. As Socialist Workers party leader Fred Halstead recalls, "We watched while about 600 Vietnam veterans filed by the steps. One by one they called out the names of buddies who had been killed and they flung at the base of the capitol medals and decorations they had been awarded for fighting in Vietnam. Some broke down and wept. Some hurled the decorations shouting curses at the government, their faces distorted with rage."[82] On April 11 and 14, the *New York Times* carried a full-page ad signed by forty-nine members of the First Air Cavalry Division, who declared, "We urge you to march for peace April 24. We'd do it ourselves but we're in Vietnam."

The Mass Protests: Despite the proliferation of antiwar factions during the Nixon years, the Movement managed to mobilize several massive demonstrations against the war during this time. On October 15, 1969, the liberal Moratorium Committee launched the first national Vietnam Moratorium Day of antiwar observations in communities across the nation. Millions of citizens in all walks of life participated in a variety of public observances.

In November, the Moratorium joined with the New Mobilization Committee to End the War in Vietnam (New Mobe) to sponsor a two-day interruption of normal activities. The New Mobe organized mass demonstrations in Washington, D.C. The weekend began with a somber March Against Death on Friday the fourteenth. Over 42,000 marched in single file past the White House, each carrying a candle and placard bearing the name of an American who had died in the war. As they passed the White House, they called out the names of the deceased. The march proceeded without a hitch for over forty hours. On Saturday, a mass march attracted unprecedented numbers to the Washington Monument. Activist Brad Lyttle recalled:

> The sky was overcast, the temperature about freezing. A chill, hard, unrelenting wind drove over the Mall from the northwest. . . . By about 8:30, people began to arrive in small groups. The wind abated. The sun broke out from behind purple clouds. By 9:30, people were flowing in from all sides, and I thought about 20,000 were there. By noon Pennsylvania Avenue was filled and the Monument area was two thirds full. Waves of marchers, many carrying banners that billowed and waved, were surging up from buses parked near the Potomac. . . . From then on, people poured in from every point on the compass. The entire grassy Mall and Monument area seemed overrun. All these people came in about six hours.[83]

It was the largest antiwar rally in U.S. history. The New Mobe estimated that 750,000 attended the Washington demonstration, while another 250,000 attended a rally in San Francisco. For his part, President Nixon stayed in a White House surrounded by two solid walls of buses, watching a football game. After the rally, a spin-off group eager to confront the government battled with police outside the Justice Department.

On April 30, 1970, President Nixon publically acknowledged what he had previously denied—that U.S. troops had invaded Cambodia, allegedly to destroy a major military headquarters of the North Vietnamese army. Much of the public saw the new strategy as another escalation of the war, justified as all others had been on the grounds of shortening the war. The response was instantaneous. Some 2,500 students and faculty at Princeton met and voted to strike. A New Haven protest called for a nationwide student strike based on three demands: immediate U.S. withdrawal from Southeast Asia, freedom for political prisoners, and an end to university complicity in the war. Students at Oberlin College took over the administration building, demanding a faculty meeting to discuss the invasion. Students at the University of California at Santa Barbara took over the university center and closed down Highway 101 for over an hour. A strike center was established at Brandeis University. By Monday, four days after Nixon's announcement, nearly one hundred campuses were on strike or planning for a strike.

Then lightning struck at the improbable location of Kent State University.

After the four students were slain, millions of television viewers watched in shocked silence as student protesters and bereaved parents of the slain students bitterly denounced the government. The student strike spread like wildfire. The nation

> came fully awake to the horror of both her foreign war and her war at home, and higher education—and much secondary and elementary education as well—came to a halt. . . . More than five hundred campuses canceled classes and fifty-one of them did not reopen at all that semester. Protest of some kind occurred at more than 50 percent of the nation's campuses; over four million students were involved. . . . [The Carnegie Commission report] stated that the Cambodia protests were without precedent, unparalleled by any previous crisis in the history of American education. Violence flared—arson, bombings, battles with police. Hundreds were arrested. In the week of the Kent State killings thirty ROTC buildings were destroyed by fire or bombs. The National Guard, heavily armed, was called out at twenty-one campuses.[84]

Long-time antiwar leader Norma Becker reflected, "Those two weeks were *the* high point of activism. I'm talking about the spontaneous upsurge *all over.* The schools closed down, junior highs, highs, colleges—everyone was in the streets protesting."[85] The student strike of spring 1970 was the largest strike action in American history. According to the President's Commission on Student Unrest, roughly 75 percent of all students supported the goals of the strike. George Katsiaficas notes that

> once the antiwar movement had won over the vast majority of students, the entire country became increasingly polarized and politicized, setting the stage for Watergate. At the same time as Nixon, Agnew, and Company were applauding the National Guard and making their "enemies list," a split developed in the nation's governing elite, a division which was originally revealed by the campus eruption of 1970. After the student strike, the split grew, extending beyond the university's establishment to include the media . . . and Congress in a power struggle against the executive and the military establishment.[86]

On February 10, 1971, a wave of demonstrations took place nationwide as word of a clandestine invasion and massive bombing leaked through a tight government news blackout. Yet movement divisiveness over goals and tactics, the understandable lack of a coherent ideological perspective on the war, an administration campaign of planned repression and harassment, and a state of growing psychological weariness were taking their toll on antiwar activists. Zaroulis and Sullivan note, "For the countervailing forces of public inertia and denial on the one hand and presidential cunning on the other stood ready to overwhelm a political audacity that could not demonstrate perceptible, steady increase: without mass, no momentum; without growth, decline." [87]

Nonetheless, the last great mass demonstrations of the war were held in spring 1971. On April 24, following the veterans' demonstrations, joint marches in Washington and San Francisco exceeded the record turnout of 1969. The breadth of antiwar sentiment was also unprecedented:

Almost every element of the American population had its representation. Present were older veterans of earlier wars, along with Vietnam vets and GIs. There was an all-Black contingent and a Third World section embracing Blacks, Latinos, Asian Americans, Iranians, and Palestinians, each bearing their own banners. There was also a group of left-Zionists. In the procession in addition were a delegation of Native Americans; religious groupings; students from scores of colleges; political parties and organizations; hundreds of local and regional antiwar committees and coalitions; pacifists, gays, lesbians; Women Strike for Peace, Another Mother for Peace; Women's International League for Peace and Freedom; the National Welfare Rights Organization; Business Executives Move for Peace; professional bodies of doctors, teachers, lawyers, and law and medical students; multitudes of government workers; a contingent of reservists and national guardsmen; high school students, handicapped people, and others.

All these groups carried banners against the war. [88]

Seven days later, the May Day Tribe, reflecting Rennie Davis's input, held the May Day actions designed to stop the government until it signed the "People's Peace Treaty." These included civil disobedience at the Pentagon and Justice Department, and mobile tactics aimed at stopping rush hour traffic. In all, about 12,000 were arrested. Few of the mass arrests held up in court, and the American Civil Liberties Union later won a $12 million damages ruling against the Justice Department.

On May 8, 1972, Nixon announced that the United States had undertaken the blockade and mining of Haiphong Harbor, Hanoi's primary outlet to the outside world. Although this was one of four actions long deemed too risky by administration planners, Nixon appealed for public support, noting, "It is you most of all that the world will be watching." The spontaneous national demonstrations that erupted were, in the words of the *New York Times*, "the most turbulent since May, 1970." Protesters abandoned cars on Chicago's expressways, tieing up traffic for hours. Three hundred chanting demonstrators caused the visitors' gallery of the House of Representatives to be closed. Some 300 students blocked the main highway into Boulder, Colorado all night. Five hundred protesters, including John Ward, vice-president of Amherst College, were arrested for blocking the entrance to nearby Westover Air Force Base. Twenty-five thousand marched through the rain in Minneapolis in one of several mass marches nationwide.

In December 1972, after Henry Kissinger had announced "peace is at hand" and Richard Nixon was re-elected, Nixon unleashed the infamous Christmas bombing of North Vietnam. As Fred Halstead described it, "In approximately ten days, 100,000 tons of bombs were dropped in these raids, the equivalent of five Hiroshima-type bombs. Hanoi and Haiphong had already been two-thirds evacuated, but the toll in human life was still severe. On December 26, for example, Kham Thien Street, one of Hanoi's major thoroughfares, was hit by B-52s. An Agence France-Presse dispatch from Hanoi reported that when clean-up squads got to the area, they found 1,445 bodies."[89] Protesters again took to the streets, although many felt too numb to respond. One recalled, "By that time it was just one blow after another after another and you just get numb and know you have to keep on working. You don't feel any particular surge of rage because it's spent. It was a kind of quiet dull horror—what are these people capable of? What next?"[90]

In these later years, Movement veterans felt battered; nothing seemed to work, and the frustration only fueled bitter strategy arguments. Their sense of acting morally was challenged by the violence that had come to be an inevitable presence at antiwar actions. Their sense of patriotism, of trying to make their country more noble, was assaulted by an administration that not only failed to listen to them but actively sought to turn the silent majority against them.

■ An Antiwar Legacy

The end of the war revealed what many in the antiwar movement had believed all along; that it was a war of horribly destructive futility. The peace terms signed in 1973 were not only practically identical to those informally agreed upon in 1972 prior to Nixon's Christmas bombing, but they approximated the original Vietminh objectives authenticated by the 1954 Geneva Conference accord. Had G.I.'s fought for nothing? Had America saved face? Had U.S. intervention prevented the dangerous dominoes from falling by demonstrating the costs of wars of national liberation? Would our government do it again? These questions were the burning residue of a struggle Americans quickly tried to forget.

The antiwar movement was obviously not without its flaws, its moments of mindless excess, its rage that turned to brutality, its periodic blindness to the suffering of American G.I.'s, and its internal divisiveness. Yet despite these shortcomings, and despite the fact that the war ground on and on seemingly impervious to antiwar sentiments, the antiwar movement so effectively charged the domestic political atmosphere that *it* became the problem for the Johnson and Nixon administrations bent on carrying out their policies. Given the incredible doggedness of the North Vietnamese and the National Liberation Front[91] that denied the United States a victory, the antiwar movement caused Lyndon Johnson to withdraw from the presidential race, and forever shifted the focus of the war to the quest for withdrawal. Thus the way was paved for an end to the war.

The struggle to end the war in Vietnam sharpened the critical edge of Sixties movements and raised their radical consciousness. Originally, the Movement was grounded on an insistence that politics must respond to morality, an instinctive sympathy for Vietnam's democratic right of self-determination, and an effort to empower the American people in the making of foreign policy. The war shattered the veil of government rhetoric and mythology. More than any other experience of the Sixties, it enabled many to see through the veneer of phrases like "defending freedom" or "fighting for democracy." It revealed an intransigent government bent on the pursuit of its policy objectives regardless of critics' appeal to moral principles. With all the bludgeoning force of a sledgehammer, the war drove home the era's hard lesson that American institutions were not compatible with this democratic vision. As Norman Birnbaum has observed, "The immediacy of Americans' immersion in an imperial society . . . compensated them for the lack of generations of radicalism."[92]

The antiwar movement left a legacy of activist opposition to American interventionism, and a public resistant to military involvement overseas, the so-called "Vietnam syndrome" anathema to recent administrations. Gabriel Kolko remarks that

> the antiwar constituency barred a return to the pre-1964 era of social passivity and naiveté, spilling over into all areas of American foreign policy opposition and creating a much larger base of committed and relatively experienced activists. In effect, the antiwar movement became a prepolitical force transforming attitudes and laying the foundation for a critical and cumulative political consciousness that in the 1960s was only in its earliest stage of development. . . . The political environment the war produced also created an imperative for a philosophy of action, imposing choices between collaboration and resistance to the war for many which evoked responses ranging from the holding of candles at vigils to sabotage. Without clear options, this amorphous, unprecedented movement existed because of the growing alienation of a significant sector of the public from the political goals of American imperialism and because of its unwillingness to accept the claims of successive administrations.[93]

Evidence of this legacy can be seen today in the myriad of activist organizations opposing American intervention in Central America and in the growth of a radical academic critique of American foreign policy.[94] This consciousness may be the basis of hope for a future without Vietnams. For a time, however, the antiwar experience was so harsh, so alienating, so full of defeats, that quite a few young people opted to drop out.

5

Retreating Inward
The Countercultural
Revolution

The society of alienation must disappear from history. We are
inventing a new and original world. Imagination is
seizing power.
—from a sign at the entrance to the Sorbonne, 1968

There's always a little bit of heaven in a disaster area.
—"Wavy Gravy," at the Woodstock Festival

Of all the phenomena of the Sixties, few were more
widely feared and loathed by mainstream America than the counterculture.
Longhairs, "mod" Edwardian costumes, public nudity, uninhibited sexuality,
passing the joint, flower children, shabby dress, dropping acid, the Love Generation, communes, rock festivals, Eastern mysticism, group marriage, street
theater, light shows, open form poetry, be-ins, underground papers, speed
freaks, bumming around the country, acid rock, free clinics, and cooperatives—all were manifestations of a distinct culture that emerged from the creative, prefigurative politics of the young and retreated from a violent American
society that seemed beyond redemption.

The counterculture celebrated its contradictions. Often bright, innocent,
tender, spontaneous, playful, joyful, spiritual, mystical, sensual, and full of
reverence, it could just as easily be dark, dirty, terrifying, mindless, self-
indulgent, lonely, mad, and hurtful. It throbbed with feeling; it anesthetized
feeling. It abhorred violence, yet it attracted violence. It rejected technology,
but its music depended upon electronics. Its rejection of politics was implicitly
political. It was both holy and satanic. It was Woodstock; it was Altamont.

The counterculture became both the most time-bound phenomenon of the
1960s and the most timeless and universal. It was one of the decade's most
radical counterpoints to mainstream America, but was easily coopted by that
mainstream. Although the counterculture faded into history, many of its atti-

tudes and values have been absorbed into American life. Noting this, Morris Dickstein has remarked, "In some respects our society will never be the same; in other ways it never really changed."[1]

The counterculture was also diverse. One major study of those attracted to Haight-Ashbury during the 1967 Summer of Love distinguished three types of participants: a psychotic or religious obsessive "fringe" (about 15 percent), true believers in the mystique of Haight-Ashbury as a model for the world (40 percent), and those "attracted by the no-hassle lifestyle of the dropout" (45 percent).[2] In an article on drug users, the psychologist Kenneth Keniston distinguished between "heads" who were thoroughly alienated from society and "seekers" who were "struggling to experience the world more intensely."[3] Chronologically, one can distinguish two waves of the counterculture: an early group of pioneers who weathered the political shockwaves of the early and mid-Sixties, and a later teenage wave attracted by the vision of freedom, community, and self-gratification.

The extreme, self-indulgent, and sometimes destructive behaviors exhibited by countercultural youth were and are an easy target for criticism, especially on the part of those eager to belittle the decade's significance. These behaviors were also vivid copy for the mass media who instinctively honed in on the strangest aberrations, thereby attracting countless drifters in search of "kicks" or something to give meaning to their lives.[4]

The most flagrant and bizarre manifestations of the counterculture stemmed from three qualities: the youth, inexperience, and immaturity of participants; its largely middle-class makeup; and a self-indulgent narcissism that itself mirrored the mainstream culture. At its most weird, the counterculture was, in Theodore Roszak's words, "A culture so radically disaffiliated from the mainstream assumptions of our society that it scarcely looks to many as a culture at all, but takes on the alarming appearance of a barbaric intrusion."[5] Or as Peter Marin declared, "They lack the resonance of cultural continuity or connection. Instead, they seem to pass among us like buffalo, like alien beasts; the reverse image of ourselves, strange weddings of the elements bred out of our lives and returned to haunt us with the irony of Greek tragedy."[6]

However, the counterculture was more than simply bizarre and self-indulgent. Roszak could also accurately describe it as "a remarkable defection from the long-standing tradition of skeptical, secular intellectuality which has served as the prime vehicle for three hundred years of scientific and technical work in the West."[7] It embodied what Herbert Marcuse termed the "great refusal," an opting out of the acquisitive and technocratic consumer culture of the industrial, capitalist world. Beneath its many manifestations the counterculture rejected much of postwar American life, its materialism, technocratic rationality, atomistic loneliness, repression of feeling, and fear of experimentation and personal growth. In its experimentation with hallucinogenic drugs and its embrace of Eastern mysticism and Zen Buddhism, the counterculture explored the inner, subjective world, while recoiling from an objective or outer world gone mad. In back-to-the-earth communes, American Indian rites, and belief in magic, the counterculture sought the primitive while fleeing the modern. In its quest for an inner light, for expressiveness, it reflected the sensibility of the artist rather than the engineer. In pursuit of sexual liberation, it rejected postponed gratification for immediate pleasure.

Through it all the counterculture explored a new epistemology, a way of knowing that lay outside traditional Western culture. For the most part, it was a gut rejection of society's instrumental rationality, its linear goal orientation, and above all its worship of objectified knowledge. Instead of dualistic, analytical thought, the counterculture was holistic. It perceived reality as interconnected rather than as isolated pieces or categories. It was integrative in that it sought to break down the barriers within the self and between the self and others. It focused on a person as inherently valuable rather than a person as agent in a world of instrumental or utilitarian reasoning. As a whole, the counterculture reversed the priorities of the old culture of scarcity which, in Philip Slater's characterization, tended to "choose property rights over personal rights, technological requirements over human needs, competition over cooperation, violence over sexuality, concentration over distribution, producers over consumers, means over ends, secrecy over openness, social forms over personal expression, striving over gratification, Oedipal love over communal love, and so on."[8]

■ The Roots and Evolution of the Counterculture

> In the past there were always some elders who knew more than any children
> in terms of their experience of having grown up within a culture system.
> Today there are none. . . . There are no elders who know what those who
> have been reared within the last twenty years know about the world into
> which they have been born.
> —Margaret Mead, *Youth Revolt: The Future Is Now*

In some of its manifestations, the counterculture shared a common vision with literary and intellectual traditions like the New England transcendentalists, the ecstatic poetry of William Blake and Walt Whitman, and nineteenth-century anarchism. As a mass generational phenomenon, however, it evolved more directly from an outlook profoundly alienated from the modern world of post–World War II America.

The foremost expression of that outlook in the United States, and the one with the most obvious parallels in the counterculture,[9] was that of the Beats—the mad "howl" of Allen Ginsberg, Jack Kerouac's existential vision of life "on the road," the political sensibility of Lawrence Ferlinghetti, and Gary Snyder's Zen Buddhism. Gathering in Greenwich Village and San Francisco, the beatniks (as they were labelled by the mainstream media) shared an alienation from the "insane demands" of America; they were drawn to the black culture of jazz and nightclubs, open-form poetry and coffee houses, experimentation with drugs and sex. Like Charlie Parker, Dylan Thomas, and Jackson Pollock, they celebrated creativity, believing, as poet Kenneth Rexroth observed, "Against the ruin of the world, there is only one defense—the creative act."[10] In raging against the American "Moloch" that destroys all that is holy, Ginsberg's vision is ultimately more apocalyptic than political.

Despite its many parallels with the Beats, the counterculture was different, a new generation's version of bohemianism. As Haight-Ashbury chronicler Charles Perry observes of the early hippies, "The Zeitgeist of the sixties avant-garde was markedly different from that of the fifties. The leading art form, the art to which all other arts aspired, had been abstract painting; now it was a sort of theater . . . an idea of uniting all arts into a performance."[11] The Beats' style and milieu were also different. Haight-Ashbury observer Leonard Wolf notes, "Beat was dark, silent, moody, lonely, sad—and its music was jazz. Hippie is bright, vivacious, ecstatic, crowd-loving, joyful—and its music is rock. Beat was the *Lonely Crowd*; hippie, the crowd tired of being lonely."[12]

The counterculture also reflected other symptoms of rebelliousness during the quiescent Fifties. The emergence of rock and roll music was perhaps the primary influence. The foremost bands of the 1960s "British invasion"—the Beatles and the Rolling Stones—were heavily influenced by Fifties rock and roll figures like Chuck Berry, while Bob Dylan followed in the footsteps of the folk underground of the Fifties. Together with rock and roll's driving, kinetic sound, the rebellious culture represented by Elvis Presley and film stars James Dean ("Rebel Without a Cause") and Marlon Brando ("The Wild

One") openly defied the prohibitions of adult society.[13] Finally, older teenagers and college students of the Fifties were exposed to the biting antiestablishment satire of Mort Sahl and Lenny Bruce, while their younger siblings were attracted to a new magazine, *Mad*, that exposed the absurd hypocrisy of everything from education and social manners to mass media, advertising, and politics. Popular books such as Joseph Heller's *Catch-22* and Kurt Vonnegut's *Cat's Cradle* and *Mother Night* captured the madness of a world in which "the arbitrary, the terrible, and the irrational have become *routinized*."[14]

John Kennedy's assassination was the first trauma that undermined young people's tentative connection with the social mainstream. The escalation of the Vietnam War confirmed this unease. By 1965, when the civil rights movement was driving toward culmination and the Vietnam War was beginning to escalate, the first clear signs of a counterculture were emerging in San Francisco, along with places like London, New York, Amsterdam, and Paris. As Charles Perry notes, "There was a strange feeling of desolation in the middle of all this activity. Maybe it was the persisting shock effect of President Kennedy's assassination or residual terror from the nuclear confrontation over Cuban missile emplacements. Whatever the reasons, it sometimes seemed that despite all the noise the party was over, and the world was settled, compartmentalized and devoid of high deeds and adventures."[15]

The counterculture was a direct extension of the expressive politics that had begun to emerge in the civil rights movement and New Left. In its own way, it carried on the four strains of the democratic vision of the Sixties: an implicit democratic faith in the intuitive wisdom of the people, the liberation and integration of repressed personality, a moral outlook that celebrated the person as sacred, and the quest for community.

The counterculture also blossomed because of young people's severe alienation from a technocratic culture "gone mad." In Vietnam, young people saw a system based on the "rational" (that is, functional) relationship among its separate parts as totally *irrational* when viewed as a whole. In their educational experiences, they found the goal-oriented extrinsic reward system to be a structure of control rather than a guide to learning. As the Movement encountered increasingly violent resistance and began to abandon its own emphasis on nonviolence, the counterculture became a refuge from instrumental politics of all kinds. It was first and foremost an expression of radical disassociation from society, comparable to the cultural nationalism of the black power movement. The young escaped by embracing those "irrational" elements that could not fit into society's rationality—the subjective, the mystical, the unconscious or intuitive.[16] Yet, at the same time that the counterculture retreated, all its trademarks came to permeate much of the political New Left.

Although consciously apolitical, the counterculture was implicitly democratic. The technocracy so visible in the Vietnam War reversed the order of democracy by elevating the allegedly objective knowledge of expertise over the people's intuitive wisdom. Experts are those who have privileged access to objective knowledge. By contrast, there are no experts in intuitive wisdom or experience. In rejecting the authority of expertise, the counterculture sought its polar opposite, the wisdom of subjective experience. As Steven Tipton put it,

> The counterculture ethic relies on an intuitive, affectively centered self-awareness, an empathic feeling for others, and a relaxed, nonanalytical attention to the present situation. "Be here now," it exhorts, "Get in touch with yourself." By contrast, the utilitarian's maximizing calculus and his technical reason are always aimed toward calculating future consequences. . . . The counterculture's cardinal virtue is sensitivity of feeling, not utilitarian efficiency or biblical obedience.[17]

From this perspective, the counterculture viewed the detached mainstream press as utterly lacking in imagination. Those who held power in society were seen as its most alienated members. Even the old Left was viewed as goal-oriented and capable of instrumental manipulation; there was "no place for dancing" in organized Marxism until "after the revolution." Rebelling against "uptight" adulthood, much of the counterculture celebrated childlike innocence. Symbolic gestures like placing flowers in the barrels of National Guard guns, or dancing through the ranks of ROTC cadets, expressed innocent play in the face of the forces of death.

This innocence extended to the counterculture's postscarcity stance toward money. Feeling assured that material needs could be met, and sharply alienated from a culture that revolved around the quest for ever more material comfort, middle-class young people groped their way toward higher ends.[18] They therefore rejected the monetary standard of value and the broader social ethic based on self-interest. The theme of free goods reverberated throughout the early counterculture: free food handouts by the Diggers in Haight-Ashbury, free concerts by rock groups like the Grateful Dead in San Francisco's Panhandle, free clinics, and recycled old clothing. As one of the early Diggers asserted, "Wherever you want to go everything revolves around profit and private property. Those are the premises and you can't question the logic. The logic is consistent. . . . But there's a passion for religious meaning, for spirituality that's just been squelched for so long: people are dying for spirituality. Me. I'm dying." [19]

From sexual experimentation to rock music, from drug use to holistic health, the counterculture also reflected efforts to discover aspects of the self denied in the objectified technocratic culture. Actual experimentation may have frequently relied on short-cuts to intimacy, mystical insight, or bodily intuition, but the *quest* for something missing remained at its core. Whereas technocracy and capitalism devalue the inherent, present meaning of personal experience, young people sought to live in the here and now. More basically they sought to enlarge their "capacity to experience: to know ourselves and others more deeply." [20]

Beneath the emphasis on personal discovery lay a basic optimism about people's capacity to grow and interact in a healthy manner once liberated from the repressions imposed by society. In singer Joni Mitchell's words, "Life is for learning." Nature, human and otherwise, is inherently good or benign. Echoing Rousseau, this outlook cherished the natural person and the simple environment with all its flaws. It viewed society's efforts to shape or master the natural as the primary cause of human alienation.

This perspective viewed mainstream culture as fundamentally fear-based and destructive. Writing in 1969, Peter Marin asked his fellow adults:

> Has there ever been a community of adults so conscious and envious of children—and so fearful of growth? We seem mired in guilt. The family, each adult life, which might at best be like a vessel, an adventure, is instead a fort established on a hostile plain—and the child is its natural enemy, for he brings to it all the energy (that wind of chaos) that threatens it with change. Say the same for schools. Anyone who has known [young people] intimately can sense their combined strength and fragility, a recurrent brittleness that stems from what is paradoxically an excessive exposure to culture and a dearth of participation. [21]

Or as the Beat poet Gary Snyder argued, "A law to work must have a hook into the social psyche—and the most effective way to achieve this is to make people doubt their natural worth and instincts, especially sexual." [22] In casting off society's bureaucratic regulations, sexual taboos, and impersonal masks, young people experienced exhilarating freedom from fear-induced conventionality.

Finally, the counterculture reverberated with the quest for community amidst the impersonal wasteland of the modern industrialized world. Objectivity is legitimized, claims historian Theodore Roszak, because society

> confuses the impersonality of scientific objectivity with the simple virtue of unselfishness. There is a sense in which both involve a denial of self; but the psychological mode is very different in each case. Objectivity involves a breaking off of personal contact between observer and observed; there is an act of psychic contraction back and away from what is studied for the sake of a sharp, undistracted focus. In contrast, moral unselfishness means to identify with the other, to reach out and embrace and feel with. Far from being a contraction of the self, here we have an expansion, a profoundly personal activity of the soul. [23]

The postwar, modern world fled by the young was experienced as a place of human beings increasingly separated from each other. As Philip Slater wrote,

> We seek a private house, a private means of transportation, a private garden, a private laundry, self-serviced stores, and do-it-yourself skills of every kind. An enormous technology seems to have set itself the task of making it unnecessary for one human being ever to ask anything of another in the course of going about his or her daily business. Even within the family Americans are unique in their feeling that each member should have a separate room, and even a separate telephone, television, and car, when economically possible. We seek more and more privacy, and feel more and more alienated and lonely when we get it. And what accidental contacts we do have seem more intrusive, not only because they're unsought, but because they're not connected with any familiar pattern of interdependence. [24]

Of course, mainstream capitalist culture fills this void through the fixation on the occupational treadmill and the "next rung on the ladder" or obscures it with anesthetics like alcohol, commercial drugs, and television.

In rejecting these, young people of the counterculture opened themselves to the full experience of the "lonely crowd." As a result, they persistently sought to integrate rather than separate, to fuse rather than polarize, to eliminate distances that separated people in functional relationships. As Jay Stevens wrote of Haight-Ashbury, "Everything was pooled—money, food, drugs, living arrangements. The underlying ethic was that the hippies were all members of an extended family, although the preferred word was *the tribe.*"[25] The Living Theater broke down traditional barriers between actors and audiences; the entire street scene in Haight-Ashbury from Ken Kesey's Acid Tests to the Diggers' embellishments of their free food was a form of participatory theater. The New Journalism and some of the more prominent Sixties literature resonated with personal reflection while relating its story. In the view of Haight-Ashbury social critic Chester Anderson, rock music became the "glue" of the new society, "erasing false categories of art, class, race, privatism, and the gap between audience and performer."[26] Huge rock festivals expressed the vision of unity, as performers and audience were fused in cathartic experience. LSD fed a holistic view of reality—"all is one."

Communal living was another current that ran through the youth movements of the Sixties, echoing the freedom houses of SNCC and urban collectives of SDS. For several years, the underground press provided an important communication network for the community called the Movement. The commitment to simple living, the move to the country, and the rising popularity of organic farming, natural healing and childbirth, and vegetarian and macrobiotic diets all reflected a need to break away from living in an unhealthy, packaged environment that anesthetized feeling.

The striving for community was no doubt intensified by young people's estrangement from mainstream culture and their sudden freedom from traditional structures. The pain of feeling betrayed by a culture turned violent, coupled with self-isolating lifestyles and the residues of hallucinogenic drug experiences, left the young with a sense of urgency, in some cases of desperation, for union with others.[27]

The counterculture pursued these ends in a way that was alienated from and alienating to the mainstream culture. Its rejection of instrumental politics was, in the end, responsible for its greatest failings. Uninformed by a sufficient political consciousness, it lapsed into a politics of style easily co-opted by the market society. Furthermore, rejecting politics and retreating into a world diametrically opposed to society's central values and conventions, the counterculture was often contemptuous of those who admonished it to be concerned about political impact. And finally, subjective feeling, communal living, sexual fusion, and an emphasis on personal and spiritual growth were often expressed in extremis, in a void, without their complements: empirical attention to objective reality, individual privacy, personal autonomy, and attention to the political and economic context of personal repression.

Disillusioned with repressive politics and the more violent forms of dissent, the counterculture retained the early New Left's refusal to elevate doctrine over human beings. Its answer, at least temporarily, was to flee politics. In its search for an alternative way of living, however, the counterculture became a place of experimentation that nurtured the transition to the Sixties' "new beginnings"—to the feminist and ecological critique of dualistic Western culture, the feminist emphasis on personal (including sexual) assertiveness, the human potential movement's focus on personal growth and interpersonal relations, and the ecological respect for nature and technological simplicity.

THE HAIGHT-ASHBURY SCENE

If you're going to San Francisco
Be sure to wear some flowers in your hair. . . .
All across the nation, such a strange vibration,
People in motion.
There's a whole generation, with a new explanation,
People in motion.
—John Phillips, "San Francisco (Be Sure to Wear Some Flowers in
Your Hair)"

Beginning in 1965, the diverse manifestations of the counterculture came together for a brief time in the Haight-Ashbury section of San Francisco, which was an attractive and inexpensive residential area not far from Golden Gate Park. In many respects, the Haight represented a countercultural microcosm. It anticipated the history of counterculture communities across the country.

During the two years prior to the infamous Summer of Love in 1967, the hippie community of the Bay area gravitated toward early community defining experiences like Ken Kesey's Acid Tests and the initial Trips Festival and early hangouts like the Blue Unicorn and the Psychedelic Shop. A sense of community self-consciousness grew, symbolically expressed in the "Prophecy of a Declaration of Independence":

When in the flow of human events it becomes necessary for the people
to cease to recognize the obsolete social patterns which had isolated man

from his consciousness and to create with the youthful energies of the world revolutionary communities to which the two-billion-year-old life process entitles them, a decent respect to the opinions of mankind should declare the causes which impel them to this creation.

We hold these experiences to be self-evident, that all is equal, that the creation endows us with certain inalienable rights, that among these are: the freedom of the body, the pursuit of joy, and the expansion of consciousness, and that to secure these rights, we the citizens of the earth declare our love and compassion for all conflicting hate-carrying men and women of the world.[28]

Above all else, young people were drawn to the dances, the emerging sound of Bay area bands, and accompanying psychedelia. One of the first new-style dances occurred on the evening of an antiwar march on the Oakland Army induction center. The dance bore no resemblance to teenage sock hops regularly held in places like the Cow Palace. Called "A Tribute to Dr. Strange," it was organized by a communal group who called themselves the Family Dog and starred two San Francisco bands, the Charlatans and Jefferson Airplane. Many of the musicians had evolved out of the early Sixties folk music environment.[29] The Charlatans had made their mark as an American response to the British sound, bedecked in mod Edwardian clothing. The Airplane drew their name from an irreverent invention of the Berkeley culture, legendary blues musician "Blind Thomas Jefferson Airplane." Perry describes the scene:

> Here was a rock and roll dance, featuring groups with weird names and MCed by the pothead's favorite DJ, dedicated to Dr. Strange. For a couple of hundred people it was something they'd been waiting for without realizing it.
>
> They came as if there might never be anything like it again. They were in Mod clothes, Victorian suits and granny gowns, Old West outfits, pirate costumes, free-form costumes. . . . Behind [the band called] the Great Society stood a poster showing an American eagle, clutching a bunch of bombs in one claw, labeled "Peace," and a bunch of dollar bills in the other, labeled "Freedom"; over the eagle's head was a banner that read, "Bad Taste."[30]

Word spread fast. The Family Dog held two more dances at Longshoreman's Hall, attracting visiting bands like the Lovin' Spoonful and the Mothers (later Mothers of Invention), while the avant-garde San Francisco Mime Troupe held a fundraising dance under the direction of Bill Graham in a loft it shared with the local SDS. The phenomenon of psychedelic dances was growing. Other bands emerged: Big Brother and the Holding Company, the Warlocks (soon to change their name to the Grateful Dead), and Quicksilver Messenger Service. Psychedelic posters, walls painted with pop art sound effects ("Poww!"), and a stoned gathering of dancers accompanied the loud music. Light shows, multi-colored lighting or visual images projected on screens, walls, or human bodies, were added, making the dances a multimedia happening. Before long, the dances became regular events, most commonly produced by either Bill Graham at the Fillmore or by Chet Helms' Family Dog at the Avalon Ballroom. Some enthusiasts could hear the new sound of rock music on FM radio where a few enterprising souls catered to the interests of the psychedelic subculture rather than playing the top-40 tunes of the AM airwaves.

In addition to the dances, rock bands, and light shows, the psychedelic culture began to permeate the Haight. Ken Kesey, the author of *One Flew Over the Cuckoo's Nest,* and his coterie of friends and hangers-on known as the Merry Pranksters went public with their LSD parties, issuing public invitations that asked, "Can You Pass the Acid Test?" Guests danced to the Grateful Dead or Kesey's musicians (playing simultaneously at opposite ends of the hall), helped themselves to prominently placed tubs of LSD-spiked punch, and milled around the floor in various states of consciousness. Perry writes of "the sea-floor riot of blinking electronic equipment, stoned people reeling around blowing whistles, counting their toes, looking for their lost minds in the Thunder Machine. Two electrified guitar bands were playing at cross-purposes; slides and swirls of color were being projected on the walls."[31] The ultimate Trips Festival was planned as a weekend-long happening featuring the usual dancing and acid test, as well as avant-garde theater by America Needs Indians, nude projections called Revelations produced by the Open Theater, a shopping bag of LSD manufactured by the infamous local chemist Augustus Owsley Stanley III (known simply as Owsley), and innumerable spontaneous events and electronic gadgets. The apocalyptic tone suggested that a revolutionary break in consciousness would result from the convergence of human celebration, rock music, and hallucinogenic drugs.

LSD became a staple of Haight life, but it wasn't always treated frivolously. Timothy Leary's *Psychedelic Review* emphasized careful preparation for an LSD experience to minimize the chance of "freaking out" and to maximize spiritual insight. Although based on Long Island, Leary became a kind of traveling salesman for the hallucinogenic experience and appeared frequently in the Haight. Religious rituals or spiritual pursuits were also highly visible, from solstice celebrations to Buddhist sects and Krishna groups, from followers of American Indian lore to those who used the *I Ching* or Tibetan prayer wheels.

Another group that made its mark was the anarchistic spin-off of the San Francisco Mime Troupe known as the Diggers, who were, in Jay Stevens' terms, the "conscience of the Haight." With more of a political conscious-ness than either the Pranksters or Leary, the Diggers rejected the "credit-card revolutionaries" of the Berkeley SDS and New Left and angrily railed against Haight-Ashbury's hip merchants for profiteering at the expense of the young hippies. Theirs was a "revolutionary alternative," a negation of the basic "profit, private property, and power" premises of mainstream culture. The Diggers operated a garage called the Free Frame of Reference and invited passersby to help themselves to clothes or household items, which were free, "because it's yours." They began daily free food handouts, drawing not only old-time panhandlers but the numbers of young people who were beginning to swell the Haight-Ashbury. In Peter Berg's words, they "assumed freedom," which meant, among other things, that they had little respect for merchants who didn't feel like donating food for the feeds. They burned money and held a Death of Money parade. Some of their stunts caught the media's attention, anticipating the subsequent media exploitation tactics of the Yippies.

Another Haight-Ashbury institution of note was the underground psyche-delic newspaper, the *Oracle*, which became a community voice for the psy-chedelic faction of San Francisco's counterculture and saw itself as "an attempt to create an open voice for those involved in a 'life of art.'" Sample articles focused on dialogues between the community and police, information about police busts, yoga and the psychedelic mind, and a panel discussion among Allen Ginsberg, Alan Watts, Gary Snyder, and Timothy Leary. In addition to information about Haight and Bay area events, the *Oracle* ran regular columns like the "Gossiping Guru" and the "Babbling Bodhisattva." One distinctive feature of its graphic art was the psychedelic design that subordinated sub-stance to form. Psychedelic posters that advertised dances, rock concerts, and local merchants became the primary visual art form of the Haight and the counterculture generally. The posters featured incongruous imagery that only made sense to those who were stoned, with cartoon figures like Mr. Zig-Zag of Zig-Zag smoking papers, and the roller-style block printing of Wes Wilson that emphasized design over content. Before long, posters were salvaged and collected as a form of people's art.

The first "Human Be-In," held in January 1967, was advertised as a gathering of the tribes—heads, anarchists, spiritualists, politicos—for music, speeches, poetry readings, and theatrical happenings. With so many people in such a rich variety of costumes and styles the gathering itself became the main event. People milled around or sat and watched others. Be-ins became a countercultural trademark, followed by more specialized events like chalk-ins for sidewalk art, clean-ins, and walk-ins to tie up automobile traffic on Haight Street.

The Be-ins were only one of many Haight-Ashbury happenings. Free rock concerts, free food, organized cleanups and street sweeping, the connecting institutions of FM radio and the *Oracle*, theater or rock performances donated as fund-raisers for those arrested in drug busts or Vietnam protests, the anarchy of styles, the common language—all gave some sense of unity to residents of the Haight. New institutions cropped up: small businesses like the Print Shop (which commissioned political posters) and a cafe aptly called the Drugstore (until police pressure caused the name to be changed to Drogstore). Happening House, a kind of alternative adult education center, offered courses in yoga, weaving, sitar, and natural childbirth while sponsoring be-ins and other activities in the community.

However, all was not joy and playfulness. Outbreaks of venereal disease and hepatitis and innumerable "bad trips" were evidence of the dark underside of casual sex and drug use. Two additional problems came from outside the Haight population, one of which was ultimately fatal. The mainstream culture's rising intolerance of the hippies' lifestyle posed the first threat. Ordinances were quickly passed in the state legislature outlawing LSD, and police harassment and drug arrests occurred daily.[32] Health inspections became more common in 1967, some for legitimate reasons, others as pure harassment that targeted publicly known groups like the Diggers. And finally, nudity and sexuality were arbitrary targets of censorship; the poet Lenore Kandel's collection *The Love Book* was seized as pornographic at the same time that topless and bottomless nightclubs were thriving in a tourist area of the city.

Success ultimately killed Haight-Ashbury. From the start, the mass media were drawn to the exotica of Haight, yet were incapable of communicating the meaning of the Haight to the rest of America, since their job was largely to distill and capture its essence in a few pithy sentences and graphic images. Some, like Timothy Leary, knew how to play the press's game, with press conferences and staged visual effects. For the most part, though, the Haight scene, and the counterculture generally, was ripe for media plucking. The freewheeling style of the Haight lent itself nicely to the imperatives of mass media. As Marty Balin of the Jefferson Airplane recalled, "I remember one time talking to a guy at *Time* magazine, when it was just hitting and Haight Street was like a tourist attraction and people were dressed in colorful costumes like you see at the Renaissance Fair. I told him, it's great you're publicizing this and telling people about all this spirit and everything that exists here. He looked at me and said, 'Fastest way to kill it.' He sure was right."[33] Hollywood soon got into the act with "Hallucination Generation," the first of a series of counterculture exploitation films.

With media attention came hordes of tourists. The Gray Line Bus Company instituted a "San Francisco Haight-Ashbury District 'Hippie-Hop' Tour" in April 1967, advertised as "the only foreign tour within the continental limits of the United States." Two-hour tours were offered with drivers "especially trained in the sociological significance" of the Haight and a "glossary of hippie terms" to help the uninitiated.

The integrity of the Haight experiment was more seriously threatened by the hordes of transient young people drawn by the media hype about the Haight scene, especially the so-called Summer of Love. Perry observes,

> When the press repeated these shallow gleanings [like "flower power"], the result was in effect an advertisement for the neighborhood, but not the kind that had been hoped for. The press advertised free love, free lunch in the Panhandle, tolerance for the crazy and the outcast, and a New Age governed by the power of love and innocence. So it brought in not only visionaries but insecure young people unable to find a place for themselves, dropouts content with the basics of life, outcasts and crazies, and—with the dissolution of the idea of bohemia—a sort of redneck bohemian indistinguishable from a wild kid attracted by the thrills of bohemia and its freedom from middle-class morality.[34]

The result was that by the Summer of Love in 1967, the Haight had changed. The second wave was in full sway. Not only did thousands of younger kids come to the Haight,[35] but the drug scene was changing. Speed was replacing LSD as a drug of choice for many (the acid itself was sometimes cut with speed or was eclipsed by more dangerous hallucinogens like STP). The *Oracle*'s Allen Cohen recalled the drug scene spreading from "creative people" to "the disenchanted, the disabled, the neurotics, the psychotic people who were too young or too scared, and had a lot of pain."[36]

The sense of community was fast disappearing, relying on the false illusion that anyone who took LSD was "on the same trip." In the Summer of Love,

> To live in Haight was to meet masses of people all the time, endless masses. . . . There were some real exotics in the throng these days. A fellow who wore a door knocker strung around his neck and wouldn't speak to you unless you knocked first. Another who wore a poncho with one of his arms sticking out of one sleeve and a plastic baby doll's arm sticking out of the other. As the Straight Theater built its dance floor, it had given away the old theater seats as it tore them out. Most had gone to furnish the vans that many people were living in, but the Psychedelic Shop took two and mounted them in its front window so you could sit and watch the passing parade on Haight Street.[37]

As the numbers of young transients grew, darker forces were drawn to the Haight. Entrepreneurs fed on the naiveté and money of the middle-class young, while corporate money moved into the rock scene, promoting the big star system and filtering out much of its raw energy. Free rock concerts were banned in the Panhandle. The mob allegedly dumped heroin on the Haight in an effort to regain control of the drug trade. Vicious criminals and satanic cults were in evidence; the body of a highly visible drug dealer, Superspade, was found mutilated. As Ed Sanders wrote of the counterculture, "there was a weakness: from the standpoint of vulnerability the flower movement was like a valley of thousands of plump white rabbits surrounded by wounded coyotes."[38] Although it didn't occur until two years later, the Charles Manson phenomenon had become possible. In October 1967, a collective Death of Hippie ceremony was held, complete with an oversized coffin, pallbearers, and a parade through the neighborhood streets—a ritual of public mourning for the distortion of original hippie values.

As the Haight became more crowded and the urban hassles grew, many of the early pioneers left for rural communes like the Diggers' Morning Star Ranch. Anticipating a trend that spread throughout the counterculture, Haight emigres sought to "get together," as the Youngbloods' song title put it, to return to the soil. The Haight-Ashbury experiment gradually subsided, endured a heroin epidemic in 1969, rallied to prevent urban redevelopment, and left behind a few lasting institutions like the Free Clinic.

Although Haight-Ashbury was a singular countercultural community with its own peculiar history, it reflected or anticipated countercultural strains that also emerged in major cities like New York and Chicago, countless university-linked communities like Cambridge and Ann Arbor, and countercultural magnets like the Big Sur coast of California, the Colorado Rockies, and communities of northern New England. No other identifiable phenomenon of the counterculture, including Woodstock and People's Park, so fully captured the many diverse manifestations of the counterculture.

PEOPLE'S PARK

While Haight-Ashbury was the heart of the countercultural scene in the Bay area, across the bay in Berkeley the youth culture remained more self-consciously political. Still, the counterculture's influence was plainly visible by 1969. Berkeley's Telegraph Avenue had become an area of cafes, bookstores, and moviehouses that Todd Gitlin has suggested "prefigure[d] a society in which the arts and crafts would flourish, and people would sip cappuccino in the morning, criticize in the afternoon, smoke dope and make love at night."[39]

The history of police clashes, the spreading influence of the counterculture, and the growth of community institutions like the Berkeley *Barb* all contributed to a sense of a community besieged by hostile external forces. Writing in July 1968, Berkeley veteran Michael Rossman characterized Berkeley as a kind of "youth ghetto" needing to "liberate territory" for the "life-functions of community and culture."[40] In 1969, vacant land that officially belonged to the University of California was "liberated" by a number of "Telegraph Avenue revolutionaries" who "simply moved onto the land, to use and defend it in the spirit, they said, of the Costanoan Indians who had owned the land before Spanish missionaries, Mexican troops, American settlers, the U.S. government, and the University of California in turn had expropriated it."[41] The squatters claimed that the land had not been put to good use by the University, which had condemned and cleared housing in the area, leaving a large abandoned tract. They began to convert the land into a usable community park. The larger Berkeley community was soon caught up in the project:

Within days hundreds of people were working in this improvised utopia. Work was joy, not a job. Local longhairs tamped down the sod next to students, housewives, neighbors, parents. Fraternity boys mixed with freaks; professors shopped for shrubs, graduate students in landscape architecture came by to propose designs. On weekends up to three thousand people a day came to carry sod, to plant, to install swings, slides, a wading pool and a sandbox, to cook and eat huge vats of stew and soup, to drink and to smoke marijuana, to play; someone made seven-foot-high letters spelling K N O W, straight out of *Yellow Submarine*.[42]

Inspired by the spirit of building an alternative communal space, some believed the university would not contest the park; others anticipated yet another clash. There is no evidence that anyone in the community had anticipated what occurred in the aftermath of May 15, 1969, when police sealed off the surrounding area, bulldozed the shrubs and gardens, and erected an eight-foot fence around the park. A crowd of several thousand students and community people moved from a rally on the Berkeley campus toward the fenced-in park. Along the way, a Bank of America window was smashed and a fire hydrant opened. A special unit of the Alameda County sheriff's deputies, armed with shotguns, met the approaching crowd. To participants' utter disbelief, the police opened fire, and continued to blast fleeing demonstrators, bystanders, and reporters with buckshot for several hours. One visitor to Berkeley, James Rector, was killed. Dozens of demonstrators were wounded, and one was blinded.

The park area came under martial law, policed by National Guardsmen with bayonets drawn; it became the first largely white community of the decade to be militarily occupied. Skirmishes continued for over two weeks as community residents tried to create new parks, leafleted, and demonstrated their outrage.[43] At one point, a helicopter blanketed a trapped campus demonstration with tear gas; at another, hundreds of demonstrators were herded into a parking lot and arrested en masse. The community's fear was palpable.

In the end, People's Park brought the metaphor of Vietnam home to the Berkeley community. Some were moved to call for armed rebellion. A group of Bay Area radicals issued a "Berkeley Liberation Program" that enumerated a thirteen-point struggle, including not only a confrontational challenge to free the Telegraph Avenue area but a call for liberated community education, a revolutionary culture free from "puritanical restraints" and the destruction of nature, the full liberation of women, protection and expansion of the drug culture, and a "soulful socialism"—in effect a perfect prop for Governor Ronald Reagan's escalating rhetoric.[44]

Others, drained and horrified by the brutality, sought refuge away from bitter struggles with the power structure. Ironically, People's Park, the very action that had brought together radicals and hippies, polarized them further, with considerable help from Governor Reagan and the police.

■ Hallmarks of the Counterculture

Something is happening here
And you don't know what it is.
Do you, Mr. Jones?
—Bob Dylan, "Ballad of a Thin Man"

The countercultural quest for spiritual connection, bodily awareness, personal growth, intimacy, and community erupted in many corners of life: academic study, literature, graphic and visual arts, theater and poetry, music, the social sciences, journalism, religious institutions, health and medicine, farming and nutrition, small business, local politics, and even, in distorted form, in the corporate world and the mass media. For a brief time, the repressed underside of American culture burst to the surface.

In all its diverse manifestations, the counterculture consisted of five related phenomena that, to varying degrees, were pervasive in the experience of growing up in the latter 1960s and early 1970s: rock music, drug use and religious mysticism, sexual experimentation, underground journalism, and communal living and flight to the country. Although closely interrelated, each reflects a distinct piece of the countercultural quest.

THE ROCK "REVOLUTION"

They must think that song can make a revolution. . . . I wish it could.
—Mick Jagger, in Mitchell Goodman, *The Movement Toward a New America*

The rock music of the mid-1960s to early 1970s enjoyed such a central place in the counterculture that it has been the subject of considerable hyperbole. Morris Dickstein has asserted, "Rock was the organized religion of the sixties—the nexus not only of music and language but also of dance, sex, and dope, which all came together into a single ritual of self-expression and spiritual tripping."[45] Because the various signposts of the counterculture came together in the dominant presence of rock music, rock became a kind of focal point for an apocalyptic vision.[46] More important, rock reflected and expressed the subjective impulses that permeated the counterculture. It also fused contending factions of the youth culture in the late Sixties; it became the common language of the young regardless of whether they were inclined to protest in the streets, drop out, work quietly within the system, or fight in Vietnam.

In part, the universality of rock can be traced to its fusion of musical antecedents. Rock music of the middle to late Sixties evolved from two sources: the rock and roll craze of the Fifties and the folk revival of the early Sixties. Those who were in their late teens and twenties around 1965 were likely to have been caught up in the Fifties rock and roll music of black musicians like Chuck Berry, Little Richard, and numerous rhythm and blues groups, to say nothing of white musicians like Elvis Presley, Jerry Lee Lewis, Bill Haley, Buddy Holly, and the Everly Brothers. The rock and roll phenomenon itself represented a merging of such traditional strains as black blues, jazz, gospel, and white country music.

The other source of rock music was the folk revival that emanated from the Gaslight and other clubs of Greenwich Village, as well as such outposts as Club 47 in the Cambridge–Boston area, the Gilded Cage in Philadelphia, and the "hungry i" in San Francisco at the beginning of the decade. Reflecting its roots in traditional folk music—protest songs from the labor movement and antiwar tradition, ballads, and folk-blues—the folk revival shared the critical, alienated vision of the Beat movement. Following in the steps of Woody Guthrie, Jack Elliott, and Pete Seeger and the Weavers, a new generation of folk performers emerged. Some like the Kingston Trio; Peter, Paul and Mary; the Limelighters; and the Chad Mitchell Trio were smooth and commercially successful in the early years. Others labored, at least for a while, in the relative obscurity of coffeehouses and the Newport Folk Festival; among these were Bob Dylan, Phil Ochs, Tom Paxton, Tim Buckley, Tim Hardin, Dave Van Ronk, Oscar Brand, Tom Lehrer, Joan Baez, Richie Havens, Odetta, Eric Von Schmidt, Tom Rush, Judy Collins, Richard and Mimi Fariña, John Sebastian, and Eric Andersen. Their message was a combination of traditional folk—with its strain of authentic, down-and-out alienation—and a new political consciousness tuned to the civil rights movement, the arms race, and repressive social mores.

At the beginning of the decade, the folk revival remained fairly autonomous. The acoustic sound occasionally made it big; by 1962, Peter, Paul, and
Mary had made gold records of Dylan's "Blowin' in the Wind" and Seeger's
"Where Have all the Flowers Gone," while Joan Baez had appeared on the
cover of *Time* magazine. Meanwhile, American rock and roll atrophied. Elvis
was drafted, Chuck Berry was arrested under the Mann Act, Jerry Lee Lewis
and Bill Haley were squeezed from the airwaves; Chuck Willis, Buddy Holly,
the Big Bopper, and Richie Valens all died in accidents. The top-40 stations
were immersed in a seemingly endless string of "teeny-bopper" artists and teen
romance songs.

Two events stimulated the wave of popular music that came to be known
simply as rock. The first of these was the "British invasion" led by the Beatles,
the Rolling Stones, and a variety of other groups like the Kinks, the Yardbirds,
the Animals, and eventually the Who. Bypassing the more tepid rock and roll
imitations, the British groups reached back to the blues roots of rock and roll
and figures like Chuck Berry. Together with a kind of working-class stance and
each group's distinctive signature—the Beatles' path-breaking chord combi-
nations and harmonies, the Rolling Stones' swaggering alienation—the result
was a burst of new energy in popular music.

The other event was the fusion of folk and rock music in 1965, symbolized
most dramatically by Dylan's "going electric" at the Newport Folk Festival.[47]
That same year, the folk–rock sound emerged. The Los Angeles–based band
the Byrds fused the socio-political lyrics of the folk tradition ("Turn, Turn,
Turn," "Mr. Tambourine Man") with Beatle-like harmonizing and electric
instruments. Explicitly political songs like Barry McGuire's "The Eve of Destruction" typified the fusion of political sensibility and rock music, and anticipated Buffalo Springfield's "For What it's Worth" and the music of Crosby,
Stills, Nash, and Young. About the same time as the escalation of American
involvement in Vietnam, the racial confrontation at Selma, and the Watts
riot, rock music began to reflect deeper, darker forces in society. The Beatles
released their "Rubber Soul" album, the Rolling Stones' 1965 hits expressed
an anti-commercial tone—"(I Can't Get No) Satisfaction" and "Get off my
Cloud"—while Bob Dylan began to embrace a new freedom rooted in the
rejection of politics. The San Francisco Bay area bands emerged: Jefferson
Airplane, Big Brother and the Holding Company, Quicksilver Messenger Service, Country Joe and the Fish, and the Grateful Dead. Rock music was in
full swing.

From that point on, rock was central to the experiences of the Sixties. The energy and tone of rock music closely paralleled the social and political events of the time. From 1965 through 1967, rock music was at its highest level of creative energy just as the political movements were swelling and spinning off into all areas of life. Soul music re-emerged, ranging from the Motown sound of the Supremes, Miracles, Temptations, and others to Sam and Dave's assertive "Soul Man" and Aretha Franklin's "Respect." Drug-influenced lyrics appeared, from the Stones' early satire "Mother's Little Helper" to the Beatles' acid-tripping "Strawberry Fields Forever," Dylan's "Rainy Day Woman #12 & 35," and Jefferson Airplane's "White Rabbit." Nostalgia, escapism, and childlike innocence could be heard in the Beatles' "Penny Lane" and "Yellow Submarine," Peter, Paul, and Mary's "Puff the Magic Dragon," and the Lovin' Spoonful's "I Had a Dream." Songs frequently and explicitly celebrated sex: Jefferson Airplane's "Somebody to Love," the Beatles' "Why Don't We Do It In the Road?" and the Doors' "Light My Fire." The retreat to the country was echoed in Dylan's *Nashville Skyline* and *New Morning* albums, Buffy St. Marie's "I'm Gonna Be a Country Girl Again," Canned Heat's "Goin' Up the Country," and the popularity of groups like Creedence Clearwater Revival and the Band.

As the counterculture swirled away from the social mainstream, the themes of collective fusion, fantasy, and loneliness became more prominent (the Stones' "2000 light years from home"). The countercultural themes of the mid-Sixties came together in the decade's most important album: the Beatles' *Sgt. Pepper's Lonely Hearts Club Band*, with its musical complexity, multi-track recording, and lyrics. As David Pichaske contends, the album "made a remarkably coherent statement on modern society and on the pervasive emptiness of all our lives and on the assorted methods we use to cope with that emptiness."[48]

By 1968–1969, the energy began to change. The political heaviness of 1968 began to be mirrored in rock lyrics: the Stones' "Street Fighting Man," Sly and the Family Stone's "There's a Riot Goin' On," James Brown's "Say it Loud: I'm Black and I'm Proud," Arthur Brown's "Fire," Jefferson Airplane's "Volunteers," the MC5's "Kick Out the Jams." Revolution and violence were in the air and on the airwaves. Some groups embraced the new feeling, others stepped back. While the Rolling Stones sang "Street Fighting Man," the Beatles objected to a violent "Revolution." Original movement troubadour Phil Ochs distanced himself from the polarizing politics of the day and simply declared, "The War Is Over."

In the rough climate of the late Sixties, the raw energy of rock encountered the political realities of the rock business. The economic imperatives of commercial music had always filtered out the more overtly sexual or political messages. Many explicit rhythm and blues songs were kept off the airwaves until a sanitized "cover" was cut by another artist; performers as diverse as Billie Holiday, the Weavers, and Jerry Lee Lewis were effectively blacklisted. Some critics considered the whole rock and roll phenomenon of the Fifties to be subversive; rock was attacked by the Christian Crusade, Art Linkletter, and even Spiro Agnew. Rock musicians like Mick Jagger and Keith Richards of the Rolling Stones and the Beatles' John Lennon were busted for marijuana possession. Like the mass media generally, the popular music business winnowed and filtered the message heard by the American public until it became "safe."[49]

The breakthrough to FM radio gave freer play to the critical messages of the mid-Sixties because the smaller, young audience of FM rock was enthusiastically receptive. Still, countercultural themes like drug use were often covered by double meanings and disconnected imagery. Even on FM, explicitly revolutionary lyrics often meant a song would not get wide airplay, or a performer would lose access to the recording industry, as happened with the MC5. Jefferson Airplane's *Volunteer* album, with its frontal challenge to the system, was blacklisted from top-40 play:

> All your private property is target for your enemy
> And your enemy is "we."
> We are forces of chaos and anarchy,
> Everything they say we are, we are,
> And we are very proud of ourselves.
> Up against the wall,
> Up against the wall, motherfucker.
> Tear down the walls,
> Tear down the walls.[50]

Similarly, the antiwar lyrics of Earth Opera's "American Eagle Tragedy" were largely absent from mainstream programming:

> And call out the border guards, the kingdom is crumbling.
> The king is in the counting house, laughing and stumbling.
> His armies are extended way beyond the shore,
> As he sends our lovely boys to die in a foreign jungle war.[51]

The cooptive effect of rock capitalism was more subtle, but equally decisive. In 1967, the first great rock festival at Monterey illuminated tensions within rock music. Musicians like John Phillips of the Mamas and Papas and Paul Simon disassociated themselves from the initial idea of a commercial festival until it shifted to a nonprofit format; the Grateful Dead refused to participate altogether if the festival were not free. Ultimately profits were donated to educational and musical charities, although the concert promoters were so casual with the festival revenues that their bookkeeper easily embezzled $50,000.

However, the Monterey Pop Festival also revealed the profit-making potential of the new rock music and festival scene. The energy unveiled at Monterey drew the attention of major record scouts. Columbia's Clive Davis recalled that Monterey revealed a "very idealistic, very innocent and beautiful philosophy of life" and "a dramatic change in pop-music group playing that I would bet on." [52] Davis subsequently signed Janis Joplin, Chicago, and Santana to lucrative contracts. As Robert Santelli observes of the Monterey aftermath,

Monterey set off a widespread hunt for more talent all over the United States and England. The pop establishment was overthrown as rock forced its way to the center of the stage. Top-40 AM stations were besieged with songs by bands formerly considered too radical for their playlists. FM stations began springing up regularly and played the music that had been heard at Monterey. Moby Grape, the Electric Flag, and Country Joe and the Fish, among others quickly became national acts. Joplin, The Who, and Jimi Hendrix began a speedy rise to superstardom. . . .

But the unveiling of the new rock and the new counterculture was not without a price. The roots of Monterey Pop . . . and the nonprofit, celebratory theme were soon debauched, distorted, and forgotten. The vision of large profits that arose from the excitement over the commercial viability of the new music and the festival format caused the perversion. Things would never really be the same again. [53]

With the exception of groups like the Grateful Dead (whom Davis called "noneconomically motivated"), the almighty dollar took over the rock scene with the same destructive effects as the mass media's attention to Haight-Ashbury. It promoted the big star system, fed and distorted the ego needs of rock musicians performing in front of ever-larger crowds, [54] and simply burned out some performers. Singer Tracy Nelson recalls, "The amounts of money that were given to people who would have accepted so much less were just extraordinary, and, in most cases, unjustified. There was total self-indulgence for a long period, and it was nearly the ruination of me."[55] Grace Slick of the Jefferson Airplane recalls the pressures of working under promoter Bill Graham:

> "His instinct was always You better keep at it, you better get it while it's hot. And we always thought he was nuts, going crazy trying to get the bucks, not because he was totally money oriented, just because Bill's instinct was to make sure of everything, watch everything, control every-thing; it could all fall apart at any second. We didn't have that attitude. We never went on the road every day of the year, really pushing hard. . . . We had a looser attitude. We were very conscious of not overloading. At least the rest of the band was. . . . I'm probably still around now partially because they were more laid back."[56]

Others like Janis Joplin, Jimi Hendrix, the Rolling Stones' Brian Jones, and Jim Morrison of the Doors were less lucky; all died from drug-related causes between 1969 and 1971.

Few on the Left entertained the possibility that rock music was truly revo-lutionary. As the *Guardian*'s cultural critic, Irwin Silber, wrote, "Our goal is not to get our message out on 10 million Columbia records, but to take over Columbia Records and make it part of a people's socialist system based on human need and human expression."[57] In a rebellious gesture, the counter-culture fought back against the big money of rock as bootleg records of major stars became popular. In the end, the rock music industry put an end to the myth of rock as revolutionary. As former activist Jim Fouratt recalled of his employment as "house freak" at CBS, "We really believed that the music was coming out of a community, and if that community was expanded because they got our major-label distribution, the message was going to be clear and we were going to take over the world. Capitalism does not work that way. The money cut the artists off from the community."[58]

The importance of Sixties rock music lies in its connection with other as-pects of the counterculture, as part of the search for personal liberation and community. Rock was kinetic, it was physical; in Richard Goldstein's straight-forward characterization, "It makes you want to move." As Eldridge Cleaver observed, rock music from Elvis Presley to the Twist to the Beatles liberated young whites from the repressive separation of mind and body; "it afforded them the possibility of reclaiming their Bodies again after generations of alienated and disembodied existence."[59] In its raw physicality, its erotic rhythms, rock was a kind of primitive, countermodern force. Again, Cleaver observed:

> In the increasingly mechanized, automated, cybernated environment of the modern world—a cold, bodiless world of wheels, smooth plastic surfaces, tubes, pushbuttons, transistors, computers, jet propulsion, rockets to the moon, atomic energy—man's need for affirmation of his biology has become that much more intense. He feels need for a clear definition of where his body ends and the machine begins, where man ends and the *extensions* of man begin. . . . It is against this backdrop that America's attempt to unite its Mind with its Body, to save its soul, is taking place.[60]

Like so much of the counterculture, rock was both intensely individualistic and communal, both introspective and participatory. Writing of rock dances, Albert Goldman remarked, "Here there is a feeling of total immersion: one is inside the mob, inside the skull, inside the music, which comes from all sides, buffeting the dancers like a powerful surf. Strangest of all, in the midst of all this frantic activity, one soon feels supremely alone; and this aloneness produces a giddy sense of freedom, even of exultation. At last one is free to move and act and mime the secret motions of his mind."[61] Or as Morris Dickstein observed, played at ear-piercing volume, "the music seemed to come from within rather than without, . . . emanating from one's own guts and vitals."[62] Rock slipped past cerebral defenses to connect with and unlock feelings that were exhilarating, giddy, erotic, even angry.

The rock experience also reflected a kind of communal fusion, nowhere more than at the major rock festivals that began at Monterey in 1967, peaked at Woodstock in 1969, and fractured a few months later at Altamont, only to re-emerge nostalgically at Watkins Glen in 1974. The festivals combined a kind of tribalistic bonding with the driving force of rock music. Throughout the festival period, the internal tensions of rock—liberation and destruction, anarchism and capitalism—were visible. The first real problems emerged at Newport Beach, California in 1968 when enormous crowds overwhelmed the facilities. A year later, high-priced admissions at "Newport '69" fueled gate-crashing efforts and resulted in sporadic violence.

The high point of the festival phenomenon, and some would say of the counterculture, was the three-day Woodstock festival attended by approximately 500,000 people, which made it, for the weekend, the third largest city in New York. The New York State thruway was bottled up for a full day before the festival began; many left their cars by the side of the highway and hiked the remaining miles. (New York police estimated over a million people were on the highways in the festival vicinity on Friday.) The vastness of the crowd in the face of torrential rain and a sea of mud gave participants a sense of being part of an historic occasion. Together with the peace-loving mood of the crowd, the numbers impressed those in the mainstream culture who came in contact with the festival. The *New York Times* reversed its initial, critical editorial and praised the "courteous, considerate, and well-behaved kids," while a Short Line bus driver commented, "I don't understand why they wear long hair, but now I don't care. . . . They're the most no-griping, no-complaining, patient and generous, respectful bunch of kids I've ever met." [63]

Like the counterculture generally, Woodstock was a study of opposites. In Abe Peck's recollection, "Speaker-tower technology was juxtaposed to skinny-dipping and backpacks. The bands' playing was often as chaotic as the scene around them, but the music became a soundtrack for tribal neighborhoods—freaks, bikers, college towns of mud, blankets, and tents." [64] An underground writer labeled Woodstock "the largest gathering of youth in the nation's history. A hip capitalist fiasco (so far). A religious experience. A glimpse of communism. The pinnacle of passive consumerism. First free dope territory in Amerika. 'Three days of music and peace.' And mud, and acid, and hunger, and freedom, and thirst, and community, and boredom. Containment—revolution." [65]

The crowd lent its full-throated energy to the participatory music, chanting the "Fish Cheer" with Country Joe and the Fish, shrieking "higher!" in response to Sly and the Family Stone's "Let Me Take You Higher," spontaneously chanting "No Rain," and lighting matches in unison in the dark hours of early Sunday morning.

Despite the obstacles, or perhaps because of them, a spirit of communal voluntarism was everywhere in evidence. Contributions from townspeople, free handouts, and special airlifts resolved an acute food shortage. Local medical personnel staffed the first aid stations. Members of the California commune the Hog Farm helped maintain order in addition to assisting with food, medical care, and bad trips.

If Woodstock was a glimpse of the counterculture's heaven, Altamont revealed its hell, the raw, aggressive underside of rock and the tendency of the naive counterculture to attract violent elements. The Altamont debacle featured the prancing, taunting Mick Jagger with the decade's best and baddest rock and roll band, a poorly planned free concert located at the last minute at Altamont Speedway, and, most of all, the ill-fated decision to hire the Hell's Angels as the festival security force. The Angels began to rough up the bois-terous crowd during early sets by Santana and the Jefferson Airplane (beating the Airplane's singer Marty Balin when he came to the assistance of a stricken man). They seemed on the verge of going out of control. After sets by Crosby, Stills, Nash, and Young and the Grateful Dead the violence culminated in the Angels' stabbing a black man named Meredith Hunter to death, right in front of a stunned Mick Jagger.

In the aftermath of Altamont, it was clear that the Woodstock spirit was dead. The heady frenzy of rock music had unleashed dark forces that, in the violent days of the late Sixties, had brought the rock revolution to an end. In the Seventies, a new musical mood would emerge. Eulogizing the rock festivals, Robert Santelli wrote,

> the "me" decade (the post-Watergate seventies) spawned a collection of rock groups and performers who simply advanced a counterfestival mood with their music and stage antics. A metamorphosis had indeed taken place; rock began to symbolize the decadence and technological domi-nation of society in more frightening ways than ever before. A musical style was created that was highly dissimilar to the format and philoso-phy of rock when festivals were in their heyday. The second half of the 1970s witnessed the increased popularity of groups that featured acts of violence onstage . . . and a generally self-oriented, self-centered lyrical expression.[66]

In the end, rock reflected the rise and fall of the counterculture; it was a lot of fun and it may have stimulated breakthroughs in personal insight, but by itself it in no way led to a qualitatively different world.

DRUGS: A REJECTION, AND REFLECTION, OF SOCIETY

Our real choice is between holy and unholy madness.
—Norman O. Brown, in Mitchell Goodman, *The Movement Toward a New America*

In the counterculture's quest to break out of a repressive state of mind, drugs became an experience-enhancing complement to the immersion in rock music. Once invited to be free, the generation of seekers would no longer accommodate themselves to a dry, impersonal existence.

> On the contrary, they are continually struggling to experience the world more intensely, to make themselves capable of greater intimacy and love, to find some "rock bottom," some "gut level," from which they can sally forth to social and interpersonal commitments. Such students characteristically make enormously high demands upon themselves, upon experience, and upon life; contrasted with their demands, their current experience often seems barren, flat, and dull.[67]

Writing in 1969, psychologist Robert Jay Lifton observed, "there is a current in contemporary youth movements that is more Nietzchean than Marxist-Leninist. It consists of a stress upon what I call experiential transcendence, upon the cultivation of states of feelings so intense and so absorbing that time and death cease to exist."[68]

As with rock, drug use was embellished with hyperbole. Drugs were a shortcut to peace and love, a means of transcending objective reality, a path to God, a way to enhance sexual enjoyment, in short, a panacea for life in a repressed, uptight society. Timothy Leary peddled the "turn on, tune in, drop out" message of acid as a quick path to nirvana: "The LSD kick is a spiritual ecstasy. The LSD trip is a religious pilgrimage."[69] Leary not only emphasized the religious quality of LSD, he also maintained that drug use was the key to a radical political change in the mainstream culture. Since a change in the prevailing consciousness would change the world, and drug use dramatically altered consciousness, drugs were the key to the revolution.

One reason for the hyperbolic emphasis on drugs is of course that drug use was a very intense and powerful experience. Initial marijuana use was commonly eye-opening and pleasurable. One Sixties veteran recalls, "My first reaction to being high was 'Why is this stuff illegal?'"[70] LSD was a more powerful total experience. Haight-Ashbury resident Patrick Gleeson remembers his first use of acid:

> I got very far out, the first time I took it. I had hallucinations that had no relation to the particular reality I was in for about three hours. I was soaring through time and space. I saw this fantastic dream creature with my whole body . . . like from my forehead down to my toes. I got very, very vibrant. . . . When I came back down I thought, "Jesus Christ, I'm going to have to spend the rest of my life telling people about it."[71]

A writer in the *Oracle* compared the effects of marijuana to LSD: "Marijuana . . . is an expanding lens. L.S.D. is an electron microscope for the ethereal."[72] Psychedelic drug users repeatedly testified not only to the power of their experiences, but to the vision, insight, and consciousness of a transcendent reality they encountered while using drugs like LSD, mescaline, and peyote.

Like the rock revolution, however, the drug panacea proved transitory and largely illusory. One reason is that, like rock, drug use had its dark side. As Leonard Wolf observed, "To disorder the mind as a means of ordering the spirit appears to be a venture that is both paradoxical and dangerous."[73] Bad trips, acid "panic," the more damaging psychotic breaks, and even suicides revealed the dangers that lurked in the quest for ecstasy and meaning. Furthermore, there was some empirical basis for mainstream society's claims that marijuana use was frequently followed by LSD, in turn followed by more serious or addictive drugs like speed (methedrine) and heroin.[74] Heavy drug experimentation in the Sixties led some to addiction, others to retreat. The Byrds singer Roger McGuinn commented, "I've reevaluated some of my drug-culture mentality. We thought acid was a panacea: it would make dull people bright, take hateful people and make them loving. It didn't work that way. I don't do drugs at all anymore."[75] Regular LSD users realized that, in Charles Perry's words, "there was a point of diminishing returns, after which it was just a hall of mirrors."[76]

Another reason for the illusory nature of the drug revolution was that its claims were simply wrong. The belief that the drug experience would lead to a change in consciousness and thence to revolutionary change in society reflected the power of the drug experience and its links to the counterculture's overall break from mainstream society, but little more. In Sandy Darlington's words, "Middle class values are deeper than acid."[77] On the other hand, as Jay Stevens observes, "One couldn't, for example, after a serious immersion in LSD, go back to the 9-to-5 world of sales managers and upward mobility. Better to work for yourself, doing something simple and useful, which was why so many hippies became entrepreneurs, farmers, craftspeople. For most, the psychedelic experience dealt a serious blow to their desire for power, and all those buttresses to the power urge that go by the name ambition."[78]

Still, a generally hostile American mainstream scapegoated drugs. Horror stories were routinely generalized in the mainstream press. Drug busts became so common that the underground L.A. *Free Press* once ran a cover story publicizing the names, addresses, and phone numbers of eighty California State

Bureau of Narcotics agents. Highly visible rock stars became targets. One infamous bust in 1967 nabbed the Rolling Stones' Mick Jagger (for possession of four amphetamine tablets) and Keith Richards (for allowing his house to be used for the purpose of smoking marijuana). Not surprisingly, the political system conveniently confused the symptom for the cause. Patrick Gleeson noted that "adults have responded to kids who have long hair and bells as if the drug was making it [*sic*] that way, which is a cop-out." [79]

In attacking drug use, the political mainstream further alienated the young. The swift passage of laws banning LSD and the crackdown on possession and use of marijuana struck the young as another hypocrisy in a culture which gave free play to such addictive and highly profitable drugs as alcohol and nicotine. Furthermore, by outlawing a counterculture staple like marijuana, mainstream America reinforced the counterculture's own sense of being outlaws in America.

However, the explicitly political struggle over drugs was less significant than the basic schism between countercultural and mainstream outlooks. Drugs provided an opening to the countercultural epistemology, an intense, spontaneous kind of deconditioning that opened one's senses to a different reality, or a different awareness of reality. From the mildly hallucinogenic marijuana to mescaline and LSD, drug use suppressed the normal discriminatory functioning of the mind, a process that had two significant effects. First, it eliminated the normal hierarchy of stimuli, the mind's preconditions that certain sounds, sights, or tastes were more important than others (a trait echoed in the counterculture's "do your own thing" relativism). Instead of filtering the thousands of stimuli for important cues, the mind would fix on a seemingly random stimulus and ignore everything else. The effect was to break away from the utilitarian way of seeing the world. Perry observes,

> The stronger the psychedelic, the more strongly it suppresses the faculty of discrimination, right up to a featureless experience called the White Light, in which all details are equally important and all connections equally valid. In a sea of perpetually changing impressions, the meaning of anything can differ wildly from moment to moment. The exaltation of being stoned might be the dawn of birth, the moment of death or a mystical unity of the two. . . . A place might disclose its utter uniqueness, or it might reveal itself as being beyond time and space. [80]

In more ways than one, the "trip" revived the fresh, subjective, and wide-open eyes of childhood. Instead of imposing an order on the world, the tripping person would experience openness and wonder toward phenomena, lingering in the pleasurable experience. It is not surprising, then, that drug use often became an integral part of absorbing experiences like sexual relations or rock concerts.

The other effect of suppressed discriminatory faculties was the holistic experience of the universe. The perception that "all is one" fed the countercultural ethic: "love your brothers and sisters," a compassionate and gentle stance toward other people and the natural world in general. Peck observes that "many people found LSD a way to sense communality with others and to encounter seemingly primal images, or even a spiritual oneness."[81]

Psychedelic perception therefore reinforced feelings of horror at human destructiveness—the bombing of Vietnamese villages, the grinding desperation of the ghetto, an oil spill that turned fragile wetlands into a death swamp. All were violations of the oneness of life. In this respect hallucinogens heightened the subjective experience of events otherwise made dry and abstract by technocratic verbiage; they fed the drive for simplicity and naturalness, they were a catalyst for the ecology movement, and for the notion of a *Whole Earth Catalog*.[82] This holistic perception reinforced the counterculture's tendency to break down barriers, unite the inner and outer, and merge with the cosmos— not that everyone had to use psychedelic drugs to embrace the countercultural way of seeing, just that the use of psychedelics intensified this perception in many participants.

Because of the intensity of LSD in particular, drug use often bordered on religious experience. Peter Marin wrote of

> a confrontation with some kind of power within an unfamiliar landscape involving sensation and risk. It is there, I suppose, that [the young] hope to find . . . through their adventures the *ground* of reality, the resonance of life we deny them. . . . [Their world] is dramatic, it enchants them; its existence forms a strange brotherhood among them and they cling to it— as though they alone had been to a fierce land and back. It is that which draws them together and makes of them a loose tribe.[83]

As a doorway to perception, LSD spawned a continuing quest for a visionary state and transcendant meaning. Mystical and often authoritarian gurus came from the East to respond to the drug-fed demand for a monistic vision. Drugs reinforced the counterculture's nontraditional religious quest, the emphasis on magic and the occult, rituals and the exotic, Hare Krishna, the *I Ching*,

Zen Buddhism, Carlos Casteneda's journeys with Don Juan and A *Yaqui Way of Knowledge*, American Indian lore, astrology, the solstice, the novels of Herman Hesse, and eventually evangelical, charismatic Christianity. As Roszak noted of young people's search for religious immediacy,

> If the young seized on Zen with shallow understanding, they grasped it with a healthy instinct. . . . Perhaps what the young took Zen to be has little relationship to that venerable and elusive tradition; but what they readily adopted *was* a gentle and gay rejection of the positivistic and the compulsively cerebral. It was the beginning of a youth culture that continues to be shot through with the spontaneous urge to counter the joyless, rapacious, and egomaniacal order of our technological society.[84]

THE "SEXUAL REVOLUTION"

The more I make love, the more I want to make revolution.
—Graffiti in Paris, 1968

An open frankness about sexual pleasure and experimentation went hand in hand with the culture of rock music and drug use. In many respects, the sexual experimentation of the young was nothing new, but had been going on from time immemorial. Yet something in the air seemed different. Some claimed that there was a great deal more sexual freedom. In one very important way, this was true, thanks to the discovery and distribution of birth control pills, a most significant event. Although it is practically impossible to make definitive cross-generational comparisons, it is likely that sexual behavior was significantly less restrained among the young of the 1960s and 1970s than among their predecessors. From narrative accounts, it is clear that large numbers of the young in countercultural communities like Haight-Ashbury experimented widely in the number and gender of sexual partners, frequency of sexual encounters, and nature of the sexual act. Furthermore, it seemed that a wider slice of the younger generation was sexually active, and at a younger age.[85]

The sexual revolution eradicated the climate of puritanical moralizing that was part of growing up in the Fifties and early Sixties. Rock lyrics were freed from their earlier covers, and song titles openly suggested sex: "Love the One You're With," "Let's Spend the Night Together," "Why Don't We Do It in the Road?" Underground papers initiated personals columns, while the papers

Screw and *Kiss* exploited the politics of eroticism. Sexuality and open nudity became prevalent on the avant-garde stage. Sex was often fused with drug use, and many claimed to enjoy their sexual experiences more when high on marijuana, mescaline, or LSD. Group sex and orgies became commonplace in some circles. Singer Essra Mohawk recalls, "It was real easy to find an orgy in the sixties, if you were a girl. I always remember being recruited for them. People would say, 'Hey, let's get in a pile.' My first awakening was to that kind of thing—open, multisexual situations. To me that was perfectly normal." [86] To some degree, of course, the appearance of pervasive sexuality and experimentation was the product of the mass media's gravitation toward anything provocative. "The rebels of the 60's are adrift in a sea of permissiveness," observed a *Time* cover story as early as 1964.

Like other countercultural phenomena, sexual experimentation rebelled against the utilitarian ethic of postponed gratification and the whole array of social taboos that restricted personal expression. "Why wait?" queried the young, who were beginning to sense that postponed gratification meant hypocrisy, deceit, and atrophy of the self. In emphasizing the natural and open enjoyment of sexuality, the counterculture struck a blow against society's repressive desublimation, the combination of sexual titillation and social control built on messages of personal inadequacy that pervade mass marketing in the capitalist culture. [87] In the mainstream culture, sexual energy is intensified, yet sexuality is distorted and channeled into the quest for material acquisition; accordingly, the erotic landscape is diminished while pornography spreads. Although the practice did not always live up to the ideal, the counterculture opened the way to a more erotic connection with self and others, a quest continued by feminism.

Despite its emphasis on sexual enjoyment, the counterculture deviated from the sexual commoditization represented by the *Playboy* mentality. Like the norm of postponed sexuality, the latter played into the stimulus-and-denial, consumer dynamic of the mainstream culture. As Jeff Shero of the underground Austin *Rag* commented, "The real Playboy philosophy . . . appears throughout the magazine in the cartoons, photos, and advertising. This advertising-promoted view of sex is so blatant and sterile that one would think it would be taken as a joke." [88] At its core, the counterculture rejected the repression, titillation, and distortion of sexuality endemic in the American mainstream. Yet, not surprisingly, the counterculture itself was not free of sexually-based commercialism; *Screw* and *Kiss* were only the most blatant examples.

The counterculture's notion of sexuality reflected the belief in getting out of one's head and in touch with one's body, in being natural. Sexual gratification was viewed as inherent in human relationships, not a kind of scarce commodity that needed to be hunted and horded. It embodied the counterculture's holistic vision, fusion with the other, and the ethic of love. One of the most common of Sixties slogans was "make love, not war."

However, sexual "freedom" had its ugly side. Despite appearances, open sexual experimentation was not the same thing as sexual liberation, for the young *were* young and had also grown up in a culture that distorted sexuality. As more than one commentator has observed, the sexual emphasis remained genital, with a fixation on orgasm. Patrick Gleeson commented on the dark side of the Haight scene:

> What I feel is happening with a lot of young kids is pretty rough. There are a lot of young girls who are coming in from the suburbs who really want to get laid and be liked and be loved. And they're getting fucked but they're not getting loved. And that's because the young males in the Haight-Ashbury still have their own hangups. They can't love everybody. Or they can't see that to embrace somebody is to love them. So like I know a couple of communal places . . . that have had more and more meth-heads going all the time, and girls are getting stoned on meth and get fucked for a couple of days until they freak out. But that's not sexual freedom, that's sexual compulsion.[89]

In effect, the push to the fringes of sexual experience suffered from the same flaws as the reliance on intense drug experiences, and both reflected the youth of many in the counterculture. As poet and Fugs musician Tuli Kupferberg put it: "Much of the sexual revolution had validity and had to be gone through, but it didn't come anywhere near solving the problem. As I look at it now, a common basis for a lot of the mistakes was that, since it was so much of a youth movement, people didn't realize that what's sexually wonderful at nineteen, may not be what you would want when you're thirty or thirty-five."[90]

Perhaps the most significant characteristic of the sexual revolution was the manner in which it redefined the relation between the sexes. While much of the early women's movement that appeared in the 1960s focused on the unequal treatment of women within Sixties movements, the counterculture opened the door to ways in which both women and men could break out of restrictive gender-based behavioral patterns. Pollock observed of sexuality in the counterculture, "The sexual revolution depended on a radical redefinition of women's sexuality."[91] While much of this redefinition was not to come until the Seventies (the button "Girls Say Yes to Men Who Say No" was still popular in 1967), there was evidence of change. Weiner and Stillman's survey led them to cite women's new freedom to initiate sexual relationships and to find sexual satisfaction as "the real sexual revolution."[92] The unisex styles and men's long hair also anticipated the theory of androgyny that became more prevalent in the Seventies. The gay liberation movement also emerged during the late Sixties, reflecting both the counterculture's openness about sexuality and the decade's equal rights movements.

PARTICIPATORY JOURNALISM:
THE UNDERGROUND PRESS

We broke down a lot of barriers to honest thought.
—Max Scherr, Berkeley *Barb*

I think that the illusion of objectivity is very important for getting your views across. That's why the New York *Times* is so effective—and effective propaganda.
—Alan Howard, Liberation News Service

The underground newspapers that emerged in mid-decade quickly became the voice of the youth movement and a crucial communications link among geographically separated individuals and communities. Underground journalism reflected all the major characteristics of the counterculture and the New Left: the assertion of subjectivity in all its manifestations, the search for community, and a critical, advocacy stance toward mainstream society.

Abe Peck's comprehensive treatment of the underground press traces this quintessentially Sixties movement from the half dozen or so first wave papers that emerged in 1964 and 1965 through the highwater mark of 1969, when "at least five hundred papers served communities and constituencies worldwide, with five hundred to a thousand more dissenting papers in high schools alone," to 1973 when the press, "like the movements it covered, had both succeeded and withered."[93]

Underground papers became a staple of life for the youth movement. They featured political exposés and news of movement activities; articles about drug use, inner growth, or mystical experiences; profiles of activists or counterculture communities; opportunities for personal and sexual contacts with likeminded others; and information and reviews of the plethora of arts and music events. Two alternative news services, the Liberation News Service and Underground Press Syndicate, brought together editors and activists in a series of movement conferences and provided national news coverage to smaller papers. Some papers like the Berkeley *Barb*, the L.A. *Free Press*, and *Win* emphasized the more instrumental politics of New Left activism, while others like the *Oracle*, the *East Village Other*, and the *Seed* were caught up in the expressive counterculture.

In the latter years of the decade, all the divisions within the Movement were visible in the underground press. Underground papers were vulnerable to the tension between fomenting radical political change and prefiguring the new, post-revolutionary society. Financial and censorship pressures and personnel clashes accentuated the divisions. Anti-capitalist and feminist challenges fed rebellions on some of the more successful papers. The staff of the Berkeley *Barb* charged that editor–owner Max Scherr's policies had violated movement values by exploiting staffers, running sexist ads, and reaping personal profits; they subsequently began a paper of their own called the Berkeley *Tribe*. Confronted by leftist heavies, Liberation News Service's Marshall Bloom disappeared in the night with LNS's subscriber lists and equipment. Radical feminists took over the New York *Rat* after denouncing its contents as pornographic and sexist.

The underground press, in short, mirrored the Movement it covered. It flourished; it gave voice to important radical criticism and powerful personal expression. It could also be silly, offensive, excessive, and, like everything else, susceptible to greed and the drive for ego gratification. It filled a social and political vacuum and fed on the energy of its times. It opened the door to journalistic alternatives and broadened the scope of traditional journalism, yet the alternative newspapers all but disappeared by the mid-Seventies.

The most radical characteristic of the new journalism was its fusion of the personal with the political. The underground press arose out of disillusionment with an innocuous mainstream press—a "dead form" in the view of *East Village Other* journalist Allen Katzman—and the felt need to express the critical viewpoint of the movement. As such it expressed the personal perspective of its writers, many of whom were themselves participants in social activism. Especially in the early going, its stance was explicitly amateur rather than professional, written for love more than for money. The L.A. *Free Press* reflected editor Art Kunkin's desire for "a primarily reader-written paper where, when people expressed their opinions, there would be a dialogue with them, and finally the emergence of a program (and party) from what students and so forth were talking about."[94] In the tradition of Sixties movements, the underground press was essentially participatory.

The implicit target of the underground press was the "objectivity" of mainstream journalism. Newspaper policies and the professional ethics of mainstream reporters, like those of social scientists, require writers to detach themselves from the external reality of the story. The result is presumably detached and balanced reporting. This reportorial stance had three results that were anathema to young people involved in the Movement. First, it reinforced the separation of the professional reporter from the community of readers, in precisely the kind of hierarchical relation criticized by those involved in the antiwar, black power, and campus movements. This detachment meant, in short, that reporters failed to write much of value about the youth movements themselves.

Second, the repression of the reporters' personal feelings and experiences resulted in a kind of lifeless nonpartisan style that became irrelevant at best in a time of intense feeling like the Sixties. Detachment from feelings reduced the writers' involvement in their stories and therefore their ability to understand the full import of the story, since part of a story's importance was its effect on viewers' feelings. Nowhere was this more crucial than in coverage of the Vietnam War. The "objective" stance of mainstream reporters, difficult as it was to maintain, meant that at best their stories failed to connect with the antiwar young who felt deep rage and frustration about the war.

By contrast, the underground press was full of "feel" pieces, first-person accounts of experiences in the antiwar movement and confessional stories about personal lifestyle. Most simply assumed a partisan involvement on the part of both writer and reader. Sometimes the result was a kind of mindless diatribe of unattributed assertions or uncritical acclaim for movement heroes, especially when the objective was to provoke readers to political action. At other times, the result was an immature irresponsibility; as Lester Dore of both the *Oracle* and *Seed* observed, "A lot of things we said and did in the *Seed* were not responsible. Now I see that everything you do has a consequence."[95]

However, the best of the underground writing reflected an openness about the writer's self. Anticipating the feminist stance toward objectivity, it embodied both "social confrontation and *self*-confrontation." In Dickstein's words, "The trivial side of this [subjective] tendency, the mere impulse toward self-display, had been evident from the first. . . . But the serious side of this new subjectivity was far more important. A writer was now free to admit his fallibility; his biases and idiosyncrasies could be out on the table."[96] Norman Mailer's two accounts of antiwar activity, *The Armies of the Night* and *Miami and the Siege of Chicago* were the most widely read, mainstream examples of this journalistic style.

Finally, the detached style of traditional reporting was not anathema solely because it was lifeless and impersonal. Objectivity, as opposed to simply good reporting, was in effect a smokescreen behind which the ideological assumptions and financial and career interests of the press were hidden. Jack Newfield of the *Village Voice* spoke of a "rhetoric of objectivity" in the mainstream press, shared by liberals and conservatives alike, that obscured "a belief in welfare capitalism, God, the West, Puritanism, the Law, the family, property, the two-party system, and perhaps most crucially, in the notion that violence is only defensible when employed by the State."[97] Points of view unpalatable to those who shared these beliefs were largely ignored or effectively filtered. The fact that the mainstream press consisted primarily of upper-middle-class white males reinforced the drive to include women and minorities on underground reporting staffs (gender and race had previously been regarded as irrelevant to objective reporting).

The gap between the "objective" mainstream and the underground press stood out most graphically in stories on the Movement itself. As Dickstein observed, the mainstream press reflected an "insider mentality that kept the reporter dependent on his sources and virtually a fixture in the institution he covered, with an ethical neutrality that turned hostile whenever the new culture of the sixties came in for attention."[98] Countless examples of mainstream press coverage of antiwar activities reflected the insider mentality, just as most mainstream stories on the war reflected their dependency on government sources. In a typical case, the *New York Times* coverage of the 1967 March on the Pentagon emphasized the low crowd estimates supplied by the police, at first promulgated police claims that tear gas use had been initiated by the protesters, and focused on arrests, permit deadlines, and the arrest record of protest leader Dave Dellinger. There was little discussion of the war-related issues that provoked the protest in the first place. By contrast, the Liberation News Service packet mixed "freak and radical perspectives, politics and celebration, and, most of all, demonstrators' experience. . . . Demonstrators were hailed as politically correct and morally superior."[99]

The point is not that the underground press told the *whole* story, but rather that it told a story, including objective facts, essentially left out of the mainstream press. As Todd Gitlin observed of the contrast between the *New York Times* and *National Guardian* coverage of the 1965 SDS demonstration, "It would be *de rigueur* to observe that the *Guardian's* coverage was ideological. The *Times's* coverage was no less so."[100] To the degree that the underground press was open about its own purposes, it was grounded in a belief that subjective involvement would ultimately produce better, if sometimes more ragged, journalism, with writing that was more alive, more real, and ultimately more accurate. It was the same belief in personal growth and empowerment that underlay the New Left's embrace of participatory democracy.

In the end, much of the underground press, like the more flamboyant expressions of the counterculture, faded from view, but not without leaving a legacy. Mainstream reporting now often includes a more open participant–observer perspective. As freelance writer Tom Miller notes, "Stories I would have done for the underground press I'm now doing for the daily papers. So either I'm slowing down or they're catching up."[101] On the other hand, most mainstream political reporting seems remarkably untouched. Mainstream news coverage, to say nothing of congressional debate, of U.S. policy toward Nicaragua and El Salvador echoes earlier coverage of the Vietnam conflict. As a result, a demand persists for alternative news sources like *In These Times*, *Mother Jones*, and *Z*, to say nothing of perennial sources like the *Nation*, the *Progressive*, the *Village Voice*, *Dissent*, and the *Guardian*. It may be, as Abe Peck argues, that there are as many dissident papers now as there were during the Sixties, albeit with a single-issue rather than comprehensive focus. What is inescapably different is that the collective energy and confidence has declined. As Peck observes, "Too many lack the spark that comes with thinking your ideas are actually changing the world."[102]

COMING TOGETHER: COMMUNAL LIVING

What do they mean by *love*? I think they mean a quality of attention to each other, to all that is around them. Through the senses—an appetite, a reverence. Love of life, of living things, of what's held in common. A sharing, a communion, a community. Members of one another.
—Mitchell Goodman, *The Movement Toward a New America*

The counterculture's quest for a tribal or kinship-based community was most visible in the profusion of communal living arrangements, intentional communities, cooperatives, and political collectives that sprang up in the late 1960s and early 1970s. Many pursued a utopian fantasy and were short-lived; others have persisted through struggles of group decision-making, personal growth, and economic hardship. While the number of intentional communities has declined from an estimated 20,000 in the late Sixties and early Seventies, some 3,000 to 5,000 contemporary communities are linked through network organizations, magazines, and newsletters.[103]

In their initial stages, Sixties communes were frequently arrangements of habit and convenience for mobile young people gravitating to the more active urban areas. Drawn together by economic necessity, political or social compatibility, accessible sex, and a vague desire to replicate the closeness of family, many of the young simply lived together and explored the lifestyle of the counterculture. Most fundamentally, the communal movement reflected deep-seated alienation from a lonely, atomistic society.

The evolution of widespread communal living became more complex than a mere groping for togetherness. As Jack Whalen and Richard Flacks have observed,

> The sixties youth culture was hardly unique in celebrating friendship, for such celebration has always been integral to the experience of youth. But the counterculture heightened the moral centrality of sharing one's fate with one's peers and constructed a vision of such community as a long-term possibility. That vision was acted out in vast celebratory assemblies such as Woodstock, in self-consciously communal households, and in the movement of considerable numbers in the late 1960s and early 1970s into full-time communes.[104]

Individual communes embodied a wide range of unifying themes, from Christian pacifism to sexual liberation, from Eastern mysticism to organic farming and vegetarianism, and from group marriage to political activism. Names like Tolstoy Farm, Yellow Submarine, Harrad West, The Family, Peace Action Farm, The Vale, Magic Forest Farm, the Hog Farm, Greenfeel, and Catholic Worker Farm reveal this diversity. Starting a commune also varied from a relatively spontaneous decision among friends, to a careful, interview-based selection process, to the more structured requirements of religious organizations. Most communes evolved a set of commitment-inducing rituals like meditation and yoga, mutual criticism, drug ingestion, singing, dancing, or chanting.[105]

While individual communes varied widely, most reflected two basic drives: a psychological retreat from a combative environment, and an effort to implement alternative values and lifestyles. In these respects, the communal movement of the late Sixties and early Seventies was linked to an American tradition of utopian communities like Brook Farm, New Harmony, and Oneida. As the nation polarized and turbulence grew, the notion of living collectively became more intentional and more widespread.

Eventually, the decision to start a commune was often linked to the decision to move from urban centers to the country. In its later stages, the communal movement became virtually inseparable from the back-to-the-earth and ecology movements of the early 1970s. The quest for a new form of community was therefore combined with the search for greater simplicity and a new imperative attuned to the rhythms of the earth, rather than the requirements of the political and economic order. It also reflected a desire for rootedness, for a sense of place. In the Haight-Ashbury, as police hassles grew, the drug scene deteriorated, and waves of thrill-seekers invaded, the old-timers looked to a future in the country. An *Oracle* column observed, "The return to the land is happening. . . . Land is being made available at a time when many of us in the Haight-Ashbury and elsewhere are voicing our need to return to the soil, to straighten our heads in a natural environment, to straighten our bodies with healthier foods and Pan's work, toe to toe with the physical world, just doing what must be done."[106] Even those urban anarchists, the Diggers, moved to their new farm, Morning Star Ranch, while Marshall Bloom packed up the Liberation News Service and moved to rural Montague, Massachusetts.

However consciously or unconsciously communes were started, they invariably struggled with issues of sexuality and love, couple integrity, privacy, and financial stability. In Whalen and Flacks' view, "By now it seems obvious enough that counterculturalists were, initially, extraordinarily naive in imagining that long-established cultural principles and social logics—such as those supporting hierarchical authority, role specialization, personal possession and privacy, monogamy, and professional expertise—could be replaced simply because people ardently desired such change."[107] One surviving communard observed, "It can be very hard. You have to be committed to making it work. I think the reason so many communes fell apart was that they didn't have this commitment, and when they hit the rough spots people just gave up."[108] As a long-time communal resident observed, "The problem with the 60's was that we all knew what we didn't like and what we wanted to get away from, but we had no clear focus of what we wanted."[109]

Communal beginners sometimes assumed that communal property, shared sexuality, and openness to outsiders were essential to an existence free from the mainstream culture's "hangups." Only later did they struggle with the need to find private space within the collective or to establish rules governing visits by outsiders. Decision-making procedures, often consensus-based, evolved through practice. Most difficult for many were the issues of intimacy and couple integrity. Some communes like Greenfeel began with the explicit purpose of enjoying full sexual freedom among its members; others experimented in sexual relationships as group intimacy grew. Commune newsletters are full of candid exchanges among those who struggled with feelings of possessiveness and insecurity, as well as the competing value of monogamy. It appears that monogamy, at least serial monogamy, became the prevailing pattern, with "group marriages" the not-infrequent exception.

The fusion impulse expressed in communes also emerged in other forms in the Seventies, from local communal activities like Berkeley's People's Park to the rising popularity of encounter groups. Virtually all such communal experiences involved a withdrawal of time and space from a culture viewed as inimical to community. The more openly these experiences confronted society, the more likely they were to encounter hostility and harassment. At the same time, the mainstream culture became more flexible and innovative, leading many to explore interpersonal relations outside the communal setting.

The communes that have persisted since the early Seventies have been largely transformed. They are as ideologically diverse as they were in the Sixties, perhaps more so. However, their persistence reflects a seriousness of commitment to an alternative way of life that combines in varying degrees spiritual growth, kinship, politics, and subsistence through farming, small business, or craft enterprises. "Twenty years ago," Charles Betterton claims, "communal groups united together against something. Now the shift has been to cooperative efforts, to working for instead of against."[110] Furthermore, communes today are more likely to involve a lifestyle consisting of long-term couple relationships, nonsexual group commitment, natural health and drug abstinence, and acoustic music, than they are the countercultural staples of sex, drugs, and rock and roll. While their form has changed, communal living arrangements and community cooperatives remain, for many, a compelling alternative to the atomistic society.

■ The Counterculture as Transition

Living on the edge took its toll.
—Abe Peck, *Uncovering the Sixties*

At its best, the counterculture was a conscious statement of opposition to a society in which technocratic reasoning and social mythology obscured criminal aggression in Vietnam, the fear-driven suppression of dissent, a vacuous consumerism, and the get-ahead rat race. The counterculture sought a society that rejected violence, intensified human connectedness, and enriched personal development and expression. Because the ills of society emerged so dramatically in the violent days of the late 1960s, and because the political system was so impervious to fundamental change, the counterculture sought to distance itself from conventionality in all forms. Following Rousseau, it rejected the alienation of the modern world and sought the authenticity of the natural person. It sought refuge in a totally new society within the old, a stance fraught with tension.

At its worst, the counterculture traveled so far from the center of American life that it lost its bearings. As the counterculture attracted a second wave of younger teenagers, much of its potential for mindless self-indulgence and destructiveness was realized: sexual encounters that were compulsive and joyless; drug abuse; total immersion in revolutionary rock music; episodic commitment to relationships, community, or political causes; forms of expression that were so grotesque that their only value was to shock.

This counterculture acted unconsciously, believing it expressed personality when in fact it was searching narcissistically for identity.[111] The quest for personal meaning, the often gnawing, anxious need to fill internal emptiness, mirrored the alienation of modern life.[112] In its separation from society, a separation reinforced by the pain of feeling devalued, by the emotion of anger, the counterculture was self-absorbed, unaware of the injury it afflicted on others or the destructive side-effects of its panaceas. Its rejection of postponed gratification infuriated working- and middle-class people who gave up personal gratification in the struggle to make ends meet; its postscarcity ethic isolated its participants from society's dispossessed who wanted their share of society's goods.

The counterculture's greatest limitations as a movement derived from this disassociation from political engagement in the larger community. Without political experience, many lacked political consciousness. Whereas the early counterculture pioneers retained their political awareness and gravitated toward nonviolent, local political movements in the Seventies and the Eighties, the second wave may have been more readily absorbed into the acquisitive culture of the Yuppie. Lacking an adequate political consciousness meant that the counterculture too easily deteriorated into a politics of style not unlike Madison Avenue's manipulated fashions. As Whalen and Flacks observe,

> By the mid-1970s, most of America was wearing blue jeans. Water beds and granola became staples in middle-class suburbia, and Bob Dylan tunes were programmed on supermarket Muzak. The commodification and absorption of countercultural symbols and styles and practices represented, for many, a kind of relief; instead of waging war on the young, the society and culture were integrating them. But what was remarkable was how little such inclusion changed the central logics of market, bureaucracy, state, and media.[113]

A revolution of style was simply not revolutionary at all. As Julius Lester put it, "The system will not disappear because we say 'fuck the system.' "[114] The counterculture's lack of political consciousness meant that the system would swallow it up, which is precisely what happened. The forces of capitalism feasted on the money-making potential of the youth market.[115]

Furthermore, as Marxist critics like Eugene Genovese and Irwin Silber contended, to argue that "politics is one of the games that people invented because they had nothing better to do with their heads,"[116] is to ignore systematic human oppression. The same could be said in reverse. The counterculture recoiled from an instrumental Left tradition and the hard-edged, centralized machinations of the Weathermen and PL. Thus, for example, Marvin Garson criticized the Left's narrow focus on ideology and organization as the primary basis of solidarity, arguing "that is why revolutionary parties quarrel and split so much about the 'correct program' because in the final analysis, that's all they have."[117]

In the end, the counterculture's radical disassociation revealed the extreme difficulty of retaining the Movement's prefigurative and instrumental politics at a time when society was becoming more repressive, less susceptible to change. The unique contribution of the New Left and civil rights struggles was the high-energy combination of these two strains. The New Left believed that fundamental political change cannot result from a movement that is attentive solely to the hard-edged, external world of politics, nor from an exclusively internal focus. One can become neither an authoritarian vanguardist nor a psychological drop-out, neither a bomb-thrower nor a hedonist. Ironically, the seeds for a revived movement that combined prefigurative and instrumental politics were nourished in the radical disassociation of the counterculture.

The struggle to synthesize these forces has proceeded on several fronts: the evolution of feminist thought and democratic–socialist criticism, the ecological struggle to protect the natural world and humankind's connection to it, the continuing struggle against racism and imperialism, the movement for healthy integration of personality, and a variety of participatory, communal experiments devoted to both meaning and empowerment. These carry forward the unfinished legacy of the 1960s.

PART THREE

Since the Sixties:

Lessons and Legacies

New Beginnings

Feminism, Ecology, and a
Revived Left Critique

> We refuse to remain on the margins of society, and we refuse
> to enter that society on its terms. . . . The human values that
> women were assigned to preserve [must] expand out of the
> confines of private life and become the organizing principles of
> society. . . . The Market, with its financial abstractions,
> deformed science, and obsession with dead things—must be
> pushed back to the margins. And the "womanly" values of
> community and caring must rise to the center as the only
> *human* principles.
> —Barbara Ehrenreich and Deirdre English, *For Her
>   Own Good*

Consumed by the war overseas, rebuffed by a resistant
mainstream culture, battered by repression at home, and spinning out of control, the Movement lost its sense of euphoria, its belief that it could save the
world while simultaneously saving its soul. Despite the countercultural quest
for community, the late Sixties and early Seventies were a time of chaos and
division rather than purpose and unity.

Yet new Movement energy was being born in the midst of this chaos. As the
black power movement and New Left spiraled into their apocalyptic phases,
women claimed center stage in the evolution of the Sixties' vision, embracing
and extending the fusion of prefigurative and instrumental politics. Women in
the civil rights movement and New Left challenged their male counterparts'
failure to live up to their political values.

The counterculture was fertile ground for women to liberate themselves
from mainstream cultural constraints. Yet, as Michele Ryan recalled, it was a
double-edged liberation:

It came in with the hippie thing, that we're all free, men and women,
there should be no inhibitions. You could make love as and when you

felt like it. As a woman one really believed that at the time. And for a while it *was* liberating to feel you no longer had to obey any conventions or inhibitions, that you could sleep with anyone because you were on the pill. If you fell in love or felt desire, you could actually say it. But the other side of the coin was that, having said it, it was used totally to the man's satisfaction. Nothing seemed to have changed very much.[1]

With its emphasis on sexual expression and domestic communality, the counterculture provided small, symbolic openings for both genders' liberation from confining sex stereotypes. Struggles between men and women on the editorial boards of underground papers or in communal kitchens set in motion dynamics that, for some, led to more fundamental attitude changes. At a theoretical level, much of the counterculture's opposition to mainstream values was an assertion of the same "domestic" values—nurturance and love, feeling, kinship and family, the natural—with which feminists later countered male dominance and female subordination in a patriarchal society. Indeed, the counterculture's instinctive hostility toward technocracy and scientific objectivity was consistent with the feminist critique that evolved during the 1970s.

The counterculture also stimulated the other major new beginning of Sixties' activism—the environmental–ecology movement.[2] Rejecting material acquisitiveness and instrumental utility, the counterculture embraced simplicity and respect for the primitive and natural. Its sensitivity to human destructiveness extended to the earth, indeed, to the universe that many sensed themselves part of. The back-to-the-earth movement spun off the urban counterculture at about the same time that the environmental movement held the first Earth Day and began the struggle to end the plunder of natural resources. "Live simply that others may simply live" read one slogan that both hippies and ecologists could endorse.

Finally, the apocalyptic New Left not only alienated many who had been drawn to movements of the Sixties, but it also led to an intellectual dead end. One result of the radicalization of Sixties' activists was that the vanguardist traditions of Marxism–Leninism and Maoism were transposed by self-styled revolutionaries to a nonrevolutionary United States, with predictable results. However, the radicalizing experience of the Sixties also awakened a new awareness of the contradictions between capitalism and democracy, resulting in a reassessment of Marxism and the blossoming of neo-Marxian studies in a wide range of academic disciplines.[3] One product of this reawakening was fresh awareness of the link between Sixties concerns and the imperatives of American and global capitalism.

Feminist, ecology, and neo-Marxian critiques have continued to evolve since their formative experiences in the late 1960s and early 1970s. Their continuing challenge to the mainstream culture remains one of the most direct legacies of the Sixties. Together they provide crucial insights into the mainstream culture and its dominant institutions, extending our understanding of the hard lessons that decade can teach us. In the process, they broaden and enrich the democratic vision of the Sixties in ways that are necessary if it is ever to be realized.

◼ The Women's Movement

Like the women's rights and women's suffrage movements of the nineteenth and early twentieth centuries, the contemporary women's movement grew out of a culture embroiled in the struggle for human liberation. Earlier women's rights activism was rooted in the abolitionist movement, women's liberation in civil rights. The social transformation that followed World War II and the growing sensitivity to injustice that flourished in the Sixties provided fertile ground for a new wave of feminist criticism.

There were, and are, many versions of feminism, each reflecting the racial, class, and ideological experience of its proponents. Thus while white middle-class women have experienced gender-grounded oppression, working-class and black women have experienced forms of oppression exacerbated by the conditions of class inequality and racism. As feminist writers Gloria Joseph and Jill Lewis maintain, "The women's movement . . . includes a wide range of groups operating in different contexts, with differing priorities and political visions. . . . The movement itself represents a multiplicity of confrontational activities and organizational strategies which address different aspects of women's oppression and stress different dimensions of male domination."[4]

The postwar "adjustment" of millions of women—the "Rosie-the-Riveters" who sustained the economy during the war and lost their jobs or job status afterward—spawned a new, modern form of female oppression. Forced by postwar social and economic adjustments to shift their energies fulltime to the domestic sphere, middle-class women learned to sublimate their self-expression in their children's development and their husbands' status. Poor and working-class women could not afford to leave the labor force, yet were often relegated to unskilled and low-paying jobs by returning male workers. The life of domestic "super-Moms," so central to television advertising, contradicted the heady world that increasing numbers of middle-class women glimpsed in college. Seminal books like Simone de Beauvoir's *Second Sex* and Betty Friedan's *The Feminine Mystique* articulated the growing contradictions of middle-class women's lives, the sense that something was wrong. As Friedan described the "problem with no name,"

> The problem lay buried, unspoken, for many years in the minds of American women. It was a strange stirring, a sense of dissatisfaction, a yearning that women suffered in the middle of the twentieth century United States. Each suburban wife struggled with it alone. As she made the beds, shopped for groceries, matched slipcover material, ate peanut butter sandwiches with her children, chauffered Cub Scouts and Brownies, lay beside her husband at night—she was afraid to ask even the silent question—"It this all?"[5]

More directly, the movement for black liberation provided the spark, and in some cases the training ground, for a new women's consciousness. As Juliet Mitchell argued, "The Black Movement was probably the greatest single inspiration to the growth of Women's Liberation."[6] Its liberal integrationist wing and more radical separatist wing also anticipated developments within the women's movement.

Echoing the earlier women's rights movement, liberal feminism began to emerge in the early 1960s among professional and upper-middle-class women. Its viewpoint was articulated in groups organized during the Sixties: President Kennedy's Commission on the Status of Women, the National Organization for Women (NOW), the Women's Equity Action League that fought sex discrimination through the courts, the National Black Feminist Organization, and the Women's Lobby, Inc. that mobilized the Equal Rights Amendment campaign.

Throughout its various manifestations, liberal feminism has viewed female oppression as rooted in the social customs and legal constraints that blocked women's access to the public world of careers and politics. In its manifestation as "sex-role" feminism, it views socially induced gender differences as a crucial source of on-going female oppression. In its pure form, liberal feminism maintains that treating men and women equally will bring this oppression to an end. It has thereby sustained the salience of equal rights through affirmative action and comparable worth initiatives.

Other strains of early or first-wave feminism objected to the universalist assumptions of white middle-class women and liberal feminism's inadequate appreciation of the sources of female oppression.[7] Black and white working-class women expressed the unique perspective of multiple oppression; many were drawn into the black liberation, welfare rights, and labor movements. Some feminist radicals sought to connect their awakening feminist consciousness to the socialist tradition; some were themselves daughters of politically active women or radical parents. One of the more significant socialist feminist groups was the Chicago Women's Liberation Union. Still other radical feminists, perceiving *men* to be the source of female oppression, denounced the intrinsic sexism of the patriarchal mainstream and, echoing the black separatism of the mid-to-late Sixties, advocated a separate women's movement. One notable group was New York's Redstockings.

The perspectives of these post-liberal feminisms developed from experiences within Sixties movements. They shared the Sixties democratic vision: "the importance of the personal; the need to change human relationships; the belief in participatory democracy and the importance of equality."[8] More crucially, the urge to disassociate from male counterparts stemmed from the growing frustration many women felt with the sexism of male civil rights activists and New Leftists. Dorothy Dinnerstein has maintained that men involved in civil rights and New Left activism had, unwittingly, begun to redefine the traditional male role.

> The program these men set themselves involved incorporating into their own relation to societal reality vital features of what had always been the female side of the collaboratively maintained ambivalence toward world-making [affirming life, opposing death forces in society]. . . . But this program did not involve working, or living, with women whose relation to societal reality would incorporate vital features of the male side of that ambivalence.[9]

Men, in short, continued to want "maternal applause, menial services, and body contact" from women in the Movement.

Experiences in SNCC and SDS opened many women's eyes to the depth of sexist stereotyping in American culture. As Sara Evans and Harry Boyte observe, "[Women] discovered the realities of sexual inequality within the

very settings which had taught them the value of egalitarian community." [10]
Women who had been deeply involved in the civil rights struggle, at the
forefront of community organizing efforts, and in the middle of antiwar activism experienced a grating second class citizenship within these movements.
Men dominated Movement decision-making and its public face—the collective gatherings and media-attracting public demonstrations—as well as its
private realm of sexual relationships. For a while, women's grievances sim-
mered amidst self-doubt and the gnawing sense that it was wrong to distract
the Movement from the urgent issues of racism and the war. However, as
the black liberation movement and New Left lost momentum, and as women
came together to share their experiences, the women's movement took off.

Participation in the civil rights movement influenced the women's movement in two ways. The first was the inspirational role played by black women.
For years, black "mamas" had courageously confronted local white power
structures. These women often harbored the young SNCC workers and impressed them with their toughness. Charles Sherrod recalled "Mama Dolly:"
"a gray haired old lady of about seventy who can pick more cotton, 'slop more
pigs,' plow more ground, chop more wood, and do a hundred more things
better than the best farmer in the area. . . . There is always a 'mama.' She is
usually a militant woman in the community, outspoken, understanding and
willing to catch hell, having already caught her share." [11] Furthermore, figures like Ella Baker, Septima Clark, Diane Nash, and Ruby Doris Smith were
powerful role models for the white women who joined SNCC as well as for
subsequent generations of activists in the civil rights movement.

Young white women like Casey Hayden and Mary King were also sensitized
to the subtleties of racial prejudice and condescension. In response to similar
treatment at the hands of white and black men in SNCC, Hayden and King
wrote an anonymous memo to their colleagues decrying the "sexual caste system. . . . Having learned from the [civil rights] movement to think radically
about the personal worth and abilities of people whose role in society had gone
unchallenged before, a lot of women in the movement have begun trying to
apply those lessons to their own relations to men." [12]

Antagonisms between men and women grew as SNCC's communal bonds
loosened. Hayden and King's memo argued that, like blacks generally, women
in SNCC were largely excluded from the "hierarchical structures of power"
and placed in the same position of assumed subordination in personal relations. Subsequently Stokely Carmichael infuriated women activists with his

infamous quip, "The only position for women in SNCC is prone."[13] Prophetically Hayden and King observed that "maybe sometime in the future the whole of the women in this movement will become so alert as to force the rest of the movement to stop the discrimination and start the slow process of changing values and ideas so that all of us gradually come to understand that this is no more a man's world than it is a white world."[14]

The experience of women in SDS was little different. Shortly after reading the Hayden–King memo, women in SDS organized the first workshop on women at SDS's December "rethinking conference." Discussions focused on the problems ERAP women faced in their projects, job sharing within SDS, sexual relations, and women's identity in a male-dominated culture. As Sara Evans put it, the all-female sub-groups "talked for the first time as women" about "women's problems," anticipating the consciousness-raising groups that would soon nurture a growing sense of collective awareness. Barbara Haber recalls of one meeting with SDS men,

> I heard men talking and I suddenly understood that they had a point of view about the world . . . that was totally wrong. I found myself saying things I didn't have any idea I knew, thought, or felt. Within an hour I discovered I was a feminist. Bohngg! A woman friend put forth the view that it was natural for women to wear a wedding ring, to do the dishes, and a man not, because of the nature of her genitalia. I got angry, and put forth a counter-notion of myself as a sexual being, a being that acted. The meeting went on for eight hours. It was one of the six great evenings of my life. I just felt I could see the light, and that I was telling it without any self-consciousness.[15]

As Ann Popkin put it, "the fog before our eyes began to lift."[16]

By 1967 a growing number of women had participated in various forms of New Left activism. At the same time, SDS felt less and less democratic: "It made me feel like other people were making decisions for me and were making assumptions about me, as to who I was and what my political views were," remarked Betty Chewning.[17] Furthermore, women were marginalized by the emergence of the draft and draft resistance as central antiwar issues. While continuing to participate fully in antiwar and New Left activities, women found themselves turning more and more to issues of their own oppression. In 1967, the militant group WITCH (Women's International Conspiracy from Hell) was formed.[18]

As New Left radicalism hardened during 1967 to 1969, the tension between men and women in the Movement grew. SDS member Rayna Rapp recalls of her first contacts with the women's movement, "Once I let feminism in, I reorganized everything I understood about the world. That was my conversion experience—it was natural and it was quick. Afterwards I was so angry about the number of mimeograph machines I had turned and the number of phone calls I had made and the number of cups of coffee I had brought for other people."[19] Marge Piercy decried the changing tone of the New Left in 1969:

> For a while, people were generally willing to put effort into their relation-ships with each other and human liberation was felt as something to be acted out rather than occasionally flourished like a worn red flag. . . . It is not necessary to recount the history of the last two years to figure out what happened. Repression brings hardening. It is unlikely that the Movement could have gone along with the same degree of involvement in personal relationships. . . . But there is also a point beyond which cutting off sensitivity to others and honesty to what one is doing does not produce a more efficient revolutionary, but only a more efficient son of a bitch. We are growing some dandy men of steel nowadays.[20]

Infuriating encounters with abusive sexism accelerated the separatist trend. One illuminating example occurred at a National Mobilization Committee gathering in January 1969. One of two women speakers on the platform, SDS veteran Marilyn Saltzman Webb, was shouted down by unruly men in the crowd yelling "Take her off the stage and fuck her!" and "Take it off!" Webb's women's group, which had up to that point resisted the separatist urgings of the radical feminists, subsequently withdrew from New Left politics and orga-nized an abortion counseling center and a feminist newspaper called *off our backs* that is still in circulation.[21] Piercing expressions of the radical femi-nist critique were published in underground papers, notably Marge Piercy's "Grand Coolie Damn" in *Leviathan* in 1969 and Robin Morgan's "Goodbye to All That" in the first "liberated" edition of *The Rat* in 1970. Both recounted ways in which the militant left of SDS reflected the same sexually demeaning stereotypes as the mainstream culture it supposedly condemned. It is hardly surprising that, in their anger, radical feminists came to see "man" (as black separatists before them saw "white") as the enemy. As Marge Piercy observed, "There is much anger here at Movement men, but I know they have been warped and programmed by the same society that has damn near crippled us.

My anger is because they have created in the Movement a microcosm of that oppression and are proud of it."[22] Or as Robin Morgan put it, "We have met the enemy and he's our friend."

CONSCIOUSNESS-RAISING:
THE PERSONAL IS POLITICAL

The years 1968 to 1971 were, as Todd Gitlin has observed, a time of deeply divided experience, "agonizing for movement men, exhilarating for tens of thousands of women."[23] Women were angry, sometimes struggling, but "riding high" in their newfound, independent empowerment; small groups and collectives with names like Cell 16, Bread and Roses, and Sudsofloppen sprang up in Chicago, Boston, New York, Washington, and Berkeley and spread to additional cities via a women's network. Women organized health collectives, newspapers, women's shelters and clinics, abortion counseling services, natural childbirth classes, therapy groups, and, through it all, consciousness-raising groups.

Thousands of young women joined consciousness-raising groups—the very embodiment of prefigurative politics—in the late 1960s and early 1970s. As Sara Evans notes, the emphasis on the personal experience of oppression

> led to the creation of small groups within which women could share with mutual trust the intimate details of their lives. Formed almost instinctively at first as radical women gathered in each others' living rooms to discuss their needs, these small groups quickly became the primary structure of the women's revolt. They provided a place, a "free space," in which women could examine the nature of their own oppression and share the growing knowledge that they were not alone.[24]

Through consciousness-raising groups, the idea of personal politics took on new meaning. Sharing experiences of male domination meant sharing personal traumas of rape, childhood abuse, spouse abuse, and other forms of sexual exploitation.[25] These most intimate details of life were political; as Annie Popkin put it, "Personal life did not merely reflect politics, it *was* politics."[26] Jo Freeman described consciousness-raising as follows:

> The process is very simple. Women come together in small groups to share personal experiences, problems, and feelings. From this public

sharing comes the realization that what was thought to be individual is in fact common; that what was thought to be a personal problem has a social cause and a political solution. The rap group attacks the effects of *psychological* oppression and helps women to put it into a feminist context. Women learn to see how social structures and attitudes have molded them from birth and limited their opportunities. They ascertain the extent to which women have been denigrated in this society and how they have developed prejudices against themselves and other women. They learn to develop self-esteem and to appreciate the value of group solidarity. . . . Most women find this experience both irreversible and contagious.[27]

Like others recoiling from social strait-jackets in the Sixties, women spoke with the authority of experience.

Consciousness-raising (CR) groups spread rapidly. Internally, the women's movement was alive with the exhilaration of discovering one's shared oppression, one's authentic voice and personal power—"power to" rather than "power over" in Marilyn French's terms. In this exhilaration, the early days of women's liberation were similar to the awakening of civil rights activism in the South.

Many CR groups also echoed the New Left's mistrust of authority. The Redstockings went one step further in an effort to avoid "masculinist" domination by vocal members. Each woman was provided with a supply of chips. Each time she spoke, she would give up a chip; when they were all gone, she was not allowed to speak for the rest of the group session.

Encouraged by the collective support of sisterhood, women felt empowered to confront both the personal and social roots of their own denigration. Prefigurative politics were linked to instrumental objectives. Consciousness-raising accentuated ways in which women's reproductive rights were largely controlled by men or the male-dominated medical profession, a realization that had obvious political outcomes in the abortion rights movement as well as in the movement for changes in health care delivery and childbirth practices. Women challenged the attitudes of those outside their groups by confronting family members, lovers, or bosses. The process of consciousness-raising thus had both internal and external dimensions, erasing the traditional liberal demarcation between public/political and private/personal, and revealing ways in which maintaining privacy and separateness perpetuates the very social order that demeans women. Once the blinders were off, women saw how the privateness of their personal experiences, feelings, and doubts kept them in a subordinate position.

In many cases, separation from men became more profound. Radical feminists reversed the traditional conservative belief that biology is destiny, arguing that something in the makeup of men caused them to diverge from female priorities and aesthetics. Many came to view male supremacy and female subjugation as the root form of oppression in society. As the Redstockings Manifesto put it, "We identify the agents of our oppression as men. Male supremacy is the oldest, most basic form of domination. All other forms of exploitation and oppression (racism, capitalism, imperialism, etc.) are extensions of male supremacy: men dominate women, a few men dominate the rest." [28] Radical feminists advocated a separate women's culture based on uniquely female experience. Mary Daly prescribed a spiritual female journey in which all traces of patriarchy are exorcised. With an effort to breathe life into language deadened by patriarchy, Daly wrote:

> Breaking through the Male Maze is both exorcism and ecstasy. It is spinning through and beyond the fathers' foreground which is the arena of games. This spinning involves encountering the demons who block the various thresholds as we move through gateway after gateway into the deepest chambers of our homeland, which is the Background of our Selves. . . . Each time we move into deeper space, these numbing ghostly gases work to paralyze us, to trap us, so that we will be unable to move further. Each time we succeed in overcoming their numbing effect, more dormant senses come alive. Our inner eyes open, our inner ears become unblocked. We are strengthened to move through the next gateway and the next. This movement inward/outward is be-ing. It is spinning cosmic tapestries. It is spinning and whirling into the Background. [29]

The lesbian movement that emerged in the late 1960s was linked to the growing separatism of radical feminism. Ann Popkin recalls,

> As women turned to each other for affection and support that we had previously sought in men, many sensual feelings were liberated. At meetings we gave each other hugs and backrubs; in the streets we began to walk arm in arm. We felt a new freedom to explore our feelings for each other. Some of us made love with women we loved; some of us "came out." For

some women lesbianism was an extension of the desire to be completely self-sufficient.[30]

Daly distinguished between a strictly gay rights lesbianism ("relating genitally to women" while retaining "allegiance to men and male myths") and radical feminist lesbianism ("woman-identified, having rejected false loyalties to men on all levels").[31] For some groups like the Radicalesbians, lesbianism was the ultimate feminist metaphor ("feminism is the theory, lesbianism the practice"). For a while, the women's movement struggled with an internal tension between lesbian vanguardism and tolerance for diverse sexual lifestyles.[32]

■ The Feminist Critique

> The Achilles' heel of human civilization, which today has reached global genocidal and ecocidal proportions, resides in [the] false development of maleness through the repression of the female.
> —Rosemary Radford Ruether, *New Woman, New Earth*

The prefigurative politics of consciousness-raising provided the crucial psychological foundation of empowerment. Psychologist Jean Baker Miller argued that "feminine" traits considered weaknesses by masculine society— vulnerability, attunement to emotions, cooperativeness—were strengths desperately needed by society. "Yet, she maintained, in a situation of inequality and powerlessness, these characteristics can lead to subservience and to complex psychological problems."[33] Thus a second wave of feminism moved from *rejecting* to *celebrating* the differences between men and women in much the same manner that black nationalism celebrated the roots of black identity in black culture.[34] Adrienne Rich wrote that "it is precisely this culture and its political institutions which have split us off from itself. In so doing it has also split itself off from life, becoming the death culture of quantification, abstraction, and the will to power. . . . It is this culture and politics of abstraction which women are talking of changing, of bringing into accountability in human terms."[35]

Early consciousness-raising experiences led women to challenge the traditional division of labor on both the personal level of domestic responsibilities and in society at large. Different feminisms have followed different instrumental paths to free women (and the culture) from masculinist oppression.

Middle-class women organized and lobbied for child care services that would support their career ambitions. The effort to balance work and domestic responsibilities jarred relationships with men. Working-class and black women drew attention to the class and racial roots of economic deprivation and feminized poverty. One of the more universal feminist targets was male control of female reproductivity and the male- and technology-dominated medical profession. From abortion rights to natural childbirth and the revival of midwifery to feminist clinics, health collectives, and self-help practices, women sought to take control of the most personal arenas of sexual domination. Some radical feminists denounced motherhood as the root of women's oppression; others distinguished between the dominant social institution of motherhood and the deep grounding of feminist values in mothering.[36]

Various feminist strains converged in their critique of masculinity as a repressed and distorted form of human development dominating virtually all cultures. Feminists pointed to innumerable targets: man as hunter when feminists sought to protect natural resources, man as warrior when feminists joined peace movements, man as repressed technocrat when feminists targeted bureaucratic policy makers in government and the corporate sector, man as compulsive competitor when feminists infiltrated the corporate boardroom or the locker room, man as rapist when feminists attacked the sexual intimidation and domination of women, man as aloof parent when women empathized with the needs of their children, man as detached and incapable of intimacy when women asked their mates for more meaningful contact.

These qualities come back to a human personality viewed as out of balance and out of touch with much of its essential humanness—man alienated from, and abusive of, his body, his spirituality, his need for intimacy; man denying his own mortality while repressing his connection with nature; man projecting his own cerebral, disconnected self onto women, children, the needy, nature, the cosmos. Ultimately, this feminist challenge became a catalyst for a men's movement, in which men grappled with their sexist assumptions and their own personal repression.[37]

Within feminism's second wave, some liberal feminists questioned their old integrative assumptions. Thus, witnessing women training as West Point cadets, Betty Friedan asked if feminism had "simply delivered women into the militaristic, materialistic bowels of late capitalist American imperialism? Must the women's movement for equality come into ultimate conflict with the profound values of life that, for me as for others, have always been associated with women?"[38] Liberal feminism's weakness reflects liberalism's assumption that oppression is rooted in discriminatory customs or laws that can be changed by legislation and education. Sex role socialization helps to sustain the oppression of both sexes, and the organization of female maternity has deep psychological implications for male and female development.[39] Yet to focus solely on these contributing forces masks independently powerful social forces like racism, class exploitation, and the incentives of capitalism that block the liberation of women and men.

All versions of feminism converge in the revelation that misogyny and female oppression are a central form of domination that poisons all human relations and affects all other forms of domination. Yet, in seeking the transformation of society, different feminisms employ different methodologies, focus on different targets, and gravitate toward different strategies. Whereas liberal feminism views women's liberation as the incorporation of women into the present structures of late twentieth century capitalism, radical and socialist feminisms issue more fundamental critiques of this society and inevitably connect with other liberatory theories and movements. As Gloria Joseph and Jill Lewis maintain, "We have heard Black women's voices claiming that the struggle for women's liberation cannot be divorced from the struggle for Black liberation."[40] Postmodern feminists maintain there is no single true feminist perspective; there are many.[41] Socialist feminists rightly point to the ways in which gender domination, like racism and class exploitation, is functionally grounded in and greatly exacerbated by the imperatives of capitalism. Amidst an on-going debate about the relative importance of patriarchy and capitalism, some socialist feminists have attempted to integrate the sources of female oppression into a coherent theory.[42] As Lydia Sargent puts it, "Socialist feminists agreed with radical feminists that there was a system of oppression called patriarchy, and they agreed with marxist feminists that there was a class oppression defining the situation for all workers. They attempted to combine the two approaches in their analysis of society."[43]

Finally, feminism joins with new scientific paradigms and the non-Western traditions explored in the counterculture to challenge the entire Western scientific edifice built on dualism, objectivity, and the suppression of *eros*.[44] It converges with the ecology movement in rejecting the misogynist tradition of man dominating nature that dates back to Francis Bacon. As ecofeminism points out to other ecologically radical movements, women and nature have long been linked as the "other" in the distorted perceptions of masculinist

Western culture. Ecofeminist Ynestra King argues, "If male ecological scientists and social ecologists fail to deal with misogyny—the deepest manifestation of nature-hating in their own lives—they are not living the ecological lives or creating the ecological society they claim."[45] To be ecologically conscious, in short, requires an end to the domination of women.

■ The Ecology Movement

> We are for an economic system oriented toward the vital requirements of people and of future generations, toward the preservation of nature and the judicious handling of natural resources. We have in mind a society in which interpersonal relationships and the relationships between humans and nature become ever more the subject of conscious consideration, a society where attention to nature's life cycles, the development and use of technology, and the relationship between production and consumption become the business of all those concerned.
> —The Federal Program of the Greens (*die Grünen*)

Like the women's movement, and the civil rights and antiwar movements before it, the modern ecology movement that emerged at the end of the 1960s encompassed both a liberal, reformist wing rooted in the political mainstream, and a more radical wing grounded in the Sixties vision of community and the counterculture's rejection of materialist Western culture. Mainstream environmentalism encompasses a variety of ideological viewpoints, from conservative claims of enlightened corporatism to liberal reformism to a more radical critique of capitalism.

The more radical ecology stance builds on ecological science and its focus on relations between organisms and their environment. As ecofeminism, it draws on woman's connectedness with the *oikos* or home, and critiques the patriarchal characterization of both women and nature as "other." As social ecology it links hierarchical domination in human society to destruction of the nonhuman environment and attempts to bring biological and social aspects of ecology into harmony.[46] As deep ecology it draws on Eastern spiritual traditions, the study of Native Americans, and a variety of eco-philosophers to advocate a "gestalt of 'person in nature.'"[47] Deep ecology converges with strains of cultural ethnicity to advocate a decentralized bioregional future that emphasizes the physical, spiritual, and communal significance of place.[48]

Finally, the Green's socialism urges, along with local democratic participation and feminist liberation, the transformation of inherently destructive economic imperatives.[49]

The various ecological perspectives differ (and sometimes conflict) in significant ways. Yet they converge in their radical perspective that harmony between human and nonhuman nature requires both the transformation of the prevailing Western and masculinist mindset and restructuring of global political and economic institutions. Like many environmentalists, radical ecologists believe that nothing less than the survival of the earth is at stake.

Both mainstream environmentalism and the more radical ecology perspective are rooted in the twentieth century tradition of conservation that dates back to the Progressive era. In contemporary form, both reflect the revival of environmental concerns that began to emerge in the 1960s and took off after Earth Day in 1970. The 1963 publication of Rachel Carson's *Silent Spring*, which documented the spread of DDT throughout the biosphere, stimulated a growing ecological consciousness within the biological sciences that in turn helped to generate environmental activism. During the 1960s, Lyndon Johnson's Great Society included clean air and clean water legislation, and in 1969, Congress passed the National Environmental Policy Act. By requiring environmental impact statements for proposed new development and creating a Council on Environmental Quality charged with monitoring pollution and collecting environmental data, the new law eased the way for subsequent challenges to environmental despoliation.

Like the antiwar movement, environmental activism was triggered by events that brought the silent perils of ecological destruction graphically to light. One of the first of these was the explosion of an oil well off the coast of Santa Barbara, California in January 1969; the resulting spill ran unchecked for ten days, coating the beaches of greater Santa Barbara and killing vast quantities of sea creatures.[50] As Ross MacDonald recalled in 1972, "The blowout shook industry and the federal bureaucracy, whose rules and safeguards had failed to prevent it. . . . It triggered a social movement and helped to create a new politics, the politics of ecology, which is likely to exert a decisive influence on future elections and on our lives."[51] Dramatic examples of ecological damage and threats to human health drew increasing attention in the next several years; these included the blanket of smog enveloping Los Angeles, a dying Lake Erie, the burning Cuyahoga River outside Cleveland, and the controversial project to construct a trans-Alaskan oil pipeline.

Movement frustration intensified as reformist hopes were dashed by the continuing horrors of the Vietnam war and state repression.

13. Vietnamese children flee in terror from napalm. The girl in the center ripped off her burning clothes as she fled. AP/Wide World Photos

14. A 1967 march in Chicago revealed the breadth of antiwar sentiment. Copyright by Jo Freeman

15. Two sides of a generation divided by the Vietnam war confront each other at the 1967 March on the Pentagon. Photo by and © Paul Conklin, from Monkmeyer Press Photo Service

16. Oberlin College protesters were hosed and gassed while surrounding a Navy recruiter's car in 1967. © Peter Martyn

17. Chicago police assaulted protesters in Grant Park during the Democratic National Convention in 1968. This particular attack was provoked when a police infiltrator ripped down an American flag. Brian Shannon/reprinted by permission of Pathfinder Press

18. For a three-day weekend celebration in 1969, the Woodstock rock festival became the third largest city in New York State. © Ken Heyman

19. In this common counterculture scene, the New Mexico "Hog Farm" commune gathered for a meal in a New York City loft. Photo by Bonnie Freer. © Freer

20. A nation divided in 1969. The limousine bearing President Richard Nixon sped past thousands of "counter-inaugural" protesters restrained by a wall of U.S. troops. The Bettmann Archive. UPI/Bettmann

21. The massive National Moratorium demonstration at the Washington Monument in 1969. © Larry Fink

23. (Opposite) Feminist and antiwar anger converged in Gloria Steinem's poster of the women and children killed by American forces in the 1969 My Lai massacre in Vietnam. © Bonnie Freer 1970

22. (Above) An early women's liberation protest targeted society's sexual exploitation of women at the 1968 Miss America pageant. AP/Wide World Photos

24. A Black Panther peers out from Chicago headquarters riddled with bullet holes from a police assault that killed Panther leader Fred Hampton. The Bettmann Archive. UPI/ Bettmann

25. Flag-waving protester Alan Canfora faced down the barrels of National Guard rifles moments before the murder of four students at Kent State.
© John Filo

The ecology movement began to mobilize with the first of several annual Earth Days held in April 1970. As the *Christian Science Monitor* anticipated the event, "Mark the date: April 22. On that day, if the present indicators produce the expected snowballing effect, this nation will witness the largest expression of public concern in history over what is happening to the environment."[52] Well over 100,000 Americans observed the first Earth Day, and far larger numbers became involved in one or more aspects of the initial Earth Week. Originally conceived by Senator Gaylord Nelson of Wisconsin as a kind of national teach-in modelled on the antiwar movement, Earth Week combined local community cleanup projects, large demonstrations in urban centers, and a one-day "liberation" of downtown streets from the automobile. It became a nationwide celebration of environmental awareness reminiscent of the Vietnam Moratorium, drawing attention to rising public concern and highlighting widespread local initiatives.

Speakers across the nation ranged from the New Left to the business community. Not surprisingly, they blamed diverse sources for environmental destruction and offered a confusing array of solutions. Not everyone was enthusiastic about the new environmental initiative. Black protesters criticized students at San Jose State College when they buried a brand new car as part of Earth Week. George Wiley, chair of the National Welfare Rights Organization, anticipated future debates when he argued, "You must not embark on programs to curb economic growth without placing a priority on maintaining income, so that the poorest people won't simply be further depressed in their condition but will have a share, and be able to live decently."[53] Some activists warned that the Nixon administration would use the environmental movement to drain energy from antiwar and racial struggles. And for the establishment, Atomic Energy Commission chair Glenn Seaborg hedged against ecology scare tactics: "What is most disturbing to me is that this trend of thinking is filled with enough logic and truth to suggest that many of the nightmares projected by today's doomsayers could come true—if we were to continue unresponsively and irresponsibly on our current course."[54] While some business people supported Earth Day concerns, others like Thomas Shepard, publisher of *Look* magazine, argued that "we are solving most of our problems . . . conditions are getting better not worse."[55]

Earth Day was closely followed by publication of the Ralph Nader study group report "Vanishing Air," which documented air pollution and pointedly criticized congressional inaction (particularly the "environmental Senator"

Edmund Muskie of Maine, then the leading Democratic presidential con-
tender). In 1970, publication of influential books like Barry Commoner's *The
Closing Circle* and Lewis Mumford's *The Myth of the Machine* broadened the
ecological critique.

As popular concern for the environment grew, politicians responded. Some,
like Senator Muskie, spoke at the original Earth Day celebrations. President
Nixon embraced the new wave of concern when he signed the new National
Environmental Policy Act into law, proclaiming, "The nineteen-seventies
absolutely must be the years when America pays its debt to the past by reclaiming the purity of its air, its waters, and our living environment. It is
literally now or never."[56] Symbolizing the degree to which environmentalism
had penetrated mainstream consciousness, California State Assembly leader
Jesse Unruh claimed, "Ecology has become the political substitute for the
word 'motherhood.'"[57]

The early 1970s were the heyday of environmentalism. The Clean Air Act
Amendments of 1970 called for sharply reduced emission levels for such pol-
lutants as carbon monoxide, sulfur dioxide, and nitrogen oxide. New emission
level restrictions were to be phased in for automobiles, utilities, and fossil
fuel burning industries. The Clean Water Act imposed similar restrictions on
pollution of the nation's waterways and water supplies. Several states, most
notably California, passed tough new pollution control laws.

Like the Great Society programs of the Johnson administration, the political
history of this phase of environmental legislation is instructive. First, the issue
of environmental pollution passed from the invisible realm of "non-decisions"
onto the political agenda as a legitimate public policy concern. In good part,
the new attention to pollution reflected the fact that public opinion had been
mobilized by the activists' rallies, projects, and confrontational tactics, and by
newspaper editorials and letters to the editor.[58]

Second, the political system responded to pollution in classic liberal fashion. Amidst surging public attention, much was made of the massive legislative effort to clean up the environment. Public officials were aglow with
hopeful rhetoric about the new public priority. Yet all was not rosy; it soon
became clear that environmental protection was not in "everyone's interest"
as some had claimed. One year after President Nixon's glowing pronounce-
ment, he reappraised his environmental policies and informed an audience
of auto industry executives that he would not allow environmental concern
"to be used sometimes falsely and sometimes in a demagogic way to destroy

the system."[59] Behind the scenes in Congress, the industrial polluters lobbied hard and successfully to postpone the implementation of new emission limits. Within mainstream imperatives of economic growth, centralized energy, and corporate power, the OPEC oil cartel and the recession of 1973–1975 produced a crisis that virtually killed progress on environmental regulation. Congress explicitly waived the environmental impact statement requirement to expedite construction of the Alaskan oil pipeline, an act that was to reap bitter fruit in the 1988 Exxon Valdez oil spill. By 1979, President Carter had proposed an Energy Mobilization Board empowered to waive local environmental regulations that might block energy development. With the ascendancy of the Reagan administration in 1980, the effort to roll back environmental safeguards accelerated.

THE EVOLUTION OF ECOLOGICAL ACTIVISM

Man poisons Nature; Nature poisons man in return.
—John Rodman, "The Dolphin Papers"

As the legislative struggles of the Seventies proceeded, a more radical ecological perspective was developing on two fronts. First, increasing awareness of ultimate limits on the earth's resources clashed with the prevailing growth fixation of industrialized nations. Second, activists influenced by antiwar experiences turned their attention to the nuclear power industry in 1974, one year after U.S. troops were withdrawn from Vietnam.

Both fronts reflected the Sixties climate of disenchantment with the modernist dream. In 1968, Stewart Brand's *Whole Earth Catalog* conveyed the prefigurative vision of the Sixties in announcing that "a realm of intimate, personal power is developing—power of the individual to conduct his own education, find his own inspiration, shape his own environment, and share his adventure with whoever [sic] is interested."[60] Repelled by the horror of technological war in Vietnam, drawn to a simpler communal "back-to-the-earth" lifestyle, and intrigued by Eastern spiritualism and Native American culture, many young people were predisposed to carry an environmental ethic to its more radical conclusions. As Langdon Winner has observed, "Many of the same concerns and passions that fueled activism in civil rights, the New Left, antiwar protests, counterculture, and environmentalism led eventually to a critical reexamination of the foundations of modern industrial society."[61]

The Antinuclear Movement: One of the primary early targets of ecological activism was the nuclear power industry. In fact, of all forms of environmental politics, the antinuclear movement was the most directly reminiscent of Sixties activism. With citizens' referenda, lobbying, litigation, and
administrative intervention; civil disobedience and other forms of direct action;
and mass rallies aglow with countercultural trappings, the antinuclear movement recalled the antiwar movement that had just ended. In its early days, it
was largely populated by former peace activists as well as feminists, assorted
environmentalists, and counterculture communards. As writer Anna Gyorgy
observed,

> In the mid to late 70s, as the nuclear program spread across the coun-
> try, people who had been politically active in the late 60s began to get
> involved in the nuclear issue. The new nuclear opponents found the
> same kinds of cover-ups, lies, vested corporate interests and inhumanity
> involved in nuclear power as in the war issue. In fact, nuclear power
> seemed in many ways to be "the Vietnam war brought home." By aiding
> the nuclear industry while assuring the public it had nothing to fear, the
> government was supporting an energy source that could prove as lethal as
> any war.[62]

The antinuclear movement also took on international overtones as antinuclear protests spread through Europe. Along with a growing peace movement, the European antinuclear movement helped spawn the West German
Green movement. Public opposition to nuclear power has grown in the wake
of accidents like those at Pennsylvania's Three Mile Island facility in 1979
and the Soviet Union's Chernobyl plant in 1986, as well as long-term leaks at
nuclear weapons facilities at Savannah River, South Carolina, and Hanford,
Washington.

One catalyst for the antinuclear movement was the energy crunch of 1973–
1974 and President Gerald Ford's Project Independence, aimed at freeing the
United States from its dependence on Middle Eastern oil. Among Ford's recommendations was the construction of 200 new nuclear power plants, despite
growing evidence of health hazards associated with nuclear power. Citizens
intervened in administrative hearings before the Atomic Energy Commission
and Nuclear Regulatory Commission, eventually leading to a National Inter-
venors coalition made up of scientists and other professionals. Ralph Nader's
first Critical Mass conference on alternative energy was held in 1974.

Amidst rising public concern, the dramatic direct action of one individual in Montague, Massachusetts, galvanized the antinuclear movement:

On 22 February 1974 [less than two months after Northeast Utilities announced plans to build a dual-reactor nuclear plant in Montague], organic farmer Sam Lovejoy took a crowbar to the support structure of a weather-monitoring tower NU had put up at the site. With its bright blinking lights, the 550-foot tower symbolized the impending nuke. Lovejoy felled 349 feet of the tower and turned himself in to the local police. He presented a statement in which he took full responsibility for the action.[63]

Like antiwar protesters before him, Lovejoy's civil disobedience was aimed at putting the nuclear industry and a corrupt political process on trial. In testimony regarding Lovejoy's action, Howard Zinn maintained,

These governmental institutions have not been very adequate to protect people, and from time to time, when grievances became too deep, groups of people had to go outside the machinery of government, had to break the law, had to commit civil disobedience, in order to dramatize something that was happening. And it seemed to me that after the most recent acts of civil disobedience, that is against the Vietnam War, maybe the time is right now for people to look closer to home at the dangers to our lives posed by corporate control of our lives.[64]

Antinuclear momentum grew rapidly in the months after Lovejoy's action. Typically, antinuclear actions were locally based and coordinated by an alliance or coalition of peace, environmental, and feminist activists. As Gyorgy notes, "Most intervention efforts have been organized by women. . . . The new groups stress democratic decision-making and open participation. They are consciously non-sexist and non-hierarchical. Responsibilities are shared, with no elected "officers" or designed [sic] leadership. People who do the work make decisions, and, given varying (volunteer) time commitments, people share the organizational work and direction setting."[65]

The first such collective action was the Clamshell Alliance's campaign against the proposed Seabrook nuclear plant on the New Hampshire coast. Inspired by a citizen occupation that blocked construction of a West German plant, the "Clams" consisted of several dozen New England affinity groups trained in nonviolent civil disobedience, coordinated by a representative committee and governed by consensus decision making. Beginning with a Seabrook march on April 10, 1976, the Clamshell Alliance engaged in a variety of actions over the next several years, including an occupation in May 1977 that resulted in over 1,400 arrests.[66] Many of those arrested refused to pay bail and were held in national guard armories. Echoing the perceptions of SNCC field hands over a decade earlier, one detainee noted, "It was like the state had given us five free conference centers."[67] Over 18,000 appeared at a Stop Seabrook rally in 1978. As protests continued apace, Seabrook opponents challenged each stage in the approval process through administrative hearings and litigation.

In the aftermath of the initial Clamshell Alliance action, groups with similarly colorful names reflecting potential nuclear victims cropped up across the country. The SHAD (Sound and Hudson against Atomic Development) Alliance opposed the Shoreham plant on Long Island. Pennsylvania's Susquehanna Alliance fought unsuccessfully against the Berwick and Limerick plants and joined with West Virginia's Panhandle Alliance to confront Three Mile Island. Major extended actions were held by the Abalone Alliance against the Diablo Canyon plant in California and by the Rocky Flats Action Group against that weapons facility in Colorado. The Potomac Alliance concentrated on federal government officials.[68]

The watchword of all these groups was local grassroots organizing. Newsletters like *No Nukes Left!* and Abalone Alliance's *Radioactive Times* provided an information link among activists and outreach to the general public. Local canvassing and public meetings continued alongside more dramatic nonviolent civil disobedience like the Seabrook occupation and the Abalone Alliance's "Declaration of Nuclear Resistance."

The antinuclear movement was the opening salvo in a campaign to shift from traditional American reliance on fossil fuel and nuclear energy sources. The preference for decentralized, community-based institutions, concern for natural resources and pollution, and the oil crisis all stimulated initiatives for solar, wind, and hydroelectric energy. On April 18, 1977, President Carter presented his National Energy Plan to the nation. Carter's strong initial emphasis on energy conservation, "the moral equivalent of war," was subsequently scuttled in the Senate and by 1978 was replaced by energy growth through natural gas price deregulation and new support for nuclear energy. After the Three Mile Island accident in 1979 and the Iran hostage crisis, the Reagan administration took power and began its assault on the environmental regulations of the 1970s.

TOWARD A RADICAL ECOLOGY

The 1972 publication of the Club of Rome report, *The Limits to Growth*, provided the first spark for a debate that continues to the present-day concern for sustainable growth.[69] Using a computer model that projected trends in population, agriculture, industry, natural resources, and pollution, the authors forecast a grim future. In less than one hundred years, the earth's limits would be exceeded, resulting in precipitous declines in population and industrial capacity. Although *The Limits to Growth* was highly controversial,[70] it had a major impact on ecological thinking. It confirmed the more intuitive, "feel-it-in-our-bones" understanding of those who would later call themselves ecofeminists and deep ecologists.

The theme of limits inspired visionary statements like E. F. Schumacher's *Small is Beautiful*, incisive logical metaphors like Garret Hardin's "The Tragedy of the Commons," and more radical political tracts like William Ophuls' *Ecology and the Politics of Scarcity*.[71] Along with the decentralist impulses of the counterculture, it fostered a movement for appropriate technology and soft energy. The latter, as articulated in Amory Lovins' *Soft Energy Paths*, emphasized decentralized, renewable energy and low technology matched to "end-use needs" instead of the highly polluting, centralized, and corporate fossil fuel and nuclear industries.[72]

Soft energy is grounded in a vision that replaces the traditional Western view of man over nature with a communitarian ethic of human and non-human nature in ecological balance.[73] Along with other variants of radical ecology, this vision builds on the counterculture's exploration of noncerebral ways of knowing and echoes the Sixties belief in participatory democracy while rejecting the priesthood of technocratic experts. It recoils in aesthetic and empathic horror at environmental destruction wrought by imposing an aggressive human technology on nature. Thus Langdon Winner wrote of the Diablo Canyon nuclear plant:

> To put the matter bluntly, in that place, on that beach, against those rocks, mountains, sands, and seas, the power plant at Diablo Canyon is simply a hideous mistake. It is out of place, out of proportion, out of reason. It stands as a permanent insult to its natural and cultural surroundings. The thing should never have been put there, regardless of what the most elegant cost/benefit, risk/benefit calculations may have shown. Its presence is a tribute to those who cherish power and profit over everything in nature and our common humanity.[74]

The ecological vision is made radical because it is irreconcilable with the interlocking institutions of the American mainstream. As Amory Lovins has written of the contradiction between soft and hard energy paths:

> These two directions of development are mutually exclusive: the pattern of commitments of resources and time required for the hard energy path and the pervasive infrastructure that it accretes gradually make the soft path less and less attainable. That is, our two sets of choices compete not only in what they accomplish, but also in what they allow us to contemplate later. They are logistically competitive, institutionally incompatible, and culturally antithetical.[75]

The quest for renewable, soft energy contains an implicitly radical challenge to the undemocratic economic control underlying the nuclear industry, as well as the consolidated power of the giant oil corporations. As H. Nowotny argued, "Opposition against nuclear power in its social structures roots is *opposition against those who will benefit from further economic and political concentration and centralization*. It is directed against "big" industry, seen in collusion with "big" government and "big" science. It is the opposition coming from those who feel *powerless and small* in the face of these developments."[76] In brief, society cannot adequately pursue the soft energy path without the radical transformation of political, technical, and most of all economic institutions.

However, the radical ecological vision goes further. It identifies the ultimate dynamic of ecocide in the very fabric of modernity: in liberal individualism and corporate capitalism, nationalism, and the competitive global economy. As William Ophuls has argued, "the tragedy of commons radically challenge[s] fundamental American and Western values. Under conditions of ecological scarcity the individual, possessing an inalienable right to pursue happiness as he defines it and exercising his liberty in a basically laissez-faire system, will *inevitably* produce the ruin of the commons."[77] Francis Carney observed this conflict in the smog-filled Los Angeles basin:

> Every person who lives in this basin knows that for twenty-five years he has been living through a disaster. We have all watched it happen, have participated in it with full knowledge just as men and women once went knowingly and willingly into the "dark Satanic mills." The smog is the result of ten million individual pursuits of private gratification. But there is absolutely nothing that any individual can do to stop its spread. Each Angeleno is totally powerless to end what he hates. An individual act of

renunciation is now nearly impossible, and, in any case, would be meaningless unless everyone else did the same thing. But he has no way of
getting everyone else to do it. He does not even have any way to talk about
such a course.[78]

Ultimately, Garrett Hardin's metaphor of the commons applies to the ecosphere as a whole. It requires a fundamental transformation in political and
economic institutions around the globe if ecological disaster is to be avoided.

Hardin and Ophuls' analysis points toward a kind of ascetic authoritarianism on a planetary scale, which is one clear counterpoint to the indulgent
privatism of the marketplace. However, nothing could be more antithetical
to the democratic vision of the 1960s, or for that matter to ecofeminism or
bioregionalism. Critics from the Left maintain that ecocide may be avoided
through a combination of forces: growing global awareness of impending disaster, the mobilization of community activism against forces that endanger the
environment, and the transformation of economies away from the imperatives
of capitalism. Social ecologist Murray Bookchin identifies a basic contradiction of capitalism, namely, that it simultaneously promises an end to material
scarcity and creates appetites that can never be fulfilled, thereby accelerating the exploitation of natural resources and the destruction of community:
"Having demolished all the ethical and moral limits that once kept it in hand,
market society in turn has demolished almost every historic relationship between nature, technics, and material well-being. . . . We have arrived at a point
in history's account of need where the very *capacity* to select needs, which
freedom from material scarcity was expected to create, has been subverted by
a strictly appetitive sensibility."[79]

Despite a major environmental protection effort in the 1970s, the world is
no closer to the vision of a healthy and unpolluted ecosphere. Instead, as the
World Commission on Environment and Development observed in 1987:

Each year another 6 million hectares of productive dryland turns into
worthless desert. Over three decades, this would amount to an area
roughly as large as Saudi Arabia. More than 11 million hectares of forests are destroyed yearly, and this, over three decades, would equal an
area about the size of India. Much of this forest is converted to low-grade
farmland unable to support the farmers who settle it. In Europe, acid pre-
cipitation kills forests and lakes and damages the artistic and architectural
heritage of nations; it may have acidified vast tracts of soil beyond reason-

able hope of repair. The burning of fossil fuels puts into the atmosphere carbon dioxide, which is causing gradual global warming. This "greenhouse effect" may by early next century have increased average global temperatures enough to shift agricultural production areas, raise sea levels to flood coastal cities, and disrupt national economies. Other industrial gases threaten to deplete the planet's protective ozone shield to such an extent that the number of human and animal cancers would rise sharply and the oceans' food chain would be disrupted. Industry and agriculture put toxic substances into the human food chain and into underground water tables beyond reach of cleansing.[80]

Each year seems to bring new, sobering reminders of the earth's fragility. The accelerating global crisis virtually insures that the ecology movement will be an enduring legacy of the Sixties. As William Ophuls has contended, "The crisis is real, and it does indeed challenge our institutions and values in a most profound way—more profoundly, in fact, than some of the most ardent environmentalists are willing to admit."[81]

■ A Revived Left Critique

One clear legacy of the 1960s experience was the revival of neo-Marxian criticism. Many who were radicalized by their experiences during the Sixties joined and extended the critical perspective of the Old Left, largely unencumbered by the latter's turbulent preoccupation with the Soviet Union. As political scientist Mark Kesselman observes, "The defeat of the left in the 1970's provided a forced opportunity for theoretical reflection. . . . The few years since the late 1960's have been the most fertile period of Marxist political analysis."[82] The explosion in Marxist political research, publication of radical textbooks in American government, and organization of a radical "Caucus for a New Political Science" were echoed in all the social sciences and in disciplines like philosophy, literature, art history, biology, women's and ethnic studies, and education.[83] Liberation theology emerged, especially in Latin American and black churches, as a formidable opponent to hierarchical Catholicism and the traditional Church.

The resulting Left brought to the participatory movements of the Sixties, and to feminism and ecology, a neo-Marxian critique refined by the transformation of American and global capitalism in the postwar years. Distinguishable from instrumental Marxist–Leninism and the thoroughly discredited Stalinism, neo-Marxism also rejects the narrow economic determinism long associated with "vulgar" Marxism. Yet it retains a methodology attentive to the material grounding of human (and natural) oppression and it highlights the ever-present significance of class.

Neo-Marxism contributes significantly to the legacy of the 1960s by distinguishing the unmistakable impact of capitalism in producing or reinforcing the ills targeted by Sixties movements—poverty, racial and sexual inequality, elite dominated pluralism, the war in Vietnam, the decline of community and growth of impersonal public space, and the specter of ecological destruction— as well as elite efforts to retrench since the 1960s. In brief, capitalism is what links these forces together. Failure to attend to this link means we fail to learn crucial lessons the 1960s can teach us.

CAPITALISM AND INEQUALITY

In the latter years of the civil rights movement, increasing numbers of black leaders focused on the role of capitalism in sustaining racial inequality despite the gains wrought by activism.[84] Neo-Marxist economists examined the symbiotic relationship between racism and capitalism. In 1966, Paul Baran and Paul Sweezy contended that a permanent black underclass benefits capitalism in three ways: through residential and social benefits associated with a segregated poor population, through the status anxieties exacerbated by capitalism's stratification, and through capitalist development that left the black migrants out of the job structure.[85]

Similarly, the capitalist marketplace operates to reinforce and rigidify the forces of patriarchy that oppress women. The impersonal exchange-value produced by men in the workforce is given clear priority over the use-value produced (and reproduced) by women in the home. Public decision-making is freed from the intrusion of private concerns, and the separation between the two is rigidified. The distorted masculine personality is conducive to the supposed neutrality of the marketplace and the formal-legal ethic of rights upon which capitalism depends for its ethical justification.[86]

Through its preoccupation with price and cost, capitalism reinforces the masculinist view of women as things. Sex as commodity, like labor as commodity, oppresses women as it oppresses workers. In fact, as many feminists argue, the masculine sexuality of dominance and subordination rather than erotic communion reduces and depersonalizes women so that men will not have to face the threat of intimacy and vulnerability. In the process, capitalism lays the groundowrk for its perpetuation in future generations.

Racial and gender inequality are psychologically significant variants of the poverty and inequality inherent in capitalism generally. One of the main contributions of the Marxian tradition has been its attention to class exploitation and inequality embedded in the private ownership and control of the means of production. Not only does capitalism produce enormous disparities in wealth and income, it depends on inequality for incentives that reinforce workplace control and spur private acquisition, resulting in an acquiescent, consuming public. In sum, to drive the personal aspirations of those who make it work, capitalism requires a highly visible inequality, the visible threat of poverty and misery on the one hand and the lure of material well-being on the other.

Radical theories of poverty that evolved out of the Great Society era spoke of the structural foundation of poverty. Not only do the poor fulfill the same psychological needs as a racially outcast group, but poverty itself is grounded in an unequal labor market. Those factors normally seen as the causes of poverty by liberal and conservative critics can, in fact, be seen as poverty's manifestations more deeply rooted in the occupational structure and powerlessness of working people.[87]

In the end, maintaining a capitalist economy ensures that poverty and pervasive inequality will persist. A political system wedded to capitalism and responsive to powerful elites will, in the best of times, produce benign social welfare programs that soften some of the harshest edges for some of the poor, and civil rights legislation that largely benefits the black middle class. From the radical perspective, that is essentially what happened with the Great Society programs and the civil rights movement in the 1960s.

The inequality inherent in capitalism is reinforced by uneven development in the marketplace, with profound implications for the Third World, American foreign ventures like Vietnam, and the global ecosphere. Briefly, those with capital are able to develop, prosper, and accumulate additional capital, whereas those without are left behind. One direct effect is regional inequality, exacerbating the inequality between classes of people. Globally, the impact is more profound. Third World development is retarded by the Third World's role in global capitalism of providing raw materials and markets for the industrialized "core" economies. The Third World is thereby plagued by severe poverty, hunger, and malnutrition. Overpopulation is essentially a *response* to these conditions, not their cause, as mainstream critics contend.[88] Overpopulation, in turn, feeds the problem of scarce global resources. Those left behind are caught in a vicious cycle.

One typical response of capitalist nations to Third World underdevelopment is Western style development that

> never seeks to enhance the specific, generic, original features of "undeveloped" countries and their peoples, treating them rather as if they were a kind of undifferentiated clay to be moulded to the standard requirements of the world market and of world capital, to the uniform tastes of international bureaucrats and national ones trained in their image. Hunger is one result. People who will not, or cannot, become consumers in the global food system will not get enough to eat. Militarization is another. Masses of miserable people with little to lose are prone to revolt. Armed forces (including the police) in Third World countries are used as often internally as against outsiders.[89]

Another inherent by-product of uneven development is imperialism; in the postwar era, the effort to maintain the *pax Americana* led to a consistent and often bloody pattern of American intervention. The most devastating example was the war in Vietnam.

VIETNAM AND GLOBAL HEGEMONY

The radical critique of the American war in Vietnam shares the moral horror and indignation expressed by liberal critics in the antiwar movement. However, the radical view targets structural imperatives that made the war, or one like it, virtually inevitable. Radicals have stepped outside the official mythology that sees the post–World War II global role of the United States as essentially benevolent.

As the European colonial empires broke up in the postwar years, and as the United States became the world's foremost economic and military power, the myth of benign American hegemony began to take hold. American global interventionism went hand-in-hand with the need to protect a world-wide stability necessary to the vitality of American corporations within the competitive global economy. Dependent on the Third World for cheap but essential raw materials, perpetually in search of markets for U.S. exports, and driven to grow in order to survive in the competitive world market, American corporations have required a global environment conducive to their expansion. Stability, in short, means an integrated world system that maximizes the economic freedom of American corporations. As Gabriel Kolko argued, "Intangibly, it is really the political and psychological assurance of total freedom of development of national economic power that is vital to American economic growth. . . . anything that undermines that condition presents a danger to [America's] present hegemony. Countering, neutralizing, and containing the disturbing political and social trends thus becomes the most imperative objective of its foreign policy."[90]

Vietnam was crucially and symbolically important for the maintenance of this global system, not so much for its tangible resources.[91] The Eisenhower–Dulles domino theory and John Kennedy's "finger in the dike" metaphor reflect the *integrated* quality of the global system. If Vietnam's war of national liberation were to succeed, if Vietnam were to develop independent of this system, the Vietnamese struggle would have, in Noam Chomsky's words, a powerful "demonstration effect" for all other Third World nations exploited by the system of global capitalism. As Kolko has argued, "It is logical to regard Vietnam, therefore, as the inevitable cost of maintaining United States imperial power, a step toward saving the future in something akin to its present form by revealing to others in the Third World what they too may encounter should they also seek to control their own development."[92]

Not surprisingly, the domino metaphor has been applied to American intervention in Nicaragua and El Salvador with bloody results.[93] In one case, an American-dependent mercenary force cooperated with American economic and political aggression to insure that the leftist–nationalist, and largely democratic, Sandinista experiment would fail.[94] In the other, a direct echo of Vietnam, American military aid has sustained a brutal reign of terror against an impoverished peasantry and an indigenous guerrilla movement.[95]

Maintaining the integrated world system is, in Kolko's words, "utterly incompatible" with the "irrepressible belief that men can control their own fate and transform their own societies."[96] In short, it is incompatible with democratic self-determination.

The contradiction between global hegemony and democracy is, of course, clouded by official rhetoric that habitually invokes the name of democracy for American overseas intervention. This strategy could not work were it not for the campaign against the communist "menace," which for years was the ultimate threat to American "democracy." As has been widely documented, anticommunism is a crucial filter in the American propaganda machine.[97] Throughout the post–World War II period, inflammatory anticommunist rhetoric and exaggerated claims of Soviet intentions proved highly functional in fostering public quiescence and quelling dissent, especially when that dissent might be critical of American corporate hegemony. The absence of a believable Soviet threat poses an extraordinary new challenge to the propaganda machine.

CAPITALISM AND ENVIRONMENTAL DESTRUCTION

The dynamic of global inequality and uneven development not only necessitates the use of force to sustain the hegemony of developed countries, it accelerates the eco-destructive imperatives built into capitalism. In contrast to the mainstream argument that ecology and equality are conflicting objectives, inequality and environmental destruction go hand in hand to the degree that *inequality* is the driving force for growth and development. Capital mobility, or the freedom of capital to move in order to maximize profitability, causes localities, states, and nations to bid against each other for new industrial development. The more fiscally strapped the community, the more likely it is to disregard long-term implications like environmental pollution or infrastructure costs. In exchange for their community service, corporations are able to extract promises (if indeed they are needed) of a desirable environment for business activity, including cheap, nonunion labor and minimal workplace, health, or environmental safeguards.

The realities of market competition relegate most "have-nots" to a perpetual catch-up effort that accelerates global environmental degradation, as can be seen in the rain forest destruction occuring in debt-saddled Brazil. The environmental implications for distressed urban areas in the United States, to say nothing of the Third World and the global ecosphere, are profound. And, despite the ideological claim that growth will translate into the reduction of poverty, new capital inevitably fails to remedy gross inequalities.[98] The outcome is that U.S. (or developed world) firms sustain their profitability, Third World oligarchs get richer, a small middle class may prosper, while the ecosphere deteriorates, and vast Third World masses remain deeply impoverished and hungry.

More generally, the capitalist market exacerbates the tragedy of the commons whereby it is in each firm's or each individual's interest to maximize resource use even if the aggregate social costs are devastating. In the competitive marketplace, increased profits mean more capital; more capital translates into an advantageous position vis-à-vis one's competitors. At the micro-level of the firm, or the macro-level of a nation's economy, nongrowth is equivalent to economic crisis.[99] Moreover, capitalist growth must respond primarily to the availability of capital and the potential for profit, not to human need or ecological vulnerability.

Furthermore, the private control of production and investment decisions renders environmental considerations marginal in precisely those industrial settings that pose the greatest potential threat to the environment. The bottom line is the most powerful imperative of capitalist enterprise. The rest consists of externals. Consequently, air and water pollution costs are not calculated as part of industrial or energy production. Topsoil erosion, declining groundwater, and long-term pesticide or fertilizer pollution do not figure into agricultural production computations. Opportunities for profit maximization chew up unused land. Quick-buck developers swallow up less profitable, older enterprises like small family farms and convert them into cheaply constructed suburban developments or shopping malls.

In short, we have Hardin's "tragedy of the commons." What makes perfect sense at the micro-level of the firm adds up to disaster at the macro-level of society, indeed of the earth. Exchange value pre-empts use value. "New" repeatedly and rapidly replaces "old." Quality declines, quantity increases, and waste is multiplied. The cumulative effect of thousands of isolated microdecisions is the macro-destruction of the environment.[100]

CAPITALISM VERSUS DEMOCRACY: ELITE-DOMINATED POLITICS

In the American liberal tradition, politics is based on the power of private groups to influence government.[101] The result is, as economists Samuel Bowles and Herbert Gintis argue, that liberalism "would seem to make democracy safe for elites—democracy is confined to a realm (the state) relatively unlikely to interfere with the wielding of economic power and limited to forms (representative government) insufficient for the consolidation of popular power."[102]

Efforts by governments to intervene in the economy in ways that threaten to reduce the profitability of private firms have a long history of at best limited success. Effective government intervention has usually come in response to intense crises in which public awareness is at a high level (that is, *after* economic activity has produced substantial and demonstrable damage), and often when private businesses have limited clout or are in some way vulnerable. Even in these cases, much government intervention has been more symbolic than truly effective.[103]

One obvious reason for corporate power lies in the enormous financial, organizational, and technical resources that the corporate sector brings to bear on the political process—resources that are unmatched, indeed unmatchable, by any competing interests or coalition of interests. This is not only true in the traditional realms of interest-group liberalism, legislative and administrative lobbying, but in the ever-increasing centrality of money and political action committees, or PACs, in political campaigns.

A second and more subtle reason for the public power of private economic enterprise lies in capital mobility, or the power inherent in the private firm's choice of location. Capital mobility affects the public realm at the local, state, and national level in a variety of ways. Almost all of the effects enhance the power of business at the expense of the local community, the workforce, or the environment. A private business cannot be easily refuted when it claims that increased costs of production will force it to close the local plant if new restrictions are enacted or if local taxes are not waived. Bowles and Gintis point out that

> capital has a kind of veto power over public policy that is quite independent of its ability to intervene directly in elections or in state decision making. . . . [T]he power of capital—its command over state policy—thus derives not so much from what it does but from what it might not do. As in many other situations, power resides with the party that can effectively (and without great cost) withdraw resources and thereby inflict large costs on an opponent. . . . The power of capital is based in large part on the fact that it is free to move. In this respect, . . . capital is quite unlike labor. Capital is owned by people and alienable from them; it can be invested or withdrawn or sent around the world by nothing more than the touch of a computer keyboard. Labor is embodied in people.[104]

More pervasively, capital mobility reinforces the popular ideology that "what's good for General Motors is good for the country." Because a business can move freely, its interests become equated with the public's interests, thereby disarming public support for the regulation of business. The potential presence of a firm means visible and imminent economic activity in a community. Through the vehicle of job creation, business enterprises make the claim of acting in the community interest regardless of the tangible private interests that are the raison d'etre of business. Sociologist Robert Bellah and his associates reveal how distorted this perception can become in a town meeting member's claim that

> it is legitimate for a group like the chamber of commerce to organize vigorously to promote town meeting decisions that would make it easier to do business in town. Such policies would merely assure a framework of regulations that would enable individual businesses to *make a contribution to the community* by providing products or jobs needed by individual community members. If individual businesses fail to provide desired products, they will go out of business. Groups like school teachers, however, are using their organizations to gain higher salaries for the same work they have been doing all along. . . . That is what makes them "special interest groups" rather than "community service organizations."[105]

Such a view is ironic at best. The private interests of a for-profit enterprise are bathed with the moral light of community service. By contrast, the financial and career concerns of the teacher engaged in an intrinsically community-serving activity are dismissed as selfish.

Ultimately, capital mobility produces multinational corporations increasingly free of any popular or even state control. As Charles Lindblom concludes in his study of world political economies:

> It has been a curious feature of democratic thought that it has not faced up to the private corporation as a peculiar organization in an ostensible democracy. Enormously large, rich in resources, the big corporations, we have seen, command more resources than do most government units. They can also, over a broad range, insist that government meet their demands, even if these demands run counter to those of citizens. . . . The large private corporation fits oddly into democratic theory and vision. Indeed, it does not fit.[106]

In sum, the inequality inherent in capitalism is counterdemocratic at both ends, legitimizing both the powerlessness of the poor and marginal groups and the immense wealth and power of the elite.

CAPITALISM VERSUS DEMOCRACY:
THE DECLINE OF COMMUNITY

Finally, capitalism undermines democracy through the cultural forces it unleashes. The common denominator of materialist acquisitiveness, compulsive consumerism, social fragmentation, aggressive competitiveness, emotional repression, centralized authority, and destruction of the landscape is capitalism; the technocratic culture is fueled by capitalism and global competition. The drive of young people in the 1960s to create new ways of living was their response to a world made meaningless to the degree that it served the imperatives of a capitalist economy.

Student restlessness derived in part from the prospect of meaningless work in the expanding corporate–bureaucratic sector. In the neo-Marxian view, work that is (and must be) controlled from the top, stratified, abstracted from workers' concerns, and shaped by its functional relationship to the larger enterprise is inherently alienating. The less workers internalize the norms of the firm (that is, the lower they are in the hierarchy), the more their work fits this description. Instead of personal gratification and a sense of self-worth, they gain a sense of their own powerlessness and the meaninglessness of their work. Their only reward is extrinsic, usually in the form of a paycheck. Concern for this extrinsic reward is heightened by its unequal distribution, thus the link between inequality and social control. The groundwork for the work experience is prepared through compulsory schooling that accentuates extrinsic learning incentives (grades) and unequal outcomes.[107]

The postwar corporate "truce" in which workers agreed to higher wages in exchange for diminished labor unrest fed the growth of a consumer society at the precise time that another postwar development, television and the acceleration of mass marketing, allowed consumerism to take off. Higher wages made workers more affluent consumers. Simultaneously, mass marketing's appeal was based on its promise to compensate for the sense of inadequacy fed by alienating work. The resulting consumer ideology

> not only fabricates false needs, it panders in a false way to real ones. The desire for companionship, love, approval, and pleasure, the need to escape from drudgery and boredom, the search for security for oneself and one's family. . . . [C]onsumerism plays on real human needs in deceptive and ultimately unfulfilling ways.
>
> [By turning] the consumer's critical perception away from the product—and away from the system that produces it—and toward herself or

himself . . . industry confines the social imagination and cultural experience of millions, teaching people to define their needs and life styles according to the dictates of the commodity market.[108]

Consumerism is one way that capitalism permeates all social life, for commodities invade all personal space—love, sex, sleep, personal health, and the like. And of course, since one cannot truly buy love, friendship, or a sense of self-worth, the needs are never met, the desires never satisfied, especially when new products continually become available, promising to do the job better.[109] Nor can they be satisfied, since declining consumption would bring on economic crisis. Together with pervasive inequality, escalating consumerism sustains the engines of capitalism. It also produces the monotonous, standardized, and repressed culture rejected by young people in the 1960s.

The dynamics of the marketplace also have dire effects on local communities. The scourge of unguided or unrestrained development is everywhere visible, from the proliferation of fast-food "strips" to vast tracts of identical, cheaply constructed split-level homes, to that albatross of inner cities, the shopping mall. The last, arguably, is an appropriate metaphor for the anti-ecological, profit-driven community of the late twentieth century

> The shopping mall is the *agora* of modern society, the civic center of a totally economic and inorganic world. The highways that lead to its parking lots and its production centers devour communities and neighborhoods; its massive command of retail trade devours the family-owned store; the subdivisions that cluster around it devour farmland; the motor vehicles that carry worshippers to its temples are self-enclosed capsules that preclude all human contact.[110]

The force of the market marginalizes whatever is not functional—personal morality, local tradition, natural landscape, or individual aesthetic expression. It is inherently antagonistic to community. As political theorist Christian Bay observes, "A fixation on free enterprise and the system upholding it bars one from real human contact with persons of different life experience; it makes one fear people who are different instead of becoming enriched by adding their sensitivity and knowledge to one's own."[111]

The drive for profitability, competitiveness, and efficiency invariably strengthens the hand of the technocrat and the technological solution. Technology, in turn, facilitates centralization and scale of organization. It produces labor-saving devices and new commodities for the insatiable consumer that increase the profitability of business, thereby accelerating ecodestruction[112] and the proliferation of waste.[113] Propelled by market forces, and freed from dysfunctional human or communal constraints, the technocratic culture becomes the dominant paradigm challenged by the student and countercultural rebels of the Sixties.

This technocratic culture is profoundly antidemocratic. By facilitating the increased scale of organization, by speaking a standardized language, by elevating the role of expert, technology reduces the meaning of public participation and undermines the emotive glue of community even as it expands its scope. It reduces the everyday person to the role of spectator or consumer. It emasculates politics by reducing political discourse to abstract issues of technique or cost-benefit analysis, instead of concern for what is good, beautiful, or simply right.

Encountering public space that has lost its richness of meaning, the individual person becomes increasingly prone to withdraw to the private realm. This inclination is enormously facilitated by technologies that are adaptive to individual wants and autonomous space, the automobile, television, the personal computer, and the "Walkman" headset. Deprived of public experience that enriches personal meaning, faced with a staggering pace of technological change, the individual retreats inward. Participatory democracy disappears as community declines. In Murray Bookchin's dark vision:

> If we take for granted and accept unreflectively that community consists of an aggregate of unrelated, monadic, self-enclosed, and highly privatized egos; that the telephone, radio, television set, and night letter constitute our principal windows to the world; that the shopping mall and its parking lots are our normal terrain for public intercourse; that processed and packaged foods, transported thousands of miles from remote areas of the country, are our major sources of nutriment; that "time is money," "fast-talking" is a paying skill, and speed-reading is a desideratum; that, above all, bureaucracy comprises the sinews of social life, gigantism is the measure of success, and clientage to professionals and centralized authority is evidence of a public sphere—then we will be irretrievably lost as individuals, will-less as egos, and formless as personalities. Like the natural world around us, we will become the victims of a simplification process that renders us as inorganic and mineral as the ores that feed our foundries and the sand that feeds our glass furnaces.[114]

As the first phase of the 1960s movements spun apart, they generated the new beginnings of feminism, radical ecology, and a revived neo-Marxian criticism. In effect, all three grew out of both the liberatory spirit and the limitations of earlier Sixties movements. All three have expanded the scope of targeted social ills and have greatly compensated for one of the Sixties' greatest inadequacies, the lack of a theoretical understanding of the sources of human oppression. They thereby extend the lessons the Sixties can teach us.

In the process, these critical perspectives add up to a dark picture of how much must be transformed if the democratic vision of the 1960s is to be realized. The symbiotic relationship between powerful structural forces and deeply rooted personal accomodation to these forces lends an air of inevitability to the status quo that Sixties movements struggled to change, especially given the reassertion of right-wing hegemony in much of the Western world. Yet, these new beginnings join with an enormous array of grassroots democratic awakenings and collective experiments, including the upheaval in the communist world, to provide a ray of hope that the structural impediments can be overcome. The passage of time also makes this more imperative.

7

A New Awakening?
Lessons and Legacies
of the Sixties

We see clearly where we are now, and we know that it is
winter. And suddenly, through this shocking cold, we
remember the beauty of the forest lying under this whiteness.
And that we will survive this snow if we are aware, if we
continue. And now we are shouting with all our strength to
the other sleepers, now we are laboring in earnest to
waken them.
—Susan Griffin, *Women and Nature*

As we start to see, in Alwyn Rees's phrase, that when we have
come to the edge of an abyss, the only progressive move we
can make is to step backward, we begin to realize that we can
instead turn around and then step forward, and that the
turning around—the transition to a future unlike anything we
have ever known—will be supremely interesting, an
unprecedented central project for our species.
—Amory Lovins, *Soft Energy Paths*

At their best, Sixties movements were inspired by a hope-
ful idealism that envisioned a better, more democratic world, and by a determined morality that refused to elevate power as an end over respect for human
personality. For participants, these qualities made the struggles of the Sixties
profoundly meaningful despite the experience of violence and human suffering, pain and disappointment, and moments of human weakness or excess.

Although Sixties movements often lacked a sufficient understanding of the
system they opposed, they accomplished a great deal. They unleashed a deep-
seated faith in the democratic community. They drove a permanent wedge
into the racially exclusive social mainstream. They helped limit the ability of
the powerful to involve the United States in foreign wars. They expressed a
fresh and insightful critique of education at all levels. They broke free from the

constraints of Western objectivism. They broke down old sexual stereotypes that oppress both sexes. They generated a new consciousness of our common ecological fate. And, through their fundamental break from "business as usual," Sixties movements anticipated an alternative future.

These are significant accomplishments in themselves. Their long-term implications, the legacies of the Sixties, are highly speculative in a world vulnerable to sudden shifts of fortune. Much depends on the degree to which we learn the lessons the Sixties can teach us about political and social change in liberal-capitalist America. This means learning how and why American institutions are resistant to change and hostile to democracy. And it means learning from the shortcomings of Sixties movements themselves.

Through their Sixties experiences, activists gained a radical appreciation that their democratic vision could not be realized within the systemic constraints of mainstream institutions—that the two were incompatible. In place of effective equality, they discovered deeply rooted systemic inequality. In place of personal empowerment, they found bureaucracies that taught their clients demeaning dependency and a marketplace that eroded individuality through a smothering conformity. Instead of politics infused with a moral vision, they found a technical relativism in which morality was equated with system maintenance. In lieu of community, they saw a system grounded on "micromotives" that accelerated human isolation, competitive interaction, and destruction of traditional and natural communities.

Nothing has confirmed this basic lesson more forcefully than the reassertion of right-wing hegemony, the so called "right turn" that began with Richard Nixon's election in 1968 and culminated in the Reagan–Bush administration of the 1980s.[1] The shift to the right can be seen as an attempt by powerful elites to stabilize a system threatened by the events and movements, indeed, the democratic vision, of the 1960s. In restoring system hegemony, its primary effect has been to aggravate the very conditions targeted by Sixties movements—poverty and inequality, overt and institutional racism and sexism, technocratic schooling, American interventionism, the decline of community, and environmental destruction.

■ The "Right Turn" and Sixties-Bashing

Ten years after the end of the 1960s, and sixteen years after Barry Goldwater's ignominious defeat by Lyndon Johnson, Ronald Reagan was elected president of the United States in a major victory for the American right wing. Many of the reasons for Reagan's stunning victory and subsequent legislative success lie beyond the scope of this book. However, we need to assess what the shift to the right says about the 1960s.

First, the revitalization of the Right began in 1968 at a time when the Vietnam War was in full sway and the majority of Americans wanted American troops out of Vietnam. The domestic order was deeply fractured; the country was more polarized than it had been in a century. Millions of Americans feared the changes promised by the 1960s liberal tide. They were disenchanted with the social chaos and resented self-indulgent hippies, antiwar activists, and liberal programs that "coddled" black or young Americans. In part, the movements of the Sixties contributed to this resentment.

Richard Nixon was the first presidential candidate to appeal to anti-Sixties sentiment. Despite campaign rhetoric about bringing the American people together, Nixon fed the nation's polarization by appealing to the resentments of those "left out" in the Sixties. The old South resented both the pro–civil rights Supreme Court and the Democratic national leaders, while the booming Southwest and the Midwestern hinterland resented Northeastern economic and media elites, and blue-collar laborers were alienated by the social programs of the Great Society and the antiwar protests of more affluent college students. No doubt many also believed Nixon's promise of an honorable end to the Vietnam war.

The Sixties were a convenient scapegoat. Urban riots, gun-toting black militants, countercultural freaks, and antiwar "trashings" provided ample fodder for Nixon's appeal. Student protesters were conveniently labelled "bums," affirmative action was "reverse discrimination," and "law and order" was a coded appeal to keep targeted groups like dissident blacks or self-indulgent young whites under tight control. And Nixon didn't disappoint his backers. He pushed the COINTELPRO surveillance and repression effort into high gear while also subscribing to Daniel Patrick Moynihan's recommended "benign neglect" of black Americans. Although continuing many liberal programs, Nixon began to shift policy in a more conservative direction through his federal court appointments and by eliminating the more redistributive poverty programs.

However, a great deal more than public disaffection with Sixties movements was at work in the Right's resurgence. In fact, 1968 began a period of global reaction against democracy. Soviet tanks rolled into Prague to crush the first, premature blossoming of reform, thereby solidifying the Brezhnev era of Soviet elite and bureaucratic hegemony. Conservative movements eventually gained power in Helmut Kohl's West Germany, Margaret Thatcher's Great Britain, and Ronald Reagan's America. From the outset, the right turn was grounded on the ability of national political leaders to create an alliance of convenience between social conservatives (the constituency of resentment) and economic conservatives representing, at least in the West, capitalism's elite.

The imperatives of capitalism required the United States and other Western powers to restore the economic profitability that had been enjoyed from the immediate postwar years into the 1960s. In their critique of the postwar corporate system, Bowles, Gordon, and Weisskopf suggest that postwar affluence rested on three "buttresses of private power": the *pax Americana* in which the United States dominated world markets and worked its will in the Third World, a capital–labor accord that traded wages for labor docility, and a capital–citizen accord that equated corporate profitability with the public good.

During the 1960s, all three foundations of postwar capitalism eroded.[2] The *pax Americana* had rested on a productive U.S. economy, growing overseas investment, and aggressive U.S. military power used forcefully to topple reformist regimes in places like Iran and Guatemala. Yet the mutual reinforcement of economic expansion and military intervention contained the seeds of decline. The hegemony of American multinational corporations meant that the United States was increasingly targeted by angry nationalist or socialist movements in the Third World (thereby requiring additional military expenditures); simultaneously, the enormous drain on productive capacity of the military budget contributed to the American economy's declining competitiveness.[3] The Vietnam War ushered in the decline of *pax Americana*.

On the domestic front, those excluded from the capital–labor truce—small businesses; the elderly; and women, minority, and young workers who dominated the nonunion secondary job market—all began to flex their political muscle. The result was the vast array of social legislation in the 1960s and government regulation in the early 1970s. While the economy was booming and social service support was at its peak, managerial control over the workforce diminished. Simultaneously, the central premise of the postwar corporate system, "If it's profitable it's desirable," began to erode as labor, consumer, and environmental interests targeted the health and environmental costs of profitability and shifted some of these costs onto the producers of these hazards.

Bowles, Gordon, and Weisskopf describe the end result of this erosion on all three fronts:

These challenges led to a realignment of political and economic power. This realignment reduced the effectiveness of U.S. corporate power, raising the real costs of imported materials and labor for U.S. corporations, reducing their ability to burden the domestic citizenry with the social costs of private capitalist development and slowing the rate of productivity growth. With this realignment, U.S. corporations suffered a sharp reverse on the front that most concerns them: their profitability fell.[4]

The outcome was predictable. The corporate sector fought back to reestablish the profitability of private enterprise. In a 1975 study entitled *The Crisis of Democracy*, the Trilateral Commission viewed the 1960s as a time of excess democracy or "democratic distemper": "In recent years, the operations of the democratic process do indeed appear to have generated a breakdown of traditional means of social control, a delegitimation of political and other forms of authority, and an overload of demands on government, exceeding its capacity to respond."[5] The Commission's aim was to "make democracy stronger" by reducing democracy (public demands and equality) and reversing the international trends that threatened U.S. corporate profitability. As Noam Chomsky observes, one

> task that had to be undertaken in the "post-Vietnam era" was to return the domestic population to a proper state of apathy and obedience, to overcome "the crisis of democracy" and the "Vietnam syndrome." These are the technical terms that have been devised to refer, respectively, to the efforts of formerly passive groups to engage in the political process, and to the general unwillingness of the population to bear the material costs and the moral burden of aggression and massacre. It has been the responsibility of the system of ideological control and propaganda to accomplish this dual task, and there is no doubt that, in part at least, the goals have been achieved. Throughout this period, it has been clear enough that when the time appeared to be ripe, there would be moves to reconstruct the capacity to intervene and subvert, and with it, the Cold War system along with its domestic counterpart, the militarization of the economy. Such steps were being taken in the latter part of the Carter Administration, and constitute the central thrust of the Reagan program.[6]

Sensing liberals' vulnerability in the chaotic aftermath of the Sixties and feeling the pinch of economic stagflation in the Seventies, corporate interests saw an opportunity to fill the ideological vacuum with their critique of active liberal government. Political scientist John Schwartz observes,

> After stagflation's appearance, many corporations and other producer interests expended vast amounts of money pounding the new arguments home. Almost daily, these interests publicized allegation after allegation about the negative economic effects of the size, power, and inefficiencies of government. They did so through television, newspaper, and magazine advertising, by way of think-tank publications, and in political-action committee advertising on behalf of favored candidates. . . . Facts to contradict the new ideology were there, the means to focus those facts was not.[7]

One reason the right turn monopolized much of the public agenda was that the "opposition" Democratic party was itself subject to pressures from corporate magnates, neoconservatives, and powerful political action committees determined to pull the party machinery away from the "dangerous" elements awakened during the 1960s.[8]

RIGHT TURN EFFECTS: OBSCURING THE DEMOCRATIC VISION

> Long ago we gave up ourselves. Now, if we are dying by increments, we have ceased to be aware of this death. . . . Instead of fighting for our lives, we bend all our efforts to defend delusion. We deny all evidence at hand that this civilization, which has shaped our minds, is also destroying the earth. . . . We are at the edge of death, and yet, like one who contemplates suicide, we are our own enemies. We think with the very mind that has brought disaster on us. And this mind, taught and trained by this civilization, does not know itself. This is a mind in exile from its own wisdom.
> —Susan Griffin, "Split Culture"

The right turn culminated in the ascendancy of Ronald Reagan and George Bush. The Reagan era was marked by increasing poverty and inequality; flashbacks to the overt racism and sexism of an earlier time; growth in corporate political power; aggressive intervention in Central America, the Caribbean, and the Middle East; social deterioration accompanied by new manifestations of personal greed; and the reversal of the environmental improvements of the 1970s.

Reagan has been the Right's most effective propagandist. Through symbolic communist-bashing in Grenada and Nicaragua, rallying cries for "freedom fighters" who are the "moral equivalent of our founding fathers," inflammatory rhetoric about the "evil empire," scathing dismissal of welfare freeloaders, reverent genuflection toward traditional family and religious values, and rhetorical support for Poland's Solidarity Union, Reagan was able to corral electoral support by demonizing threats to Americans' personal and national security.[9] He appealed successfully to both economically conservative elites and social conservatives who felt threatened by the social changes of the Sixties. In so doing, he effectively resurrected the veil of mythology obscuring the less palatable effects of American policy.

Americans have been deluged with good news about the successes of this right turn: "corporate profitability is back"; "thousands of new jobs have been created"; "more Americans enjoy visible affluence"; "America is standing tall again"; we enjoy the "longest peacetime prosperity"; and, most crucially, "we won the Cold War." These claims contain enough truth to make them appear credible. Yet together they divert attention from a flawed system and from growing signs of deterioration, which is precisely what they are supposed to do as system-integrating propaganda.[10] Through political rhetoric and a conscious effort to minimize the extent of our societal and global problems, through manipulative advertising and new technologies, Americans are offered the illusion of progress and human empowerment.

The blend of domestic spending cutbacks, tax cuts for corporations and the wealthy, huge military spending increases, and government deregulation known as Reaganomics increased corporate profitability, widened the range in income and wealth inequality, vastly increased the number of poor Americans, aggressively asserted U.S. corporate and military interests overseas, and reversed the modest environmental gains of the 1970s.[11] Corporate profitability has produced enormous wealth for the wealthiest fraction of the population, resulting in self-indulgent rather than productive investment. Flagrant consumption by the wealthy stands in stark contrast to the increased misery of the poor, to say nothing of the belt-tightening of working- and middle-class Americans. The bulk of new employment occured in the low-wage, dead-end secondary labor market. Union-busting tactics resurfaced, from the PATCO air traffic controllers' strike in 1981 to the 1989 Pittston coal miners' strike.

If the United States again "stands tall," it does so largely in the imaginations of Americans who take pride in "big stick" policies in Grenada and Central

America and ignore or remain ignorant of the brutal effects of these policies in nations like El Salvador and Nicaragua and the Third World's growing enmity. The United States continues to fight a rear-guard action against the tide of popular insurrection and self-determination of Third World peoples, all the time applauding the pro-democracy movement in Eastern Europe.

The much-heralded end to the Cold War reflects the remarkable defossilization of the Stalinist Eastern bloc. As propaganda, however, legitimizing and suggesting the "victory" of American capitalism, these claims are little more than disingenuous self-congratulation. They fail to address the role of American imperialism and aggression as a catalyst for the sustained Cold War. They overlook the systemic flaws and global decline of American capitalism unrelated to the communist "threat." And they suggest that the only alternative to Stalinist communism is the American model of state capitalism, thereby obscuring any left-democratic critique of both the Soviet and American models.

Domestically, Reagan rhetoric nurtured the hostility and discontent of those who had felt disempowered during the 1960s. Whereas John Kennedy's rhetoric was a catalyst for public participation on the part of the young, Reagan's rhetoric about welfare freeloaders, unpatriotic critics, and the virtues of greed only succeeded in bringing deeply-rooted resentments out of the closet. Its effects can be seen in the general decline in civility, increasingly visible racial hostility, an emboldened Ku Klux Klan, groups like the skin-heads, a new breed of TV "scream" shows, an increasingly violent pro-life movement, private counterinsurgency mercenaries in the Third World, pervasive vocationalism on college and university campuses, and the allure of Wall Street wealth and the Yuppie lifestyle.

Meanwhile, the connecting web of community and public trust continues to unravel in an increasingly violent and litigious culture. The ranks of the poor, the homeless, the underemployed, and those who have given up on finding work have swollen; alcoholism, drug dependency, and youth suicides grow alarmingly while debilitating diseases like AIDS spread on an epidemic scale. Families disintegrate as distances grow and emotional needs go unmet. Those who are lucky enough to be middle class commute alone in their cars from development-tract homes through grid-lock traffic jams and into the impersonal concrete and glass of urban public space. Residential developments and innumerable shopping malls replace old communities and family farms. Increasingly, the easiest retreat from the rat-race is the numbed suppression of the six-pack or the experience-intensifying thrill of cocaine. Meanwhile human needs continue to be displaced onto the shiny new gadgets that Americans consume.

The ascendancy of the Right has also accelerated the global crises we face. The ecosphere suffers from increasing, not reduced, levels of pollution, to the point that the planet's ability to sustain life is showing signs of being endangered. Disappearing species not only reduce the rich diversity of the ecosphere, they foreshadow our own demise, like the canary in the mineshaft. Meanwhile the pressures of global competition and increased production have generated a self-sustaining dynamic of technological innovation that exceeds the limits of human morality and imagination.[12] While competing economies continue to stimulate economic growth, waste is generated at an ever increasing rate while we are simultaneously running out of places to put it.[13] Nuclear and other forms of toxic waste with no safe repository continue to be produced.

Kirkpatrick Sale offers the metaphor for this crumbling world in the decaying ruins of the Parthenon, an expression of aesthetic and spiritual human sensibility and a symbolic reminder of the ancient Athenian experiment in democracy. Standing as an inspiring monument for nearly twenty-four centuries, the Parthenon, like many ancient artifacts, has suffered irreversibly from the perils of modern pollution in the last thirty years. As Sale puts it, "The onslaught on the Parthenon is not of course the worst offense of the contemporary world. But it is a symbol, for me a haunting one: as the Parthenon so fittingly embodies the heritage of Western civilization, so it displays as well the condition to which that civilization has been brought over the last few decades and the crises with which, I think one can say without hyperbole, it is now imperilled."[14]

In the end, with the help of television, Americans get a rhetorical flourish from their leaders that obscures the deep-seated, systemic roots to these problems. We don't discover answers, we create technical fixes that postpone our "high noon." We don't enrich the human community by advertising morning in America, we destroy it with the vast sprawl of development. Our economy isn't thriving. While the rich get richer, the bill for corporate excess is coming due in the form of declining industries, regressive taxation, and federal debt. We don't help to spread democracy in the world as much as we help to crush it. The forces unleashed by Reagan's emphasis on privatism threaten to erode, not build, conditions that foster a sense of community and reinforce the viability of family and personal values.

These visible trends are anathema to those who glimpsed the democratic vision of the 1960s. They also are grounded in the very institutions that resisted the pro-democracy movements of the 1960s. It is not surprising, then, that mainstream conservative and liberal responses to these social ills are inadequate.

WHAT TO DO? MAINSTREAM RESPONSES

Conservatives respond to the human unease caused by powerlessness and the decline of community by appealing to traditional values and a return to community. Both are traditional and legitimate conservative propositions. However, within the American liberal tradition, the conservative claim of community masks two important realities. One is repression in the form of racism, religious authoritarianism, or physical violence that occurs in the local community, family, or workplace. The other is the conservative embrace of capitalism and the same "free" market that has accelerated development, bigness, uniformity, and efficiency-worship, all terribly destructive of the traditional community.

For their part, liberals respond to the conservative position by employing the state to intervene in local communities to prevent overt repression and to intervene in the economy to prevent the more ugly excesses of capitalism. However, this response also escalates bigness, standardization, and development, especially to the degree that the state serves the interests of corporate capital. The liberal response strips local communities of their need to confront and struggle with human oppression, and it creates Big Government to counteract Big Business. In the end individuals are disempowered by the very institutions that supposedly liberate their powers; human freedom is increasingly stripped of its meaning as these institutions redefine human needs to fit *their* imperatives. As Carl Boggs maintains,

> In this context liberal ideas inevitably lost their relevance to social change. . . . Liberal states . . . are no longer capable of ideological renewal and political innovation. They preside over bureaucratic centers of power, tied to a declining economic order, in which the historical tension between capitalism and democracy has been weighted decisively in favor of the former, thereby laying the basis for something akin to state capitalism.[15]

In sum, the archetypal conservative blueprint is to return to a mythical time before the 1960s. The tepid liberal rejoinder is to reassert technocratic government management tinged with greater compassion. Conservatives urge us to ignore our intransigent crises, while liberals offer us the "incremental politics of running repairs."[16] Both conservative and liberal positions frustrate the democratic impulse. The traditional community and family become a regressive place of refuge from a threatening world, while both corporate capitalism and bureaucratic government intervention distort and repress development of the whole person. Bellah and associates have stated our dilemma well: "We thus face a profound impasse. Modern individualism seems to be producing a way of life that is neither individually or socially viable, yet a return to traditional forms would be to return to intolerable discrimination and oppression."[17]

If we take liberals' concern about local repression seriously, we should transform those forces that feed mistrust and distorted human development in a way that trusts human beings' capacity for compassion and growth. If we take the conservative call for community seriously, we need to transform those institutions that threaten community, including, most fundamentally, the capitalist economy. Otherwise, we leave virtually untouched the forces that accelerate the deepening social, economic, and ecological crises we face. A system based on the lowest common denominator gradually erodes everything that is not the lowest common denominator. Madisonian liberalism created an American politics that sets interest against interest and mistrusts the political sentiments of the people. Capitalism is grounded on the micromotive of maximizing material self-interest. Bureaucratic organization calls on little more than adherence to minimal standards applicable to everyone.

Young people in the 1960s responded to the desire for something more. They embraced a democratic vision rooted in American experience that lay outside the dominant institutional paradigm. In short, the democratic movements of the 1960s, together with feminism, ecology, and a neo-Marxian critique of capitalism, propel us toward a third path. The same is true globally. The dissolution of the Stalinist monopoly in the Eastern bloc opens the way for democratization, "socialism with a human face," and both Green activism and ethnic bioregionalism. The decline of the "communist menace" means that Western regimes, especially in the United States, will have to find persuasive new demons like Saddam Hussein, Third World terrorists, or the scourge of drugs that threaten us and draw our attention away from the flaws of our own state capitalist systems.

In 1969, shortly after the student takeover at Columbia, Immanuel Wallerstein observed of the period of détente that began in 1963:

"Consensus politics" had thrived, intellectually and politically, throughout the United States and Western Europe during the Cold War because it was not really consensus politics: it was conflict politics. "Consensus politics" in that period was the ideology of the "free world" in combat with the "Communist world." . . . When, however, many intellectuals of Europe and North America began to feel that the "enemy" of their governments was the underdeveloped world, they found it more difficult (for some it was impossible) to collaborate against such an enemy. As a result, they began to call upon their universities to limit or to cease co-operation. . . . Thus, the universities of Europe and North America have been turned into battlegrounds over government policy.[18] ·

The partial thaw in Cold War tensions that occurred in the 1960s opened the way for many to begin questioning the American system, and we have seen where that questioning led. Where the end of the Cold War may lead is highly speculative. It seems plausible, however, that a second-wave, Western pro-democracy movement may reawaken once again and make life uncomfortable for powerful elites.

■ ### Toward a Third Path:
A Global Pro-Democracy Movement

The utopians, in the negative sense of that term, are the pragmatists who mystically believe that society can survive political, economic, social, and military upheavals—can cope with what is a transition to a new civilization—by squatting in the middle of the road.
—Michael Harrington, Democratic Socialists of America

In the early 1960s, buoyed by the civil rights movement and the rhetoric and image of the Kennedy administration, young people chose to fight against the forces of darkness in society. Late in the Reagan era, buffeted on all sides by destructive imagery, increasingly cynical about the Reagan presidency, sadder and wiser because the Sixties revolt did not deliver the Eden it promised, middle-class young people were more prone to flee into the private world of acquisitiveness, the one reliable if ultimately dehumanizing thing they felt they could hold onto.[19]

There are, however, innumerable signs that the vision of the 1960s persists, reinvigorated by the very oppressiveness of the right turn. As Doug McAdam has observed of veterans of the Mississippi Freedom Summer project,

> They may yet play a role in the resurgence of leftist activism in this country. . . . It is only in popular parlance that social movements "die" or political eras "come to a close." The finality of these phrases is rarely borne out in reality. Movements do not so much die as survive on a much smaller scale. More often than not, it is the media's interest in the movement that lapses, creating the impression that the movement has died. But rarely is this the case. . . . [T]he New Left lives on in contemporary America in the lives and political involvements of people like the Freedom Summer veterans. They are keepers of the leftist flame. . . . [T]he likes of the Freedom Summer veterans will have constructed ideological and organizational bridges linking the New (by then Old) Left to the next major upsurge in leftist activism.[20]

Popular press reports notwithstanding, the "best" of the 1960s—the determined, idealistic activism that confronted injustice, meaninglessness, and the horrors of war—is very much alive in a myriad of movements and struggles around the globe. As Carl Boggs observes,

> The spirit of the new left, if not its precise form, was preserved throughout the 1970's and early 1980's by a proliferation of community-based groups that embodied the interests and values of the earlier period. . . . Whereas the 1960's version of radicalism was diffuse and spontaneous, the popular formations of a decade or more later took on a clearer identity, along with a deeper commitment to build new institutions, even if a radical strategic orientation was still missing.[21]

Antiapartheid, peace, sanctuary, feminist, ecology and bioregional, consumer, labor, community organizing, and neighborhood movements; protest against United States policy in Central America; experiments in collective enterprise; and a variety of counterinstitutional movements in the health and mental health fields[22]—all bear witness to the quest for a personally empowering, morally grounded alternative.

At the very least, these movements offer a healthy alternative to the myopic reassertion of technocratic capitalism and resigned public fatalism. More ambitiously, they converge to sustain and broaden the democratic vision of the 1960s, anticipating a third path. It is at least highly plausible that a widely acknowledged thirty-year pendulum shift from right to left will occur, helped along by the children of the Sixties generation and by the need to confront deepening economic, ecological, and social crises. Meanwhile feminist, ecological, and left-democratic activism have been complemented by efforts to develop more comprehensive theoretical explanations of the sources of human oppression.[23] The convergence of global crises and theoretical development have led some to anticipate a historic paradigm shift.[24] It is also possible that democratic impulses from the East and West may converge.

LEARNING FROM THE SIXTIES

> More remains than memories, than the sense of the limits of politics. There remains a generation not entirely cynical, not entirely without a conviction that things can change. Privatization has not quite provided a substitute: career, family, routine have brought the generation of the sixties, everywhere, to confront problems insoluble by private means.
> —Norman Birnbaum, "Hope's End Or Hope's Beginning? 1968 and After"

Populated largely by students, Sixties movements reflected the strengths and limitations of youth, its energy, impatience, idealism, and free time on the one hand; its isolation, a tendency toward apocalyptic vision, and short-sightedness on the other. Arguably the major defects of Sixties movements reflected the youthfulness of most activists and the pressing immediacy of events.

Many activists entered the fray of political action with a naive expectation that the system would deliver on the promise of democracy, an expectation grounded on faith in mainstream electoral politics. However, the 1960s clearly demonstrated that elected officials had to be continually pushed and prodded by activists agitating from outside the electoral process. Even then, the most fundamental lesson of the Sixties experience was that the very institutions that raise hopes for equality, empowerment, and enhanced personal meaning will not and cannot deliver more than marginally on these promises.

Young activists also suffered from a quick-fix impatience for immediate success that was a product of youth, events, and the consumer society's emphasis on quick remedies for personal and social problems. This sense of impatience was initially a strength of Sixties activism; it was part of the refusal to tolerate injustice and a catalyst for change. However, the belief that injustices had to be erased and wars ended immediately led activists further and further away from an ability to be political, to expand their base and work with others of different backgrounds, and to take time to explore and articulate a theoretical perspective. Critic Michael Neumann argues that at the extremes this tendency led to a form of politically counterproductive, but psychologically gratifying, rebellion.[25] As many middle-aged Sixties veterans probably realize, the trick is to fuse the sense of urgency with a recognition that the struggle for personal democracy will continue well after our lifetimes, while at the same time realizing that participating in the struggle is what makes a life fulfilling.

Finally, the initial proactive movements for civil rights and a New Student Left were swamped by the war in Vietnam, growing domestic violence, and unanticipated organizational tensions. A considerable amount of activism became *reactive*, reacting to blatant racial oppression, a horrible war of aggression against a largely peasant society, pressures to repress one's self in order to fit into society, sexual abuse and domination, and the visible destruction of the natural world. Because of the frenzy of the times, especially in the mid-to-late Sixties, little attention was given to articulating a vision of an alternative order, or to the means of effecting that order. Instead, the climate of reaction and rage produced countless tales of personal tragedy or excess. The process of articulating a more systematic critique and envisioning an alternative future began in earnest only as the frenzy of the Sixties died down.

In part because of unrealistic expectations and youthful impatience, in part because of horrors encountered and society's brutal response, Sixties movements contained a powerful impulse to disassociate that was manifested in the counterculture, the separatism of black militants and radical feminists,[26] and the "purer than thou" ideological tensions within movement factions. This disassociation sometimes bordered on paranoia. Fears of co-optation became legendary in the late 1960s, to the point that virtually *any* interaction with mainstream officials was viewed as selling out. Carl Oglesby decried this trend, observing that "it instructs people to reject what their fight has made possible on the grounds that it falls short of what they wanted." Oglesby redefined co-optation: "You are co-opted when the adversary puts his goals on your power; you are *not* co-opted when your power allows you to exploit his means (or contradictions) in behalf of your goals."[27]

Perhaps most damaging to Sixties movements was their tendency to pull back from a growth-inducing engagement with society, in effect, a rejection of democratic participation. The most destructive examples of this arose in the student rebellion and antiwar struggle. Many in these largely upper-middle-class movements became intolerant of, or took out their frustrations on, working-class men who filled the ranks of police departments, the National Guard, and the military in Vietnam. The middle-class young vented their rage toward an impersonal system on the lower-strata agents of oppression, who were arguably more victimized by that system than the students were. While the feelings of rage are readily understandable, especially when one is attacked by the system's agents, this class-bound behavior revealed an inadequate reading of the systemic forces of repression in society as well as an inability to empathize with other human beings, in other words, a rejection of the nonviolent community envisioned by Martin Luther King, Jr. As Ronald Fraser has observed, "the inability to see beyond a specific age group and student experience led to more than organizational failure. Lack of a discourse which took in the real (as distinct from the theoretically assumed) experience of the other social strata left the movements bereft of a valuable and historical corrective."[28] And as activist Rayna Rapp put it, "I think all our flamboyant 'politics and culture' and 'politics as confrontation' and 'politics as theater' stretched the boundaries in the U.S. and was useful—but it wasn't a strategy for reaching people who were different from us, who were either older or more ensconced in working-class or even middle-class jobs. That was a tremendous mistake."[29]

In its extreme form, disassociation meant withdrawal from membership in community with others—a *loss* of connection, not its opposite. The rage and frenzy of the moment led some to lose their moorings, to excessive immersion in drugs or aggressive violence against others—all of which widened the gap between activists and the rest of society. Clearly anger is a legitimate and powerful inducement to action. Yet, as protest movements have demonstrated, the genius of effective action is to build a confrontation in which the protest audience feels closer to the protesters than to their targets. This was relatively easy (though enormously costly) in Birmingham and Selma, when many in the U.S. audience felt more connected to the protesters than to those who oppressed them. It was and is infinitely more challenging when the audience has been bombarded with propaganda welding them to the very system being challenged, as was the case with the Vietnam War or the attack on economic racial inequality. The deepening ecological crisis, however, would seem to enhance the potential for establishing common ground with others.

Another facet of the quest for common ground is the need to transcend the divisiveness of the Movement itself. While scattered leftists of various shades

continue to vilify each other, there are signs of convergence in recent theoretical writing, in the European effort to bring "Reds" and "Greens" together,
and in the ecofeminist movement. In theory, the Movement for democracy
could transcend the limitations of distinct fragments.[30] Thus it can embrace
Marxian insights into the alienation and commoditization of human beings,
into the material basis of consciousness, and into the systemic defects of capitalism without a reductionist preoccupation with economics as the sole basis
of oppression or an overly simplistic class analysis. Such a movement can
embrace feminism's insights into the patriarchal sources of the masculine–
feminine dichotomy and emphasis on a feminized culture without embracing
the radical rejection of males. It can embrace the ecological insight into human
connectedness with the biosphere, the aesthetic and spiritual significance of
this connectedness, and the inherent ecological destructiveness of capitalism,
while rejecting the ascetic, Malthusian view of global hunger as "nature's way."
The Movement can even embrace liberalism's emphasis on individual human
agency and antiauthoritarianism, while rejecting its emphasis on neutral and
atomistic public space, expertise-based technocracy and hierarchy, and segmented personality. These convergent themes are the subject of on-going
dialogues among progressives of various allegiances.

■ The Sixties Democratic Vision Revisited

> To remain in control of ourselves, we must be able to acknowledge
> continuously that nothing less than self-government based on self-
> knowledge will ever do.
> —Henry Kariel, *Beyond Liberalism: Where Relations Grow*

> People need institutions that belong to them, that they can experiment with
> and shape.
> —Casey Hayden, SNCC

In concluding a work on the Sixties experience, it seems fitting to
construct a speculative prescription for this alternative future drawn from
movements of the 1960s. At the heart of the decade's legacy is the vision of
democracy that inspired initial activism and weathered the shocks and refine-
ments caused by the diverse experiences of that decade. I would characterize
this as both a personal democracy that emphasizes human empowerment

through action, exchange, and growth, and asserts the primacy of relations, community, learning, and work as the basis of this growth; and also as a global democracy conscious of the integral link to the larger community, including the largest community of all, the ecosphere.

The Sixties experience showed that efforts to realize the democratic vision within constraints imposed by mainstream social, political, and economic institutions were doomed to frustration. One lesson of the 1960s is that a democratic future cannot be attained by absorbing this democratic vision *into* prevailing institutions. Another lesson is that simply rejecting prevailing institutions and all values on which they rest is also inadequate.

Consequently, the struggle for a democratic future agitates toward, and ultimately take place within, a new political paradigm that reverses old priorities. On several dimensions, dominant institutional and masculinist values of separation, aggression, competition, analytic rationality, and objectivity must be constrained by and responsive to what are currently subordinate and feminist values—connection, receptivity, nurturance, intuition, and experience. Economic control must be reversed from the top down to the bottom up, producing a democratic economy or a participatory variant of socialism. The struggle for personal and global democracy seeks to transform the person-denying, eco-destructive imperatives of capitalism. It requires a dynamic of sustainable growth based on the ecological recognition that something good is only good within limits; more of something good is not necessarily better.

This democratic vision therefore challenges both Western dualism and the large, impersonal institutions that grow ever larger in the modern world. It challenges the prevailing ideological separation of public and private, and the analytical segmentation of political and psychological. It rests on widely held values of human integrity, community, and compassion, yet it challenges virtually everyone's experience of everyday life and requires the radical transformation of the institutions of education, work, and government. It requires a sharply limited range of income and wealth inequality. It implies decentralization of institutions and their reduction in scale. It rests on a broadened vision of politics infused with moral concern for the person. And it is grounded in the human community. Personal democracy means an active, person-enriching interchange with others as expressions of creative human agency.

Democracy sees the bedrock of the universal human condition not in the modern metaphor of calculating one's interests in competitive exchange with others, but in the fundamental human quest to achieve a sense of dignity, to find meaning in one's life, to love and be loved, to create, to nurture children, and to express an aesthetic sensibility. Humans are alike not only in their capacity to reason, but in their experience of emotions such as grief, anger, joy, and affection. These comprise the foundation of our universal citizenship, our "in-commonness" that allows us to feel empathy for strangers, and our openness that strengthens our connection to nature. They are the glue of our biotic community, the basis for what Jefferson called our "moral sense" and Rousseau, our "pity." Democracy shifts the meaning of personal freedom from one that emphasizes separateness to one that emphasizes enhanced self-knowledge through action and exchange with others.

The black and women's liberation movements opened doors to a personal praxis of empowerment, a key to the personal side of democracy. As Jean Baker Miller argues, "Within a framework of inequality the existence of conflict is denied and the means to engage openly in conflict are excluded. . . . Instead, inequality generates hidden conflict around elements that inequality itself has set in motion. In sum, both sides are diverted from open conflict around real differences, by which they could grow, and are channeled into hidden conflict around falsifications."[31] The feminist notion that the personal is political celebrated a journey of self-discovery from awareness of one's oppression, to consciousness of its external sources and internal reinforcement, to confrontation of one's oppressors.

Like Martin Luther King's belief in nonviolent action, the feminist praxis is both a process for challenging and changing power relations in society and a model for interpersonal relations in a democracy.[32] With its focus on personal assertiveness, feminism emphasizes the expression rather than repression of thoughts and feelings. Yet like King's philosophy, it channels expression in a manner that neither negates the humanity of the other, nor severs the connection with the larger community. It is thereby strikingly different from both masculinist aggressiveness and the repression of feelings that perpetuates the denial of one's personhood.

Finally, and centrally, democracy transforms the small-scale, face-to-face community from what is "left over" between the private family and modern macro-institutions to its rightful, preeminent place at the core of politics. Democracy is rooted in face-to-face exchange, the workplace, the local community—precisely those spheres of activity that large-scale, impersonal institutions of the modern world undermine.[33] By definition, community is where people are participants, not spectators. Democracy also requires that community be progressively transformed so that it nurtures rather than retards human development.[34] Absent repressive forces (or in struggle against them), participation in a community is an indispensable vehicle for development of an integrated sense of self. In a variety of respects—ethical, spiritual, aesthetic, and social—the community is the source for much of the meaning individuals find in their diverse lives.

The link between democracy and small-scale community reflects an appreciation of place in human lives, the sense of groundedness that is increasingly fleeting in mobile, urban America. Community provides what Simone Weil called the "culture bed" for empathy and civic-mindedness—the "watchful and tender concern" toward's one's social and natural environment.[35] The concrete world of experience is also the cognitive and political basis for understanding the larger world. Micro-education provides the basis for macro-awareness.

Sixties movements converged in expressing the quest for community, a moral vision of politics, personal liberation, and the struggle against inequality and oppression. Yet the central dilemma experienced again and again by Sixties activists was posed by their combination of prefigurative and instrumental politics: how can one act in a way that is both true to one's vision *and* politically effective, especially as society's deeply rooted resistance to change becomes manifest? Or, when resistance wanes, how does one effectively agitate for radical change in an open society permeated by subtle persuaders? How do we get from here to there?

The dissonance between moral vision and effective action became a powerfully disruptive force during the turbulent Sixties. It continues to be a stumbling block for progressive democratic movements, for example, in the growth versus no-growth debate among left unionists and Greens, the emphasis on electoral versus nonelectoral politics, and the question of progressive liberal reform versus liberal co-optation.[36] Electoral politics and activity within the system invite inevitable co-optation *in the absence of an aroused and aware public.* The inside or outside the system dilemma that so preoccupied Sixties activists can be reconceived as a choice between trying to influence those in power *directly* as opposed to trying to draw a larger audience into critical activism. A critical, self-empowered public becomes a force that those in power have to heed. The latter course is obviously more democratic, since it is grounded in the collective will and values of the people. It was also the course that generated the movements of the 1960s. All began outside the system.

However, it is also clear that both courses can be productive. Leaders can generate powerful symbols to support change, as John Kennedy did, so to this degree it matters greatly who we choose as our leaders. Yet progressives cannot lose sight of the co-optive forces that necessarily impinge on those who hold power; it is terribly naive and contradictory to hope that the powerful can lead us to democracy. The 1960s convincingly demonstrated that they cannot.

The tension between pragmatic short-term considerations and long-term visions has persistently plagued the Left in the United States and, no doubt, will be at the forefront of progressive struggles yet to come. This tension is itself linked to two underlying structural tensions facing the movement for democracy. One is the dilemma of scale. As the world catapults its way toward ever-greater connectedness among increasingly large entities, it becomes increasingly difficult to imagine *how* institutions can be brought down to a size that allows human control. In short, how can one decentralize and devolve global-scale institutions when many of the imperatives of modernity, including centralized power, militate in the opposite direction? The other tension is the dilemma of power and inequality. Reversing the locus of control means that those who now disproportionately enjoy the fruits of power will have to yield a healthy share of that power.

Tactical questions will recur again and again. Ultimately, it would seem, resolution of the dilemma of scale is grounded on the educative effect of participation or consciousness-raising, on the increasing ability of individuals to make connections between the local and immediate and more global and long-term. Ultimately, the resolution of the dilemma of power rests on the inherent attractiveness of democracy, the deteriorating attractiveness of the modern paradigm, and the implicit power of majority sentiment.[37]

The potential power of a mobilized majority returns us again to democratic education, to participation that enhances self-awareness and self-confidence while also raising consciousness of oppressive forces in society. To realize potential support for fundamental change requires transforming a fear-based dynamic into one grounded on taking risks in order to make qualitative gains. The only way to learn that risks can pay off is to take them. As Sixties movements demonstrated, inspirational leadership, the example of others' actions, and a supportive community all played an important role in the myriad of individual decisions to act. Empowerment is both a personal and communal experience. It is also self-sustaining and contagious.

**NOTES
AND
INDEX**

Notes

Chapter 1

1. Aldon D. Morris, *The Origins of the Civil Rights Movement* (New York: The Free Press, 1984), p. 195.

2. As quoted in Stephen Spender, *The Year of the Young Rebels* (New York: Vintage, 1969), p. 111.

3. Michael Arlen, Jr., "Television and the Press in Vietnam; Or, Yes, I Can Hear You Very Well—Just What Was It You Were Saying?" in Michael Arlen, Jr., *Living Room War* (New York: Penguin Books, 1982), p. 106.

4. Theories that stressed *maturation* drew on sociological, anthropological, and psychological studies of generational conflict and personal development. While emphasizing developmental traits, these studies were also attentive to the distinctive maturation of the young Sixties rebels. Notable works in this genre included Erik Erikson, *Identity: Youth and Crisis* (New York: Norton, 1968); Margaret Mead, *Culture and Commitment: A Study of the Generation Gap* (New York: Basic Books, 1970); Bruno Bettelheim, "The Problem of Generations," in Erik Erikson, ed., *The Challenge of Youth* (New York: Anchor, 1965); and Lewis Feuer, *The Conflict of Generations: The Character and Significance of Student Movements* (New York: Basic Books, 1969). Some, like Mead, were sympathetic toward Sixties young people; others, like Bettelheim and Feuer, denounced the immaturity or emotional instability of activists while ignoring the content of their revolt.

5. This perspective ranged from interpretations that focused on the theory of child-raising advocated by Dr. Benjamin Spock and followed by parents of the baby boom, to works that focused on value congruence between Sixties activists and their parents. Notable among the former was Philip Slater's sympathetic *The Pursuit of Loneliness* (Boston: Beacon, 1970). Among the latter were studies by Kenneth Keniston, *Young Radicals: Notes on Committed Youth* (New York: Harcourt, Brace and World, 1968); Richard E. Flacks, "The Liberated Generation: An Exploration of the Roots of Student Protest," *Journal of Social Issues* 23 (1967): 52–75; and Seymour Martin Lipset, "The Activists: A Profile," *The Public Interest* (Fall 1968): 39–61. Keniston's "young radicals" were "personalistic," "focused on face-to-face, direct and open relationships with other people," and "hostile to formally structured roles and traditional bureaucratic patterns of power and authority." Significantly, they had close maternal relationships, tended to identify academic achievement with maternal pressure and "the feminine," and identified with the principled sides of their fathers—all of which gives credence to Dorothy

Dinnerstein's thesis that the New Left was unknowingly (and imperfectly) grounded in feminism.

6. I use the terms "liberal" and "conservative" to refer to the left and right wings of the American political mainstream. Both accept the basic parameters of political liberalism that defines and justifies American political and economic institutions, and was a major target of the more radical critiques of the 1960s.

7. Liberal interpretations of the 1960s vary widely. Some, like John Schwartz's *America's Hidden Successes: A Reassessment of Public Policy from Kennedy to Reagan*, rev. ed. (New York: Norton, 1988), defend the gains of liberal programs against the conservative attack launched in the Seventies and Eighties. Others, like Samuel Huntington's *American Politics: The Promise of Disharmony* (Cambridge, Mass.: Belknap Press, 1981), reinforce a more conservative swing back to "normalcy." Interestingly, the liberal argument that the system worked has also been forwarded by Sixties "radicals" like Tom Hayden. See Hayden, *Reunion: A Memoir* (New York: Random House, 1988).

8. For instance, *Time* magazine of August 15, 1977, referred to the "long hallucination of the 1960's" (p. 68).

9. Conservative critiques of the "failure" of Sixties liberalism include George Gilder, *Wealth and Poverty* (New York: Basic Books, 1980), and Charles Murray, *Losing Ground: American Social Policy, 1950–1980* (New York: Basic Books, 1984).

10. Critiques of the self-indulgent Sixties include Herbert I. London, *The Overheated Decade* (New York: New York University Press, 1976); Joseph Conlin, *The Troubles: A Jaundiced Glance Back at the Movement of the Sixties* (New York: Franklin Watts, 1982); and Stanley Rothman and S. Robert Lichter, *Roots of Radicalism: Jews, Christians, and the New Left* (New York: Oxford University Press, 1982). A more recent critique that implicates the Sixties in the rise of pervasive cultural relativism is Allan Bloom's *The Closing of the American Mind* (New York: Simon & Schuster, 1987).

11. See especially Peter Collier and David Horowitz, *The Destructive Generation* (New York: Summit, 1989).

12. The tension between these two strains posed the central dilemma of Sixties movements. See Wini Breines' analysis of the New Left in *Community and Organization in the New Left, 1962–1968: The Great Refusal*, 2nd ed. (New Brunswick, N.J.: Rutgers University Press, 1989).

13. As Breines contends, "The desire for connectedness, meaningful personal relationships and direct participation and control over economic, political and social institutions on the basis of the needs of the individual and community takes on radical meaning in a period such as ours." See *Community and Organization*, p. 7.

14. I do not mean to imply that these movements always lived up to these values, just that the values lay at the heart of their efforts to create a prefigurative politics for a transformed America. Obvious shortcomings of these and other movements are discussed later.

15. Murray Bookchin, *The Ecology of Freedom* (Palo Alto, Calif.: Cheshire, 1982), p. 339.

16. Quoted in Doug McAdam, *Freedom Summer* (New York: Oxford University Press, 1988), p. 231. Emphasis in original.

17. Also recalling Major Smedley Butler's remarks about his military career in Central America in the early part of this century: "I helped in the rape of half a dozen Central American republics for the benefit of Wall Street." Quoted by Noam Chomsky, *Turning the Tide: U.S. Intervention in Central America and the Struggle for Peace* (Boston: South End Press, 1985), p. 95.

18. Godfrey Hodgson has argued that American politics in the post-War era was governed by a liberal consensus consisting of six beliefs: By creating abundance, American free enterprise capitalism creates the potential for social justice; the key to this potential is increased production and economic growth; American society is characterized by a natural harmony of interests rather than traditional class conflict; social problems, like industrial problems, can be solved by social science that identifies the problems and points the way to policy solutions administered by experts; the main threat to this beneficent system is posed by the "deluded adherents of Marxism", who are engaged in a prolonged struggle with the Free World; and it is the duty of the United States to bring its humane system to the rest of the world. Godfrey Hodgson, *America in Our Time: From World War II to Nixon, What Happened and Why* (New York: Vintage, 1976), p. 76.

19. Greg Calvert and Carol Neiman dissect neocapitalism in *A Disrupted History: The New Left and the New Capitalism* (New York: Random House, 1972), ch. 3. Samuel Bowles, David M. Gordon, and Thomas E. Weisskopf analyze the postwar corporate system in *Beyond the Waste Land: A Democratic Alternative to Economic Decline* (Garden City, N.Y.: Anchor, 1984), ch. 4.

20. Langdon Winner, *The Whale and the Reactor: A Search for Limits in an Age of High Technology* (Chicago: University of Chicago Press, 1986), p. 170.

21. Richard Flacks, "On the New Working Class and Strategies for Social Change," in Philip G. Altbach and Robert S. Laufer, *The New Pilgrims: Youth Protest in Transition* (New York: David McKay, 1972), pp. 88–89.

22. James Gibson observes, "Politics, economics, and science were now united in a new way. Just as the state changed capitalism and changed the practice of science, so too did the now vastly expanded economy and scientific apparatus change the nature and practice of politics, particularly the conduct of foreign policy. . . . A deeply mechanistic worldview emerged among the political and economic elite and their intellectual advisers." James William Gibson, *The Perfect War: The War We Couldn't Lose and How We Did* (New York: Vintage, 1988), p. 14.

23. Calvert and Neiman, *A Disrupted History*, p. 80. The authors go on to contend, "It is a revolt of being, of Eros, against the plastic, boring, dehumanizing world, with its values of domination and exploitation, which brutalizes two-thirds of the world's people in order to maintain power and profit abroad while creating an anesthetized and de-eroticized plastic population in the midst of a garbage heap at home."

24. Barry Commoner has contended, "Most of our environmental problems are

the inevitable result of sweeping changes in the technology of production after World War II: the use of new, large, high-powered, smog-generating automobiles; the shift from fuel-efficient trains to gas-guzzling trucks and cars; the replacement of bio-degradable and less toxic natural products with non-degradable and hazardous petro-chemical products; and the substitution of chemical fertilizers for manure and crop rotation. By 1970 it was clear that these changes in the technology of production were the *root cause* of modern environmental pollution." "The Failure of the Environmental Effort," *Harper's* 276 (May 1988): 28.

25. For accounts of the relations between the Old and New Left, see Maurice Isserman, *If I Had a Hammer . . . The Death of the Old Left and the Birth of the New Left* (New York: Basic Books, 1987); Paul Buhle, *Marxism in America* (New York: Verso, 1987); and George R. Vickers, *The Formation of the New Left* (Lexington, Mass.: Lexington Books, 1975).

26. Paul Goodman, "The Poverty of the Great Society," in Marvin E. Gettelman and David Mermelstein, *The Great Society Reader* (New York: Random House, 1967), p. 518.

27. Norman Mailer, "Superman Comes to the Supermarket," in Gerald Howard, ed., *The Sixties* (New York: Washington Square Press, 1982), pp. 158, 146.

28. Activists who later took to the streets testified to Kennedy's role as a catalyst for their initial political involvement. Tom Hayden, referring to Kennedy's ability to give young people a sense of hope and vision of what might be, observed, "I was, in part, tied to the Kennedy image." Cited in Milton Viorst, *Fire in the Streets: America in the 1960's* (New York: Simon & Schuster, 1979), p. 171. Paul Cowan noted that "his Presidency would inspire thousands of young people like me to leave their middle-class environments and work in the Peace Corps or the civil rights movement." Paul Cowan, *The Making of an Un-American* (New York: Viking, 1967), p. 10.

29. Carl Oglesby, "Notes on a Decade Ready for the Dustbin," in Mitchell Goodman, ed., *The Movement Toward a New America* (Philadelphia: Pilgrim Press, 1970), p. 737.

30. Hayden, *Reunion*, p. 74.

31. Morris Dickstein, *The Gates of Eden* (New York: Basic Books, 1977), p. 188.

32. Breines, *Community and Organization*, pp. 40, 65.

33. Quoted in Lewis Feuer, *Conflict of Generations*, p. 441.

34. Quoted in McAdam, *Freedom Summer*, p. 231.

35. The phrases are all Keniston's, summarizing his observations about New Left activists working in the Vietnam Summer project in 1967. See Keniston, *Young Radicals*, pp. 287–88.

36. Allen J. Matusow, *The Unraveling of America: A History of Liberalism in the 1960's* (New York: Harper and Row), p. 127.

37. George Katsiaficas, *The Imagination of the New Left: A Global Analysis of 1968* (Boston: South End Press, 1987), p. 10.

38. Thus McAdam writes of the Freedom Summer, "What the volunteers had discovered in Mississippi was nothing less than the political significance of the personal.

Encoded in this discovery was an ideology and rhetoric of personal liberation that, when fused with the earlier emphasis on political change, were to give the Sixties their distinctive cast." *Freedom Summer*, p. 234.

39. Hans Koning, *Nineteen Sixty-Eight: A Personal Report* (New York: Norton, 1987), pp. 16–17.

40. For me, this moment came when I found myself cornered by a phalanx of bayonetted federal troops at the 1967 March on the Pentagon. Beyond the anxiety of the moment, the more sobering effect of this experience was my sudden realization that I was considered an enemy of my government in this symbolic showdown.

41. Ann Oakley, "Feminism, Motherhood, and Medicine," in Juliet Mitchell and Ann Oakley, eds., *What is Feminism?* (New York: Pantheon, 1986), p. 140. As Eric Hobsbawm observed, "Liberty, equality, and above all fraternity may become real for the moment in those stages of the great social revolution which revolutionaries who live through them describe in terms reserved for romantic love." *Primitive Rebels* (New York: Norton, 1965), p. 61.

42. Quoted in Breines, *Community and Organization*, p. 85.

43. Quoted in Abe Peck, *Uncovering the Sixties: The Life and Times of the Underground Press* (New York: Pantheon, 1985), p. 307.

44. Koning, *Nineteen Sixty-Eight*, p. 13.

45. Richard Flacks, "Whatever Happened to the New Left?" in Breines, *Community and Organization*, p. 120.

46. In 1976, the Senate Select Committee to Study Government Operations with Respect to Intelligence Activities, under Senator Frank Church, published its report documenting the sweeping COINTELPRO effort to spy on, infiltrate, harass, discredit, and eradicate the movement. For historical documentation of government repression during this era, see Robert J. Goldstein, *Political Repression in Modern America: From 1870 to the Present* (Cambridge, Mass.: Schenkman, 1978), ch. 11.

47. Peck, *Uncovering the Sixties*, p. 258.

48. It is telling that, in generalizing about the Sixties, the second thoughts of Sixties converts Peter Collier and David Horowitz focus almost exclusively on the most militant and fractured period of the Black Panthers, the Weathermen, and their heirs. See Collier and Horowitz, *The Destructive Generation*. It is also important to note that the escalating violence of factions like the Weathermen drew strong criticism from Movement leaders like Dave Dellinger who had long been committed to nonviolence. See Dellinger's *More Power than We Know: The People's Movement Toward Democracy* (Garden City, N.Y.: Anchor, 1975), chs. 13–16.

49. Koning, *Nineteen Sixty-Eight*, p. 14.

50. This radical critique has evolved along a variety of paths: revisionist treatments of John Kennedy and Lyndon Johnson's Great Society, a flourishing neo-Marxian literature, and critical theories arising within the feminist and ecology traditions.

51. Bruce Miroff, *Pragmatic Illusions: The Presidential Politics of John Kennedy* (New York: David McKay, 1976), p. 44.

52. For instance, President Johnson presented the Gulf of Tonkin incident as an

attack by the North Vietnamese against an innocent U.S. destroyer in order to rally Congress to approve a resolution (prepared in advance of the incident) that legitimized administration escalation of the war. In fact, as subsequent hearings and studies revealed, the administration had begun to plan American aggression against and provocation of the North Vietnamese almost immediately after Johnson assumed the presidency, yet curiously the plans were not implemented until *after* the 1964 election. A 1965 State Department White Paper, which asserted North Vietnamese aggression against the South, was contradicted by evidence in its own appendix. Ground troops were deployed in 1965 in small enough units that the press and public would not suspect that the administration was planning a fundamental shift in strategy—a shift that included an open-ended commitment to engage in ground warfare. The attack on Pleiku became the pretext for implementing the planned bombing of North Vietnam. The deception of the public escalated along with the war, later taking on the peculiar Nixon signature.

53. In taking his case for foreign aid to Congress, Kennedy stressed accurately, "Foreign aid is in our economic self-interest. It provides more than half a million jobs for workers in every State. It finances a rising share of our exports and builds new and growing export markets. It generates the purchase of military and civilian equipment by other governments in this country. It makes possible the stationing of 3½ million troops along the Communist periphery at a price one-tenth the cost of maintaining a comparable number of American troops." Cited in Jim F. Heath, *Decade of Disillusionment: The Kennedy–Johnson Years* (Bloomington: Indiana University Press, 1976), pp. 147–48.

54. Thus Kennedy was slow to respond to activists' demands for civil rights legislation, followed political tradition in appointing segregationist southern judges to the federal bench, and initially discouraged the March on Washington. Johnson undercut the Mississippi Freedom Democratic Party's efforts to gain seating at the 1964 presidential convention. See Chapter 2.

55. As Secretary of Defense McNamara declared, "Every quantitative measure we have shows us we're winning this war." As one South Vietnamese general remarked, "*Ah, les statistiques!* Your Secretary of Defense loves statistics. We Vietnamese can give him all he wants. If you want them to go up, they will go up. If you want them to go down, they will go down." Both quotes in Loren Baritz, *Backfire: A History of How American Culture Led Us into Vietnam and Made Us Fight the Way We Did* (New York: William Morrow, 1985), pp. 116–17. For a systematic critique of the technocratic mindset in the Vietnam War, see Gibson, *Perfect War*.

56. Another candidate was John McNaughton's conclusion, "We had to be there because we would be embarrassed to lose there." Gibson, *Perfect War*, p. 159. The war's irrationality was, of course, most brutally encountered by the men who served in Vietnam. As one G.I. put it, "We don't take any land. We don't give it back. We just mutilate bodies. What the fuck are we doing here?" Quoted in Robert Jay Lifton, *Home from the War* (New York: Simon & Schuster, 1973), p. 33.

Chapter 2

1. As Aldon Morris has written, "Prior to the movement the system of segregation forced blacks to live in a separate and limited world characterized by poverty, racial discrimination, powerlessness, symbolic subordination, and imperative acts of deference to white supremacy. The South is a different place today. Most of the 'white' schools, washrooms, theaters, swimming pools, parks, bus seats and other facilities are either integrated or at least not segregated by law. This does not mean that the races are thoroughly integrated in the South, because economic and residential segregation, which lead to segregation in other spheres of life, is widespread nationally." In *The Origins of the Civil Rights Movement* (New York: The Free Press, 1984), p. 287. Or as Stokely Carmichael (Kwame Touré) told a young questioner, "Blacks in Montgomery will never go to the back of the bus again. That is the essence of the change." From a speech given in Ann Arbor, Michigan on October 29, 1981, as quoted in Morris, *Origins*, p. 287.

2. Reflecting this pattern, the petitioners in the historic *Brown v. Board of Education* case refiled their suit against the "voluntary" resegregation of the original school systems. Schools are now more segregated in the North than in the South.

3. Initial voting rights efforts produced an increase in the percentage of southern blacks registered to vote, from 29 percent in 1960 to 43 percent in 1964. By 1968, black voter registration had increased to 62 percent, including 300,000 newly registered voters in the seven months after the Voting Rights Act passed. In counties where federal examiners and registers were active, registration increased by 50 percent; in counties where they were not sent it increased by only 22.3 percent. See Harrell R. Rodgers, Jr., and Charles S. Bullock, III, *Law and Social Change: Civil Rights Laws and Their Consequences* (New York: McGraw Hill, 1972), p. 31.

4. For example, the number of black elected officials in the United States grew from 103 to 5,115 between 1964 and 1982. From the U.S. Bureau of the Census, cited in Harrell R. Rodgers, Jr., and Michael Harrington, *Unfinished Democracy: The American Political System* (Glenview, Ill.: Scott, Foresman, 1985), p. 427.

5. David Garrow, *Protest at Selma* (New Haven, Conn.: Yale University Press, 1978), p. xii.

6. Jerry Watts, "The Left's Silent South," in Sohnya Sayres, et al., *The 60's Without Apology* (Minneapolis: University of Minnesota Press, 1984), p. 263.

7. Quoted in Juan Williams, *Eyes on the Prize: America's Civil Rights Years, 1954–1965* (New York: Penguin Books, 1988), p. 76.

8. Quoted in Howell Raines, *My Soul is Rested* (New York: Penguin Books, 1983), p. 151.

9. Letter written by Margaret Aley, quoted in Doug McAdam, *Freedom Summer* (New York: Oxford University Press, 1988), p. 68.

10. McAdam, *Freedom Summer*, p. 137.

11. Vincent Harding, "Black Radicalism: The Road from Montgomery," in Alfred F.

Young, ed., *Dissent: Explorations in the History of American Radicalism* (DeKalb: Northern Illinois University Press, 1968), p. 326.

12. Quoted in Williams, *Eyes on the Prize*, p. 79.

13. McAdam, *Freedom Summer*, p. 71.

14. James Baldwin, *The Fire Next Time* (New York: Dell, 1963), p. 136.

15. Sara Evans observed of the white students who joined the voter registration drive, "Their experiences had an impact far beyond the borders of the south, . . . for the white youth who joined the civil rights movement were crucial to the mobilization of the 'new left.' Their involvement in the south forced the white student movement to shift from cerebral concerns to community organizing and direct action demonstrations. Students who had been to the south provided the leadership, tactics, and ideology for the developing movements against the Vietnam War, for 'student power,' and for women's liberation." *Personal Politics: The Roots of Women's Liberation in the Civil Rights Movement and the New Left* (New York: Vintage, 1980), p. 61.

16. Mario Savio, "An End to History," in Massimo Teodori, ed., *The New Left: A Documentary History* (Indianapolis, Ind.: Bobbs-Merrill, 1969), p. 159.

17. Doug McAdam documents the radicalizing effect of the Mississippi Freedom Summer, noting, "The most immediate consequence of this process was the transformation of many of the volunteers from conventional liberals into leftist radicals. Having been denied (or spared) the annealing process, most of the [Freedom Summer] no-shows emerged from the summer with their liberalism intact." McAdam, *Freedom Summer*, p. 186.

18. King's radical critique of American capitalism is largely obscured by the media-hyped adoration of this American hero. See David J. Garrow, *Bearing the Cross: Martin Luther King, Jr., and the Southern Christian Leadership Conference* (New York: Vintage, 1988).

19. See Baldwin, *Fire Next Time*, 73–74.

20. See Richard Kluger, *Simple Justice* (New York: Vintage, 1977), p. 710.

21. Morris writes, "The black minister, because of his occupation, listened to and counseled people about their financial woes, family problems, and health problems, as well as problems stemming from discrimination, prejudice, and powerlessness. . . . The ministers listened to the educational and occupational aspirations of countless black children, along with the pleas of their parents. . . . Thus the black ministers of the 1950s knew black people because they had shared their innermost secrets and turmoils." In *Origins*, p. 10.

22. Lerone Bennett, Jr., "When the Man and the Hour Are Met," in C. Eric Lincoln, ed., *Martin Luther King, Jr.* (New York: Hill and Wang, 1970), pp. 7–39.

23. Quoted in Morris, *Origins*, p. 47.

24. James Lawson, from an interview with Aldon Morris, quoted in *Origins*, p. 124.

25. Morris notes, "During the bus boycotts in Montgomery and Tallahassee the revenues of the bus companies plummeted, and the entire white business community was adversely affected." *Origins*, p. 49.

26. *Origins*, pp. 62–63. In response to the shifting stance of the movement, Montgomery Mayor Gayle declared, "There seems to be a belief on the part of the Negroes that they have the white people hemmed up in a corner and they are not going to give an inch until they can force the white people of our community to submit to their demands—in fact, swallow all of them." Gayle denounced the boycott leaders as "a group of Negro radicals." Quoted in Williams, *Eyes on the Prize*, p. 81.

27. Quoted in Williams, *Eyes on the Prize*, p. 88.

28. One of the more prominent affiliates of the SCLC was the Nashville Christian Leadership Conference. NCLC classes and workshops at the First Baptist Church and the presence of four black higher education institutions generated a disproportionately large number of the leaders in the student movement of 1960; John Lewis, Diane Nash (Bevel), James Bevel, Marion Barry, Cordell Reagon, Bernard Lafayette, and Matthew Jones all played instrumental roles in either the sit-in movement or the subsequent leadership of SNCC or both. See Morris, *Origins* pp. 176–77.

29. Howard Zinn wrote of the personal impact the sit-ins had on the future leaders of SNCC: "To these young people, the Supreme Court decision of 1954 was a childhood memory. The Montgomery bus boycott of 1955 . . . , though also dimly remembered, was an inspiration. The trouble at Little Rock in 1957 was more vivid, with the unforgettable photos of the young Negro girl walking past screaming crowds toward Central High School. The Greensboro sit-ins struck a special chord of repressed emotion, and excitement ran across the Negro college campuses of the South." Howard Zinn, *SNCC: The New Abolitionists* (Boston: Beacon Press, 1965), p. 18.

30. In one typical "blame the victim" instance in Nashville, after the seated students were physically assaulted by white teenagers, eighty-one of the nonviolent protesters were arrested for disorderly conduct. The local white establishment subsequently denounced the *black* "rioters."

31. Evans, *Personal Politics*, p. 39. Evans also describes students' later amazement in reflecting on their decision to act.

32. Clayborne Carson, *In Struggle: SNCC and the Black Awakening of the 1960's* (Cambridge, Mass.: Harvard University Press, 1981), p. 14.

33. John Lewis remarked of Ella Baker, "She was much older [than the students] in terms of age, but I think in terms of ideas and philosophy and commitment she was one of the youngest persons in the movement." As quoted in Carson, *In Struggle*, p. 24.

34. Zinn, *SNCC*, p. 38.

35. Sherrod quoted in Carson, *In Struggle*, p. 33.

36. Milton Viorst, *Fire in the Streets: America in the 1960's* (New York: Simon & Schuster, 1979), pp. 144–5. One rider, Hank Thomas, recalled the fear riders felt inside the attacked bus. "When the bus was burning, . . . panic did get ahold of me. Needless to say, I couldn't survive that burning bus. There was a possibility I could have survived the mob, but I was just so afraid of the mob that I was gonna stay on that bus." Quoted in Raines, *My Soul is Rested*, p. 114.

37. Bull Connor claimed that protection wasn't available since many of his men

were off duty for Mother's Day. Many years later, congressional testimony revealed that the Birmingham police had promised the Ku Klux Klan enough time to carry out their attack. See Viorst, *Fire in the Streets*, p. 145.

38. Carson, *In Struggle*, p. 37.

39. The strain between alternate approaches can be seen in this exchange between Gloster Current of the NAACP and Courtland Cox of SNCC at a strategy session following the 1964 Democratic convention. Current: "The whole program must be reviewed. We need a summit meeting of different groups to evaluate the whole situation." Cox: "The need is for a low-level meeting. Get expression from the people so we can help develop programs which speak to their needs." Quoted in James Forman, *The Making of Black Revolutionaries* (Washington, D.C.: Open Hand, 1985), p. 404.

40. Garrow cites repeated instances of King's critique of capitalism. At a press conference during the Poor People's Campaign in 1968, King spoke off the record and, in one participant's recollection, "Talked about the fact that he didn't believe that capitalism as it was constructed could meet the needs of the poor people, and that what we might need to look at was a kind of socialism, but a democratic form of socialism." Quoted in Garrow, *Bearing the Cross*, p. 592.

41. Morris, *Origins*, p. 242.

42. As Kennedy put it on national television, "The U.S. government is involved in sitting down at Geneva with the Soviet Union. I can't understand why the . . . city council of Albany . . . can't do the same for American citizens." Quoted in Williams, *Eyes on the Prize*, p. 172.

43. Quoted in Carson, *In Struggle*, p. 61.

44. Connor was known to have direct contact with the violent White Citizens Council, the Ku Klux Klan, and with Governor George Wallace, famous for his pledge of "segregation now, segregation tomorrow, segregation forever!" At the time of the Birmingham demonstration, however, Connor was contesting his electoral defeat for mayor, evidence of a crack in his armor. See Morris, *Origins*, p. 262.

45. Martin Luther King, Jr., *Why We Can't Wait* (New York: Signet, 1964), p. 61.

46. *Ibid.*, pp. 80–81.

47. *Ibid.*, p. 85.

48. Morris notes, "The economic elites of Birmingham were vulnerable to outside pressure, because Northern capitalists owned most of the businesses they managed. But pressure from Northern capitalists to change racial exploitation in Birmingham was nonexistent as long as the profits kept rolling northward. Northern capitalists became concerned with racial problems in the South only after the movement began choking off their profits." *Origins*, p. 266.

49. John F. Kennedy, "Address to the Nation on Civil Rights," in Leon Friedman, ed., *The Civil Rights Reader: Basic Documents of the Civil Rights Movement* (New York: Walker, 1967), p. 65. As Reverend Fred Shuttlesworth remarked to the Birmingham community, "Yes, my friend[s], the New Frontier is trying to catch up with the Negro frontier." Fred Shuttlesworth, as quoted in Morris, *Origins*, p. 274.

50. Quoted in Viorst, *Fire in the Streets*, p. 229.

51. Quoted in Carson, *In Struggle*, p. 94.

52. For more detailed accounts, see Zinn, SNCC, and Carson, *In Struggle*. See also autobiographical accounts like Forman, *The Making of Black Revolutionaries*; Cleveland Sellers with Robert Terrell, *The River of No Return: The Autobiography of a Black Militant and the Life and Death of SNCC* (New York: William Morrow, 1973); and the more recent analyses of Mary King in *Freedom Song* (New York: William Morrow, 1987) and of Doug McAdam in *Freedom Summer*.

53. Zinn, SNCC, pp. 1, 8. The latter trait was reflected in SNCC's open-mindedness about participants in the civil rights struggle. Unlike more established groups but like its SDS counterpart, SNCC leaders initially welcomed all sympathetic participants, including members of the Communist party. This policy, of course, fueled the usual anticommunist scare tactics on the part of conservatives like J. Edgar Hoover.

54. Emily Stoper, "The Student Non-Violent Coordinating Committee: Rise and Fall of a Redemptive Organization," in Jo Freeman, ed., *Social Movements of the Sixties and Seventies* (New York: Longman, 1983), pp. 320–34.

55. Moses recalled, "I remember reading very bitterly in the papers the next morning, a little item on the front page of the McComb *Enterprise Journal* said that a Negro had been shot as he was trying to attack E. H. Hurst. And that was it. Might have thought he'd been a bum. There was no mention that Lee was a farmer, that he had a family, nine kids, beautiful kids, and that he had farmed all his life in Amite County." Quoted in Zinn, SNCC, p. 73.

56. Carson, *In Struggle*, p. 74.

57. Quoted in *ibid.*, p. 54.

58. Emily Stoper, "Student Non-Violent Coordinating Committee," p. 331.

59. Quoted in Raines, *My Soul is Rested*, p. 237, emphasis in original.

60. Zinn, SNCC, p. 89.

61. Quoted in *ibid.*, pp. 93–94.

62. In addition to voter registration efforts and the Mississippi Freedom Democratic party, the Freedom Summer Project included an educational campaign that reached over 2,000 black students through forty-one "freedom schools." The latter drew on enthusiastic young volunteers, new curricula, and the experience of the Highlander Folk School. They provided an enriched learning environment and enhanced the students' political consciousness. They also helped to stimulate the school reform movement of the middle to late Sixties.

63. Personal encounters with virulent racism and violence forged in these whites an unwavering commitment to the Movement, and often radicalized them. Zellner was dragged from a line of marchers in McComb and severely beaten. "That experience had the effect of welding him to the movement by a feeling so deep that it was akin to a religious experience. For the Negro youngsters in McComb, the sight of Bob Zellner walking with them into the mob and being beaten was a jolt to their general distrust of white people, an opening wedge for a new understanding about the tyranny of race." Zinn, SNCC, p. 171.

64. This was a theme that was repeated again and again. For example, the death

of northern white minister James Reeb during the Selma march of 1965 brought an immediate and powerful national response. President Johnson was moved to denounce the violence of the white mob. Johnson never mentioned the young black worker, Jimmy Lee Jackson, who was killed by a state policeman while trying to help his mother who had been clubbed by police. With understandable feeling, Stokely Carmichael bitterly denounced the double standard: "Now, I'm not saying we shouldn't pay tribute to Rev. Reeb. What I'm saying is that if we're going to pay tribute to one, we should also pay tribute to the other. And I think we have to analyze why [Johnson] sent flowers to Mrs. Reeb, and not to Mrs. Jackson." Quoted in Carson, *In Struggle*, p. 113. Similar sentiments were expressed when the murder of James Chaney, Andrew Goodman, and James Schwerner (respectively, a black SNCC worker and two northern whites) resulted in a full-scale federal investigation.

65. Quoted in McAdam, *Freedom Summer*, p. 46.

66. *Ibid.*, p. 127.

67. Quoted in Zinn, *SNCC*, p. 232. More generally, McAdam documents the radicalization of white volunteers. See McAdam, *Freedom Summer*, pp. 127–32.

68. Quoted in McAdam, *Freedom Summer*, p. 127. Another volunteer recalled the disillusionment of meeting Senator Paul Douglas (D-Ill.), a "liberal hero of mine. . . . I'll never forget this, he said, 'This is a wonderful thing you are doing, but,' he said, 'the main thing . . . is watch out for the Commies'" (p. 130).

69. William H. Chafe, *The Unfinished Journey: America Since World War II* (New York: Oxford University Press, 1986), p. 308. Again and again, field workers who had pleaded for federal support encountered FBI agents only impassively taking notes on the violence they observed. As the sympathetic but legally constrained Justice Department official John Doar told SNCC volunteers, "There is no federal police force. The responsibility for protection is that of the local police. We can only investigate." Quoted in Viorst, *Fire in the Streets*, p. 258.

70. Paul Cowan, *The Making of an Un-American* (New York: Viking, 1967), pp. 28–32.

71. The regular state party had also passed a resolution in July 1964 that read in part, "We oppose, condemn, and deplore the Civil Rights Act of 1964. . . . We believe in separation of the races in all phases of our society." Quoted in Stokely Carmichael and Charles V. Hamilton, *Black Power: The Politics of Liberation in America* (New York: Random House, 1967), p. 93.

72. Zinn, *SNCC*, p. 254.

73. Forman, *Making of Black Revolutionaries*, p. 389.

74. *Ibid.*, pp. 395–96.

75. *Ibid.*, p. 393.

76. Charles Sherrod, "Mississippi at Atlantic City," in Carson, *In Struggle*, pp. 127–28.

77. As recently as 1986, black activists in Boston were calling for the formation of an independent municipality to be known as "Mandela."

78. No fewer than ten African nations gained their independence in 1960.

79. See note 64, Chapter 2.

80. Sellers, *River of No Return*, pp. 122–23.

81. Garrow suggests that King's decision reflected strong pressure from the administration to hold off on the second march. Both the SCLC and the Justice Department had been seeking an injunction from Judge Frank Johnson prohibiting the state from interfering in the march to Montgomery. Johnson recommended a one-day pause in the plans in order to review the petition. SCLC leaders were at this time concerned for King's life. *Bearing the Cross*, pp. 85–86.

82. Students of protest movements have maintained that the audience for political conflicts plays the crucial role in determining outcomes. Where violence is involved, the public "becomes estranged from the party it blames for the occurrence of violence." Garrow attributes the observation about violence to Harvey Seifert, *Conquest through Suffering* (Philadelphia: Westminster Press, 1965), in Garrow, *Protest at Selma*, p. 215.

83. Stoper, "Student Non-Violent Coordinating Committee," p. 329.

84. In George Breitman, ed., *Malcolm X Speaks* (New York: Grove Press, 1965), pp. 141–42.

85. The bravado of male black power advocates was subsequently criticized by feminists who decried the movement's equation of liberation with manhood. See Manning Marable, *How Capitalism Underdeveloped Black America* (Boston: South End Press, 1983), ch. 3.

86. As a young speaker in Atlanta put it, "O.K., America, Nonviolence is dead. You just killed your last chance for a peaceful revolution. We won't forget." Quoted in Harding, "Black Radicalism," p. 348.

87. Julius Lester, "The Angry Children of Malcolm X," *Sing Out* (November 1966): 25.

88. Quoted in Viorst, *Fire in the Streets*, pp. 376–77.

89. Baldwin, *Fire Next Time*, p. 130.

90. The community control experiment rejected the professionalism and paternalism of white, middle-class school bureaucracies, instead opting for direct "bottom-up" control by the indigenous community and "equal power." In the process, it raised classic technocratic–democratic issues about expertise and access to mainstream institutions. (See Edward P. Morgan, "Two Paradigms of Urban Educational Policy: The Quest for Equality and its Central Dilemma," *Polity* 15 [Fall, 1982]: 48–71.) Like the Community Action Program in Lyndon Johnson's War on Poverty, however, the school experiment was too radical to last, for it wrested power from the school bureaucracy. For useful insight into the clash between Jewish and black communities, see James Baldwin's essay "The Harlem Ghetto," in *Notes of a Native Son* (Boston: Beacon Press, 1955), pp. 57–72.

91. Quoted in Carson, *In Struggle*, p. 194; second bracketed phrase by Carson.

92. Philip S. Foner, ed., *The Black Panthers Speak* (Philadelphia: J.B. Lippincott, 1970), p. xv.

93. *Ibid.*, p.x.

94. Eldridge Cleaver, "An Open Letter to Stokely Carmichael," in Foner, *Black Panthers Speak*, pp. 105–7.

95. Quoted in Foner, *Black Panthers Speak*, p. xxi.

96. Ronald Fraser, ed., *1968: A Student Generation in Revolt* (New York: Pantheon, 1988), p. 289.

97. The *New York Times*, May 18, 1970.

98. Carl Oglesby, "Notes on a Decade Ready for the Dustbin," in Mitchell Goodman, *The Movement Toward a New America* (Philadelphia: Pilgrim Press, 1970), p. 743.

99. Despite improvements for some middle-class families, black median income has remained at 57–60 percent of white income since 1966 (when it increased from 50 percent), and black unemployment has consistently been at least twice as high as white unemployment. Job discrimination has been compounded by the rapid growth in black female-headed households (which increased by over 80 percent from 1970 to 1980), itself the result of welfare laws, sexist socialization, and imperatives of the American economy. In 1985 47 percent of all black children lived in poverty, as compared to 18 percent of all white children.

100. Stoper, "Student Non-violent Coordinating Committee," p. 331.

Chapter 3

1. For accounts of the global student movement, see Ronald Fraser, ed., *1968: A Student Generation in Revolt* (New York: Pantheon, 1988), and George Katsiaficas, *The Imagination of the New Left: A Global Analysis of 1968* (Boston: South End Press, 1987).

2. Greg Calvert and Carol Nieman, *A Disrupted History: The New Left and the New Capitalism* (New York: Random House, 1972), p. 17.

3. Kirkpatrick Sale, *SDS* (New York: Vintage, 1974), pp. 663–64. Sale also notes that the decade began with 3,789,000 students in institutions of higher education and ended with 7,852,000 enrolled (p. 21).

4. Richard Flacks, "On the New Working Class and Strategies for Social Change," in Philip G. Altbach and Robert S. Laufer, *The New Pilgrims: Youth Protest in Transition* (New York: David McKay, 1972), p. 89. Or as Robert J. Lifton noted, "The university is indeed a training ground for available occupational slots in society, as young rebels are quick to point out, and can, at its worst, approach a technical instrument in the hands of the military–industrial complex. But it can also be precisely the opposite, a training ground for undermining social institutions, as the young rebels themselves attest to by the extent to which they are campus products." From "The New History," in Altbach and Laufer, *The New Pilgrims*, p. 188.

5. Notable titles published between 1960 and 1970 included A. S. Neill, *Summerhill*; Paul Goodman, *Growing Up Absurd*; John Holt, *How Children Fail* and *How Children Learn*; Jonathan Kozol, *Death at an Early Age* and *Free Schools*; Edgar Friedenberg, *Coming of Age in America*; Nat Hentoff, *Our Children Are Dying*; Herb Kohl, *36 Children*; James Herndon, *The Way It Spozed to Be*; George Dennison, *The Lives of Children*; Charles Silberman, *Crisis in the Classroom*; Philip W. Jackson, *Life in*

Classrooms; Neil Postman and Charles Weingartner, *Teaching as a Subversive Activity*; Jules Henry, *Culture Against Man*; Jerry Farber, *Student as Nigger*; Bel Kaufman, *Up the Down Staircase*; Everett Reimer, *School is Dead*; Ivan Illich, *Deschooling Society*; and Paulo Freire, *Pedagogy of the Oppressed*. Subsequently, more radical critiques, like Samuel Bowles and Herbert Gintis, *Schooling in Capitalist America*, pointed to systemic reasons for the failure of schooling.

6. Wini Breines, *Community and Organization in the New Left, 1962–1968: The Great Refusal*, 2nd ed. (New Brunswick, N.J.: Rutgers University Press, 1989), p. 28.

7. *Ibid.*, p. 67.

8. At Oberlin College, as on many other campuses, students surrounded a Navy recruiter's car, demanding an end to military recruiting in the college's placement office. The mainstream liberal administration of Robert Carr responded forcefully, claiming that such a policy violated the free speech rights of recruiters and students interested in military careers. Activists responded that the issue was recruitment, not speech, and that through use of the placement office, Oberlin was contributing to an immoral war effort. The recruiter demonstrations brought normal campus activities to a halt. A day-long debate was held in a packed Finney Chapel amidst tense administration–faculty deliberations, student planning sessions, and abnormal media attention. The public debate was followed by a student–faculty "5-5 Committee" that negotiated a proposal for use of the recruitment office. Having served on the latter, I can attest to the hours of wrangling over what was essentially a clash between the moralistic politics of the New Left and the pragmatic liberalism of college representatives.

9. Cited in Seymour Martin Lipset and Everett Carll Ladd, Jr., "The Political Future of Activist Generations," in Altbach and Laufer, *The New Pilgrims*, p. 63.

10. Barbara G. Myerhoff, "The Revolution as a Trip: Symbol and Paradox," in Altbach and Laufer, *The New Pilgrims*, p. 263.

11. The French student leader Daniel Cohn-Bendit tried to resolve these tensions by rejecting Lenin's notion of a revolutionary vanguard that would impose a new revolutionary order, arguing instead for "an active minority, acting you might say as a permanent ferment, pushing forward without trying to control events." Quoted in Robert J. Lifton, "The New History," in Altbach and Laufer, *The New Pilgrims*, p. 185.

12. Theodore Roszak, *The Making of a Counter Culture* (New York: Anchor, 1969), p. 57.

13. Sale, *SDS*, p. 16.

14. Quoted in Milton Viorst, *Fire in the Streets: America in the 1960's* (New York: Simon and Schuster, 1979), p. 176.

15. Tom Hayden to Al Haber, "Re. SNCC meeting, Jackson, Mississippi, September 14–17, 1961," quoted in Clayborne Carson, *In Struggle: SNCC and the Black Awakening of the 1960's* (Cambridge, Mass.: Harvard University Press, 1981), p. 176.

16. Quoted from a speech delivered at a *National Guardian* dinner, in Jack Newfield, *A Prophetic Minority* (New York: Signet, 1966), p. 90.

17. Quoted in *ibid.*, p. 96.

18. *Port Huron Statement* (Chicago: Students for a Democratic Society, 1966), p. 3.

19. Quoted in Abe Peck, *Uncovering the Sixties: The Life and Times of the Underground Press* (New York: Pantheon, 1985), pp. 24–25.

20. *Port Huron Statement*, p. 6.

21. Newfield, *Prophetic Minority*, p. 93. Newfield goes on to cite a common example of early SDS moralism, "Most SDS members seem to be against the war in Vietnam not primarily because they think it is imperialistic or they fear a world war with China; they are against it because they feel they cannot participate in a war that demands they murder innocent peasants. Again, this is an invocation of the post-Nuremberg ethic— every man is responsible for his actions . . . and at some moment he must say no to the machine and the officers giving the orders to kill."

22. *Port Huron Statement*, pp. 7–8.

23. As James Miller observes, "'Participatory democracy' seemed pertinent to a variety of people. It combined a patriotic aura with a revolutionary ring. Because it remained open to different interpretations, it could unite people with different interests in a common political quest." James Miller, *"Democracy is in the Streets": From Port Huron to the Siege of Chicago* (New York: Simon & Schuster, 1987), p. 152.

24. Breines, *Community and Organization*, p. 57.

25. *Port Huron Statement*, p. 9.

26. *Ibid.*, p. 10.

27. The latter metaphor echoed the writing of Paul Goodman, whose *Compulsory Mis-education and The Community of Scholars* (New York: Vintage, 1962) was first published the same year as the Port Huron convention.

28. Speech by Paul Potter at the SDS-sponsored conference on "The Role of the Student in Social Change," Harvard, November 1962. Quoted in Sale, *SDS*, pp. 84– 85.

29. *SDS Bulletin*, March–April 1963, quoted in Breines, *Community and Organization*, p. 124.

30. Quoted in *Community and Organization*, p. 125.

31. Miller, *"Democracy,"* p. 184.

32. Haber questioned the anti-intellectualism and moral superiority implied by field organizing in the urban ghettoes, and anticipated a perennial activist's dilemma. "Is radicalism subsisting in a slum for a year or two, or is it developing your individual talents so you can function as a radical in the 'professional' fields and throughout your adult life? Can a teacher be a radical in his profession? or an artist? or a lawyer?" *SDS Bulletin*, March 1964, quoted in Breines, *Community and Organization*, p. 129.

33. Maurice Isserman, *If I Had a Hammer . . . The Death of the Old Left and the Birth of the New Left* (New York: Basic Books, 1987), p. 217.

34. Tom Hayden, *Reunion: A Memoir* (New York: Random House, 1988), pp. 145– 46.

35. Sale, *SDS*, pp. 204–5.

36. Sale, *SDS*, pp. 440–41.

37. A friend of militant SDS leader Bernardine Dohrn recalled the moment that she first heard of Martin Luther King's death. "She was really stunned. I must admit that

I was fairly jaded by then, and I remember saying that with King dead, the Panthers and the other militants would have a clear field to lead the revolution. But Bernardine was sincerely moved, and she began to cry. She cried for a while and she talked about Chicago, when she had worked with King. She said she hadn't always agreed with him, but she responded to him as a human being. Then she went home and changed her clothes. I'll never forget that—she said she was changing into her riot clothes: pants. We went up to Times Square, and there was a demonstration going on of pissed-off black kids and white radicals. We started ripping signs and getting really out of hand and then some kids trashed a jewelry store. Bernardine really dug it. She was still crying, but afterward we had a long talk about urban guerrilla warfare and what had to be done now—by any means necessary." Quoted in Sale, *SDS*, pp. 424–25.

38. This assault was duplicated by major city police departments. Ronald Fraser observes that "the evidence suggests that many police informants and FBI infiltrators themselves repeatedly broke the law by acting as provocateurs—urging activists toward violence, provoking violence themselves during demonstrations, and sometimes provoking people with weapons and explosives. In one case, after infiltrating the Northern Illinois University SDS chapter, a Chicago police agent physically attacked the university president and threw him off the stage, thus creating a pretext for official action against the chapter." In Fraser, 1968, pp. 289–90. For more systematic documentation see the Final Report of the Senate Select Committee to Study Government Operations with Respect to Intelligence Activities (Washington, D.C.: U.S. Government Printing Office, 1976); Frank J. Donner, *The Age of Surveillance* (New York: Knopf, 1980); Robert J. Goldstein, *Political Repression in Modern America* (Cambridge, Mass.: Schenkman, 1978).

39. Fraser, 1968, p. 288.

40. Quoted in Sale, *SDS*, p. 506.

41. Carl Oglesby, "Notes on a Decade Ready for the Dustbin," in Mitchell Goodman, ed., *The Movement Toward a New America* (Philadelphia: Pilgrim Press, 1970), p. 742, emphasis in original.

42. The title was drawn from a line in Bob Dylan's "Mr. Tambourine Man."

43. Quoted in Fraser, 1968, p. 312.

44. *Ibid.*, p. 314.

45. An FBI film of the protest, called "Operation Abolition," characterized the students as dupes of communist organizers. When shown on college campuses, the film had precisely the opposite effect of what J. Edgar Hoover intended. Tom Hayden recalls of the Michigan showing, "The room was packed. There were three hundred people, which at the time was unprecedented. I don't think most of them understood the formal issues, like contempt of a congressional committee. To them, Red-baiting was a new word. . . . But what the movie made clear was that there were really outdated and irrational people on congressional committees who were behaving in, you know, insane ways, and the San Francisco police were their allies. Young people like ourselves were being washed down the stairs of City Hall, getting their heads broken. Those people were like us." Quoted in Viorst, *Fire in the Streets*, p. 173.

46. A partial list of active campuses would include Antioch, Berkeley, Carleton, Chicago, City College of New York, Columbia, Cornell, Earlham, Harvard, Michigan, Minnesota, Oberlin, Radcliffe, Reed, Swarthmore, and Wisconsin.

47. The events of the Berkeley revolt are recounted in two significant books: Max Heirich, *The Beginning: Berkeley, 1964* (New York: Columbia University Press, 1970), and Hal Draper, *Berkeley: The New Student Revolt* (New York: Grove Press, 1965).

48. "Look, Ma, No Hope," in Goodman, *Movement*, p. 18.

49. Seymour Martin Lipset and Sheldon S. Wolin, *The Berkeley Student Revolt* (New York: Doubleday, 1965), pp. xi–xii.

50. Quoted in Draper, *Berkeley*, p. 60.

51. Cited in Sol Stern, "A Deeper Disenchantment," in Walt Anderson, ed., *The Age of Protest* (Pacific Palisades, Cal.: Goodyear, 1969), p. 64.

52. Breines, *Community and Organization*, p. 42.

53. Clark Kerr, *The Uses of the University* (Cambridge, Mass.: Harvard University Press, 1963), cited in Lipset and Wolin, *Berkeley Student Revolt*, pp. 47–49.

54. This is Kerr's term. In Kerr's perception, "The guild view is elitist toward the external environment, conservative toward internal change, conformist in relation to the opinion of colleagues. The socialist view is democratic toward society, radical toward change, and nonconformist. And the political liberal is drawn toward both views." By implication, of course, the technocratic manager is made to sound nobly impartial. "To make the multiversity work really effectively, the moderates need to be in control of each power center and there needs to be an attitude of tolerance between and among the power centers, with few territorial ambitions." Kerr "Problems in the Multiversity," in Lipset and Wolin, *Berkeley Student Revolt*, pp. 54, 44.

55. Lipset and Wolin, *Berkeley Student Revolt*, p. 43.

56. Bradford Cleaveland, "A Letter to Undergraduates," in Lipset and Wolin, *Berkeley Student Revolt*, p. 66.

57. Bradford Cleaveland, "Education, Revolutions, and Citadels," in Lipset and Wolin, *Berkeley Student Revolt*, p. 89.

58. For example, Harold Taylor, the former president of Sarah Lawrence College, wrote, "The big universities have changed in precisely the ways Mr. Kerr has described. They have become corporations for producing, transmitting, and marketing knowledge, and in the process have lost their intellectual and moral identity. At the time that they should have been creative centers for the development of strategies for peace, disarmament, and world unity, they were busy with defense department contracts. When the educational problem of the Negro was getting worse by the day, they were busy making admission requirements more and more favorable to the white middle-class student from privileged environments. When the social habits and material ambitions of the citizens were following the lead of the advertising agencies, the universities were producing graduates whose intellectual equipment was suited to reading advertising copy." From "The Academic Industry," in Lipset and Wolin, *Berkeley Student Revolt*, p. 62.

59. Sale, *SDS*, p. 167, emphasis in the original.

60. This phenomenon was captured by Kenneth Keniston's article, "You Have to Grow Up in Scarsdale to Know How Bad Things Really Are," in the *New York Times Magazine*, April 27, 1969.

61. Mario Savio, "An End to History," in Mitchell Cohen and Dennis Hale, *The New Student Left* (Boston: Beacon Press, 1967), p. 249. One Freedom Summer volunteer recalls the impact Mississippi apparently had on Savio: "No way he ever would have . . . stepped forward if it hadn't been for Mississippi. Part of it was confidence. He was really a pretty shy guy [but] . . . Freedom Summer tended to boost you; you felt like you had been there and you knew what you were talking about. . . . But more than that it was moral outrage. . . . Off of what he saw in McComb, there was just this . . . total commitment to the [civil rights] movement . . . and no stupid bureaucratic rules were going to get in the way." Quoted in Doug McAdam, *Freedom Summer* (New York: Oxford University Press, 1988), p. 166.

62. Carl Davidson, "The Multiversity: Crucible of the New Working Class," in Immanuel Wallerstein and Paul Starr, eds., *The University Crisis Reader*, Vol. I (New York: Vintage, 1971), pp. 89–93.

63. Drawing on the experiences of MIT students, Benson Snyder described the contrast between the formal and hidden curricula of higher education. On the academic front, he maintained, the *real* curriculum is one that emphasizes efficient time management and cue reading skills, as students seek to figure out what information is most important in their professors' eyes—all in the cause of maximizing their grades and thus their future occupational success. As Snyder's students attest, this process undermines the stated aims of intellectual growth and learning. On the social front, colleges and universities promulgated petty rules (like the infamous "three feet on the floor and wastebasket in the door") in order to reassure nervous parents that students were not engaging in sexual intercourse, when in fact students perceived university officials as not caring about their personal lives and concerns. See Benson Snyder, *The Hidden Curriculum* (Cambridge, Mass.: M.I.T. Press, 1971).

64. A study by Richard Flacks indicated that the student protesters had an average grade of B to B plus, somewhat higher (and therefore less directly threatened by the ruling) than the nonprotesting pool. Richard Flacks, "The Liberated Generation: An Exploration of the Roots of Student Protest," *Journal of Social Issues* 23 (1967): 52–75.

65. For example, one survey of the 78 most prominent colleges and universities revealed that 430 protests occurred on their campuses during the 1966–1967 academic year. Another survey of 246 campuses indicated that 90 percent had experienced protests against administrative policies, in which, on over 100 campuses, more than half the student body was involved. Over 25 percent of the 246 institutions had demonstrations against Vietnam and racial discrimination in which more than a quarter of the student body was involved. Cited in Sale, *SDS*, p. 305n.

66. *Ibid.*, pp. 371–73.

67. See Peck, *Uncovering the Sixties*, p. 95.

68. Cited in *ibid.*, p. 94.

69. According to Bill Sales, black students applauded white students' goals but were

put off by their lack of seriousness. They also encountered democratic lessons of their own from the neighboring black community: "We went down there and said, 'Look man, this line of stopping the gym is wrong. You can't stop Columbia from building it.' They looked at us and said, 'No. The gym is not going to be built and that's it.' And that's when we began to see that, because we thought we knew so much, we had missed the point altogether. We began to develop a better appreciation that 'ordinary folks,' as we saw them, are much closer in their guts to what's really happening than we were." Quoted in Fraser, 1968, pp. 195–96.

70. Stephen Spender likened the relationship between blacks and whites to that of workers and students in the upheavals simultaneously occurring in France. Because Columbia bordered West Harlem, and because the black inner-city communities had exploded after the assassination of Martin Luther King, Jr., less than a month before, the Columbia situation was the opposite of the national pattern. In Spender's view, "It was the black students who in fact controlled the situation. What the authorities most feared was a racial riot, with black victims, on the campus. They could have put up with white victims far more easily." In Stephen Spender, *The Year of the Young Rebels* (New York: Vintage, 1969).

71. Dotson Rader and Craig Anderson, "Rebellion at Columbia," in Walt Anderson, ed., *The Age of Protest* (Pacific Palisades, Calif.: Goodyear Publishing, 1969), p. 70. In the account of the Cox Commission, "The men were not ordinary plainclothesmen, as many have supposed, but middle-echelon police officers who had been called by their superiors to help prepare detailed plans for clearing the buildings. Many [Ad Hoc Faculty Group] members were young instructors; it is unlikely that the police officers knew who they were or by what authority they were blocking the path to the office to which the police had been summoned." Cox Commission, *Crisis at Columbia: Report of the Fact-Finding Commission Appointed to Investigate the Disturbances at Columbia University in April and May 1968* (New York: Vintage, 1968), p. 122.

72. See the descriptive account in *ibid.*, pp. 123–35. The mediating efforts of the Ad Hoc Faculty Group were particularly noteworthy.

73. Although the group's name was obviously selected for strategic reasons, a poll of student opinion taken at the time indicated that sizeable student majorities supported the gym and the anti-IDA demands of the protesters, while opinion was more evenly divided on the question of amnesty for the SDS leaders. See *ibid.*, p. 137.

74. Rader and Anderson, "Rebellion," in Anderson, *Age of Protest*, pp. 71–72. Another account by anthropology professor Marvin Harris resembles that of Rader and Anderson; see Harris's "Big Bust on Morningside Heights," in Goodman, *Movement*, pp. 26–30. The more detached Cox Commission Report refrained from assigning responsibility for the violence but observed, "There was great violence. Given the conditions on the campus, violence was unavoidable. . . . Outside the buildings were hundreds of strike sympathizers, many resentful of the presence of police upon any academic campus." Cox Commission, *Crisis at Columbia*, p. 140.

75. *Ibid.*, pp. 181–82.

76. Sale, *SDS*, pp. 511–12.

77. Mike York and Fred Kirsch, *May 1970: Birth of the Antiwar University* (New York: Pathfinder Press, 1971), p. 13.

78. The tragic events at Kent State are graphically described and interpreted by James Michener in *Kent State: What Happened and Why* (New York: Fawcett Crest, 1971) and by I. F. Stone in *The Killings at Kent State: How Murder Went Unpunished* (New York: New York Review of Books, 1971).

79. Sale, *SDS*, p. 636.

80. Quoted in Katsiaficas, *Imagination of the New Left*, p. 117.

Chapter 4

1. Loren Baritz, *Backfire: A History of How American Culture Led Us into Vietnam and Made Us Fight the Way We Did* (New York: William Morrow, 1985), p. 7.

2. One wounded vet recalled, "When you come home you feel like everybody you touched turned to shit. I forgot how to cry. I just buried my best friend in 1979 and I couldn't cry. I knew how before I went to Vietnam." Quoted in Myra MacPherson, *Long Time Passing* (Garden City, N.Y.: Doubleday, 1984), p. 71.

3. These figures are taken from MacPherson, *Long Time Passing*.

4. *Ibid.*, p. 336.

5. It should be remembered, however, that many G.I.'s were themselves antiwar. Their activities included individual acts of resistance, organizing on military bases, and formation of the Vietnam Veterans Against the War.

6. John Pilger, quoted in Noam Chomsky, *Towards a New Cold War: Essays on the Current Crisis and How We Got There* (New York: Pantheon, 1982), p. 25. It is now known that countless American veterans also face the health hazards caused by Agent Orange, although the government resisted efforts to provide health benefits for these unknowing victims of the chemical defoliant.

7. Ngo Vinh Long, "View from the Village," as quoted in Chomsky, *New Cold War*, p. 25. Chomsky goes on to note, "Bombing of dikes was reported by the U.S. press without comment during the war, recalling to some the fact that Nazi criminals were hanged for opening the dikes in Holland under the postwar 'victors justice'" (p. 383, note 74).

8. See David Dellinger, *Vietnam Revisited: Covert Action to Invasion to Reconstruction* (Boston: South End Press, 1986).

9. Paul Potter, "Speech to the April 17, 1965 March on Washington," in Judith Clavir Albert and Stewart Edward Albert, eds., *The Sixties Papers: Documents of a Rebellious Decade* (New York: Praeger, 1984), pp. 218–19.

10. I use the word "radical" to refer to both those who argue that the war policy was consciously pursued by the ruling economic and political powers in a calculated effort to maintain their position in the world and in American society, and those who ascribe

considerable self-delusion to many who contributed to war policy. In either case the radical views the war as an outgrowth of American multinational capitalism, an elitist national power structure, and the myth-making cover of liberal ideology.

11. For an account of Ho Chi Minh's democratic inclinations, see Gabriel Kolko, *Anatomy of a War: Vietnam, the United States, and the Modern Historical Experience* (New York: Pantheon, 1985), ch. 4.

12. Movement leadership emerged from an array of groups—from the Committee for a SANE Nuclear Policy, Americans for Democratic Action, and the liberal wing of the Democratic party, to pacifist and antiwar groups like the War Resisters' League, Fellowship of Reconciliation, and Women Strike for Peace, to social democratic groups like the Socialist party–Social Democratic Federation and the League of Industrial Democracy, to SDS and SNCC, to Stalinist groups like the American Communist party and Progressive Labor, to Trotskyists like the Socialist Workers party and the Young Socialist Alliance.

13. As ex-Marine William Ehrhart put it, "In grade school, we learned about Redcoats—the nasty British soldiers that tried to stifle our freedom, and the tyranny of George the Third, and I think subconsciously, but not very subconsciously, I began increasingly to have a feeling that I was a Redcoat. And I think it was one of the most staggering realizations of my life, to suddenly understand that I wasn't a hero, I wasn't a good guy, I wasn't handing out candy and cigarettes to the kids in the French villages, that somehow I had become everything I had learned to believe was evil." From the film "Vietnam: America Takes Charge," produced by WGBH/Boston.

14. Potter, "Speech," in Albert and Albert, *Sixties Papers*, p. 222.

15. Carl Oglesby, "Notes on a Decade Ready for the Dustbin," in Mitchell Goodman, ed., *The Movement Toward a New America* (Philadelphia: Pilgrim Press, 1970), p. 745.

16. There are innumerable analyses that focus on one or more of these traits. Notable examples include James William Gibson, *The Perfect War: The War We Couldn't Lose and How We Did* (New York: Vintage, 1988); Gabriel Kolko, *The Roots of American Foreign Policy* (Boston: Beacon Press, 1969); and Edward S. Herman and Noam Chomsky, *Manufacturing Consent: The Political Economy of the Mass Media* (New York: Pantheon, 1988).

17. Others have treated this initial period in great detail. See Leslie H. Gelb with Richard K. Betts, *The Irony of Vietnam: The System Worked* (Washington, D.C.: Brookings Institution, 1979); Archimedes Patti, *Why Viet Nam?* (Berkeley: University of California Press, 1980); Paul Kattenburg, *The Vietnam Trauma in American Foreign Policy, 1945–1975* (New Brunswick, N.J.: Transaction Books, 1980); Kolko, *Anatomy of a War*; George C. Herring, *America's Longest War: the United States and Vietnam, 1950–1975*, 2nd ed. (New York: Knopf, 1986), and Gibson, *Perfect War*.

18. In planning for President Truman's speech, a state department information officer asserted that "the only way we can sell the public on our new policy is by emphasizing the necessity of holding the line: communism vs. democracy should be the major theme." Cited in Chomsky, *New Cold War*, p. 20.

19. The nationalist–communist Ho Chi Minh sought recognition by and cooperation with the United States in his effort to throw out the occupying Japanese forces
and the last vestiges of prewar French colonialism. Through Office of Strategic Services intermediary Archimedes Patti, Ho had sought American support from a not-
unsympathetic Roosevelt administration for "the cause of a free Vietnam." However,
as Patti observed of the Truman years, "All the information that people in the field
passed to Washington ended in a dry well. . . . By the summer of 1946, the word had
reached Washington, and all official references to Ho were prefixed 'communist.'" See
Patti, *Why Viet Nam?* pp. 86, 382.

20. *Newsweek* reporter Harold Isaacs warned prophetically, "The United States
has embarked upon another ill-conceived adventure doomed to end in another self-
inflicted defeat. It will not help the United States in its struggle against Communism. It
will help the Communists in their struggle against the United States." From James C.
Thomson, Jr., Peter W. Stanley, and John Curtis Perry, *Sentimental Imperialists* (New
York: Harper Colophon Books, 1981), pp. 207–8.

21. Noam Chomsky, *Turning the Tide: U.S. Intervention in Central America and the
Struggle for Peace* (Boston: South End Press, 1985), p. 100. See also Kolko, *Anatomy
of a War*, ch. 7.

22. Kattenburg observes that few if any policy makers would have dared to say in
1950, "Ho is certainly a Communist, but he has great appeal; he is regarded as a cham-
pion of nationalism and of anti-colonialism; he is forging an unbreakable bond with his
people; he will win his revolutionary struggle regardless of the odds, for . . . the masses
of the people support him and not the French or their puppets." Kattenburg, *Vietnam
Trauma*, p. 40.

23. Baritz, *Backfire*, p. 102.

24. Kattenburg, *Vietnam Trauma*, p. 108.

25. Nancy Zaroulis and Gerald Sullivan, *Who Spoke Up? American Protest Against
the War in Vietnam, 1963–1975* (New York: Doubleday, 1984), p. 9.

26. Herman and Chomsky show how the same mass media blamed by the administration for the American loss of will after Tet actually reinforced public support for the
war through faithful adherence to administration positions from 1962 through 1967.
See Herman and Chomsky, *Manufacturing Consent*, ch. 5.

27. Kolko, *Anatomy of a War*, p. 150.

28. There are considerable doubts about the nature of the first engagement between
the PT boats and the U.S. destroyer *Maddox*. There is ample evidence of prior U.S.
provocation of North Vietnam in its Operation Plan 34A actions, and the *Maddox* had
been conducting espionage on North Vietnam within the twelve-mile territorial waters
claimed by the North. It seems highly plausible that the North Vietnamese also viewed
the *Maddox* as a support vessel for South Vietnamese commando raids on the Gulf of
Tonkin islands in the preceding days. It also seems likely that an alleged second North
Vietnamese attack never occurred. What is clear is that the incident served as a timely
and useful focus for an administration bent on escalating hostilities against the North.
And, as Daniel Hallin revealed, "On virtually every important point, the reporting of

the two Gulf of Tonkin incidents . . . was either misleading or simply false." Daniel C. Hallin, *The "Uncensored War": The Media and Vietnam* (New York: Oxford University Press, 1986), p. 19. More generally, see Joseph C. Goulden, *Truth Is the First Casualty: The Gulf of Tonkin Affair—Illusion and Reality* (New York: Rand McNally, 1969).

29. As McGeorge Bundy observed, "Pleikus are streetcars—that is, if you miss one, another one will come along." Cited in Zaroulis and Sullivan, *Who Spoke Up?* p. 33. Critics of the Bundy plan, including Vice-president Humphrey and Under Secretary of State George Ball, urged greater caution. Ball recognized from his World War II study that bombing would not break the will of Hanoi, nor would it win the war. As a result of these deliberations, Humphrey was not invited to participate in foreign policy discussions for a year, while George Ball became President Johnson's token dissenter.

30. Quoted in Godfrey Hodgson, *American in Our Time: From World War II to Nixon, What Happened and Why* (New York: Vintage, 1976), p. 286. The teach-ins were originally conceived as a one-day faculty strike by a group of forty-nine faculty, forty-six of whom were untenured. In the swirl of controversy over faculty responsibilities that followed, the strike signers decided on the all-night teach-in as a way of maintaining the focus on Vietnam.

31. Secretary of State Dean Rusk commented disparagingly on the teach-ins: "I sometimes wonder at the gullibility of educated men and the stubborn disregard of plain facts by men who are supposed to be helping our young people to learn—especially to learn how to think." From an April 23, 1965 speech to the American Society of International Law, quoted in *Facts on File: World News Digest* (April 22–28, 1965): 145.

32. Thomas Powers, *Vietnam: The War at Home* (Boston: G. K. Hall, 1984), pp. 60–61.

33. See Marvin E. Gettleman, *et al.*, eds., *Vietnam and America: A Documented History* (New York: Grove Press, 1985), p. 274.

34. Quoted in Zaroulis and Sullivan, *Who Spoke Up?* p. 38.

35. Potter, "Speech," pp. 218–25.

36. Quoted in Zaroulis and Sullivan, *Who Spoke Up?* p. 41.

37. Fred Halstead, *Out Now! A Participant's Account of the American Movement Against the Vietnam War* (New York: Monad Press, 1978), p. 43.

38. Quoted in *ibid.*, p. 57.

39. Quoted in *ibid.*, pp. 60–61.

40. The following week, *Life* magazine ran a photograph of Dave Dellinger, Robert (Moses) Parris, and Staughton Lynd being splattered with red paint thrown by a member of the American Nazi party. As Halstead notes, the heckler was released on $10 bail, while Dellinger drew 45 days in jail for his role in the sit-down. *Ibid.*, pp. 67–68.

41. The *New York Times*, November 3, 1965.

42. Quoted in Halstead, *Out Now!*, pp. 113–15.

43. Zaroulis and Sullivan, *Who Spoke Up?* p. 76.

44. *Ibid.*, p. 89.

45. Five years later, the production and use of napalm persisted despite a 1969 attack on Dow Chemical offices in Washington, D.C. by the DC9 (a group of radical Catholics), and the publication of perhaps the most famous photograph of the war—a naked Vietnamese girl screaming in agony while running toward the camera as her flesh was burning and melting from napalm. The use of napalm against civilian populations was one of the war crimes cited by the Russell War Crimes Tribunal in 1971.

46. Quoted in Zaroulis and Sullivan, *Who Spoke Up?* p. 110.

47. The *New York Times*, April 5, 1967.

48. Michael Herr describes the stress of combat conditions: "Imagine being too tired to snap a flak jacket closed, too tired to clean your rifle, too tired to guard a light, too tired to deal with the half-inch margins of safety that moving through the war often demanded, just too tired to give a fuck and then dying behind that exhaustion. . . . Once I talked for maybe five minutes with a sergeant who had just brought his squad in from a long patrol before I realized that the dopey-dummy film over his eyes and the fly abstraction of his words were coming from deep sleep. He was standing there at the bar of the NCO club with his eyes open and a beer in his hand, responding to some dream conversation far inside his head. It really gave me the creeps . . . for a second I imagined that I was talking to a dead man. When I told him about it later, he just laughed and said, 'Shit, that's nothing. I do that all the time.'" Michael Herr, *Dispatches* (New York: Avon, 1978), p. 57.

49. For example, one vet recalled a village massacre: "We were crossing a rice paddy when VC mortar fire came in. The shrapnel cut one guy across the middle. His guts spilled out. I grabbed his insides and tried to shove them back. It looked like afterbirth, and it just slid through my hands, and the guy died. Then we took some small-arms fire from a village. I don't remember if it was much, but we charged the village and started shooting. . . . There was total panic. . . . When something like that gets started, you can't stop it. There was nobody in charge and everyone was shouting and shooting, shouting, 'Shoot this! Shoot that!' and I went into a hut that was filled with people and sprayed it. We wasted everyone and everything in that village. We wasted the women and the kids and the old men and the dogs. . . . Then we burned the village to the ground. It was the most awful thing and I still dream about it. Listen, man, I dream this shit every night." Quoted in MacPherson, *Long Time Passing*, p. 195.

50. Quoted in *ibid.*, pp. 68–69.

51. *Ibid.*, p. 259. Or as founder of the Vietnam Veterans of America Robert Muller put it in words echoing Carl Oglesby's, "disillusionment over the leadership in this country and the fucking institutions that betrayed my fucking willingness to give my tender fucking ass in the service of this country." Quoted in A. D. Horne, ed., *The Wounded Generation: America After Vietnam* (Englewood Cliffs, N.J.: Prentice-Hall, 1981), p. 151.

52. One veteran recalls the reenlistment pep talk, "Jesus Christ, you dropped out of high school with a D-plus average! Listen, the stuff you did in Vietnam, if you go and reenlist now we'll give you a bonus of about $1,500, promotion to sergeant, and, man,

you're on your way up. There's no question you'll make gunnery sergeant in five years. Christ, you might be able to earn maybe as much as $10,000 *a year* and you won't have a problem in the world!" Quoted in MacPherson, *Long Time Passing*, p. 300.

53. Quoted in Wallace Terry and Janice Terry, "The War and Race," in Horne, *Wounded Generation*, p. 181. The statistics on black servicemen are drawn from the same article, p. 167.

54. McNamara worried, "The picture of the world's greatest superpower killing or seriously injuring 1,000 non-combatants a week, while trying to pound a tiny backward nation into submission on an issue whose merits are hotly disputed, is not a pretty one." He went on to observe that such a picture "could produce a costly distortion in the American national consciousness and in the world image of the United States—especially if the damage to North Vietnam is complete enough to be successful." That McNamara saw such a picture as a distortion only reveals how distorted the decision-maker's inside view can be. Quoted in Baritz, *Backfire*, p. 117.

55. From "We Refuse to Serve," in Alice Lynd, ed., *We Won't Go: Personal Accounts of War Objectors* (Boston: Beacon Press, 1968), p. 239.

56. *Ibid.*, p. 243 (emphasis in original).

57. Andrew Kopkind, "They'd Rather Be Left," in Kopkind, *America: The Mixed Curse* (Harmondsworth, England: Penguin Books, 1969), p. 73.

58. Quoted in Zaroulis and Sullivan, *Who Spoke Up?* pp. 131–32.

59. Quoted in *ibid.*, p. 140. The military formations, with fixed bayonets and a rapid-step march toward the soon to be cornered demonstrators succeeded in scattering many who had time to run for cover. See note 40 in Chapter one.

60. Quoted in *ibid.*, p. 141.

61. William L. O'Neill, *Coming Apart: An Informal History of America in the 1960's* (New York: Times Books), 1971.

62. Zaroulis and Sullivan, *Who Spoke Up?* p. 149.

63. Khe Sanh became a place of legend synonymous with hell for many of the besieged marines, and the perfect metaphor for U.S. toughness and persistence under fire for military brass. It also became one of the most heavily bombed targets in the history of warfare. See Michael Herr's powerful account in *Dispatches*. Herr reminisced with one Marine about a time "long before Khe Sanh had taken on the proportions of a siege camp and lodged itself as an obsession in the heart of the Command, long before a single round had ever fallen inside the perimeter to take off his friends and make his sleep something indistinguishable from waking. He remembered when there was time to play in the streams below the plateau of the base, when all anybody ever talked about were the six shades of green that touched the surrounding hills, when he and his friends had lived like human beings, above ground, in the light, instead of like animals who were so spaced out that they began taking pills called Diarrhea-Aid to keep their walks to exposed latrines at a minimum" (pp. 91–92).

64. For example, the military estimated that 37,000 of the Viet Cong and North Vietnamese troops were killed, along with 6,000 civilians, and 2,500 U.S. troops.

Upwards of one million South Vietnamese had probably become refugees.

65. Zaroulis and Sullivan, *Who Spoke Up?* p. 150.

66. As Herman and Chomsky argue, the attack on the media coverage of Tet not only distorts the record but diverts attention from the more pervasive role mass media played in supporting government policy. It also acts as a check on future media independence. See Herman and Chomsky, *Manufacturing Consent*, pp. 211–28.

67. Baritz, *Backfire*, p. 180.

68. Zaroulis and Sullivan, *Who Spoke Up?* p. 168.

69. Todd Gitlin, *The Whole World is Watching* (Berkeley: University of California Press, 1980), p. 196. Gitlin goes on to note that the threat of investigation had the desired effect. CBS News President Richard Salant promised, "If the set of circumstances that occurred in Chicago ever occurs again, I think we'll report it somewhat differently."

70. Kirkpatrick Sale, *SDS* (New York: Vintage, 1974), pp. 472, 476–77.

71. This polarization is captured with marvelous irony by two very different musical performances held at the time of Nixon's inauguration in 1972, as described by Zaroulis and Sullivan: "More than fifteen thousand people gathered at the Washington Cathedral of St. Peter and St. Paul to hear Haydn's *Mass in Time of War* conducted by Leonard Bernstein. Only three thousand could be accommodated inside; the rest stood in the raw, rainy night and heard the performance over a public address system. Bernstein, the soloists, and orchestra appeared in street dress. The Mass, written at a time when Napoleon was overrunning the armies of Austria, is famous for the mournful kettledrum accompaniment to the words of petition that bring the Agnus Dei, its final section, to a close: 'Dona nobis pacem' (Grant us peace). Some in the audience recalled the drumbeat of three years earlier that led off the March Against Death on a similarly chill, damp Washington night. Meanwhile, at the John F. Kennedy Center for the Performing Arts, the inaugural committee was presenting its concert to a formal dress audience, including the presidential party, that did not quite manage to fill the hall, perhaps because tickets started at $250 each. A highlight of the concert was Tchaikovsky's *1812 Overture*, a retrospective set piece, scored for cannon and celebrating the rout of Napoleon's army in Russia." *Who Spoke Up?* pp. 401–2.

72. For a detailed, documented account, see Seymour M. Hersh, *The Abuse of Power: Kissinger in the Nixon White House* (New York: Summit Books, 1983). See also Baritz, *Backfire*, pp. 188–97. Perhaps the most extreme maneuver revolved around the peace agreement itself. According to Hersh, Johnson reported that he and President Thieu of South Vietnam "had agreed on a joint statement supporting negotiations, but Thieu had suddenly backed away. Jack Valenti, one of Johnson's closest confidants, quotes Johnson in his memoirs as saying that 'hard information had come to him that representatives of Nixon reached President Thieu and urged him not to accept' any last-ditch negotiations, suggesting he would get a better deal if Nixon won the election" (Hersh, *Abuse of Power*, p. 17). Baritz reports, "Anna Chenault, a private citizen deeply involved with the right-wing China lobby, was secretly advising the South Vietnamese

to stall because the new Republican administration would not sell them down the river, as the Democrats would"—a warning that may have been painfully recalled by Thieu in 1973." (*Backfire*, p. 190).

73. The secret "Duck Hook" plan prepared in 1969 reflected the distinctive Nixon signature—a plan that included massive bombing of Hanoi and Haiphong and other key areas in North Vietnam, the mining of harbors and rivers, the bombing of the dike system, a ground invasion of North Vietnam, and the destruction, possibly with nuclear devices, of the Ho Chi Minh Trail. Zaroulis and Sullivan, *Who Spoke Up?* p. 259.

74. See Baritz, *Backfire*, p. 200–204.

75. Quoted in Zaroulis and Sullivan, *Who Spoke Up?* p. 279. Nixon's speech was a masterpiece of manipulation. While making the antiwar movement out as the scapegoat should the United States lose the war, his plans nonetheless embodied the movement's call for withdrawal, although with a timetable and a savage intensification of the war that the antiwar movement would find abhorrent. If it weren't for scapegoating the antiwar movement, Nixon's withdrawal might have been viewed by the silent majority as selling out the South Vietnamese regime. The real target of his manipulation was the silent majority.

76. As George Herring put it, Nixon not only supported intensified COINTELPRO surveillance and provocation, he "approved one of the most blatant attacks on individual freedom and privacy in American history, the so-called Huston Plan, which authorized the intelligence agencies to open mail, use electronic surveillance methods, and even burglarize to spy on Americans." See Herring, *America's Longest War*, p. 238.

77. By the "eros effect," Katsiaficas meant the "massive awakening of the instinctual human need for justice and for freedom." See George Katsiaficas, *The Imagination of the New Left: A Global Analysis of 1968* (Boston: South End Press, 1987), p. 11.

78. Neil Sheehan, *A Bright Shining Lie: John Paul Vann and America in Vietnam* (New York: Random House, 1988), p. 689.

79. *Ibid.*, p. 690. As a Defense Department investigation of civilian deaths in Quang Ngai Province put it, "the Viet Cong *are* the people." Quoted by Sheehan on p. 688, emphasis in the original. The Defense Department phrase emerged in Jonathan Schell's investigation, which found that 70 of 450 Quang Ngai hamlets had been completely destroyed, and the process was continuing. Schell's account, "The Village at Ben Suc," was later published as *The Real War* (New York: Pantheon, 1987).

80. Sheehan, *Bright Shining Lie*, p. 741.

81. MacPherson notes, "Veterans from the earlier days of the war were 20 percent less stressed than those who returned in the demoralizing dog days of 'Vietnamization.' Many veterans who went later formed a nihilistic subgroup. Often reluctant draftees surrounded by antiwar peers, by 1970 they were fighting in a war largely perceived as a failure." One veteran expressed the cynicism about Nixon's Vietnamization: "Withdrawal and Vietnamization were very tough on those of us left behind. Kissinger ought

to be hung instead of giving speeches. We were at 60 percent strength. We couldn't get spare parts. The whole thing just fell apart." In *Long Time Passing*, pp. 281, 290.

82. Halstead, *Out Now!*, p. 607.

83. Brad Lyttle, as quoted in Halstead, *Out Now!*, p. 515.

84. Zaroulis and Sullivan, *Who Spoke Up?* p. 320.

85. Quoted in *ibid.*, pp. 320–21.

86. Katsiaficas, *Imagination of New Left*, p. 125.

87. Zaroulis and Sullivan, *Who Spoke Up?* p. 300. Dave Dellinger argues that the failure to pursue a policy of massive civil disobedience at a Washington, D.C. rally following the Cambodia invasion resulted in an "illusion of impotence" that damaged the Movement and caused some to turn to violence. See Dellinger, *More Power than We Know: The People's Movement toward Democracy* (Garden City, NY: Anchor, 1975), pp. 135–45.

88. Halstead, *Out Now!* p. 611. Halstead describes a similar configuration in San Francisco including an AFL-CIO contingent and a Napa Valley group with the banner "Make Wine, Not War."

89. *Ibid.*, p. 692. Halstead cites a *New York Times* account of January 8, 1973.

90. Quoted in Zaroulis and Sullivan, *Who Spoke Up?* p. 399.

91. This was a quality recognized and begrudgingly respected by American G.I.s even as they tried to annihilate the persistent enemy. It was especially galling to G.I.s that the enemy in Vietnam fought so courageously while the troops we were supporting were commonly viewed as slackers with little interest in the war. Perhaps nothing was more potentially radicalizing than this realization. "They," after all, were fighting for their country.

92. Norman Birnbaum, "Hope's End or Hope's Beginning? 1968—And After," *Salmagundi* no. 81 (Winter 1989): 146.

93. Kolko, *Anatomy of a War*, pp. 174–75.

94. This line of criticism has traveled many productive directions, from a neo-Marxian critique of global capitalism, to analysis of the American political economy, to a critical assessment of specific American foreign policies within a hegemonic framework. See for example, Immanuel M. Wallerstein, *The Modern World System* (New York: Academic Press, 1974); Seymour Melman, *The Permanent War Economy* (New York: Simon & Schuster, 1974); and Chomsky, *Turning the Tide*.

Chapter 5

1. Morris Dickstein, *Gates of Eden* (New York: Basic Books, 1977), p. 82.

2. The Haight-Ashbury Research Project was directed by Dr. Stephen Pittel. My citation comes from Charles Perry, *The Haight-Ashbury* (New York: Vintage, 1985), p. 293, one of the few accounts to examine the cross-currents of the counterculture. The backgrounds of these three groups are particularly intriguing. The fringe group

tended to come from cold authoritarian families, the believers from supportive families with whom they maintained contact, and the dropouts from families that demanded high achievement but discouraged independence.

3. See Kenneth Keniston, "'Heads' vs. 'Seekers'," in his *Youth and Dissent: The Rise of a New Opposition* (New York: Harcourt Brace Jovanovich, 1971), p. 237.

4. Charles Perry has noted of the Haight-Ashbury phenomenon, "If the press had come to the Haight-Ashbury with the intention of doing justice to this phenomenon, reporters would have spent months reconstructing the intense period of development and amazing coincidences that had made it a magical event. As it was, reporters had only a couple of days to make sense of this roiling, incomprehensible mob of weirdos and they fell back on the stock journalistic formula of Bohemia, Menace to the Nation's Youth: a panorama of indolence, promiscuous sex and madness." See Perry, *Haight-Ashbury*, p. 271.

5. Theodore Roszak, *The Making of the Counter Culture* (New York: Anchor, 1969), p. 42. As Leonard Wolf put it, "Why should it surprise us that a new consciousness struggling into life should emerge amid stink and dismay?" Leonard Wolf, *Voices from the Love Generation* (Boston: Little Brown, 1968), p. xviii.

6. Peter Marin, "The Golden City," in Mitchell Goodman, ed., *The Movement Toward a New America* (Philadelphia: Pilgrim Press, 1970), p. 631.

7. Roszak, *Counter Culture*, p. 42.

8. Philip Slater, *The Pursuit of Loneliness*, rev. ed. (Boston: Beacon Press, 1976), p. 109.

9. Parallels are reflected in the phrases the Beats appropriated from black street culture and jazz: "ball," "bread," "cool," "far out," "funky," "groove," "hip," "roach," "turn on"; in Sixties song lyrics that echo Beat poetry; and even in the name chosen by the Beatles.

10. Kenneth Rexroth, "Disengagement: The Art of the Beat Generation," in Thomas Parkinson, ed., *A Casebook on the Beat* (New York: Thomas Y. Crowell, 1961), p. 181.

11. Perry, *Haight-Ashbury*, pp. 250–51. According to Perry, the term "hippies" itself was coined by Beats who derisively viewed the younger generation as less authentic hipsters.

12. Wolf, *Voices*, p. xxi.

13. Brando's characterization of a motorcycle outlaw in *The Wild One* epitomized this youthful rebelliousness. Asked what he was rebelling against, Brando responded, "Whadda ya got?"

14. Dickstein, *Gates of Eden*, p. 110, emphasis in original.

15. Perry, *Haight-Ashbury*, pp. 4–5.

16. It is not surprising, then, to find frequent reference to madness in the expressions of the counterculture itself, to say nothing of its critics. In the field of psychiatry, critics like R. D. Laing and Thomas Szasz articulated the view that insanity is a rational response to a world gone mad. See R. D. Laing, *The Politics of Experience* (New York: Ballantine, 1967), and *The Divided Self* (New York: Penguin Books, 1965); and

Thomas Szasz, *The Myth of Mental Illness* (New York: Dell, 1961), and *The Age of Madness* (Garden City, N.J.: Anchor, 1973).

17. Steven M. Tipton, *Getting Saved From the Sixties: Moral Meaning in Conversion and Cultural Change* (Berkeley: University of California Press, 1982), p. 16.

18. The postscarcity quest for higher needs can be seen as a reflection of Abraham Maslow's "hierarchy of needs." For a more global analysis of the "postmaterialist" revolution, see Ronald Inglehart, *The Silent Revolution: Changing Values and Political Styles among Western Publics* (Princeton, N.J.: Princeton University Press, 1977).

19. Peter Cohon (now Peter Coyote), quoted in Goodman, *Movement*, p. 25.

20. Roszak, *Counter Culture*, p. 236.

21. Marin, "Golden City," in Goodman, *Movement*, p. 631.

22. Gary Snyder, "Why Tribe?" quoted in Goodman, *Movement*, p. 662.

23. Theodore Roszak, *Where the Wasteland Ends* (New York: Anchor, 1973), p. 224.

24. Slater, *Pursuit of Loneliness*, p. 13.

25. Jay Stevens, *Storming Heaven: LSD and the American Dream* (New York: Harper and Row, 1987), p. 305.

26. As quoted by Abe Peck, *Uncovering the Sixties: The Life and Times of the Underground Press* (New York: Pantheon, 1985), p. 46.

27. As George Dennison observed of the hippies, "I have always taken their bizarre dress as a kind of confession that they have no world to live in." Quoted in Goodman, *Movement*, p. 472.

28. Quoted in Perry, *Haight-Ashbury*, p. 96.

29. One exception was Quicksilver Messenger Service's lead guitarist John Cipollina, whose recollection reflected an adolescent preoccupation of the time: "All-acoustic Martins were the mainstay; folk music was an attempt to do something 'refined.' Playing electric guitar was just another way of saying *fuck*. It was an unwritten law: It's okay to play rock 'n' roll until you were eighteen; after that it was folk." Quoted in Ed Ward, Geoffrey Stokes, and Ken Tucker, *Rock of Ages: The Rolling Stone History of Rock & Roll* (New York: Rolling Stone Press, 1986), pp. 332–33 (emphasis in original).

30. Perry, *Haight-Ashbury*, pp. 29–30.

31. *Ibid.*, p. 43.

32. The city police department estimated that it was making one hundred felony drug arrests a month by late 1966. See *ibid.*, p. 148. On an ironic note, at a cordial exchange between community members and the police, police chief Thomas Cahill unwittingly gave the Haight community a new name, asking, "You're sort of the Love Generation aren't you?"

33. Quoted in Bruce Pollock, *When the Music Mattered: Rock in the 1960s* (New York: Holt, Rinehart, and Winston, 1983), p. 113.

34. Perry, *Haight-Ashbury*, p. 271.

35. By Perry's estimation, at least 75,000 lived in the psychedelic community by fall 1967. *Ibid.*, p. 245.

36. Cited in Peck, *Uncovering the Sixties*, p. 52.

37. *Ibid.*, p. 174.

38. From Sanders' account of the Charles Manson story, *The Family*, quoted in *ibid.*, p. 51.

39. Todd Gitlin, *The Sixties: Years of Hope, Days of Rage* (New York: Bantam, 1987), p. 354.

40. Michael Rossman, "Claiming Turf in Berkeley," in Goodman, *Movement*, pp. 502–3. Originally in the San Francisco *Express Times*, July 9, 1968.

41. Todd Gitlin, "The Meaning of People's Park," in Goodman, *Movement*, p. 506. Originally published in *Liberation*, July 1969.

42. Gitlin, *The Sixties*, p. 355.

43. One incident was recorded by John Simon: "Late afternoon, Bloody Thursday, quiet south campus street, woman with baby carriage, telephone repairman, street brother grazed earlier by pellets tells girl on lawn 'they're shooting people on telegraph.' 'Are you sure?' then Blue Meanie (Alameda county sheriff) pokes his head around the corner and lets fly, wounding the brother again, missing the baby carriage and grazing the phone man who doesn't understand, 'lemme go get his badge number' he cries and has to be held back gently, 'no, he's not wearing a badge and if you go up there they'll shoot you again.'" Quoted in Goodman, *Movement*, p. 509.

44. Not long afterwards, after the Isla Vista branch of the Bank of America was burned down, Reagan declared, "Appeasement is not the answer. . . . If it's to be a blood-bath, let it be now." Quoted in Jack Whalen and Richard Flacks, *Beyond the Barricades: The Sixties Generation Grows Up* (Philadelphia: Temple University Press, 1989), p. 31; from Robert A. Potter and James J. Sullivan, *The Campus By the Sea Where the Bank Burned Down: A Report on the Disturbances at UCSB and Isla Vista, 1968–70* (Santa Barbara, Calif.: Faculty and Clergy Observers Program, 1970).

45. Dickstein, *Gates of Eden*, pp. 185–86.

46. In their self-selective survey of the Sixties generation, Weiner and Stillman reported that 62 percent of the political activists responding to the survey believed during the Sixties that rock was a "revolutionary political force." Rex Weiner and Deanne Stillman, *Woodstock Census: The Nationwide Survey of the Sixties Generation* (New York: Viking, 1979), p. 61. The degree to which this belief is a delusion is best illustrated by Jann Wenner and *Rolling Stone*, a highly successful news magazine devoted to the culture of rock and popular music. During the heat of the middle to late Sixties, Wenner retreated from both the political New Left and the more far-out drug-oriented counterculture, arguing that rock was "the revolution." However, Wenner was first and foremost a good businessman, recognizing a good market when he saw one. Not surprisingly, the majority of *Rolling Stone* readers voted for President Reagan in 1984, which suggests how much of a revolution Wenner represented.

47. The drama came when Dylan brought to Newport the electronically amplified Chicago blues sound of the Paul Butterfield Blues Band, and later when he played the rock piece "Maggie's Farm." Folklorist Alan Lomax's sarcastic introduction of the Butterfield band led to an onstage fistfight with Dylan manager Albert Grossman. The

older folk stalwarts like Pete Seeger were horrified and cried betrayal. Dylan's own performance was shouted down by an outraged audience of folk purists.

48. David Pichaske, *A Generation in Motion: Popular Music and Culture in the Sixties* (New York: Schirmer, 1979), p. 80.

49. See Paul Hirsch, *The Structure of the Popular Music Industry* (Ann Arbor: University of Michigan Press, 1970).

50. From the song by Paul Kantner, "We Can Be Together," copyright Icebag Music.

51. From the song by Peter Rowan, "The Great American Eagle Tragedy," copyright Nina Music.

52. Quoted in Peck, *Uncovering the Sixties*, p. 170.

53. Robert Santelli, *Aquarius Rising: The Rock Festival Years* (New York: Delta, 1980), p. 59.

54. According to Abe Peck, *Rat* editor Jeff Shero recalled a disconcerting encounter with the effect of the star system when he called Janis Joplin, whom he had known several years before while at the University of Texas. After Shero asked Joplin for an interview, she responded, "Well, honey, I'm talkin' to *Time* and *Newsweek*. Why do I want to do an interview with a li'l ol' hippie publication?" Shero had an answer: "Rock music is part of *our* culture." "Hell," Joplin replied, "millions of people read *Newsweek*. I'd rather do that." Quoted in Peck, *Uncovering the Sixties*, pp. 165–66.

55. Quoted in Pollock, *When the Music Mattered*, p. 119.

56. Quoted in *ibid.*, p. 116.

57. Quoted in Peck, *Uncovering the Sixties*, p. 170.

58. Quoted in *ibid.*, p. 169.

59. Eldridge Cleaver, *Soul on Ice* (New York: Delta, 1968), p. 197. In this sense, Cleaver saw rock as a kind of revolutionary force: "The Twist was a guided missile, launched from the ghetto into the very heart of suburbia. The Twist succeeded, as politics, religion, and law could never do, in writing in the heart and soul what the Supreme Court could only write on the books" (p. 197).

60. *Ibid.*, pp. 202–3.

61. Albert Goldman, "The Emergence of Rock," in Gerald Howard, ed., *The Sixties* (New York: Washington Square Press, 1982), p. 344.

62. Dickstein, *Gates of Eden*, p. 190.

63. Quoted in Goodman, *Movement*, p. 112.

64. Peck, *Uncovering the Sixties*, p. 178.

65. Quoted in *ibid.*, p. 180.

66. Santelli, *Aquarius Rising*, p. 261.

67. Keniston, *Youth and Dissent*, p. 237.

68. Robert Jay Lifton, "The New History," in Philip G. Altbach and Robert S. Laufer, *The New Pilgrims: Youth Protest in Transition* (New York: David McKay, 1972), p. 189.

69. Quoted in Roszak, *Counter Culture*, p. 167. Leary's oft-repeated phrase is explained by Leonard Wolf: "One turns on by dropping (i.e. taking) acid; tunes in by

discovering, on the acid trip and subsequent meditation, one's 'transcendence of verbal concepts, of space-time dimensions and of the ego or identity.' One drops out because, having found one's self in harmonious unity with the perfection of the cosmos, one is no longer interested in playing ego or power games." Wolf, *Voices*, p. xxv. Leary's claims knew no bounds, for example, a woman who made love while tripping could have "a hundred orgasms."

70. Cited in Weiner and Stillman, *Woodstock Census*, p. 110.

71. Quoted in Wolf, *Voices*, pp. 69–70.

72. *Ibid.*, p. xxiv.

73. *Ibid.*, pp. 200, xxiv.

74. Perry notes of the post–Summer of Love Haight: "Haight Street was speed street now, with half the hippies in the neighborhood shooting Methedrine. One out of five had tried heroin, which they used as freely as tranquilizers or barbiturates to overcome the feeling of depression that followed a week-long sleepless 'speed run' of Methedrine-fueled activity. . . . Speed freaks developed hallucinations, as if the mind were struggling to dream in the absence of sleep. These hallucinations tended to be paranoid and violent." *Haight-Ashbury*, pp. 227–28.

75. Quoted in Pollock, *When the Music Mattered*, p. 88.

76. Perry, *Haight-Ashbury*, p. 278. Perry quotes Beat poet Michael McClure: "I can't see in retrospect that anything was gained after the first couple of uses. Or whatever it takes to let that awareness and appreciation of reality in its manifold dimensions to come into being. To experience it over and over doesn't seem to lend anything. It's so beautiful and it promises so much, but there isn't any more that way" (p. 274).

77. Quoted in Peck, *Uncovering the Sixties*, p. 262. In fact, as some argued, drug use itself mirrored cocktail-numbing and pill-popping middle-class American culture that seeks easy solutions to stressful living.

78. Stevens, *Storming Heaven*, p. 368.

79. Quoted in Wolf, *Voices*, p. 70. As Roszak observed, "Ironically, it may not be the young who have suffered public obloquy because of their association with the psychedelics; it may be the psychedelics that have suffered because of their association with troublesome youngsters. Unwilling to blame themselves for the alienation of their children, mother and father have decided to blame the drugs." Roszak, *Counter Culture*, p. 172.

80. Perry, *Haight-Ashbury*, p. 254.

81. Peck, *Uncovering the Sixties*, p. 34.

82. Perry has attributed a number of late Sixties and early Seventies phenomena to the psychedelic experience: "When meaning and motivation are a mysterious whirl, and one can grasp only what is observable at the moment, it may become stunningly evident that the cupboard is badly designed, your shoes are heavy and stiff." Hence the "organic life that arose in the seventies," attempts at psychological integration like Gestalt and Esalen (which break down distinctions between inner and outer), and the ecology or small-is-beautiful movement. *Haight-Ashbury*, pp. 279–80.

83. Marin, "Golden City," in Goodman, *Movement*, p. 4.

84. Roszak, *Counter Culture*, pp. 136–37, emphasis in original.

85. Supportive evidence for the latter comes from Weiner and Stillman's Sixties generation survey. A distinction between those born before and after 1950 emerges in their voluntary responses. For example, 21 percent of the former waited until they were at least age 22 before having sex, while only 7 percent of the latter waited that long. Conversely, twice as many of the younger group had sex by age 15. The survey suggests a division between those who grew up struggling against the old environment of postponed sexuality and those who grew up in a new permissive environment. See Weiner and Stillman, *Woodstock Census*, pp. 163–70. See also Landon Y. Jones, *Great Expectations: America and the Baby Boom Generation* (New York: Ballantine, 1980), pp. 205–8.

86. Quoted in Pollock, *When the Music Mattered*, p. 181.

87. See Herbert Marcuse, *One Dimensional Man* (Boston: Beacon Press 1964), ch. 3.

88. Quoted in Weiner and Stillman, *Woodstock Census*, p. 173.

89. Quoted in Wolf, *Voices*, p. 71.

90. Quoted in Pollock, *When the Music Mattered*, p. 182.

91. *Ibid.*, p. 181.

92. See Weiner and Stillman, *Woodstock Census*, pp. 173–77. Respondents made frequent reference to the importance of the pill. One woman observed, "I knew that once I started the pill I had what I felt was to be almost limitless freedom in sexual practices. I knew this was a radical departure from the woman's traditional role as the reluctant, worried participant" (p. 173). For a lengthy autobiographical account of women's sexual liberation during the 1960s, see Sara Davidson, *Loose Change* (New York: Pocket Books, 1985).

93. Peck, *Uncovering the Sixties*, p. xv. The "first wave" papers, following the lead of the established *Village Voice* and *Liberation*, included the L.A. *Free Press*, the Berkeley *Barb*, the (New York) *East Village Other*, the (Detroit) *Fifth Estate*, the (East Lansing) *Paper*, and the San Francisco *Oracle*. Soon to follow were, among many others, the Chicago *Seed*, the (Austin) *Rag*, the New York *Rat*, the (San Quentin) *Outlaw*, the (Washington) *Quicksilver Times*, the (Houston) *Space City*, the (Cambridge) *Old Mole*, the (Jackson) *Kudzu*, the (Denver) *El Gallo*, the Madison *Kaleidoscope*, the (San Jose) *Red Eye*, and the (Boston) *Avatar*. The underground press also included muckraking magazines like *Ramparts*, the video service *Newsreel*, G.I. papers like the *Bond*, the Resistance's *Resist*, and issue- or group-specific papers like the *Black Panther*, *Gay Activist*, (New York) *Win*, and *Peace Newsletter*. The phenomenal rate of growth of underground papers is evident in the *East Village Other*'s circulation growth from 5,000 to 65,000 in four years; by contrast, it took the established *Village Voice* fourteen years to achieve a circulation half again as large. See Peck, *Uncovering the Sixties*, p. 183.

94. Quoted in *ibid.*, p. 23.

95. Quoted in *Ibid.*, p. 304.

96. Dickstein, *Gates of Eden*, p. 137.

97. Quoted in Peck, *Uncovering the Sixties*, p. 24.

98. Dickstein, *Gates of Eden*, p. 137.

99. Peck, *Uncovering the Sixties*, p. 75. Liberation New Service pronounced its stance after the Pentagon march: "Liberation News Service provides a totally different alternate medium for those of us who are fed up with hearing there were 'some 25,000 to 40,000 demonstrators' when we ourselves saw at least twice that many; hearing them say the 'police acted with appropriate restraint' when we saw the guy next to us getting his skull busted just because he had long hair; hearing that we . . . are 'sincerely working for peace' and that we are 'supporting and defending democratic government in Vietnam,' when we see our government destroying a countryside, waging an undeclared war of attrition on helpless women, children, and farmers in the name of one totalitarian puppet regime after another, with no sane end in sight" (p. 77).

100. Quoted in Peck, *Uncovering the Sixties*, p. 25.

101. Quoted in *ibid.*, p. 313.

102. *Ibid.*, p. 293.

103. According to Susan Trausch, *Communities* magazine has 3,000 subscribers, while three other organizations provide network services: the Fellowship of Intentional Communities, the Federation of Egalitarian Communities, and the National Historical Communal Societies Association. The current estimate comes from Charles Betterton, editor of *Communities*, while the earlier figure was provided by Professor Donald Pitzer of the Center for Communal Studies at Southern Indiana University. See Trausch, "Where Have All the Flower Children Gone," *Boston Globe Magazine* (August 2, 1987), pp. 12ff. In the late Sixties and early Seventies, a comparable exchange of experiences and ideological pieces could be found in magazines like *Modern Utopian* or *Alternatives Newsmagazine*.

104. Whalen and Flacks, *Beyond the Barricades*, p. 263.

105. See Benjamin D. Zablocki, "Communes, Encounter Groups, and the Search for Community," in Kurt W. Back, ed., *In Search for Community: Encounter Groups and Social Change* (Boulder, Co.: Westview, 1978), p. 130.

106. Quoted in Perry, *Haight-Ashbury*, p. 142.

107. Whalen and Flacks, *Beyond the Barricades*, p. 265.

108. Quoted in Trausch, "Flower Children," p. 52.

109. Corrine McLaughlin, a cofounder of the Sirius Community in Shutesbury, Massachusetts, quoted in *ibid.*, p. 50.

110. Trausch, "Flower Children," p. 50.

111. Important critiques of this narcissism include Edwin Schur, *The Awareness Trap: Self-Absorption instead of Social Change* (New York: Quadrangle–New York Times, 1976); Richard Sennett, *The Fall of Public Man* (New York: Knopf, 1977); and Christopher Lasch, *The Culture of Narcissism* (New York: Norton, 1978). Lasch argued that the narcissistic personality seeks "to seduce others into giving him their attention, acclaim, or sympathy and thus to shore up his faltering sense of self" (p. 21). In Lionel Trilling's characterization, the narcissism of the counterculture was comparable to an emphasis on "authenticity," "play[ing] the role of being ourselves," rather than "sin-

cerity," being "true to one's self." See Trilling, *Sincerity and Authenticity* (Cambridge, Mass.: Harvard University Press, 1972).

112. In fact, it was the very emptiness of society's dominant form of meaning in a rootless culture, the occupational treadmill, that propelled many young people on their search. As Philip Slater has argued, the counterculture's emphasis on immediate gratification was a relatively nontoxic form of narcissism when compared to the narcissism of "short-term ambition: machismo, the warrior ethos, conspicuous consumption" or of "long-run ambition: the accumulation of wealth, complex planning to gain and hold power, lifelong goals to achieve professional eminence, artistic fame, or whatever." Philip Slater, *Footholds: Understanding the Shifting Sexual and Family Tensions of Our Culture* (New York: Dutton, 1977), p. 106.

113. Whalen and Flacks, *Beyond the Barricades*, p. 270.

114. Quoted in Peck, *Uncovering the Sixties*, p. 130.

115. A Columbia record advertisement that appeared widely in underground papers and music magazines in 1968 symbolizes this phenomenon. The ad carried a photograph of a group of demonstrators in a jail cell under the heading, "But The Man can't bust our music." The small print trumpeted some Columbia recordings and argued, "And The Man can't stop you from listening. Especially if you're armed with these."

116. Maggie Gaskin, quoted in Wolf, *Voices*, p. 92.

117. Marvin Garson, "Revolutionary Gangs," in Goodman, *Movement*, p. 696.

Chapter 6

1. Quoted in Ronald Fraser, ed., *1968: A Student Generation in Revolt* (New York: Pantheon, 1988), p. 342.

2. One could well argue that the gay liberation movement was another major extension of Sixties activism. Indeed, it was, beginning symbolically with the police raid at the Stonewall Bar in New York in 1969 and extending to the current struggle over AIDS. The gay rights movement converges with feminism in its challenge to deep-seated, mainstream sexual beliefs and stereotypes; sexism and heterosexism (and, for that matter, environmental despoilation) may be seen as extensions of misogyny. Largely because of space constraints, I do not examine the gay rights movement, nor the important Native American, Chicano, and disabled rights movements that evolved out of the Sixties. Each is important as an extension of the civil rights struggle and each articulates a critique that reflects the particular cultural experience of its population. In addition to sharing these traits, the women's movement breaks new theoretical ground in its critique of virtually all cultures.

3. See Bertell Ollman and Edward Vernoff, *The Left Academy: Marxist Scholarship on American Campuses*, vol. I (New York: McGraw-Hill, 1982), vol. II (New York: Praeger, 1984), and vol. III (New York: Praeger, 1986). The neo-Marxian insights built on the work of long-time Marxists like Ollman, Stanley Aronowitz, Paul Baran, Harry Braverman, Michael Harrington, Harry Magdoff, Ralph Miliband, James O'Connor,

Paul Sweezy, and others who continued to make seminal contributions to the left critique.

4. Gloria I. Joseph and Jill Lewis, *Common Differences: Conflicts in Black and White Feminist Perspectives* (Boston: South End Press, 1981), pp. 49–50.

5. Betty Friedan, *The Feminine Mystique* (New York: Dell, 1963), p. 11.

6. Juliet Mitchell, *Women's Estate* (New York: Pantheon, 1971), p. 50.

7. As one critic noted, "America creates two kinds of women: those who can't take care of themselves and those who have to." Attributed to Sarah Small by Carol S. Robb, "A Framework for Feminist Ethics," in Barbara Hilkelt Andolsen, Christine E. Gudorf, and Mary D. Pellauer, eds., *Women's Consciousness, Women's Conscience* (Minneapolis, Minn.: Seabury, 1985), p. 227.

8. Sara Evans, *Personal Politics: The Roots of Women's Liberation in the Civil Rights Movement and the New Left* (New York: Vintage, 1980), p. 125. Evans goes on to describe the striking parallels between the SNCC–SDS ideology and that of the women's movement: "The anti-leadership bias and emphasis on internal process in ERAP found counterparts in the women's movement's experiments with rotating chairs, long, intensely personal meetings, and distrust of public spokeswomen; the theory of radicalization through discussions that revealed the social origins of personal problems took shape in the feminist practice of consciousness-raising; the belief in participatory democracy and the idea that 'in unity there is strength' helped feed the new ideas about sisterhood and the power of women united" (p. 137).

9. Dorothy Dinnerstein, *The Mermaid and the Minotaur: Sexual Arrangements and the Human Malaise* (New York: Harper Colophon, 1976), p. 269.

10. Sara M. Evans and Harry C. Boyte, *Free Spaces: The Sources of Democratic Change in America* (New York: Harper & Row, 1986), p. 104.

11. Quoted in James Forman, *The Making of Black Revolutionaries* (Washington, D.C.: Open Hand, 1985), p. 276.

12. Casey Hayden and Mary King, "Sex and Caste: A Kind of Memo," in Judith Clavir Albert and Stewart Edward Albert, *The Sixties Papers: Documents of a Rebellious Decade* (New York: Praeger, 1984), p. 134.

13. Carmichael's quote is an example of a black macho strain in the black power movement that has been criticized by feminists for equating black liberation with the assertion of manhood. See Manning Marable, *How Capitalism Underdeveloped Black America* (Boston: South End Press, 1983), ch. 3.

14. Casey Hayden and Mary King, "SNCC Position Paper: Women in the Movement," in Albert and Albert, *Documents*, p. 116.

15. Evans, *Personal Politics*, p. 165, quoted in Fraser, 1968, pp. 294–300.

16. Ann Popkin, "The Personal Is Political: The Women's Liberation Movement," in Dick Cluster, ed., *They Should Have Served That Cup of Coffee* (Boston: South End Press, 1979), p. 187.

17. Quoted in Evans, *Personal Politics*, p. 176.

18. WITCH had its own unique form of political action called the "zap." Rayna Rapp recalls the effort to pressure the Michigan legislature during its consideration of

a new abortion law: "We flew in as WITCH and we hexed these old men with a chant about how they were going to die because they were all men and they were controlling women's bodies. Then we flew out again." Quoted in Fraser, 1968, p. 300.

19. Quoted in Fraser, 1968, p. 300.

20. Marge Piercy, "The Grand Coolie Damn," in Robin Morgan, ed. *Sisterhood is Powerful: An Anthology of Writings from the Women's Liberation Movement* (New York: Vintage, 1970), p. 422.

21. See Todd Gitlin's account, *The Sixties: Years of Hope, Days of Rage* (New York: Bantam, 1987), pp. 362–64.

22. Piercy, "Grand Coolie Damn," in Morgan, *Sisterhood*, p. 438.

23. Todd Gitlin, *The Sixties*, p. 374.

24. Evans, *Personal Politics*, p. 215.

25. The public attack on sexual oppression ranged from Kate Millett's *Sexual Politics* to the feminist critique of pornography and prostitution to the analysis of rape as the most rudimentary form of male terror. See Millet, *Sexual Politics* (New York: Avon, 1971); Susan Brownmiller, *Against Our Will: Men, Women, and Rape* (New York: Simon & Schuster, 1975); Andrea Dworkin, *Pornography: Men Possessing Women* (New York: Perigree, 1981); and Laura Lederer, ed., *Take Back the Night: Women on Pornography* (New York: Bantam, 1982).

26. Annie Popkin, "An Early Moment in Women's Liberation: The Social Experience within *Bread and Roses*," *Radical America* 22:1 (Jan./Feb. 1988): 20.

27. Jo Freeman, *The Politics of Women's Liberation* (New York: David McKay, 1975), p. 118.

28. "Redstockings Manifesto," in Leslie B. Tanner, ed., *Voices from Women's Liberation* (New York: Signet, 1970), pp. 109–10.

29. Mary Daly, *Gyn/Ecology: The Metaethics of Radical Feminism* (Boston: Beacon, 1978), pp. 2–3. Typical Daly terms include "Crone-ology" (Chronology), "the/rapist," "malefunction" (malfunction), "dis-cover," "re-member," and her title "Gyn/Ecology."

30. Ann Popkin, "The Personal is Political: The Women's Liberation Movement," in Cluster, *They Should Have Served*, p. 212.

31. Daly, *Gyn/Ecology*, p. 26.

32. See Freeman, *Politics*, pp. 134–42; and Anne Koedt, "Lesbianism and Feminism," in *Women: A Journal of Liberation* 3:1 (1972): 33ff.

33. Jean Baker Miller, *Toward a New Psychology of Women*, 2nd ed. (Boston: Beacon, 1986), p. 27. For related assertions of the "feminine" see Sara Ruddick's account of "Maternal Thinking," *Feminist Studies* 6:2 (Summer 1980): 342–67, and Carol Gilligan's study of the feminist "ethic of caring," *In a Different Voice: Psychological Theory and Women's Development* (Cambridge, Mass.: Harvard University Press, 1982).

34. Josephine Donavan calls this second phase "cultural feminism," a term that encompasses distinct feminisms grounded in different theories about the roots of women's oppression. All ultimately seek to transform the world according to feminist values. See Donavan, *Feminist Theory: The Intellectual Traditions of American Feminism* (New York: Ungar, 1986), ch. 2.

35. Adrienne Rich, *Of Women Born* (New York: Norton, 1976), p. 285.

36. As Adrienne Rich has argued, there is a crucial difference between physiological differences and the way in which those differences are integrated into a system of male political and economic control: "I try to distinguish between two meanings of motherhood, one superimposed on the other: the *potential relationship* of any woman to her powers of reproduction and to children; and the *institution*, which aims at ensuring that the potential—and all women—shall remain under male control." *Ibid.*, p. 13, n. 27.

37. Although it is impossible to determine how extensive the men's liberation movement is, there are innumerable signs of feminist-style consciousness-raising among men, from innumerable books to diverse men's groups, workshops, and retreats that in many ways mirror the experiences of women's consciousness-raising and support groups.

38. Betty Friedan, *The Second Stage* (New York: Summit, 1981), pp. 164–65. For a critique of liberal feminism, see Jean Bethke Elshtain, *Public Man, Private Woman* (Princeton, N.J.: Princeton University Press, 1981), pp. 228–55.

39. Dorothy Dinnerstein and Nancy Chodorow have explored the depth of sex role differentiation in the psychic identity formed during each sex's first attachments to mother. See Dinnerstein, *Mermaid and the Minotaur*, and Chodorow, *The Reproduction of Mothering: Psychoanalysis and the Sociology of Gender* (Berkeley: University of California Press, 1978).

40. Joseph and Lewis, *Common Differences*, p. 274.

41. See Rosemary Tong's characterization of postmodern feminism in *Feminist Thought* (Boulder, Colo.: Westview, 1989), ch. 8.

42. See particularly Juliet Mitchell, *Women's Estate* (New York: Pantheon, 1971), and *Psychoanalysis and Feminism* (New York: Vintage, 1974); and Alison Jaggar, *Feminist Politics and Human Nature* (Totowa, N.J.: Rowman & Allanheld, 1983). For the debate, see Lydia Sargent, ed., *Women and Revolution: A Discussion of the Unhappy Marriage of Marxism and Feminism* (Boston: South End Press, 1981).

43. Sargent, *Women and Revolution*, p. xxi.

44. See Evelyn Fox Keller, "Gender and Science," *Psychoanalysis and Contemporary Thought* 1 (1978): 414–15. See also Fritjof Capra, *The Turning Point* (Toronto: Bantam, 1983).

45. Ynestra King, "The Ecology of Feminism and the Feminism of Ecology," in Judith Plant, ed., *Healing the Wounds: The Promise of Ecofeminism* (Philadelphia: New Society Publishers, 1989), p. 22.

46. See Murray Bookchin, *The Ecology of Freedom* (Palo Alto, Calif.: Cheshire Books, 1982).

47. See Bill Devall and George Sessions, *Deep Ecology: Living as If Nature Mattered* (Salt Lake City, Utah: Peregrine Smith, 1985).

48. See Peter Berg, *Reinhabiting a Separate Country* (San Francisco, Calif.: Planet Drum Foundation, 1978); and Kirkpatrick Sale, *Dwellers in the Land: The Bioregional Vision* (San Francisco, Calif.: Sierra Club Books, 1985).

49. See Fritjof Capra and Charlene Spretnak, *Green Politics* (New York: Dutton, 1984).

50. The spill was also the occasion for skillful manipulation of public awareness by President Nixon, who calmed public fears through a televised inspection tour filmed on an isolated segment of freshly cleaned beach. Viewers were unable to see the miles of oil-coated beach beginning a few feet from the president. See W. Lance Bennett, *News: The Politics of an Illusion*, 2nd ed. (New York: Longman, 1988), p. 84.

51. Ross MacDonald, "Introduction," in Robert Easton, *Black Tide: The Santa Barbara Oil Spill and Its Consequences* (New York: Delacorte, 1972), p. ix.

52. The *Christian Science Monitor*, January 22, 1970.

53. Quoted in Barry Commoner, *The Closing Circle: Nature, Man, and Technology* (New York: Knopf, 1971), p. 7.

54. Quoted in Charles O. Jones, *Clean Air: The Policies and Politics of Pollution Control* (Pittsburgh, Pa.: University of Pittsburgh Press, 1975), p. 154.

55. Quoted in Commoner, *Closing Circle*, p. 9.

56. Richard Nixon, quoted in Barry Commoner, "The Environment," *New Yorker* 62 (June 15, 1987): 66.

57. Quoted in Commoner, *The Closing Circle*, p. 6.

58. See Matthew Crenson's instructive analysis of why and under what circumstances air pollution moved onto the political agenda in large metropolitan areas, in *The Un-Politics of Air Pollution* (Baltimore, Md.: Johns Hopkins University Press, 1971).

59. Quoted in Commoner, "The Environment," p. 66.

60. Steward Brand et al., *The Whole Earth Catalog* (Menlo Park, Calif.: Nowels, 1968), p. 1.

61. Langdon Winner, "Building a Better Mousetrap: Appropriate Technology as a Social Movement," in Franklin A. Long and Alexandra Oleson, eds., *Appropriate Technology and Social Values: A Critical Appraisal* (Cambridge, Mass.: Ballinger, 1980), pp. 29–30.

62. Anna Gyorgy et al., *No Nukes: Everyone's Guide to Nuclear Power* (Boston: South End Press, 1979), p. 388.

63. *Ibid.*, p. 393.

64. From the Green Mt. Post film "Lovejoy's Nuclear War." Lovejoy was subsequently acquitted of the charge of "willful and malicious destruction of personal property" on the grounds that the tower was real rather than personal property. According to Gyorgy, jurists were unwilling to find Lovejoy guilty because they felt his action was not "malicious." See Gyorgy, *No Nukes*, p. 394.

65. *Ibid.*, p. 388.

66. As recently as June 1989, more than 650 protesters were arrested at the Seabrook site. Carrying signs that read "In Mourning for the Late, Great State of New Hampshire" and "Remember Chernobyl," they invaded the plant grounds in protest against the first low-power reaction at the plant. The Seabrook saga continues along both legal and extra-legal paths.

67. Gyorgy, *No Nukes*, p. 398.

68. The movement continued to spread nationwide while targeting local facilities: the Paddlewheel Alliance in Ohio, the SEA (Safe Energy Alternatives) Alliance in New Jersey and Delaware, the North Anna Environmental Coalition in Virginia, the Catfish Alliance in Alabama, the Palmetto Alliance in South Carolina, LAND (League Against Nuclear Dangers) in Wisconsin, the Twin Cities Northern Sun Alliance along with organized farmers in Minnesota, the Detroit Safe Energy Coalition, the Armadillo Alliance in Texas, the Great Plains Federation in Missouri, the Black Hills Alliance in South Dakota, the Crabshell Alliance in Washington, and the Trojan Decommissioning Alliance in Oregon.

69. Donella Meadows, et al., *The Limits to Growth: A Report for the Club of Rome's Project on the Predicament of Mankind* (New York: Universe, 1972). One aspect of the limits to growth argument had been foreshadowed by the publication of Paul Ehrlich's *Population Bomb* (New York: Ballantine, 1968).

70. The Club of Rome report brought an immediate critical response, much of which focused on the flaws in the computer model developed by the initial authors. A subsequent Club of Rome report came to virtually the same conclusions using a different computer modeling scheme. See Mihajlo Mesarovic and Eduard Pestal, *Mankind at the Turning Point: The Second Report to the Club of Rome* (New York: Dutton, 1974). For a critique, see H.S.D. Cole, *Models of Doom: A Critique of the Limits to Growth* (New York: Universal, 1973), which also contains a response by Meadows. The theme of shifting to sustainable growth characterizes the more recent World Commission on Environment and Development report, *Our Common Future* (New York: Oxford University Press, 1987).

71. E. F. Schumacher, *Small is Beautiful: Economics as If People Mattered* (New York: Harper, 1974); Garrett Hardin, "The Tragedy of the Commons," *Science* 162 (1968): 1243–48; and William Ophuls, *Ecology and the Politics of Scarcity: Prologue to a Political Theory* (San Francisco, Calif.: W. H. Freeman, 1977).

72. Amory Lovins, *Soft Energy Paths: Toward a Durable Peace* (Cambridge, Mass.: Ballinger, 1977).

73. Thus, for example, Aldo Leopold's land ethic encompassed a "community of interdependent parts" that "simply enlarges the boundaries of community to include soils, waters, plants, and animals, or collectively: the land . . . and changes the role of *Homo sapiens* from conqueror of the land-community to just plain members and citizens of it. It implies respect for his fellow members, and also respect for the community itself." Leopold, *Sand County Almanac* (New York: Oxford University Press, 1968), pp. 204, 209.

74. Langdon Winner, *The Whale and the Reactor: A Search for Limits in an Age of High Technology* (Chicago: University of Chicago Press, 1986), p. 176.

75. Lovins, *Soft Energy*, p. 49.

76. H. Nowotny, "Social Aspects of the Nuclear Power Controversy," quoted in Lovins, *Soft Energy*, p. 155. Emphasis in original.

77. Ophuls, *Ecology*, p. 152.

78. Francis Carney, "Schlockology," *New York Review of Books* (June 1, 1972): 28–29.

79. Bookchin, *Ecology of Freedom*, p. 71 (emphasis in original).

80. The World Commission, *Our Common Future*, pp. 2–3. The commission compared the ever-present threat of nuclear annihilation to this "competing if more subtle apocalyptic threat: the slow death that looms as human activities exhaust natural resources and undermine the planet's life-support systems."

81. Ophuls, *Ecology*, p. 1.

82. Mark Kesselman, "The State and Class Struggle: Trends in Marxist Political Science," in Ollman and Vernoff, *Left Academy*, vol. I., pp. 87, 84. The growth of academic Marxism has been attacked by the Right as dangerous, and by the Left as a politically impotent retreat to academic respectability. For an example of the Right's reaction see the conference of the National Association of Scholars, which in 1988 denounced the radicalization of academia. For an example of the Left's reaction, see Russell Jacoby, *The Last Intellectuals: American Culture in the Age of Academia* (New York: Basic Books, 1987).

83. For example, Richard Flacks claimed in 1982, "Marx has been restored to sociology in a way that would have been very surprising a decade ago." From Flacks, "Marxism and Sociology," in Ollman and Vernoff, *Left Academy*, p. 44. Herbert Gintis observed at the same time, "The reemergence and subsequent growth of Marxism in the latter half of the 1960's was a direct response to the civil rights, antiwar, and feminist movements which shattered the post–World War II 'consensus.'" From Gintis, "The Reemergence of Marxian Economics in America," in *ibid.*, p. 53. For other disciplines, see volumes II and III of Ollman and Vernoff's work.

84. Martin Luther King, Jr. was known to have expressed privately the view that capitalism was an underlying cause of racial inequality (see note 40 in Chapter two). See also Robert L. Allen, *Black Awakening in Capitalist America* (Garden City, N.Y.: Anchor, 1970); and Marable, *How Capitalism Underdeveloped*.

85. See Paul A. Baran and Paul M. Sweezy, *Monopoly Capital: An Essay on the American Economic and Social Order* (New York: Monthly Review Press, 1966), pp. 263–68. As Michael Reich has argued, racism flourishes in a "society which breeds an individualistic and competitive ethos, status fears among marginal groups, and the need for visible scapegoats on which to blame the alienative quality of life in America." Reich, "The Economics of Racism," in David M. Gordon, ed., *Problems in Political Economy: An Urban Perspective* (Lexington, Mass.: D. C. Heath, 1977), pp. 183–88.

86. It is not surprising to find persistent and significant male–female differences in public opinion surveys. For example, women are consistently more inclined toward conciliatory, peace-emphasizing positions, while men are more inclined to support arms buildup and a strong defense posture. More to the point, a 1987 Times-Mirror/Gallup poll carved the American public into distinct opinion clusters. The most significant male–female differences occured in two groups: 60 percent of an affluent, educated, probusiness group called "enterprisers" were men, while 62 percent of an upper-middle-class group of "60's Democrats" identifying with peace, civil rights, and environmental movements were women.

87. William Ryan has labeled the conservative–technocratic perspective "blaming the victim," a process that consists of four steps: "First, identify a social problem. Sec-

ond, study those affected by the problem and discover in what ways they are different from the rest of us as a consequence of deprivation and injustice. Third, define the differences as the cause of the social problem itself. Finally, of course, assign a government bureaucrat to invent a humanitarian action program to correct the differences." Ryan, Blaming the Victim (New York: Vintage, 1971), pp. 8–9. The more fundamental reality, that poverty is a function of income and wealth inequality built into a capitalist economy and preserved by a political system in which the poor are powerless, is neatly avoided by this perspective. While many poor are likely to lack skills and attitudes conducive to educational and economic advancement, the primary reason for the lack of skills and attitudes is their position at the bottom of the economic and political hierarchy.

88. Barry Commoner notes that "there is considerable evidence that in developing countries poverty encourages a high birth rate, for parents hope that enough children will survive the scourge of disease to support the family. The reason for malnutrition, starvation, and famine, then, is poverty, not overpopulation. *Excess population is a symptom of poverty, not the other way around.*" See "The Environment," p. 65. Emphasis added.

89. Susan George, A Fate Worse Than Debt: The World Financial Crisis and the Poor (New York: Grove Press, 1988), p. 15.

90. Gabriel Kolko, The Roots of American Foreign Policy: An Analysis of Power and Purpose (Boston: Beacon, 1969), pp. 54–55.

91. Tangible corporate economic interests were not significantly at risk in Vietnam, although as Eisenhower's "tin and tungsten" speech indicated, there *were* corporate interests in Vietnam as elsewhere. However, these were neither explicitly linked to official analyses of U.S. interests in Vietnam, nor were they substantial enough to outweigh other economic concerns, such as government spending levels. In fact, by 1968, much of the business community was urging an expeditious end to a war they saw as destabilizing both the American and global economies.

92. *Ibid.*, p. 85.

93. American hegemony was also enforced in Iran and Guatemala in the 1950s, Cuba and the Dominican Republic in the 1960s and 1970s, Chile in the 1970s and 1980s, and the Philippines from the 1950s through the 1980s.

94. Among the many sources on the American assault against Nicaragua see Noam Chomsky, Turning the Tide: U.S. Intervention in Central America and the Struggle for Peace (Boston: South End Press, 1985); Peter Kornbluh, Nicaragua and the Price of Intervention (Washington, D.C.: Institute for Policy Studies, 1987); and Holly Sklar, Washington's War on Nicaragua (Boston: South End Press, 1988). For a documented comparison of the relative level of democracy in Nicaragua and El Salvador, see Edward S. Herman and Noam Chomsky, Manufacturing Consent: The Political Economy of the Mass Media (New York: Pantheon, 1988), ch. 3.

95. For accounts of the onslaught against the people of El Salvador, see Robert Armstrong and Janet Shank, El Salvador: The Face of Revolution (Boston: South End Press, 1982); Charles Clements, Witness to War (New York: Bantam, 1984); and Ray-

mond Bonner, *Weakness and Deceit: U.S. Policy and El Salvador* (New York: New York Times Books, 1984).

96. Kolko, *American Foreign Policy*, p. xviii.

97. See Herman and Chomsky, *Manufacturing Consent*; Michael Parenti, *Inventing Reality: The Politics of Mass Media* (New York: St. Martin's, 1986); and W. Lance Bennett, *News*.

98. As Amory Lovins puts it, "three billion people offer living refutation of a theory that assured us that growing wealth would automatically enrich the poor without our having to redistribute anything." *Soft Energy*, p. 165.

99. As Gorz notes, "Capitalism can accept non-growth *as long as competition is eliminated* in favor of a general cartelization that freezes the power relations among firms, guarantees them their profits, and substitutes capitalist planning for the market." Such a scenario, of course, eliminates the legitimizing rationalization *for* capitalism. Andre Gorz, *Ecology as Politics*, trans. Jonathan Cloud and Patsy Vigderman (Boston: South End Press, 1980), p. 86 (emphasis added).

100. Similarly, the dynamics of capitalism drive energy use, posing an additional threat to the ecosphere. In Amory Lovins' words, "The energy problem, according to conventional wisdom, is how to increase energy supplies (especially domestic supplies) to meet projected demands. The solution to this problem is familiar: ever more remote and fragile places are to be ransacked, at ever greater risk and cost, for increasingly elusive fuels, which are then to be converted to premium forms—electric and fluids—in ever more costly, complex, centralized, and gigantic plants." Lovins' analysis highlights the futile illogic of an energy path wedded to a never-ending extrapolation of past and present growth trends, which wastes enormous energy by concentrating on electricity production and conversion, which is supported by massive government subsidies and favorable price regulations, which produces far fewer jobs than other forms of investment, which charges low-use poor consumers a higher rate than high-use industrial users, and which produces (in the case of nuclear-related energy) intractible hazards that society has no way of handling satisfactorily. Lovins, *Soft Energy*, p. 3.

101. One clue to the ideological nature of liberalism is its inconsistency in labeling politics "public" and economics "private," even though both reflect a similar modern dynamic of an atomistic society of individuals pursuing their enlightened self-interest. Feminists criticize the more general ideological separation between public and private in which public means politics *and* economics and is equated with masculine dominance, while private means domestic and is equated with the feminine.

102. Samuel Bowles and Herbert Gintis, *Democracy and Capitalism: Property, Community, and the Contradictions of Modern Social Thought* (New York: Basic Books, 1987), p. 17.

103. See Murray Edelman, *The Symbolic Uses of Politics* (Urbana, Ill.: University of Illinois Press, 1974). In the realm of environmental regulation, government intervention has been fought tooth and nail by private corporations and their political representatives. As Barry Commoner has demonstrated, this resistance has rendered efforts to control toxic emissions or require safe waste disposal virtually marginal in their impact.

The only dramatic successes in environmental protection have come when a *ban* on toxic materials (like DDT, PCBs, and lead in gasoline) has been imposed—in all cases after considerable damage was done and substitute materials were readily available. See Commoner, "The Environment."

104. Bowles and Gintis, *Democracy and Capitalism*, p. 88.

105. Robert Bellah et al., *Habits of the Heart: Individualism and Commitment in American Life* (New York: Harper and Row, 1986), pp. 173–74 (emphasis added).

106. Charles E. Lindblom, *Politics and Markets: The World's Political–Economic Systems* (New York: Basic Books, 1977), p. 356.

107. See Samuel Bowles and Herbert Gintis, *Schooling in Capitalist America: Education Reform and the Contradictions of Everyday Life* (New York: Basic Books, 1976); and Edward P. Morgan, *Inequality in Classroom Learning: Schooling and Democratic Citizenship* (New York: Praeger, 1977).

108. Parenti, *Inventing Reality*, p. 63.

109. As Marcuse has argued, liberal society becomes repressed if people are ostensibly "free to act as they please" while desires are shaped by consumer messages that appeal to basic private and internal needs. See Herbert Marcuse, *One Dimensional Man* (Boston: Beacon Press, 1964). Alan Wolfe argues that "the most repressive system possible in America would not be a police state, but its very opposite, one in which there were no police because there was nothing to police, everyone having the same lack of ideas." Wolfe, *The Seamy Side of Democracy: Repression in America* (New York: David McKay, 1973), p. 231.

110. Bookchin, *Ecology of Freedom*, p. 137.

111. Christian Bay, "'Freedom' as a Tool of Oppression," in C. George Benello and Dimitrios Roussopoulos, eds., *The Case for Participatory Democracy* (New York: Grossman, 1971), p. 265.

112. Again, capitalism provides the incentives. The private firm's need to accumulate capital through sales has made cheap and convenient commodities a marketing priority. For example, the petrochemical industry gave us plastic in place of paper, wood, and metal; detergent instead of soap; and nitrogen-rich fertilizer in place of organic matter or nitrogen-fixing crops. All dramatically increase environmental despoliation. Similarly, the automobile industry gave us bigger, more comfortable cars that consume far more energy; the nuclear industry offered electricity "too cheap to meter" as long as no account was taken of its potential hazards. The pattern is repeated throughout the manufacturing sector.

113. The waste crisis threatens to be one of the major environmental crises of the 1990s as municipalities across the United States run out of room for their trash. Not surprisingly, many have grabbed for the quick fix of incineration, a strategy that not only produces additional hazards like dioxins, but postpones the need for recycling and drastic changes in both production and consumption patterns.

114. Bookchin, *Ecology of Freedom*, p. 335.

Chapter 7

1. The term is used by Thomas Ferguson and Joel Rogers in their *Right Turn: The Decline of the Democrats and the Future of American Politics* (New York: Hill and Wang, 1986). The authors demonstrate that the much-touted shift to the right in American politics is not borne out by public opinion surveys. While elite opinion shifted rightward, public opinion remained essentially liberal, with a few notable exceptions. The book also documents the role played by the corporate sector in bank-rolling both parties' shift to more conservative platforms and candidates.

2. See Samuel Bowles, David M. Gordon, and Thomas E. Weisskopf, *Beyond the Waste Land: A Democratic Alternative to Economic Decline* (Garden City, N.Y.: Anchor, 1984), pp. 62–97.

3. Obviously other factors also contributed to this predicament: termination of the gold standard, growing Third World nationalism, and cartels like OPEC that strengthened the bargaining position of raw material producers. More generally, see Paul Kennedy's study, *The Rise and Fall of Great Powers: Economic Change and Military Conflict from 1500 to 2000* (New York: Random House, 1987).

4. Bowles, Gordon, and Weisskopf, *Beyond the Waste Land*, p. 64.

5. Michel Crozier, Samuel P. Huntington, and Joji Watanuki, *The Crisis of Democracy* (New York: New York University Press, 1975), p. 8. Founded by David Rockefeller, the Trilateral Commission consisted of corporate, political (Republicans and Democrats alike), and foundation figures from North America, Western Europe, and Japan concerned about the plight of global capitalism. The commission's view of democracy was so completely at odds with those of Sixties movements that it could argue that "value-oriented intellectuals who often devote themselves to the derogation of leadership, the challenging of authority, and the unmasking and delegitimation of established institutions pose a challenge to democratic government . . . as serious as those posed by aristocratic cliques, fascist movements, and communist parties" (p. 7).

6. Noam Chomsky, *Towards A New Cold War: Essays on the Current Crisis and How We Got There* (New York: Pantheon, 1982), pp. 4–5.

7. John Schwartz, *America's Hidden Success: A Reassessment of Public Policy from Kennedy to Reagan*, rev. ed. (New York: Norton, 1988), pp. 113–15.

8. See Ferguson and Rogers, *Right Turn*, especially chapter 3. The authors continue their analysis of corporate PAC funding through the 1984 campaign.

9. For a discussion of the compatibility between demonizing in Reagan's personality, American culture, and the needs of the elite, see Michael Rogin, *Ronald Reagan, The Movie* (Berkeley, Calif.: University of California Press, 1988).

10. See Jacques Ellul, *Propaganda: The Formation of Men's Attitudes* (New York: Vintage, 1973), pp. 70–79.

11. See Barry Commoner, "The Environment," *New Yorker* (June 15, 1987): 41–76; Frank Ackerman, *Reaganomics: Rhetoric and Reality* (Boston: South End Press, 1982); Sidney Blumenthal and Thomas Byrne Edsall, eds., *The Reagan Legacy* (New York: Pantheon, 1988); and John L. Palmer and Isabel V. Sawhill, eds., *The Reagan Record* (Cambridge, Mass.: Ballinger, 1984).

12. For example, new forms of dairy cattle are bred with unprecedented milk-producing capacity. Reflecting the profit imperatives of a capitalist economy, their "inventors" fight to collect "royalties" on each cow sold; meanwhile their higher cost favors the large capital enterprises of agribusiness, further handicapping the small family farmer.

13. Urban refuse and hospital waste washes onto the beaches of New Jersey and New York, while trash barges search in vain for a Third World nation financially desperate enough to accept municipal trash from American cities.

14. Kirkpatrick Sale, *Human Scale* (New York: Coward, McCann & Geoghegan, 1980), p. 16.

15. Carl Boggs, *Social Movements and Political Power: Emerging Forms of Radicalism in the West* (Philadelphia: Temple University Press, 1986), p. 7.

16. The phrase is Jean Bethke Elshtain's from her *Public Man, Private Woman: Women in Social and Political Thought* (Princeton, N.J.: Princeton University Press, 1981), p. 239.

17. Robert Bellah et al., *Habits of the Heart: Individualism and Commitment in American Life* (New York: Harper and Row, 1986), p. 144.

18. Immanuel M. Wallerstein, *The University in Turmoil: The Politics of Change* (New York: Atheneum, 1969), pp. 22–29.

19. In teaching a course on the politics of the 1960s, I have repeatedly heard students express these sentiments as they compare their world to that of young people in the 1960s. One student lamented the absence of hopeful determination so characteristic of the early to mid-1960s, commenting, "We have no emotionally charged, catalyzing issue. The scourge of drugs, the plight of the poor and homeless, South Africa, Central America, and rescuing the environment could all qualify as the most pressing issues of our day. However, *they are so widespread and hard to fight* that they do not begin to touch the poignant body bags and lynchings of the Sixties."

20. Doug McAdam, *Freedom Summer* (New York: Oxford University Press, 1988), pp. 235–36.

21. Boggs, *Social Movements*, p. 39. For book-length treatments of these movements on a global scale, see Boggs; Harry C. Boyte and Frank Riessman, *The New Populism: The Politics of Empowerment* (Philadelphia: Temple University Press, 1986); and Fritjof Capra and Charlene Spretnak, *Green Politics* (New York: Dutton, 1984).

22. One commentator observed of the democratic foundation of new holistic medical approaches, "The feeling of empowerment, of being able to do something for oneself, no matter how small, seems to be an important psychological ingredient in whatever successes the behavioral-medicine methods are having." David Coleman, "Mind Over Body," *New York Times Magazine* (September 27, 1988): 60.

23. See for example, Isaac D. Balbus, *Marxism and Domination: A Neo-Hegelian, Feminist, Psychoanalytic Theory of Sexual, Political, and Technological Liberation* (Princeton, N.J.: Princeton University Press, 1982); Alison Jagger, *Feminist Politics and Human Nature* (Totowa, N.J.: Rowman & Allanheld, 1983); and Boggs, *Social Movements*.

24. Fritjof Capra argues that we are experiencing the beginning of a historically unique turning point in which three great epochs are simultaneously coming to an end: the age of patriarchy that has dominated all cultures for at least three thousand years; the "fossil-fuel age" in which coal, oil, and natural gas have provided energy for industrial production; and the Western cultural paradigm manifest in the scientific revolution, the enlightenment, and the industrial revolution. Fritjof Capra, *The Turning Point: Science, Society, and the Rising Culture* (New York: Bantam, 1983), pp. 29–33. Popular works like Marilyn Ferguson's *The Aquarian Conspiracy* (Los Angeles: J. P. Tarcher, Inc., 1980), have reviewed new developments in science, medicine, politics, psychology, education, work, and religion that suggest the breadth and interconnectedness of change.

25. Neuman contends, "If your actions fail in their declared intent, all the better— you will get angrier. That is why it was commonplace to set unattainable strategic goals, like storming the Pentagon or keeping Dean Rusk out of New York. The notion that you might instead pursue successful strategies that made you happy and your opponents unhappy was abhorrent, because it made revolution less necessary from the only standpoint that mattered—the psychological one." Michael Neumann, *What's Left: Radical Politics and the Radical Psyche* (Peterborough, Ont., Can.: Broadview Press, 1988), p. 172.

26. Black and feminist separatism were arguably necessary both for the psychological empowerment of human beings who had internalized a position of powerlessness and for protection from the co-optive quality of modern liberal culture. Both produced a clarity of vision that generated important radical insights about that culture. In some cases, that vision has led to a conscious choice not to be political, not to rejoin the struggle with and in the cultural mainstream. The mainstream criticism of black "racism" and "anti-male" feminism glosses over these important points.

27. Carl Oglesby, "Notes on a Decade Ready for the Dustbin," in Mitchell Goodman, ed., *The Movement Toward a New America* (Philadelphia: Pilgrim Press, 1970), p. 739.

28. Fraser goes on to reason, "Thus at times it became possible for movements, or sectors within them, to conflate 'repressive tolerance' with repression full stop, parliamentary democracy with bourgeois dictatorship if not fascism, democratic rights with forms of coercion; and eventually to reach an emotional over-identification with (as distinct from militant support for) the Vietnamese revolutionaries." Ronald Fraser, ed., *1968: A Student Generation in Revolt* (New York: Pantheon, 1988), p. 358.

29. Quoted in *ibid.*, p. 358.

30. For example, feminism and Marxism highlight distinct dimensions of oppression. Feminism accentuates the personal and psychological while Marxism emphasizes the economic and political. Like the dialectic between inner and outer, public and private, the two traditions complement and enrich each other. Feminism forces some versions of Marxism out of its too-narrow preoccupation with economics, while Marxism reveals the futility of a purely inner or private liberation advocated by some feminists.

31. Jean Baker Miller, *Toward a New Psychology of Women*, 2nd. ed. (Boston: Beacon Press, 1986), p. 13.

32. It also opened the gates for the human potential movement, the myriad of therapies and practices designed to empower people by helping them overcome internal obstacles to growth. In place of the purely psychological focus on the repressed or "stuck" person, however, democracy requires attention to both the *person* and the *environment that encourages repression*. In effect, personal democracy harnesses the personal growth emphasis of the human potential movement to the requirement of external or political change. Praxis occurs when shared experiences lead to consciousness of membership in an oppressed class, which leads to awareness of the material conditions for oppression. For a more detailed discussion of the symbiosis between critical theory and humanistic education, see Lee Bell and Nancy Schniedewind, "Realizing the Promise of Humanistic Education: A Reconstructed Pedagogy for Personal and Social Change," *Journal of Humanistic Psychology* 29 (Spring 1989): 200–23.

33. For Evans and Boyte, these "particular sorts of public places in the community, what we call free spaces, are the environments in which people are able to learn a new self-respect, a deeper and more assertive group identity, public skills, and values of cooperation and civic virtue. Put simply, free spaces are settings between private lives and large-scale institutions where ordinary citizens can act with dignity, independence, and vision." Sara M. Evans and Harry C. Boyte, *Free Spaces: The Sources of Democratic Change in America* (New York: Harper & Row, 1986), p. 17.

34. Whereas the liberal paradigm solves the dilemmas of personal freedom by emphasizing privatism, democracy shifts the emphasis from the "walls" to the "connections," from the freedom to be left alone to the sphere of communal interchange. Personal democracy is grounded in the dynamic, creative, and honest interaction of people working out their conflicts, hopes, and values together. Because it emphasizes human growth and empowerment, personal democracy cannot brook the obliteration of personal autonomy and privacy. Instead it recognizes the simultaneous existence of autonomy and connection within a larger social milieu, and it focuses on a constructive dynamic between the two.

35. Simone Weil, *The Need for Roots* (Boston: Beacon Press, 1952), p. 179.

36. Andre Gorz's distinction between reformist reforms (which subordinate their objectives to a given system's criteria of practicability) and nonreformist reforms (which are conceived in terms of what "should be made possible in terms of human needs") is instructive. See Gorz, *Strategy for Labor: A Radical Proposal*, trans. Martin A. Nicolaus and Victoria Ortiz (Boston: Beacon Press, 1967), p. 7. Further, one may distinguish between structural reforms (for example, eliminating PACs—one source of enormous corporate power) and programmatic efforts to soften the edges of a capitalist economy. In both cases, however, reform thrusts will be enormously watered down in the absence of intense public pressure.

37. As the Greens' economic program declares, "A fundamental transformation must occur in all areas of society. This can be achieved only by means of a movement from below, from those affected who recognize the necessity to take further developments into their own hands." Quoted in Capra and Spretnak, *Green Politics*, p. 105.

Index